WESTMAR COLLEGE

OF
UTMOST
GOOD
FAITH

OF UTMOST GOOD FAITH

Edited by

Vine Deloria Jr.

Straight Arrow Books

San Francisco

Library of Congress Catalog Card Number: 76-141473

First Edition

STRAIGHT ARROW BOOKS

625 Third Street
San Francisco, California 94107

Distributed by the World Publishing Company

THE UTMOST GOOD FAITH shall always be observed towards the Indians; their land and property shall never be taken from them without their consent; and in their property, rights and liberty, they shall never be invaded or disturbed, unless in justified and lawful wars authorized by Congress; but laws founded in justice and humanity shall from time to time be made, for preventing wrongs being done to them, and for preserving peace and friendship with them.

—*An Ordinance for the Government of the Territory of the United States north-west of the river Ohio, 1789*

CONTENTS

Introduction   1

I - Aboriginal Title and the Doctrine of Discovery   6

II - The Changing Concept of the Tribe
    Indian Removal Act, 4 Stat. 411 (1830)   40
    The Kansas Indians, 5 Wall 737 (1866)   42
    Miami Allotment and Removal Act, 17 Stat. 631 (1873)   47
    Point Elliott Treaty, Article V 12 Stat. 927 (1854)   50
    Fort Hall Agreement, Section 10, 25 Stat. 452 (1888)   51
    Great Sioux Agreement, 25 Stat. 888 (1889)   52
    Waldron v. United States, 143 Fed. Repts. 413 (1905)   63
    Indian Reorganization Act, 48 Stat. 984 (1934)   64
    United States v. Santa Fe Pacific Railroad Co.
        314 U.S. 339 (1941)   69
    Native American Church v. Navajo Tribal Council
        272 F. 2d. 131 (1959)   75
    Menominee Tribe v. United States, 391 U.S. 404 (1968)   78

III - Diversity of Citizenship and Civil Rights
    Elk v. Wilkins, 112 U.S. 94 (1884)   85
    Ritual for Admission to Citizenship   92
    Indian Citizenship Act, 43 Stat. 253 (1924)   94
    Davis v. Sitka School Board, 3 Alaska 481 (1908)   95
    Ex Parte Crow Dog, 109 U.S. 556 (1883)   100
    The Seven Major Crimes, Section 9, Act of March 3, 1885,
        23 Stat. 362 (1885)   109
    Talton v. Mayes, 163 U.S. 376 (1896)   109
    Toledo v. Pueblo de Jemez, 119 F. Supp. 429 (1954)   114
    Colliflower v. Garland, 342 F. 2d. 369 (1965)   117

IV - Claim and Counterclaim
    The Indian Depredations Act, 26 Stat. 851 (1891)   129
    Jaeger v. the United States and the Yuma Indians,
        29 Ct. Cl. 278 (1894)   132
    The Claims of the Six Nations   134
    Indian Claims Commission Act, 60 Stat. 1049 (1946)   142
    Sioux Tribe of Indians v. United States
        146 F. Supp. 229 (1956)   147
    Unliquidated Claims
        The Baker Massacre   156
        The Sand Creek Massacre   157
        A Bill to Liquidate Liability for the
            Sand Creek Massacre   161
        The Wounded Knee Massacre   162
        A Bill to Liquidate the Liability for the
            Wounded Knee Massacre   165

V - White Defenders of Indian Rights
    Against Allotment - Senator Teller   168
    Against Allotment - Senator Morgan   170
    A Plea for Indian Citizens - Jennings Wise   175

VI - The Lonely Fight of the Indian Leader
    Protest of the Representatives of Indian Territory
        Against the Allotment Act   198
    The Fight Against Garrison Dam   200
        Testimony of Jefferson Smith, Council Member,
        Fort Berthold Tribal Council   202
        Testimony of Carl Whitman, Jr., Chairman,
        Fort Berthold Tribal Council   204
        Testimony of Martin Cross, Council Member,
        Fort Berthold Tribal Council   205
    Concerning House Report No. 2680 of the 83rd Congress - A
        Resolution of the National Congress of American Indians   208
    Senate Concurrent Resolution No. 3 (1957)   213
    Testimony of Joseph R. Garry, President, National Congress of
        American Indians in Support Senate Resolution No. 3   214
    Reaffirmed Policy Statement - National Congress of
        American Indians   216
    Statement of Earl Old Person, Chairman, Blackfeet Tribe
        Against the Omnibus Bill (1966)   219
    Testimony Against the Civil Rights Bill of 1968   221
    History of San Felipe Pueblo People   222
    Statement of Governor Robert E. Lewis, Zuni Pueblo   226

VII - Dealing With Indians
    United States v. Lucero 1 N.M. 422 (1869)   230
    The Faithful Apache Scouts   242
    An Act of Indian Territory   245
    Early Reservation Days - Martin Mitchell,
        Fort Peck Assiniboine   246
    The Campbell Ranch   248
    The Story of Hill 57   250
    The Problem With the Senecas   255
    Venning Memorandum   256
    Basil Two Bear   257

SUGGESTED READING FOR FURTHER STUDY   259

INTRODUCTION

The usual anthology of documents pertaining to Indian Affairs attempts to give a generalized and representative picture of history as seen by the editor. It alleges, therefore, to be neutral and unbiased. It is not. History must be told through the eyes of people that have experienced it and experience develops a point of view. The American reader has been led to believe that Indian history has a neutrality. It's not so. Each and every incident, every treaty, statute and case is loaded with values, viewpoints and biases. In some cases Indians fared very well. In others the deprivation was blatant and obvious. One can no more casually tiptoe through American history than walk on water.

At the outset, then, it is admitted that this selection of documents is no more unbiased than any other. It makes, for example, provocative efforts to call attention to the unresolved liabilities of the United States government for massacres of Indians at Wounded Knee and Sand Creek. It does so because the United States has admitted its responsibility for these incidents but has refused to compensate the Indian victims. This is a wrong that needs to be corrected. Instead of taking over abandoned islands to which there is tenuous claim, Indian militants could be proclaiming the admitted liability of the United States from every rooftop. White citizens, worried over the increasing brutality of the American forces in Southeast Asia should ponder the story of the Indian wars and re-examine their unshakeable faith that America is always engaged in handing out candy bars to the children of its victims.

It would be unfair, however, to overlook those whites, admittedly few, who have come forward in times of crisis to defend Indian rights at extreme cost to themselves. For that reason a chapter has been devoted to the speeches and writings of white men who have stood up to be counted when Indian people were in greatest danger.

Some of the selections are quite long. And for good reason. Many anthologies give minute portions of laws, cases, and treaties. Anyone wishing to pursue the matter must search further to find in what context the selection fits. Then he must determine if the selection is really material to his needs. The cases selected are pretty well intact with the exception of *Caldwell v. Alabama* from which extensive repetitive material has been deleted. Thus the reader can savour the entire case, roll over in his mind the various considerations which the court had to make in order to reach its decision, and understand how and why Indian legal rights have become such a maze.

The Great Sioux Agreement is quoted in full. For nearly a year sporadic incidents have marked Indian country as groups of young militants have claimed the Sioux Treaty of 1868 as legal justification for their activities. Few people have realized that the Agreement of 1889 amends the Sioux Treaty of 1868 in many strange ways. Most important for contemporary use is its subsequent characterization as a treaty and not an agreement. At the risk of being called a visionary, I would suggest that the Sioux Agreement of 1889 may eventually prove to be a pivotal document around which the militants of future years may evolve a whole new theory of Indian rights. For that reason the selection is reproduced intact with the very important case of *Waldron* following it as a complementary document.

The average citizen is frequently shaken by newspaper reports that the government has awarded portions of certain states to Indian tribes. People are shocked to learn that the major land cessions of the last century have not yet been settled. The late Senator and Attorney General Robert Kennedy, upon assuming his post as Attorney General, wrote an article for a national magazine outlining his dismay that the United States was still engaged in settlement of land claims. Almost immediately he was confronted with angry Indians who had taken affront at his apparently disparaging remarks on the Indian Claims Commission. Although he later became an active spokesman on behalf of Indian rights and did not intend a slur of Indian claims, Robert Kennedy was placed in a position of ignorance because there was so little information available to the average person on the nature and extent of Indian claims.

There are probably not a hundred Indians in the nation today who have much knowledge about the Indian Depredations Act. There are probably fewer non-Indians who know anything about it. The fact is, long before Indian tribes got a chance to present their cases, the Indian Depredations Act allowed any and every white who had any conceivable claim against an Indian tribe to present his data for compensation. Thus the tribes were held and skinned long before they got a chance to reply. It's important, therefore, for people not only to understand the nature of the Indian Claims Commission, but also to realize that the claims are a long-overdue and much belated attempt to do justice.

We've also included a great many classic speeches by Indian spokesmen. Red Jacket's reply to the missionaries, Chief Joseph's surrender speech, Tecumseh's statement on the ownership of the earth, and Crazy Horse's dying words—they are familiar and immortal. But the problem with books written about Indians is that these are usually the only speeches quoted. The average reader gets the impression that no Indian has been articulate since. This attitude is enhanced by the very scanty handling of Indian history beyond the wild cavalry charges and exciting battles. For that reason only speeches of contemporary Indian leaders are used in this book. The past two decades have been filled with struggles as desperate as many of the last century. Yet the reading and television-watching public is only aware that some movie stars and liberal lawyers are interested in Indians, with an occasional pipe-smoking anthropologist or social scientist nodding his head wisely in agreement.

Indian people have had outstanding leaders over the past two decades. These leaders have been deliberately pushed to the background by ambitious whites who have claimed to speak on behalf of a primitive people who have no sense of history or issues. The selections used in this book are representative of Indian leadership today but are certainly not all-inclusive. It is with a deep feeling that we should acknowledge our leaders while they are still among us, vigorous and fighting for our rights, that I have chosen these selections. Hopefully this chapter will inspire other people to produce a comprehensive book of contemporary speeches by today's Indian leaders.

With the passage of the 1968 Civil Rights Act, Indian Affairs has been thrown into the mainstream of legal complexities that plague and illuminate social movements. Expanding legal aid programs, turmoil over termination, and the continual tendency of non-Indians to equate Indian problems with those of other groups, make necessary an exploration of the civil rights issue in its two phases—the Indian as an American citizen and the Indian as a member of a tribal community. It will take at least another decade to resolve some of the issues now developing in this field. The selections in this area are chosen primarily to illustrate some of the paths that might be taken in the future in resolving some of these difficulties.

Finally the reader must visualize the entire field of Indian Affairs if he is to fully understand the selections in this documentary analysis. A United States general once characterized an Indian reservation as a piece of land surrounded by thieves. Imagine also, if you will, a rather gooey glob of inertia-bound career bureaucrats surrounded by well-intentioned do-gooders who flit in and out of the mess with complete misunderstanding but the best of motives. Record all of this in the special esoteric language of the academic community in which footnotes become the key to understanding and you have a fair characterization of Indian

Affairs. Now sprinkle liberally with legal phrases and pilot projects presided over by tribal councils that change every two years and you have it.

The situation is far from lost, however. There are presently in excess of 7,000 Indian students in college and graduate school. Industries are booming on many reservations. Indian people are assuming command of their own affairs at a very rapid rate. Militants are raising issues that would have been unthinkable just five years ago. Churches are setting up committees of Indian churchmen who will soon completely take over the mission fields. The level of Indian people now in government service is continually rising. The last two Commissioners of Indian Affairs have been Indians. Most of the important posts dealing with Indian Affairs are now filled with Indian people. Clearly the situation never looked so bright.

Indian people and their non-Indian friends must consolidate these gains and lay the foundation for future progress. A philosophy of Indian Affairs must be constructed by this generation of Indian people that will withstand the ravages of time. No real progress has been made in developing new concepts since the Indian Reorganization Act. That law is nearly 40 years old. Its ideas, adequately phrased for a depression America, cannot now express the realities of a space age Indian community. Thus hopefully this book will spur other Indians to begin the arduous task of creating a contemporary philosophy and life-style which can be useful to Indian people in the closing years of the twentieth century. And we also hope that by realizing the complexity of these problems, the non-Indian reader will come to better understand the differences in outlook, philosophy and legal status that distinguish Indian people from other groups in American society.

I

ABORIGINAL TITLE AND THE DOCTRINE OF DISCOVERY

At the founding of the United States, the former colonists were faced with a difficult problem. The Revolution had been based upon the right of people to throw off a despotic government and resolve for themselves how they would be governed. In conjunction with the establishment of this new American government was the definition of rights to which the United States, as successor to the crown of Great Britain, had succeeded. Particularly the vast western expanse, which someday would certainly have to lie under the flag of the fledgling republic.

During the days of government under the Articles of Confederation each state had continued its own method of treating with the Indian tribes within its claimed territory and on its borders. Thus one of the important topics at the adoption of the Constitution was the regulation of trade with the Indian tribes. Any Constitutional clauses had to be sustained by accepted tenets of international law in order for the federal government to assert its pre-eminence in the field.

For a long time after the adoption of the Constitution different states dealt with the Indian tribes on their own different terms. Thus New York continued to maintain that it had concurrent jurisdiction with the United States with respect to the Iroquois, whereas at the admission of Maine into the Union, Massachusetts merely ceded the Maine Indians and their treaty responsibilities to the new state prefering to step out of the picture altogether.

In the South the new states were faced with an unusual situation. While the state of Georgia refused to recognize any federal primacy over Indian affairs and continued to nullify Supreme Court decisions with respect to the Cherokee, other states attempted to find suitable legal solutions to reconcile their particular interests with the long history of federal rights in the field of Indian relations.

The Removal treaties with respect to the Five Civilized tribes left the state governments in even more doubt as to the exercise of their functions of jurisdiction. In most of the removal treaties, individual Indians were granted tracts of land which were technically Indian country yet given as enticement for individual Indians to break their tribal relations and become American citizens. Some of the treaties continued the dual citizenship while others seemed to indicate one or the other type of citizenship inherent in the Indian settler. At times he appeared to be a member of his tribe and responsible to federal officials, at other times he was accepted as a citizen of the state with federal officials disclaiming responsibility for him and his property.

The crucial test in the state of Alabama came in the case of *Caldwell v. the State of Alabama*. Caldwell was arrested and convicted for the murder of a Creek Indian. The crime was committed on lands of the Creek Nation which were shortly to become the lands of the state of Alabama upon the removal of the tribe to Oklahoma. Thus the question of the jurisdiction of the state courts had to be resolved.

The Supreme Court of Alabama rose to the occasion. In this extremely scholarly decision the judges reached the conclusion that Alabama had jurisdiction and that the conviction should be affirmed. In the course of their discussion the entire history of colonial-Indian relations was reviewed. The doctrine of Discovery, the justification of international law, and the comparative state of Indian-state relations at that time was reviewed. Thus in this single and sometimes obscure state case one can find the fundamental position of state governments with respect to Indian tribes. By reading this case with modern problems such as state jurisdiction, hunting and fishing, and state taxation of Indian lands in mind—one can understand how the states have developed their theories on Indian relations in opposition to existing federal law. The problem is as old as the colonial governments that once banded together to form the United States. And with the power of states and local governments now re-asserted, it's important to understand the basic theory of states' rights in regard to the lands, property rights and civil rights of American Indian people.

Caldwell v. The State of Alabama
1 Stew. & Potter (Ala.) 327 (1832)

LIPSCOMB, CHIEF JUSTICE
    It is contended that the act of the Legislature of Alabama, extending the jurisdiction of the State, and embracing that part of the Creek Nation where the offence [Caldwell had killed a Creek Indian] was committed is void, because it is in contravention of that provision in the Constitution of the United States that confers on Congress the right to regulate commerce with foreign nations, and among the several States, and with the Indian tribes.
    There is nothing in the exercise of State jurisdiction incompatible with the right of the General Government to regulate trade and commerce—each jurisdiction can be sustained, whilst operating within its legitimate sphere. Although the states may not be authorized to pass laws regulating trade and commerce, they may well take cognizance of murder, of larceny, and enforce contracts not in contravention of such regulations of trade and commerce as may be ordained by Congress. The plenary jurisdiction of the United States cannot extend beyond the subject of the grant to Congress. Trade and commerce have been subjected to its control, and to exercise it further would be destructive of all those salutary barriers, interposed for the protection of the states from federal encroachment. Admit the principle contended for, and the whole action of state jurisdiction would be arrested and subverted; for the terms used in the grant of power, refer as clearly to the states, as to the Indian tribes. This view, is on the hypothesis, that the tribes within the limits of a state are embraced by the Constitution; but its truth may well be controverted. Surrounded as our government was, at the period of the adoption of the Constitution, by numerous and barbarous tribes of Indians, not within our territorial limits, it is not to be supposed, that the power to regulate trade and commerce with them, would have been deemed too unimportant for the consideration of the framers of that instrument. The Indian tribes were a description of people not coming within any known definition of an independent sovereign nation or government; hence, they could not be embraced in the term, foreign nation. The term did not express the familiar idea entertained of those people; it was therefore essential to employ the more expressive one, Indian tribes. In connexion with this view of the subject, it is worthy of consideration, as a historical fact in federal jurisdiction, that it never has been assumed over the small tribes, within the limits of a state. I will leave it to others to determine, what is the standard of depreciation to which a tribe must be reduced, to fall below federal jurisdiction.

7

Another ground assumed, is alike destructive of federal and state jurisdiction. It claims for the Creek tribe of Indians, the high character of independent sovereignty, entitled as such, to every political right incidental thereto. The Indians, it is said, were the first occupants of the soil; and the first European discoverers, acquired no right, except such as the Indians conceded to them. That possession acquired by force, conferred no right, as it was in violation of the paramount natural right of the original occupants. We will examine this high pretension to savage sovereignty. If a people are found in the possession of a territory, in the practice of the arts of civilization; employed in the cultivation of the soil, and with an organized government, no matter what may be its form, they form an independent community; their rights should be respected, and their territorial limits not encroached on. From such a people, territory can only be acquired consistently with good faith, and national law, peaceably by treaty; by conquest, in open war; or by a forcible trespass, in violation of political right. The first mode of acquisition, would be in accordance with the soundest principles of morality; the second, sanctioned by the uniform usages of war; the last would be morally wrong; and if the power whose rights had been invaded, was too feeble to extort redress, other governments would be justified in making common cause in enforcing right against the wrong doer. But if the usurpation was acquiesced in, the political aspect of such an acquisition would be in favor of the *jus possessionis*. The code of national law, by which political societies should be tried, to establish their national rank, is not one of express enactment; nor the result of any convention of assembled nations: but it is a system of elementary principles, to which, the influence of morality and propriety, has constrained all civilized nations, tacitly to yield their assent; and is now considered as binding and obligatory as if sanctioned by the most solemn treaties. Savage tribes without a written language, or established form of government, and wholly ignorant of the customs and usages of civil society, are not capable of appreciating the principles of this code; and, (not yielding obedience to its canons) have never been looked on as parties to this compact of nations.

Were the natives of this vast continent, at the period of the advent of the first Europeans, in the possession and enjoyment of those attributes of sovereignty, to entitle them to take rank in the family of independent governments? They were composed of numerous tribes, subsisting by fishing and hunting, without any uniform or established system of government. Whatever authority exercised was adventitious and temporary, passing from one warrior to another, as accident might determine; and what was essential to national character, they had no geographical boundaries: Under such circumstances the continent is discovered by the Europeans. What ought they to have done? The fairest quarter of the globe is roamed over by the wildman, who has no permanent abiding place, but moves from camp to camp, as the pursuit of game may lead him. He knows not the value of any of the comforts of civilized life: he claims no definite boundary of territory. In what way is he to be treated with? As well might a treaty, on terms of equality, be attempted with the beast of the same forest that he inhabits. If it were possible to treat with them, and a hunting camp should be purchased, the right of purchase would not extend beyond its confines: another tribe, or the same, might settle down at the immediate door of the purchaser. The Indians, until long after the first Europeans came among them, had no idea of any actual or ideal line of demarcation, between their several tribes. Tecumseh, in his celebrated speech, declares this, and complains that boundaries between the several tribes, were the result of arbitrary European imposition; and this very tribe, that now assumes to be a sovereign, independent nation, within three quarters of a century back, claimed no territory beyond the smoke of the wig-wams; and how near them their neighbors, the Choctaws, might approach in their hunting expeditions was dependent on the relative strength of the two parties. Long continued wars had been waged between these tribes—their battle ground was wherever they chanced to meet—

until the humanity of the British government interposed, (not as one friendly neutral sovereign between two belligerents) but it was as sovereign to his subjects, the King of England, by his agent, Col. Stewart, spoke on Indian Affairs. He calls himself their great father, and informs the assembled Creeks and Choctaws, that he had resolved to put an end to those bloody rencontres; that he would in order to effect this object, mark out a line, running North and South between them—that the Creeks should not hunt West of that line, nor the Choctaws East of it. Never was there loftier, and more absolute language of command used by a Roman pro-consul, to an abject, subjugated province, than that employed by this representative of the British Crown to the Choctaws and Creeks. The line designated by him, was the first boundary line known between two tribes, then among the most numerous and warlike in North America.

The civilized nations of Europe, had either to adjust among themselves, a fair, an equitable mode of acquisition according to their own canons of morality and national law, or to leave this fair continent in the rude and savage state in which they found it. They reasoned, and reasoned correctly, that the right of the agriculturists was paramount to that of the hunter tribes.

The learned Vattel says, "the cultivation of the soil is not only to be recommended by government, on account of the extraordinary advantages that flow from it, but from its being an obligation imposed by nature on mankind; the whole earth is appointed for the nourishment of its inhabitants, but it would be incapable of doing it, was it uncultivated."

The same author again says, "It has been asked, if a nation may lawfully take possession of a part of a vast continent, in which there are found none but erratic nations, incapable by the smallness of their numbers to people the whole? We have already observed, in establishing the obligation to cultivate the earth, that those nations can not exclusively appropriate to themselves more land than they have occasion for, and which they are unable to settle and cultivate. Their removing their habitations through those immense regions, can not be taken for a true and legal possession; and the people of Europe, too closely pent up, finding land in which these nations are in no particular want, and of which they make no actual and constant use, may lawfully possess it and establish colonies there."

The same author again says, "If each nation had resolved from the beginning, to appropriate to itself a vast country, that the people might live only by fishing, hunting and wild fruits, our globe would not be sufficient to maintain a tenth of its present inhabitants."

The European powers acted on these principles: they found the country uncultivated, and inhabited by only hunter tribes. Their own dominions were surcharged with population, and they appropriated a part of the uncultivated land of this continent to their own use, as well as they might do. If treaties were had with the nations, we have seen that more could not be acquired by them than the savages actually occupied. Those treaties were no admission of the Indians' right to the lands over which they occasionally wandered, in search of game or wild fruits. They were holden for the purpose of conciliating the savages, and was no more an acknowledgement of their right than the contribution levied by the Barbary cruisers, from many of the Christian powers. They were never considered by the Europeans, as independent sovereignties: they adjusted the boundaries of their different clans on this continent, without consulting the Indian tribes that might be included in those boundaries.

In the case of *Johnson v. McIntosh,* Chief-Justice Marshall says, "the United States maintain, as all others have maintained, that discovery gave an exclusive right to extinguish the Indian title of occupancy, either by purchase or by conquest, and gave them also a right to such a degree of sovereignty as the circumstances of the people would allow them to exercise." This is placing the tribes in their true condition of privilege, under our government—making it a question of policy, at what time, and to what extent, jurisdiction should be exercised.

If their numbers were small, and the action of civilized institutions could be brought directly to bear on them, jurisdiction has invariably been exercised, by the State, within whose limits they resided. If numerous, and detached from the vicinity of the white man, policy inculcated the propriety of treating their ignorance and their prejudices with lenity and forbearance, until they should become capable of appreciating the superior advantages of the arts and institutions of civilized society; but how long a particular line of policy should be pursued, and when and how changed, are political, and not judicial enquiries.

It has been the uniform practice of the United States, and of all European powers, claiming possessions on this continent, to assert their sovereignty over such Indian tribes as resided within their respective limits; and in this, they have only acted in accordance with the principles, of the Laws of Nations: it is wholly impossible to embrace them in the family of National Governments, either on the ground of right of domain, or of empire.

The state of Georgia, before she ceded the territory now composing the two states of Alabama and Mississippi, to the United States, exercised, in her sovereign capacity, not only her political right of empire, but asserted her right to the soil, over the very territory from which it is now attempted to exclude the jurisdiction of Alabama. This was done by selling the fee of the soil, to certain purchasers called and generally known as the Yazoo speculators. When this sale was made, the Creek Indians were, as now, in the quiet possession, as far as Indian occupancy could give such possession of the land sold. And they were then much more powerful, and from their numbers and warlike character, better entitled to rank among independent nations, than they are at present. Yet the Supreme Court of the United States, in the case of *Fletcher and Peck,* sustained the validity of the sale. If the United States have formed treaties with Indian tribes, residing within the limits of states incompatible with the right of state jurisdiction over them, the authority to enter into such arrangements with the Indians, must be derived from the Constitution; otherwise those quasi treaties can avail nothing against the rights of the state. We have shown that the Constitution gives no such authority. The enquiry therefore, how far any of them may interpose a bar to the exercise of jurisdiction, will be waived, if, however, it were admitted, for the sake of argument, that those treaties, at the time they were entered into, were valid, it might well be contended, that so far as Alabama is concerned, they have been abrogated. It is competent for Congress to annul a treaty, and this may be done expressly or impliedly. The making of treaties and the breaking them, are acts of political sovereignty in the government; and whether the principles of private or public justice has been violated, can not be enquired into by the judicial tribunals of the country.

Whatever the obligations might have been, subsisting between the United States and the Creek Indians, if capable of being characterised at all, must have been of a political character. In treating with the people of the now state of Alabama, on the subject of their assuming the rank of an independent state of the Union, no reservation is made in favor of the rights of the Creeks, and no reference to the relations that might then be subsisting between that tribe and the United States.

*　　　　　　*　　　　　　*

The only condition imposed by the act of admission, on the people of Alabama, in favor of the United States, is, that they shall relinquish all right to the waste and unappropriated lands within her limits.

The British government, before the revolution, exercised absolute dominion over the Indians within her limits in such was as policy dictated: —that all the right of sovereignty exercised by that government vested in the states, not collectively, but severally, within their respective limits: that this sovereignty remains with the states to the full extent exercised by the British Crown, if not abridged by concessions made to the Federal Government; that the state of Georgia, prior to the act of Cession, could lawfully have exercised jurisdiction, and that all the right of jurisdiction is now in the state of Alabama, are the conclusions that I have arrived at. The conviction must be affirmed.

SAFFOLD, JUDGE OF THE SUPREME COURT

No view of the case can be more material to the question than that which relates to the true character of national grade of the Creek tribe within the chartered limits of Alabama at the date of the statute—whether they should be regarded as a foreign nation, or State of the Union; or if neither, what other title is descriptive of their state and condition?

It is essential to the enquiry to investigate not only the right of the tribe to distinct sovereignty and the extent of federal power over their territory, but also in illustration of those to examine their title of interest in the soil they occupy. The latter question has been frequently adjudicated by the highest tribunals in the United States. These decisions maintain that on the discovery of this immense continent, all the great nations of Europe who had thereby acquired what they considered titles to distinct portions of it, concurred in establishing the principles "that discovery gave title to the goverrment by whose subjects, or by whose authority it was made, against all other European governments, which title might be consummated by possession." Also, that "the exclusion of all other Europeans necessarily gave to the nation making the discovery, the sole right of acquiring the soil from the natives, and establishing settlements upon it."

Each nation claimed the right to regulate for itself, in exclusion of all others, the relation which was to subsist between the discoverer and the Indians. —That relation necessarily impaired to a considerable extent, the right of the original inhabitants; and an ascendancy was asserted, in consequence of the superior genius of the Europeans, founded on civilization and Christianity, and of their superiority in the means, and in the art of war. The nations which respectively established colonies in America, assumed the ultimate dominion to be in themselves, and claimed the right of occupancy. The history of America, from its earliest discovery, and especially the practice of Spain, France, Holland and England, prove the general recognition of this principle.

The same authorities show that the United States adopted the same principle; they also declare the exclusive right to exist in the general or state governments, (according to subsisting relations between them) to extinguish the Indian title by purchase or conquest—to grant the soil, and to exercise such degrees of sovereignty over the territory, as circumstances may require; and that this right has never been judicially questioned. The case of *Goodell v. Jackson* decided at Albany, about the same time with that of *Johnson v. McIntosh,* at Washington, maintained that the government of New York had always claimed the exclusive right to extinguish the Indian title to lands within their jurisdiction, and that all purchases made by others were null and void.

The legislature of Virginia, in 1779, says Chancellor Kent, "asserted the same exclusive right of pre-emption; and the colonial and state authorities throughout the Union always negotiated with the Indians, within their respective territories, as dependent tribes, governed, nevertheless, by their own chiefs and usages, and competent to act in a national character, but placed under the protection of the whites, and owing a qualified subjection, so far was requisite for the public safety. The Indian tribes within the territorial jurisdiction of the government of the United States, are treated in the same manner; and the numerous treaties, ordinances, and acts of Congress, from the era of our independence, down to the present time, establish the fact."

In order more perfectly to comprehend and appreciate the principles of right, as established by the potentates of Europe, and to determine the relative state of the tribe in question, it is necessary briefly to investigate the early history of the title of the Indians to the soil, and the stipulations of various treaties to which they were parties.

The territory in question, having been a part of the colony chartered to Georgia, it was, in 1802, dissevered, by the articles of agreement and cession between that State and the United States; consequently the origin of title to the Creek land, as well as its subsequent state in most respects, has been the same in Georgia and Alabama. The charter of the British King, in reference to these lands, contained, among other grants, the following declaration: "that it is our royal will and pleasure, for the present as aforesaid, to reserve (the land aforesaid) unto our sovereignty, protection and dominion, for the use of said Indians, and we do hereby strictly forbid, on pain of our displeasure, all our loving subjects from making any purchases, or settlements whatever, or taking possession of any of the lands above reserved, without our special leave and license, for that purpose first obtained." This language is a clear indication of the assumed right of the British government to grant the future license, at pleasure.

The construction of this charter, by the Supreme Court of the United States—*Fletcher v. Peck*—as declared by the Chief Justice, is, "that the reservation for the use of the Indians, appears to have been a temporary arrangement, suspending, for a time, the settlement of the country reserved, and the powers of the Royal Governor within the territory reserved; but is not conceived to amount to an alteration of the boundaries of the colony." He further remarks, "if the language of the proclamation be in itself doubtful, the commissions subsequent thereto, which were given to the Governors of Georgia, entirely remove the doubt."

Looking to treaties, which may be considered obsolete, except for the purpose mentioned, is found in the one between Georgia and the Creek Nation, concluded at Galphinton, in 1784, art. 1, the admission, on the part of the Creeks, "that the said Indians, for themselves, and all the tribes, or towns, within their respective nations within the limits of the state of Georgia, have been, and now are, members of the same, since the day and date of the [original!] Constitution of said state of Georgia." The 4th article stipulated, if any citizen of Georgia, or other white person, committed any capital crime, on any Indian, he should be delivered up and tried by the laws of Georgia. And by the 5th article, the nation bound themselves to inflict adequate punishment on all like offences by Indians on white persons. The treaty at Shoulderbone, the succeeding year, did not vary the relations in any material respect.

By the treaty of New York, in 1790, between the Creeks and United States, the latter having become the proper party, in virtue of the Federal Constitution, then recently adopted, the Nation acknowledged themselves under the protection of the United States alone; and stipulated not to hold any treaty with any individual State, nor with individuals of any State. By the same, the United States guaranteed to the Nation all their lands in the United States; it stipulated that any citizen of the United States, who should attempt to settle on any of the Creek land, should forfeit their protection, and the Creeks might punish such at pleasure; and further, that no citizen of the United States should attempt to hunt or destroy game on the Creek land; nor should any go into their country without a passport. This treaty further provided, if any Indian should commit any capital crime on any citizen, the offender should be delivered up to be punished by the law of the United States; it was the same if any citizen should commit such crime in the Nation.

The treaty of Colerain, in 1796, authorised the President to establish trading, or military posts on the Indian lands; that the same, with land five miles square, to each hould be under the government of the United States; but when they ceased to be necessary, they should revert to the Indians: provided nothing therein should "be construed to affect any claim of the State of Georgia to the right of pre-emption," &c., "or to give to the United States, without the consent of Georgia, any right to the soil, or to exclusive legislation over the same, or any other right" than those mentioned.

Nothing contained in the treaty of 1803, or that of 1806, cited in argument for the prisoner, is thought material; unless it can be, that the latter allows to the United States a horse path from Ocmulgee to Mobile.

The authorities remaining to be reviewed, are deemed more material. By the articles of agreement and cession, between the United States and Georgia, all the right, title, and claim, which the said State had to the jurisdiction and soil of the territory, part of which composes Alabama, was ceded by Georgia to the United States, on, and subject to, express conditions—one of which was, that the territory thus ceded, should form a State, and be admitted as such into the Union in an event that has occurred on the same conditions and restrictions with the same privileges and in the same manner as is provided in the ordinance of Congress of the 13th of July, 1787, for the government of the western territory of the United States; which ordinance it was agreed should in all respects extend to the ceded territory.

*   *   *

As respects the pretension of empire in the Indian tribes, within the chartered limits of the states, it is a claim which has been found to involve incalculable difficulty and embarrassment; and such must be the unavoidable consequences of it, so long as the evils of conflicting sovereignty are perpetuated. It is, however, a subject, concerning which, the Supreme Court of the Union has recognized principles assumed by the states, which that court cannot retract, and which the states cannot yield.

In "The Cherokee Case," (Jan. 1831) Marshall, Chief Justice, in declaring the opinion of the Court, remarks, "the bill requires us to control the legislation of Georgia, and to restrain the execution of its physical force. The propriety of such an interposition, by the Court, may be well questioned. It savours too much of exercise of political power, to be within the province of judicial department."

In the same case, and in reference to the same claim of Indian sovereignty, in opposition to that of the state, Johnson, Justice, observes, "I cannot entertain a doubt that it is one of a political character altogether, and wholly unfit for the cognizance of a judicial tribunal: there is no possible view of the subject that I can perceive, in which a Court of justice can take jurisdiction of the questions made in the bill."

The fact that the Indian tribes, while remaining in their truly anomalous state and condition, have been, *ex necessitate,* allowed to maintain the relations of peace and war, does not prove their right to general empire. The general government has been, and must remain, incompetent to the extension of general municipal authority over tribes in the situation of these; because, the power has not been delegated by the states, and to do so, would violate state sovereignty. In this state, as well as some others, it had, until recently, been considered, by the ruling power, impracticable, or inexpedient, (and perhaps some thought it unconstitutional) to extend state jurisdiction over the resident tribes. While, therefore, such has been the situation of the tribe, and they were necessarily left to govern themselves as they chose, the United States have occasionally exercised the relations of peace and war with them; but in doing so, the nation has never thought it necessary to observe the checks and restraints which the Constitution has thrown around the war-making power. By the Constitution, Congress alone has power "to declare war;" but after many wars have been waged with various tribes, our Code of statutes contains no declaration of war against Indians. The several tribes having been placed under subjection to the United States, and located within the same, the power to suppress resistance, or any internal commotion by them, and to punish any hostilities they may commit, is necessarily incident to the national sovereignty; and to the duties of the commander-in-chief, in preserving, protecting and defending the Constitution.

No founder of any American colony has been more generally, or perhaps more justly eulogised, for his moderation and humanity to the Indians, than William Penn. He has rendered his fame immortal by his acknowledged generosity or magnanimity in purchasing lands of the Indians, instead of taking them under his British charter, as all concede he, and others, had authority to do, and as they must have had, to entitle them to encomium for forbearing to do so.

The same writer says, "we can not help praising the moderation of the English Puritans, who first settled in New-England; who notwithstanding their being furnished with a charter from their sovereign, purchased of the Indians, the lands of which they intended to take possession. This laudable example was followed by William Penn, and the colony of Quakers that he conducted to Pennsylvania."

We can not, however, suppress the reflection, as the fact constitutes part of our authentic history, that the prices given by the Puritans, (Penn and others) were scarcely more than nominal, compared with the then value of the lands: or with the prices which the United States have repeatedly offered to the various tribes in different states. The prices originally given, were doubtless, in most instances, less, and so considered, than would have been the expense of occupying the same lands, forcibly, against the consent of the Indians; nor is it to be forgotten, that the Indians were then numerous and formidable; and that policy may have been strongly united with humanity in dictating the terms by which the Indian titles were extinguished.

It is gratifying to know, that liberal and humane as the United States have uniformly been in relation to the aboriginal inhabitants, the course of the Federal Government, continues to evince no less magnanimity; that, (notwithstanding complaints of some to the contrary) the national character in this respect, never shone with more lustre than at present: That from motives of humanity, and a regard to long usage and custom, the General and State Governments acknowledge the right of all the tribes, as well in the States as Territories, to the occupancy of their lands; their right to cede them to the United States or an individual State, according to the circumstances; and their right to protection, &c.

The facts are also identified with the history of our country, that the government continues its uniform practice of tendering to the Indians, (such as have not yet accepted) more than just and liberal inducements to relinquish their right of occupancy within the States, and emigrate to the west; that it has evinced the utmost solicitude to avoid coercion against them; that among other means used to avoid the necessity, and tempt them to move, it has tendered an extensive grant of lands west of the Mississippi—one, not included within the chartered limits of any State—better adapted to the habits and pursuits of the Indians than their present restricted and exhausted possessions; and where they can have, not only the absolute right of soil, but different and higher assurances of less restricted empire.

It has long been the settled policy of the government, to prevent, if possible, by negociation with the tribes, any conflict of sovereignty, or other rights, between them and the States they inhabit.

To maintain the position I assume, that the propriety of extending the jurisdiction of the State, involves a question of expediency, the fact is material, that by various cessions, by the Creeks, and the consequent separation of their tribe from all others except the Cherokees, the size of their territory had been greatly reduced; and that by emigration the same effect had been produced on the number of inhabitants. The reduction had been such before the date of the statute in question, that this tribe were not, I conceive, distinguishable, in principle, from many of the tribes, or remnants of Indians, remaining in many of the States of the Union, over which the respective governments have long exercised jurisdiction.

The fact has not escaped me, that there is nothing in the record shewing the original size or reduction of the Creek Nation; but it is equally true, that there is nothing shewing that they are not the smallest remnant, totally incapable of the most abject government.

Hence, if the size of the tribe be material, reference to the history of the country is unavoidable, and may be rightfully had in all such cases. That the size is material, to sustain the argument, that the question is one of expediency, to be decided by the Legislature, appears to me to be evident, from the known fact, that the different States and Territories of the Union, contain tribes of every grade and number, from the most powerful to the most insignificant, imaginable.

It will be seen from the statutes of the different states, that many of them, before and since the adoption of the Federal Constitution, have exercised the right of passing laws in relation to the Indians within their limits; not only to secure and protect the lands, and regulate commerce between them and the whites; but, in many instances, they have subjected the Indians to ordinary municipal regulations; and more generally, have extended criminal jurisdiction alone, over their territory.

Of the various acts of the kind referred to a few only need be noticed; and first, one of New York, passed in 1822, entitled "an act declaring the jurisdiction of the Courts of the State," and pardoning Tommy Jemmy. The preamble recites, among other state rights, that "the sole and exclusive cognizance of all crimes and offences, committed with this state, belongs, of right, to Courts holden·under the Constitution and laws thereof, as a necessary attribute of sovereignty, except only crimes and offences, cognizable in the Courts deriving jurisdiction under the Constitution and Laws of the United States." —And further, that "it has become necessary, as well to protect the said Indian tribes, as to assert and maintain the jurisdiction of the Courts of the State, that provision should be made in the premises" —therefore, the act proceeds to declare full power and jurisdiction accordingly. By the same act it was declared, that Tommy Jemmy, an Indian of the Seneca tribe, having been indicted for the murder of an Indian woman of the same tribe, committed within the same reservation; and it having been represented, that the alleged murder had been committed under pretence of Indian authority—therefore, he should be pardoned.

Consistently with the spirit of our Federal and State Governments, the acts of Congress, as well as various treaties referred to must have been, mainly intended, as far as respects the exercise of judicial power over Indian territory to establish the relation between the United States and Indian tribes, while the latter occupied lands embraced only by territorial forms of government; and which from their recent organization, sparce population, and subjection to, and dependence on the general government, were incompetent to the efficient exercise of full sovereignty. Far different, according to the fundamental principles of the union, are the powers and privileges of the state governments. If, however, it be conceded, that the treaties and statutes referred to, were partially intended to apply also to tribes of Indians inhabiting the states, it could only have been, as already suggested, for a limited time, during the infancy of the states; or, while any particular tribe should remain so savage, fierce, or formidable, as to render it impracticable, or inexpedient, to subject them to state empire. Such, we find, is not the relative condition of this state and the Creeks.

The position, with others, has been assumed in argument, that the admission of Alabama into the union, with defined boundaries, cannot confer jurisdiction commensurate with these limits; because, it would be to confer greater powers on the grantee than the grantor possessed. The tendency of this argument would be to prove that the jurisdiction belongs to the Creek tribe. It would be an intolerable proposition that a citizen of the United States under the Constitution thereof, and of this state, should be subjected to the Creek mode and manner of trial and punishment. It is a power claimed, perhaps, by no tribe, but yielded to the United States by either the express or implied stipulations of various compacts or treaties, and which the latter have claimed, so far as such jurisdiction was deemed compatible with federal and state empire. The fact, that such power has never been claimed, or tolerated, in favor of any tribe, by any American treaty, furnishes a strong argument against the existence of Indian right of sovereignty, in any respect, after the earliest time when the state, inhabited by them, finds it expedient to extend its jurisdiction over them.

The 19th section of the intercourse law, seems to have contemplated the neccessity of such a reservation of state authority—it provides, that the act "shall not be construed to prevent any trade or intercourse with Indians living on lands surrounded by settlements of the citizens of the United States, and being within the ordinary jurisdiction of any of the individual states." Statutes are to be construed according to their reason and spirit, without a scrupulous regard to their literal expressions. The reason and necessity for the extension of the jurisdiction over the Creek country, in its present state, is substantially such as above contemplated. The Creek tribe, as also the Cherokees adjoining, "are surrounded by settlements of the citizens of the United States." It cannot be required, that they should be inhabitants of the same state; nor that the surrounded Indians should be of the same tribe—neither requisition could be made without the grossest absurdity. Surely, the Indian authority cannot derive strength, from the circumstance of their being located on a line, or lines, dividing two, three, or more states; nor from any given number of Indians being divided into two, or more distinct tribes. If such construction prevail, the consequence must be, that the very circumstances which render them more obnoxious and embarrassing to the citizens, by bringing their governments into conflict with those of several states, instead of one; or by leaving them a more impotent and degenerate community, from their division into distinct tribes, would have the effect to rivet them permanently on the state, or states. The Creek claim to distinct empire is, in principle, but the same that it would have been, had their territory been removed on the east, a few miles from the Georgia line, and on the north, as many from the Cherokees; and if the intermediate spaces had been occupied by freeholders, or intruders, citizens of the United States. The argument, that this provision can only apply to tribes that were, at the passage of the law, (1802) thus surrounded by citizens, would appear equally refined and preposterous. The law is general in relation to the Indians in the states, and territories of the union. The government was the only party to it. It is not in the nature of a compact, operating on the parties only, and to be varied by their mutual consent; but it stands as a law of the union, establishing rules uniform and universal, requiring a construction to suppress the evils and advance the remedy—to be applied to each tribe, whenever its state and condition shall justify and require it. The law imports no designation of the individual tribes, or nations, to which it does, or does not apply, but merely defines the general principle of its application; the most important of which is, that it does not apply to prevent trade, or intercourse, with Indians living "within the ordinary jurisdiction of any of the individual states," at the time when the question of sovereignty, or jurisdiction may arise.

In all the British charters for American colonies, and in the articles of agreement and cession between the United States and Georgia, (though including Indian tribes,) are to be found express cessions of sovereignty to the grantees; on the contrary, it has never been deemed necessary, nor is there an instance of a cession from any Indian tribe, in which the right of sovereignty is expressed as a part of the rights ceded.

In determination of these vexed questions of conflicting empire, it may not be irrelevant to notice, briefly, how they stood under the confederation; and what changes have been since effected in the political relations of the parties.

It is declared, (Article 2) that "each state retains its sovereignty, freedom and independence, and every power, jurisdiction, and right, which is not by this confederation expressly delegated to the United States in Congress assembled."

(Article 9) "The United States in Congress assembled, shall have the sole and exclusive right and power of regulating the trade and managing all the affairs with the Indians, not members of any of the states: provided the legislative right of any state, within its own limits, be not infringed, or violated."

The Constitution subsequently adopted, contemplated the extension of jurisdiction over, at least, some of the tribes; (as many, and at such times, according to reasonable inference, as the states might deem expedient;) one evidence of it is, that Indians subjected to state taxation, are authorised to be included in the federal census.

Nor is there found in the Federal Constitution, more than in that of our state, any authority in the United States, to exercise the right of sovereignty over, or regulate intercourse with, the Indian tribes. The relative powers of the federal and state governments have been permanently established, by the sacred fundamental principles of the union; so that they cannot be essentially varied, even by mutual consent, unless by an alteration of the Constitution, in the manner therein prescribed.

The relation is strongly demonstrated by the 3d section, 4th article of the Constitution, which provides, "that new states may be admitted by the Congress into the union; but no new state shall be formed, or erected, within the jurisdiction of any other state, nor any state be formed by the junction of two or more states, or parts of states, without the consent of the legislatures of the states concerned, as well as of the Congress." It further declares, that "Congress shall have power to dispose of, and make all needful rules and regulations, respecting the territory, or other property, belonging to the United States; and nothing in this Constitution shall be so construed as to prejudice any claim of the United States, or of any particular state."

The Supreme Court of the Union, in the case of the *Cherokee Nation v. Georgia,* appears to have left the relation of the Indian tribes to the United States, in an awkward dilemma. The opinion delivered by Marshall, Chief Justice, raised the preliminary question, whether that Court had jurisdiction of the case. He remarks, "the 3d article of the Constitution describes the extent of the judicial power. The second section closes an enumeration of the cases to which it is extended, with 'controversies' between a state, or the citizens thereof, and foreign states, citizens, or subjects"—that a subsequent clause of the same, gives the Supreme Court original jurisdiction in all cases in which a state shall be a party. The party defendant may then unquestionably be such in this Court. May the plaintiff sue in it? Is the Cherokee nation a foreign. state, in the sense in which that term is used in the Constitution?"

He continues, "their counsel have shewn conclusively, that they are not a state of the union, and insist that, individually, they are aliens, not owing allegiance to the United States." He also says, "the condition of the Indians in relation to the United States, is perhaps, unlike that of any other two people in existence. In the general, nations not owing a common allegience, are foreign to each other. The term, foreign nation, is with strict propriety, applicable by either to the other. But the relation of the Indians to the United States, is marked by peculiar and cardinal distinctions, which exist nowhere else."

After advancing other views against their claim to the capacity of a foreign nation, the Court decides, that "they may more correctly, perhaps, be denominated domestic dependent nations"—that "they occupy a territory to which we assert a title independent of their will, which must take effect in point of possession, when their right of possession ceases: meanwhile, they are in a state of pupilage. Their relation to the

17

United States resembles that of a ward to his guardian." Supposing such to be the true relation, whose right and privilege is it to terminate this wardship and pupilage? or by whom, and in what way, are they to be governed while it continues: The only way it ever has been, or can be, effectually done, is by the action of the state government, and that by the extension of its laws, as has been done by the statute in question. It was, as we have seen an authority with which the state was invested, before the adoption of the Federal Constitution, and which has never been transferred, or relinquished. The contrary was not, on that occasion, maintained by the Supreme Court.

In as much then, as the Indian nations are not to be regarded, either as foreign states, or states of the union; but are unlike any other people in existence; their right to a separate existence, and that within regular constitutional states of the union, is found to be not more anomalous, than embarrassing to the states. Locally and politically, they are excluded from every portion of the world, except the United States. They can have no alliances, confederation, intercourse, or commerce, with any foreign nation. They have yielded these rights, by various compacts, or treaties, with our general, or state governments.

In "the Cherokee case" referred to, Chief Justice Marshall, in reference to these tribes, remarks, they and their country are considered, by foreign nations, as well as by ourselves, as being so completely under the sovereignty and dominion of the United States, that any attempt to acquire their lands, or to form a political connection with them, would be considered, by all, as an invasion of our territory, and an act of hostility.

If it be suggested, that the United States government has recognized the Indian tribes as states, or nations, by holding various treaties with them, my reply is, that names may, or may not, be very material. If the government should enter into any legal agreement or compact, with an individual, corporation, or voluntary association of persons, and should entitle it a treaty, instead of agreement, compact, grant or charter, and no undue privileges were claimed under it, by virtue of the name, no injury could result from the misnomer. So, with the Indian treaties—they must have effect according to their legitimate nature, regardless of their title; and if the opinion be correct, that the tribes are not such nations, or states, as were contemplated by the Constitution; not such as the United States are authorised to form "treaties" with, in the diplomatic sense of the term, (and which may become a part of the supreme law of the land,) the title with which they have been dignified, cannot give them that virtue, nor prove that the government could not, rightfully, make such compacts as they have done, to answer other purposes as therein expressed.

The validity of these treaties has seldom come in question, nor can it often; because they are, doubtless, binding on the Indians as parties; and, generally, binding on the United States, because authorised to dispose of the public lands, or at least extinguish the Indian title to it; and regulate commerce with the Indian tribes; and also, because the latitude of this treaty-making power, with Indian tribes, is so defined and circumscribed, by rights constitutionally established, that a violation of them would scarcely be attempted. This doctrine was recognized, and forcibly expressed by the American Commissioners, during the negotiations at Ghent. "The treaty of Greenville," say they, "neither took from the Indians the right which they had not, of selling lands within the jurisdiction of the United States, to foreign governments, or subjects; nor ceded to them the right of exercising exclusive jurisdiction within the boundary line assigned. It was merely declaratory of the public law, in relation to the parties, founded on principles previously and universally recognized."

Relying on the foregoing review as establishing the positions that the Indian tribes are not states entitled to any constitutional right of empire after the individual states embracing them, deem it expedient to incorporate them; and that the Creek tribe have no

18

jurisdiction of crimes similar to the one in question; it only remains to be shewn by further illustration that the federal judiciary has not the jurisdiction, at least, exclusively of the state authority.

*   *   *

The circumstances of the United States having the ultimate right to soil, cannot impair the right of sovereignty. There is no incongruity in the proposition that the right to the public domain resides in the United States, while the ordinary right of empire, over the same territory, is vested in the state government. While the United States have possessed and exercised the right to dispose of the unappropriated lands, and even to remove intruders from them, the states, containing them, have as uniformly exercised the ordinary municipal government.

Vattel's doctrine, relative to domain, cannot fully apply to the peculiar rights and relations of our governments; but so far as it can apply, it sustains these positions. He says, "the useful domain, or the domain confined to the rights that may belong to an individual in the state, may be separated from the sovereignty; and nothing prevents the possibility of its belonging to a nation in places that are not under her jurisdiction. Thus, many sovereigns have fiefs, and other possessions, in the territories of another prince; in these cases, they possess them in the manner of private individuals." The eminent domain, he defines to be, "the right, which belongs to the society, or to the sovereign, of disposing, in cases of necessity, and for public safety, of all the wealth contained in the state."

The right to the waste, or unappropriated lands, within this state, (which must include the lands occupied by the Indians, if not before, after the extinguishment of their title,) however it might otherwise have been, was reserved to the United States, by agreement between the two governments, at the time of the admission of the state to self-government. The consequence of this state of things, according to my doctrine, is, that while the United States hold the seisin, or ultimate fee, and have guaranteed to the Indians the usufructuary interest in the soil they occupy, the state government, (without any claim to the soil,) possesses the same right of sovereignty, to the extent of our chartered limits, that is common to other states of the union, under the Constitution thereof. At the same time, the United States can rightfully exercise that degree of federal sovereignty and jurisdiction, which belongs to them, in, and over other states of the union.

The result of this investigation is, that the tribe in question cannot be regarded either as a foreign nation, or state of the union; that, if from want of rank in the community of nations, or states, they must be considered (as denominated by the Supreme Court of the United States,) "a domestic dependent nation," in a state of "pupilage," and unlike any other recognized by any nation; their wardship has general relation, as their guardian, to the state whose limits they inhabit; with the exception of the rights necessarily incident to the ultimate right of domain remaining in the United States, and the power of Congress to regulate commerce with the Indian tribes, as it may do with foreign nations, and, elsewhere, among the several states; that this guardianship over the tribe was vested in the local government, (if not before), by the admission of the territory to the powers and privileges of state government; and that the proper time and manner of exercising the trust, (and of course abolishing the Indian laws and customs), are, and have been, questions of grave duty resting in the discretion of the legislature.

TAYLOR, JUDGE OF THE SUPREME COURT

These doctrines are maintained by Martens, Montesquieu, and every respectable writer who has treated on the same subject. It. . . appears that the human family is

19

divided, by these writers, into two classes. First, Agriculturists, or those who use the earth in that way which is calculated to secure the subsistence and happiness of the greatest number of inhabitants, and whose possessions, therefore, cannot be rightfully invaded; and, 2nd, Those who are erratic in their habits, who do not use the soil over which they roam, but live either by rapine and violence, or depend upon the precarious supplies afforded by hunting, fishing, and wild fruits. The country which the latter "overrun rather than inhabit," may be lawfully occupied by those of other nations who intend to appropriate it to agricultural purposes, if they "confine themselves to just bounds:" that is, as I understand it, leave an ample territory to these nomadic tribes to subsist upon by becoming cultivators of the soil, and to furnish them with necessary supplies by their usual pursuits, until they can effect the necessary change in their mode of life.

If this is not the view which is taken of these wandering tribes and hordes, why the compliment which is paid by Vattel to the English puritans who first settled New England? If he did not consider their charters as vesting them with ample authority to possess themselves of so much of the Indian lands within their limits as they chose or were able to do, without making any compensation to the aboriginal occupants, why praise those early settlers, because "not withstanding their being furnished with a charter from the sovereign, they purchased of the Indians the land they resolved to cultivate?" But more especially, if this sovereign himself had no legal right to touch a foot of those lands, except such as he acquired by treaty, by what mode of reasoning could the author come to the conclusion, that the puritans had exhibited a moderation and forbearance towards the inhabitants of the forest, which demanded the tribute of his praise?

It is obvious that this writer believed, that the European discoverer of a country possessed by wandering tribes of Indians, had a right to appropriate to himself so much of their territory as he required, to be used for the purpose of tillage, and that he considered the charters which were granted to our ancestors by the King of Great Britain, as conveying this right.

*   *   *

Notwithstanding frequent wars took place between European nations on account of their American possessions, many of which originated in disputes about boundaries, yet the principle here laid down was never contested. The acts of the sovereigns of Europe, from the first discovery of America, show that they maintained their rights in those parts of it which were discovered by their subjects respectively, to be as ample and their jurisdiction as complete, as property in the soil, and dominion over the country could make them.

The charter granted by the King of Spain to Columbus, is expressed as follows: "In order that in the said islands and mainland, which are discovered and shall be discovered hereafter in said ocean, in the parts mentioned of the Indies, the inhabitants of all that country may be better governed, we give you such power, and civil and criminal jurisdiction," &c.

This jurisdiction, it will be recollected, was for the "better government of the inhabitants," when the only "inhabitants" were natives.

Queen Elizabeth's charter to Sir Humphrey Gilbert, authorised him, "at all times hereafter to discover, find, search out, and view such remote heathen and barbarous lands, countries, and territories, not actually possessed of any christian prince or people, as to him, his heirs and assigns, shall seem good, and the same to have, hold, occupy and enjoy, to him, his heirs, and assigns forever; with all commodities, jurisdictions, and royalties, by sea and land! And further, shall have, hold, and occupy all the soil of all such, &c., and of all cities, castles, towns, and villages in the same, with the rights, royalties, and jurisdictions," &c.

The one to Sir Walter Raleigh, grants "all the soil of all such lands, territories, and countries, to be discovered and possessed as aforesaid, and of all such cities, castles, towns, villages, and places in the same with the royalties, franchises, and jurisdictions," &c.

All the charters granted by the Kings of England, were equally ample. That to Massachusetts, gives authority "to take and to hold that part of New England, &c. and all the islands, rivers, ports, havens, waters, fisheries, mines, minerals, jurisdictions," &c.

It thus appears that the different potentates of Europe, so far from regarding the Indian tribes as sovereign nations, whose jurisdiction within their dominions was sacred, paid no respect to their internal regulations, or even their right to the soil, but proceeded to distribute the land and to exercise their own jurisdiction, as they would have done had the Indians not existed.

The charter to Connecticut gives a general power to make war on, "and upon just causes to invade and destroy the natives or other enemies of the said colony." It must be borne in mind that this charter was granted before the settlement of Connecticut, and in contemplation of that event. I would ask, what is meant by the words "just causes." Had this chartered company any right, according to the opinion of those who deny the power of the State to pass the law in question, to set a foot on the lands of the sovereign nations who resided within the limits of the Connecticut grant, and who are therein denominated "the natives?" Suppose these "natives" had refused to sell an acre of their domains to the emigrants, but permitted them to land upon their coast, and they had proceeded to erect houses to dwell in, and open plantations for cultivation, without any express permission from their landlords, and these landlords had then requested them to leave their shores, declaring that they could not consent to receive them as inmates of their country, nor permit them to possess lands within their limits; what would have been the conduct of these "moderate puritans?" Would they have felt that they were aliens in a foreign empire, and bound to comply with the requisitions of the ruling powers? Or would they have treated the demand for their departure with contempt, and viewed any attempt to enforce it as "just cause for war?" In a word, would they not have considered themselves landlords and not tenants, and an attempt to dispossess them of the fruits of their industry and toil, as ample cause, not for war, (the charter does not use this term of equality when speaking of the resident Indians,) but "to invade and destroy the natives?" And yet surely the kindness of the Indians, in extending hospitality to them in the first instance, instead of at once expelling them from their shores, could give to title to the territory which they occupied. It is a general regulation in civilized communities, that aliens shall not hold a fee simple title to land, and what is to prevent the sovereigns of the wilderness from adopting and enforcing the same policy? It appears to me absurd, that any sovereign should grant a large extent of country to a company and vest in them the fee in the soil, and extensive political privileges, uniformly including jurisdiction, over the natives of the country in express terms, when he believed that he had himself no right to exercise jurisdiction over the country nor ownership over the soil, and that both resided in distinct independent nations then inhabiting the granted territory. I know it is said, that these grants conveyed the ultimate fee, that they contemplated a purchase of the possession from the Indians, who were viewed as the rightful occupants, and who could not be dispossessed without their consent. But the whole history of the western world, contradicts this assertion. The Spaniards, the Dutch, the French, the English, all took possession of great part of the countries they discovered without regard to any title in the first inhabitants, and extended their settlements and territories as their wants required. The charters obtained by the early settlers, expressly granted the right of soil and jurisdiction, and meant what they said. A great part of Virginia, and of the other Southern States, and of Kentucky and Tennessee were taken possession of, not because the Indians agreed that it should be done, but because the whites willed to do it. It is true, that most of the country, particularly in the two latter states, was ceded by treaties, but the cessions were generally made by treaties of peace at the termination of hostilities between the white and red man, which ha been produced by the occupation of the lands of the latter by the former, and often relin quished a claim to that, great part of which had before been wrested from their possession The authority "to invade and destroy the natives," conferred by the kings of England upon the colonists, carries irresistible proof to my mind, that the grantor considered himsel lord and rightful sovereign of these domains. The power conferred was not to declare war but "invade and destroy," manifesting that no declaration of war was necessary, no con formity to the usages existing among civilized nations intended, no boundaries to be re garded, but the pursuit to be continued wherever the foe could be found, until this savag enemy was "destroyed." Would it not be a most extraordinary departure from all civilize usage, for one nation to authorise a part of its subjects "for just causes," of course to b determined on by them, "to invade and destroy," the citizens of subjects of a neighborin state, and would not such an act be justly viewed as hostile in its character?

The fact that by far the greater portion of the territory within the United States whicl has been obtained from the Indians, has been procured by purchase, can not weigh greatl in this investigation, when it is recollected, that the consideration paid for it, was always until recently, merely nominal, and that true policy required that these fierce nations which generally surrounded the settlements of the whites on every side, except the on washed by the ocean, should be conciliated. Nor is the circumstance that they were, i early days, usually left under the government of their own peculiar customs, any argumen against the right of the colonizing nations to exercise jurisdiction over them. No bene ficial effect could have resulted from an effort of this kind, and its only tendency woul have been to have aroused the jealousy of the Indians, and excited their combined effor against their new neighbors, when thus informed that the whole country was considered a subject to their sway.

Additional light may be obtained on this subject of Indian privileges, by reference to speech of Mr. Stuart, superintendent of Indian affairs, made to the Indians at Mobile, soo after the conclusion of peace in 1763. The following is an extract from that speech: "Lastly I inform you that it is the King's order to all his governors and subjects, to treat the Indian with justice and humanity, and to forbear all encroachments on the territories allotted t them; accordingly all individuals are prohibited from purchasing any of your lands. But a you know that your white brethren can not feed you when you visit them, unless you giv them ground to plant, it is expected that you will cede lands to the king for that purpose But whenever you shall be pleased to surrender any of your territories to his majesty, must be done, for the future, at a public meeting of your nation, when the governors the provinces or the superintendent shall be present, and obtain the consent of all you people. The boundaries of your hunting grounds will be accurately fixed, and no settle ment be permitted to be made upon them. As you may be assured that all treaties wit you will be faithfully kept, so it is expected that you also will be careful strictly to observ them."

Here the Indian "hunting grounds" are spoken of as being "allotted" to them by th King; a strange phraseology, if the King's lands were, in fact, to be allotted to him by th Indians. And so careful was this superintendent, lest he should compromit the rights his master, that he used the expression "Indian hunting grounds," not "Indian lands. Is it not evident that he considered the Indians as occupying these lands for the purpose hunting, by the permission, and at the discretion of the King. He has "allotted" them, la off the boundaries, and although he will not permit his subjects to encroach on these "hun ing grounds," and expects "the consent of all your people" when you agree to contract yo limits, yet as your white brethren "will want ground to plant," it is expected that you ced "lands to the King for that purpose." The amount of all which, seems to be this.—The Kir has in kindness still permitted you to occupy these lands as hunting grounds. He is pe fectly satisfied, that at the request of the governors of his provinces, or his superintendent, you will, for the merest trifle, agree to contract the limits of the country thus "allotted" to you, whenever his subjects may require more land for the extension of their settlements, and he is willing to give you this trifle, because it is much better to have your friendship on these terms, than to have your lands for nothing, but your enmity as the consequence. It may be said, that the Indians cannot be presumed to have understood the peculiar meaning of the word "allotted," and, therefore, could not have yielded any right or privilege by not objecting to the use of it. The inquiry, however, is not, how did the Indians understand this language, but how was it understood by the sovereign whose agent employed it? It has never been supposed that the wild savage tribes who inhabited this continent in the sixteenth and seventeenth centuries, considered their lands as the property, or themselves as the subjects of the different European powers who claimed them as such, nor did they doubt their right to treat and trade with whom they pleased; especially those who roamed at a distance from the white settlements. They had as little idea of the restraints which they are admitted to have been subject to, as any others. Can it be believed that the Cherokees of that day believed that the fee of their lands was vested in the King of Great Britain, subject only to their occupancy, and that he could make a valid grant of that fee even to the spot in the centre of the nation upon which they met to hold their counsels, to a citizen of London?

It is not our business to ascertain the opinions of the Indians as to the relative situation which they occupied to the European governments which planted colonies among them; but the understanding of the civilized world is what we wish to know.

The proclamation issued by the King of Great Britain in 1763, soon after the ratification of the articles of peace, contains the following sentence. "And we do further declare it to be our royal will and pleasure, for the present, to reserve under our sovereignty, protection, and dominion, for the use of the said Indians, all the lands and territories lying to the westward of the sources of the rivers which fall into the sea, from the west and north west as aforesaid."

There is contained in these words the plain reservation of a right to determine the Indians "use" at pleasure. But be this as it may, there is a manifest declaration of sovereignty and jurisdiction. To be within the "dominion" is synonymous to being within the government or jurisdiction of the author of the proclamation.

I come now, in the course which I have laid down for my government in this investigation, to an examination of the acts of some of the British colonial legislatures relative to the Indians, passed before the revolution. And I propose to embrace in this examination some of the statutes providing for the punishment of individual Indians for offences committed in the country occupied by the whites, with the view of ascertaining whether they were considered to be clothed with all the privileges of citizens or subjects of a foreign government, or were viewed as inferior beings, who from their savage nature, required a different measure of punishment from that which was meted to British subjects for similar offences. For if this be so, it will go far to prove in what light the colonists estimated Indian titles and Indian jurisdiction.

So early as the years 1660 and 1672, we find the colony of Massachusetts legislating on this subject. One of their first acts was for settling the Indian title to "lands in this jurisdiction." By this law it was provided, "That what lands any of the Indians in this jurisdiction have possessed and improved, by subduing the same, they have just right unto:

"And for the further encouragement of the hopeful work among them, for the civilizing and helping them forward to christianity, if any of the Indians shall be brought to civility and shall come among the English to inhabit in any of their plantations, and shall there live civilly and orderly, such Indians shall have allotments amongst the English, according to the custom of the English in like cases.

"No person shall sell, give, or barter, directly, or indirectly, any gun or guns, powder, bullets, shot or lead, to any Indian whatsoever, or to any person inhabiting out of this juris-diction, nor shall any amend or repair any gun belonging to any Indian, nor shall sell any armour or weapons, upon penalty of ten pounds for every gun, &c."

"In subsequent acts the following provisions are contained: Whereas the French and Dutch and other foreign nations, do ordinarily trade guns, powder, and shot, with Indians, to our great prejudice, and strengthening and animating the Indians against us, and the aforesaid French, Dutch, &c., do prohibit all trade with the Indians within their respective jurisdictions, &c.

"It is therefore ordered: That it shall not be lawful for any Frenchman or Dutchman, or any person of any other foreign nation whatsoever, or any English dwelling amongst them, to trade with any Indian or Indians within the limits of our jurisdiction, under penalty of confiscation of all such goods and vessels as shall be found so trading, &c."

And it shall be lawful for any person inhabiting within this jurisdiction, to make sei-zure of any such goods or vessels so trading with the Indians."

From these statutes it appears that Indians were prohibited from engaging in parti-cular kinds of trade with any and every person whatever; that it was considered unsafe to permit them to have arms, and that a citizen was liable to a considerable penalty for furnishing them with even a pound of shot. But the one last extracted from, proves more than this. It shows that the trade of foreigners with the Indians, throughout the whole limits of the colony, was either regulated or interdicted as was deemed proper. For it cannot be supposed that the intention of the statute, was only to prohibit this trade in arms and ammunition within the settlements of the colony. It would have been folly to have sup-posed that foreigners would thus openly attempt to excite the hostility of the Indians to-wards the colonists. We, therefore, also learn from these extracts, that the term "jurisdic-tion," when used by the legislature of Massachusetts to express the extent of country over which it was exercised by the colony, included their whole chartered limits.

In the winter of 1693-4 an act was passed in the same colony, "for the better rule and government of the Indians in their several plantations." The object of the statute is de-clared to be, "That the Indians may be forwarded in civility and Christianity, and that drunkenness and other vices may be more effectually suppressed among them."

By this law it is provided, "That his excellency the governor, by and with the advice and consent of the council, may, and is hereby empowered to appoint and commissionate one or more discreet persons within the several parts of this province, to have the inspection and more particular care and government of the Indians in their respective plantations; and to have, use, and exercise the power of a justice of the peace over them in all matters, civil and criminal, as well for the hearing and determining of pleas betwixt party and party, and to award execution thereon, as for the examining, hearing, and punishing of criminal offences, according to the acts and laws of the province, &c.

"It shall and may be lawful for any person or persons to seize any wines, strong liquors, or cider, which he or they may find in the custody of any Indian, &c.

"Every Indian convicted of drunkenness, shall suffer and pay, unto the use of the poor of the town or place where such offence is committed, the sum of five shillings, or else be openly whipped by the constable of such town or place, not exceeding ten lashes."

This statute at least proves that the Indians were measured by a rule different from that which was applied to the rest of the population. The most degrading punishment is to be inflicted upon one of them for the slightest misdemeanor: public whipping for intoxi-cation, which offence when committed by a white man was followed by a very different punishment. What would have been thought of a law which made such a distinction between the provincials, and the subjects of the King of France or of Spain? It would not have been tolerated. And yet it is urged that never until this day have the Indians been received as other than sovereign nations, collectively and individually possessing all the rights and privileges which appertain to the citizens of such nations, and entitled in other countries than their own, to all the comity and respect which would be extended to the subjects of the proudest potentate of Europe. We see, however, that the "moderate puritans" of Massachusetts Bay, viewed them as savages and outlaws, who, while they wished to civilize and reclaim them, were to be punished in the most ignominious manner for the slightest offences and to be restrained from crime, like the slave, not by incitements to good, but by the terror of the suspended whip. It cannot be believed that a people thus singled out for infamous punishment, thus subject to have the spirits, the wines, &c., which they had purchased, and of course any other articles which the legislature might have chosen to add to the catalogue, arrested from them by every petty constable; were considered as possessing all the privileges of citizens of sovereign independent communities. They were found roving bands of savages by our ancestors, who first settled the American wilderness, governed entirely by their passions, and giving a full sweep to every appetite without regard to consequences. They could not be induced to forbearance from those gratifications of the animal appetite, so destructive in their consequences, by the incentives usually addressed to the civilized man. They were treated as a peculiar people, distinct laws were enacted to govern and control them, they were addressed through their fears, and while every inducement was held out to them to change their mode of life, to give up their habits of indolence and dependence upon the chase, and to apply themselves to agriculture and the arts; the slightest offences brought upon them the degrading punishment of the lash; most degrading when inflicted upon the white man, and never prescribed except for the most heinous crime: but the Indian neither felt nor feared the disgrace, the bodily pain alone was the object of terror to him.

We have evidence amounting to demonstration of the opinion entertained by the legislature of the province of Massachusetts Bay, of the situation which the Indian tribes within the limits of their charter occupied, in relation to the government of Great Britain, in the preamble to a statute passed in 1725. It is in the following language: "Whereas the Indians in the eastern part of the province, having been some years past in hostilities and rebellion, have now submitted themselves, and recognized their subjection and obedience to the crown of Great Britain," &c. They are stated to have been in "rebellion." Who are rebels? Those who, owing obedience, take up arms against a government. Can the members of an independent nation be guilty of "rebellion," by engaging in "hostilities" with another independent nation? I presume this will not be contended. Among all the sovereign states treated of by the writers on national law, not one of the stronger or weaker, the protector or protected, whether united by alliance, league, or confederacy, is declared to be guilty of rebellion by taking up arms against the other. Rebellion implies allegiance, and if there has been no allegiance, there can be no rebellion. Yet here the tribes who had never been brought into actual subjection, as is obvious from phraseology, who had not hitherto received the justices of the peace and constables which the governor, under the paternal provisions of the laws, was authorised to appoint; who had never submitted themselves to the fatherly chastisement of the whip for getting drunk, who, as to any actual restraint, have been as free as their own native wilds, are declared to have been rebels. If rebels, they had surely been guilty of treason; and as traitors, might have been tried, condemned, and executed upon their submission, but for the mercy of their sovereign against whom they had offended.

The statutes of Connecticut keep pace with, and are, in almost all respects, similar to those of Massachusetts. The laws of the province also, restrained the intercourse and trade between the Indians and whites: prohibited the latter from selling or giving to the former spirituous liquors, &c., prescribed the punishment of whipping to be inflicted upon an Indian for drunkenness, and declared the great objects in view to be the Christianizing and civilizing the sons of the forest, and to induce them to give up the chase and turn their attention to agriculture.

The other colonies of New England exercised similar powers, but it is deemed unnecessary to make special reference to any of the statutes.

I might multiply quotations similar to those which I have made from the laws of Massachusetts, from the statutes of every colony which afterwards formed the thirteen United States, but I will content myself with a reference to some of the acts passed in Virginia.

In the year 1658, the legislature of that province enacted, "That there be no grants of land to any Englishman whatsoever *(de futuro)* until the Indians be first served with the proportion of fifty acres of land for each bowman; and the proportion of each particular town to lie together, and to be surveyed as well woodland as cleared ground; and to be laid out before patented, with liberty of all waste and unfenced, lands for hunting for the Indians."

Again—"Whereas many complaints have been brought to this assembly, touching wrong done to the Indians, in taking away their land, and forcing them into such narrow straits and places, that they cannot subsist either by planting or hunting, &c.—Be it enacted, that all the Indians of this colony shall and may hold and keep those seats of land which they now have; and that no person or persons whatsoever, be suffered to intrench or plant upon such places as the said Indians claim or desire, until full leave from the governor and council."

Here full power is recognised in the governor and council to deprive the Indians of the places they occupied, nor is the land restored which it is acknowledged had been taken from them.

In 1660, the following law was passed in the same colony:—"Whereas, the Indians of the Accomack have complained that they are very much straitened for the want of land, and that the English seat so near them, that they receive very much damage in their corn. It is ordered that the right honorable the governor give commission to two or three gentlemen, with a surveyor living on this side of the bay (that have no relation to Accomack) to go over thither, and lay out such a portion of lands for the said Indians as shall be sufficient for maintenance, with hunting and fishing excluded; and the land so laid out, to be so secured to the Indians, that they may have no power to alienate it, or any part of it, hereafter, to the English."

In 1665, the same colony enacted, that, "Whereas, at a Grand Assembly, held at James City, September 10, 1663, it was provided that where any murder was committed by the Indians upon the English, the next turn of the Indians was to use their utmost endeavors for discovering the actors and doers thereof, and in regard the same act was only limited to the northern Indians," this proceeds to make the provision general. Another section is as follows: "That the said Indians shall not have power within themselves to elect or constitute their own Werowance or chief commander, but the present honorable governor and his successors from time to time, shall constitute and authorise such persons in whose fidelity they may find the greatest cause to repose a confidence, to be the commander of the respective towns: and in case the Indians shall refuse their obedience to, or murder such persons, then that nation so refusing or offending, be accounted enemies and rebels, and to be proceeded against accordingly."

Here is evidently an innovation upon the internal regulations of the Indians, and, in fact, an abrogation of their civil institutions and customs. These must have prevailed before, and their "Werowance or commanding chief," have been constituted by their own appointment; else why the apprehension that those appointed under this statute will not be received by them?

I think enough has been said on this part of the subject to satisfy an impartial mind that neither the sovereigns of Europe who held possessions in America, nor the colonial legislatures, doubted their right to embrace within the jurisdiction of their courts any Indian tribes who were situated as to make it expedient to do so. Doubtless at the date of many of the statutes which were passed in the colonies for the government and regulation of the Indians some of the nations had been so much reduced in limits and numbers as to bring their whole country within the immediate neighborhood of the whites, and to render it perfectly convenient, and every way desirable, to embrace them directly within the operation of the laws. In Virginia, it would appear, that the territories of many of the tribes were gradually intruded upon by the colonists until the Indians had not land enough left to answer their own demands for the purposes of agriculture, hunting, &c., and the legislature was compelled frequently to interfere to prevent their entire expulsion from the home of their fathers. For it cannot be supposed that regular cessions had been made of all the country which these Indians inhabited who were the objects of the care of the legislature: if so, they as do the red men of modern times would have left the country they had parted from by treaty, and sought other places of habitation. But this was not their situation. The increasing numbers and advancing improvements of the colonists required the extension of their borders, and they pressed into the Indian countries around them as their wants required; thus we find the European and aboriginal American inhabitants of the same country, and the possessions of the latter diminishing while those of the former are enlarging.

*   *   *

The effect of acquisition by conquest is to vest all the national rights of the conquered, in the conqueror, and because all right to the soil among Indian tribes was national, none individual, the right of soil, as well as sovereignty, passed to the conqueror. The conquerors "took to themselves what was not wanted by the natives." Can we suppose they would be more scrupulous about assuming jurisdiction, than a right to, and, often, possession of the soil?

In delivering the opinion of the court in the case of *Johnson v. McIntosh,* Chief Justice Marshall says: "On the discovery of this immense continent, the great nations of Europe were eager to appropriate to themselves so much of it as they could respectively acquire. Its vast extent offered an ample field to the ambition and enterprise of all; and the character and religion of its inhabitants afforded an apology for considering them as a people over whom the superior genius of Europe might claim an ascendency. The potentates of the world found no difficulty in convincing themselves that they made ample compensation to the inhabitants of the new, by bestowing on them civilization and Christianity, in exchange for unlimited independence. But, as they were all in pursuit of the same object, it was necessary, in order to avoid conflicting settlements, and consequent war with each other, to establish a principle, which all should acknowledge as the law by which the right of acquisition, which they all asserted, should be regulated as between themselves. This principle was, that discovery gave title to the government by whose subjects, or by whose authority, it was made, against all other European governments, which title might be consummated by possession.

"Those relations which were to exist between the discoverer and the natives, were to be regulated by themselves. The rights thus acquired being exclusive, no other power could interpose between them.

"While the different nations of Europe respected the right of the natives, as occupants, they asserted the ultimate dominion to be in themselves; and claimed and exercised, as a conveyance of this ultimate dominion, a power to grant the soil, while yet in possession of the natives."

Again—"The United States have unequivocally acceded to that great and broad rule by which its civilized inhabitants now hold this country. They hold, and assert in themselves, the title by which it was acquired. They maintain, as all others have maintained, that discovery gave an exclusive right to extinguish the Indian title of occupancy, either by purchase or by conquest; and gave also a right to such a degree of sovereignty, as the circumstances of the people would allow them to exercise."

With respect to the "relations which existed between the discoverers and the natives," the Chief Justice says, "We will not enter into the controversy, whether agriculturists, merchants and manufacturers, have a right, on abstract principles, to expel hunters from the territory they possess, or to contract their limits. Conquest gives a title which the courts of the conqueror cannot deny whatever the private and speculative opinions of individuals may be, respecting the original justice of the claim which has been successfully asserted. The British government, which was then our government, and whose rights have passed to the United States, asserted a title to all the lands occupied by the Indians, within the chartered limits of the British colonies. It asserted also a limited sovereignty over them, and the exclusive right of extinguishing the title which occupancy gave to them. These claims have been maintained and established as far west as the Mississippi, by the sword. The title to a vast portion of the lands we now hold, originates in them. It is not for the courts of this country to question the validity of this title, or to sustain one which is incompatible with it.

"Although we do not mean to engage in the defence of those principles which Europeans have applied to Indian title, they may, we think, find some excuse, if not justification, in the character and habits of the people whose rights have been wrested from them.

"The title by conquest is acquired and maintained by force. The conqueror prescribes its limits. Humanity, however, acting on public opinion, has established, as a general rule, that the conquered shall not be wantonly oppressed, and that their condition shall remain as eligible as is compatible with the objects of the conquest. Most usually, they are incorporated with the victorious nation, and become subjects or citizens of the government with which they are connected. Where this incorporation is practicable, humanity demands, and a wise policy requires, that the rights of the conquered to property should remain unimpaired; that the new subjects should be governed as equitably as the old.

"But the tribes of Indians inhabiting this country were fierce savages, whose occupation was war, and whose subsistence was drawn chiefly from the forest. To leave them in possession of their country, was to leave the country a wilderness; to govern them as a distinct people, was impossible, because they were as brave and as high-spirited as they were fierce, and were ready to repel by arms, every attempt on their independence. What was the inevitable consequence of this state of things? The Europeans were under the necessity of either abandoning the country, and relinquishing their pompous claims to it, or of enforcing those claims by the sword, and by the adoption of principles adapted to the condition of a people with whom it was impossible to mix, and who could not be governed as a distinct society; or of remaining in their neighborhood, and exposing themselves and their families to the perpetual hazard of being massacred.

"Frequent and bloody wars, in which the whites were not always the aggressors, unavoidable ensued. European policy, numbers, and skill prevailed. As the white population advanced, that of the Indians necessarily receded. The country in the immediate neighborhood of agriculturists became unfit for them. The soil, to which the crown originally claimed title, being no longer occupied by its ancient inhabitants, was parcelled out according to the will of the sovereign power, and taken possession of by persons who claimed immediately from the crown, or mediately, through its grantees or deputies.

"However extravagant the pretension of converting the discovery of an inhabited country into conquest, may appear; if the principle has been asserted in the first instance, and afterwards sustained; if a country has been acquired and held under it; if the property of the great mass of the community originates in it, it becomes the law of the land, and cannot be questioned."

Comment upon the foregoing extracts, from both the argument and opinion, would seem to be unnecessary. The plain positions taken by counsel and sustained by the court are, that discovery and conquest, as they relate to the title to the lands of the North American continent, are convertible terms, the one applicable to the other civilized powers; the other to the natives. That the European power, whose subjects or citizens made the discovery, was acknowledged the sovereign of the territory thus discovered, from the fact of the discovery, by every other nation in Europe, and considered the natives as a conquered people; although from the numbers, the fierceness and warlike character of the Indians, actual possession was obtained by these new masters in the manner deemed most politic; sometimes by gradual encroachment; sometimes by what was termed a purchase, though the consideration was always very inadequate, in most instances merely nominal; and sometimes by the sword. The title in fee to the soil, even while the possession remained in the Indians, was universally admitted to be vested in the discovering state: was so recognised in this case of *Johnson v. McIntosh,* and was granted either to individuals or companies, as was thought proper, and the grantees always adjudged, by every court, to hold an indefeasible estate, not withstanding it was not convenient for the possession to accompany the grant.

And what was the situation of the sovereignty or jurisdiction? Did it not stand in precisely the same predicament? The cases to which we have referred uniformly treat the "dominion" as in the European state. It is true, actual jurisdiction was not exercised over all these erratic people, and why was it not? Because it was not politic or convenient to exercise it; but as fast as the circumstances of the whites would allow them to exercise it, it was done.

If the Indian tribes ever were independent of the states in which they lived; if at any time the states had no authority to extend their jurisdiction over them, they continued independent while having a common "habitation and a name," no matter how greatly reduced in numbers or importance, and all the old states have committed aggressions upon them by interfering with their internal policy.

By what right did Massachusetts, Connecticut, New York, Virginia, *in fine,* all the colonies, forbid individuals from purchasing lands from the Indians, if they were sovereign nations? Had they not as much right to invite emigrants among them; to offer inducements to the settlement and cultivation of their immense territories; to embrace within their bosom, and cover with the protection of their institutions and jurisdiction, those who were thus drawn to their country, as any other people? Yet it appears never to have entered the minds of either white or red, that settlers upon Indian lands became Indian citizens, and were covered by the panoply of Indian law. Surely as one of these sovereigns, an emigrant might have secured to himself such right as the rest possessed, to the use of the spot which he cultivated while he lived upon it: but no; all contracts of individuals with the Indians for their lands, were declared void, by a power which, according to the modern doctrine, had no jurisdiction over those lands.

But when the substance of things is looked to, is it not most absurd to talk about the purchases which the early settlers made of Indian lands? By the statutes of Massachusetts, &c., all contracts, agreements, &c., made with an Indian are declared to be void. These people, chiefs and all, are like infants, pronounced incapable of protecting their own interests. Yet these persons, who have not a sufficient capacity to be permitted to make a binding contract to the amount of a dollar, are intelligent enough fully to estimate their national interests; to meet the learned and wily European as diplomatists, make treaties by which they are again and again yielding up millions of acres of fertile land, and all this is done on terms perfectly reciprocal! A few strings of red beads, a hogshead or two of tobacco, with a bale or two of coarse cloth, form an ample consideration, when given by treaty, for any extent of country which the cupidity of the white man might induce him to ask, and the ignorance of the red man cause him to sell!

If this be the real state of the case, let these unholy acquisitions be immediately surrendered; let the remnants of the once numerous and powerful, but ignorant tribes, be collected together, and honestly told that our ancestors have used their superior knowledge to cheat and defraud them; we now wish to do them justice by giving back all that extensive domain which has been thus iniquitously occupied. Let us make restitution; the rents and profits will amply compensate us for first cost and improvements.

But if we believe these "roving bands" did not use the country they "overran," that, finding it in a state of nature, our forefathers were justifiable in clearing away the forests and cultivating the fields formed by their industry, and in bringing the Indians into subordination to them by the best means which policy and humanity dictated; let us continue to act in the same way, and while we enjoy the rich returns which Providence blesses our labors in this fertile region, let us do all that we can to civilize, Christianize, and perpetuate the Indians who remain among us.

After a patient and laborious investigation, I can find nothing, either in ancient charters; the conduct of any European power, or the opinion of any respectable writer of older date than 1825, which tends in the remotest degree to countenance the opinion that the Indian tribes have ever been considered as distinct and independent communities.

Whenever the Indians residing within the chartered limits of a colony, have made war upon it, they have been declared rebels, and their "destruction" authorised. No declaration of war has ever been made against them from their earliest history; and by the constant practice of the federal government, since the adoption of the constitution of the United States, the President has ordered troops against them, including those nations with which treaties have been made, without waiting for any movement in Congress on the subject, and his authority to do so has never yet been questioned. From the earliest day, we are informed by Douglass in his history of the British settlements in North America, "when the country of the Indians at war with us lies upon our own frontier, but without our grants, I call it a war, in the common acceptation; if within our grants, but without our settlements, I call it an eruption; in our proclamations against them, it is called a rebellion, as in all the New England wars with the aborigines; if intermixed with our settlements, it is an insurrection."

It might be well in taking leave of this part of the cause, to look for a moment at the consequences which would result from a decision adverse to the constitutionality of the law. Not that consequences would ever authorise a Court to shrink from its duty; but they should always have their influence where the law of a case is doubtful.

If this state has not the right to exercise jurisdiction over the Creek nation now, when will it have the right? Some tell us, whenever the number of that people dwindles down to a few hundreds, or the extent of their country to a small compass. But suppose one of these events were to take place without the other: the number of the tribe is reduced to insignificance, but they retain all their territory; or they cede three fourths or nine tenths of their country, but their population, instead of diminishing, increases; what is the consequence of this state of things? How would it be were they to establish a code of written laws, divide their lands into small tracts, and convey them to the individuals of their nation in fee simple? Are they to be permitted to form such a government among us, and to adopt a policy calculated to make this state of things perpetual? Besides, what then is to become of the paramount title to these lands, so often decided by the Supreme Court of the United States, to reside in the general government?

It is obvious that unless the act of the General Assembly which we are now consider-ng, can be carried into execution, the Creek Indians, may establish and maintain a separate government forever, and the State of Alabama would have within its borders another and a distinct sovereignty; an *imperium in emperio.*

Where such consequences would ensue, something must be wrong, and the error would be in the decision producing them.

The second question which presents itself is; have not the states, since the Declaration of Independence, all the powers on this subject, which the King of Great Britain had before, except so far as they have surrendered them to the United States? This has never been controverted. The states by that event, became sovereign and independent, and clothed with all the privileges and powers of sovereign nations. Among the powers essential to sovereignty is that of jurisdiction. Let us inquire, have the states, by the adoption of the federal constitution, relinquished their right of jurisdiction over the Indians within their limits?

By the tenth article of the amendments of the Constitution it is declared, that "the powers not delegated to the United States by the Constitution, nor prohibited by it to the states, are reserved to the states respectively, or to the people."

Have the states delegated their right to jurisdiction over the Indian tribes?

The word Indian is used only twice in the Constitution.—In the 2nd section of the 1st article, it is provided, that "representatives and direct taxes shall be appointed among numbers, which shall be determined by adding to the whole number of free persons, including those bound to service for a term of years, and excluding Indians not taxed, three fifths of all other persons."

Here certainly is no delegation of power to the United States, but rather an express recognition of the rights and sovereignty of the states, over the aborigines. So far as Indians are taxed, they are, in express terms included in apportioning representatives, and viewed as inhabitants of the states, because the apportionment is directed to be made according to the population of the states; but words of exclusion are used with respect to those not taxed; which could only have been made necessary by the belief that, being within the limits and jurisdiction of the states, they would be embraced by a general phraseology, comprehending all persons within such jurisdiction.

In the 8th section of the same article, it is declared, "the Congress shall have power to regulate commerce with foreign nations, and among the several states, and with the Indian tribes."

It has been contended in the argument, that this clause yields up every right of the states to the United States in relation to the Indians, and the domain they occupy. But where are the words which convey this meaning? The power to regulate commerce with the Indian tribes is relinquished, but what idea does that convey? It is insisted that by this expression it was intended to give to the general government, and that alone, the power to regulate all intercourse with the Indians; I do not understand it is this way. Has the Congress the power to regulate the whole intercourse between the states? To prescribe terms upon which the citizens of different states shall carry on correspondence and every communication with each other; or would this clause, unrestrained by any other, confer such a power? No one would answer in the affirmative, and yet the expression in relation to the commerce of the states, is as comprehensive as that which respects commerce with the Indian tribes—the phraseology is identical.

Commerce relates to trade; intercourse may be carried on without trade. Commerce, therefore, includes no intercourse but that which consists in trade or traffic; and certainly does not include jurisdiction. In conferring upon Congress the power "to regulate commerce with the Indian tribes," even admitting them to be the tribes within their limits, the states had no more intention to surrender their sovereignty over those tribes, than they had to divest foreign nations of jurisdiction within their own territories by placing in the hands of the federal government the power to regulate commerce with them.

And not only does a correct construction prove this, but the conduct of the states since the adoption of the Constitution. New York, Maine, &c., have governed the Indian tribes within their limits by their own laws. All the tribes living in those States have, long since, been brought under the action of their courts; nor has the first man, either in Congress or out of it, been heard to raise his voice and sound the alarm, that the Constitution of the United States had been violated.

But it is said, that these tribes are few in number and surrounded by a white population.

These circumstances, then, terminate a power vested by the Constitution, in the United States, without any declaration in that instrument that they shall produce such an effect! Such an argument is too extravagant to need an answer.

By the 10th section of the 1st article of the Constitution it is declared, that "no state shall enter into any treaty, alliance, or confederation, &c.," and by the 4th article, that "this constitution, and the laws of the United States which shall be made, under the authority of the United States, shall be the supreme law of the land."

Several treaties made with the Creek nation by the United States, by which the former have ceded considerable districts of country, contain a stipulation, by which the latter guaranty the remainder of their lands to the former.

These treaties, it is urged, form part of the supreme law of the land, as much as the Constitution itself, and strip the states of all right to interfere, in any way, with the possessions or internal government of the Indians.

It might be replied that the act extending the jurisdiction of the state over them, in no way violates this guaranty; but under the view I take of the Constitution, it is unnecessary to investigate its effect in this respect.

I can not for a moment believe, that it was ever intended, by the framers of the Constitution, or the states which ratified it, that compacts within the Indian tribes should be embraced in the above provision: conventions with independent sovereign nations, were alone contemplated. This construction, is, I think, supported by the 2nd section of the 2nd article, which is in these words: "He (the President) shall have power by and with the advice and consent of the Senate, to make treaties, provided two thirds of the Senators present concur; and he shall nominate, and, by and with the advice and consent of the Senate, shall appoint ambassadors, other public ministers, and consuls," &c.

If the Constitution had intended to give to negotiations, which had previously been conducted and concluded with so little form and solemnity, all the sanctity and the high character of treaties formed with sovereign states, and to have placed them, not on the footing of other contracts, but that of the Constitution itself, by making them, equally with it, the supreme law of the land, surely some plain expression of such intention would have been made use of, and as the power to "regulate commerce with the Indian tribes," was defined in so many words, the high character of treaties with those tribes would have been as plainly expressed.

It seems manifest to me that treaties with the Indians were never intended to be, and are not embraced by this provision of the Constitution; that the history of the intercourse between the crown, the colonies, the states, and the United States, and the Indians, proves this. The United States, however, are bound by their contracts with these tribes, and can not, either in morality or justice, violate at pleasure, the agreements they have made with them. If they have stipulated any thing they cannot perform, they must satisfy them by a reasonable equivalent. No treaty, however, contains stipulations conflicting with the exercise of jurisdiction by this state. The integrity of their country is guaranteed to the reek Indians; be it so; this state has no right to the soil in that country either present or rospective. The fee resides in the United States; to the federal government, Georgia elinquished it, and in that government it is vested. The power of the United States to ontinue the Indians in the possession of the country they now occupy in this state, and o remove intruders from among them. I have never denied; but our right of jurisdiction an not be taken from us without impairing our sovereignty.

The Constitution of the United States declares that, "no new state shall be formed or rected within the jurisdiction of any other state" without its consent.

I would ask those who contend against our right of jurisdiction, if the effect of their loctrine is not a virtual violation of this provision? If the Indians, as distinct sovereign tates, can by treaty or in any other way, be perpetuated among us; if we can not reach hem by our statutes; if they can be encouraged to adopt a regular system of laws, a vritten code for their government: is not a new state formed within this; are not our imits in truth, contracted, by so much as is included in this "new state?"

From the time Alabama has assumed the station of an independent state, as great art of the territory within her limits has been occupied by Indians of different tribes, vretchedly poor in their condition, and excessively indolent in their habits. The great nterest of the state, and the object to which she has looked with the deepest solicitude, has een the removal of the Indians, and the opening of the territory occupied by them to a valuable population. Every treaty which has been made, has, in a measure, promoted this mportant object. It could not be expected, then, that Alabama would object to those reaties. She has always looked forward with confidence to the time, and has expected hat it would soon arrive, when the whole state would be freed from its Indian population y the means which were in operation, to the mutual satisfaction of the red and the white nan, and has been desirous that, in this way, it might be done. But when the Indians have een reduced to such narrow limits, and arrived to such a condition that a sound policy equires that they shall be embraced by our laws: and when too, indications have been given by them of a disposition to cede no more of their lands, but to establish themselves s a permanent nation among us; the time has surely come when we should at once, exercise our sovereignty coextensively with our limits.

I have thus far treated this question as if Alabama were one of the original thirteen States. I have now to examine the last point which was made in the argument against he validity of the statute, viz.: that Alabama has relinquished her right to exercise this urisdiction.

The Union is formed of independent sovereign states, which have combined together o secure their own safety, and the happiness of their citizens. In forming this combina- tion, and establishing a federal government, nothing has been given up tending to destroy heir individual sovereignty. Had this been done, our general government would not be 'ederal, but consolidated. It follows from the nature of things, that whenever a new mem- ber is added to this family of states, it is received with the same sovereign rights and privileges which belonged to the older members; it does not come in as an inferior, but s an equal; and if any exaction were made of a new state at all inconsistent with its sovereignty, it would be void, because that would be stipulated to be surrendered which s essential to sovereignty; and its being received into the Union as a sovereign state, vould avoid any such suicidal stipulation.

On this subject, however, it is only necessary to appeal to the Constitution of the United States, and the different acts of Congress, by virtue of which, Alabama has been admitted into the Union.

By the 3d section of the 4th article of the Constitution of the United States, it is declared, that "new states may be admitted by Congress into this Union." If new states are admitted into "this Union," it must be as the old states have been, that is, by becoming

parties to the compact which bind the old states together. They must come in under t]
Constitution. "This Union," means the Union formed by this instrument or Conventio
none can be received unless upon relinquishing to the federal head such powers as ha
been relinquished by the states which formed the Union, and all shall be secured in eve
political right which is secured to the first members.

In the year 1787, which was before the adoption of the Constitution of the Unit
States, an ordinance was passed by Congress "for the government of the territory of t]
United States, north west of the river Ohio." By that ordinance, it was provided th
"there should be formed in the said territory not less than three, nor more than fi
states" and such states "shall be admitted, by their delegates, into the Congress of t]
United States, on an equal footing with the original states, in all respects whatever."

The ordinance. . . referred to. . . declares. . . in these words: "The utmost good fai
shall always be observed towards the Indians; their lands and property shall never]
taken from them without their consent; and in their property, rights, and liberty, th
shall never be invaded or disturbed, unless in just and lawful wars, authorized by Congres
but laws founded in justice and humanity, shall, from time to time, be made, for preventi
wrongs being done to them, and for preserving peace and friendship with them."

The object of this article, is to secure the observance of "the utmost good fait]
towards the Indians, by the new states; the subsequent clauses only specify the manner
which this "good faith" is to be observed.

1st. "Their lands and property shall never be taken from them without their co
sent."

The act of our general assembly does not take from the Creek Indians their lands
property. It does not disturb the possession of an individual, but leaves every member
the tribe in the enjoyment of his "lands and property," be they much or little.

2nd. "In their property, rights, and liberty, they shall never be invaded or disturbed."

By the words "rights and liberty," I do not suppose is meant, "rights" claimed]
them to the destruction of the rights of the states, nor a "liberty" to do every imaginab
act, unrestrained by law. I understand it to be intended that justice shall be secured
them fully and completely, and that their freedom shall be as perfect and unrestraine
as that of any citizen in the land.

It is argued, however, that the extension of our laws over them is an invasion
their "rights and liberty," as it necessarily abrogates their laws and usages which the
prefer, and which they were governed by when our constitution was adopted.

If it was intended by the framers of this article to give them rights as nations, th
most unfortunate language has been used for that purpose. They are spoken of as Indian
not as nations, and the word "liberty" has been employed in a manner which must co
vince the mind that it is individual liberty which is intended.

The substance of the whole article is, that these people shall be secured by prop
laws, and a correct administration of justice, in their persons and property; that o
account of their liability, from their ignorance, to be overreached and defrauded by th
white man, they shall be protected by suitable laws to be enacted for the purpose. The
shall be viewed somewhat as minors, and as wards of the state, receive that degree
care and attention which their situation, and peculiar liability to injury requires.

But the idea that to secure the "rights" of the Indians, the state was to relinquis
some of those most important to her, and place herself in something of a state of pupilag
to, and dependence upon the savage tribes within her boundary, can not be tolerated fo
a moment. We are almost surrounded by these children of the forest; were we to yield a
that is claimed for them, in a short time we might, and, I doubt not, would, feel th
effects of their "independence." Our citizens might be prohibited by these new sovereign
from carrying on intercourse with several of the neighboring states, except by the one

wo path ways which they have agreed with United States should be open to them; most
ntolerable exactions might, even then, be made of them. For offences, either pretended
r real, charged to be committed by them while journeying through the dominions of these
overeigns, they might be dragged before their chiefs and other head men, and upon the
nost crude and unsatisfactory testimony, be consigned to ignominious or fatal punish-
nents.

These and an hundred other causes, would produce a constantly increasing feeling
of enmity between the white and red man, especially those who lived near each other,
nd frequent affrays, riots, and homicides would be the consequence. In fact, a kind of
order warfare would always exist between them and the only effective way to comply
vith the injunction of the ordinance, "to prevent wrongs being done to the Indians, and
reserve peace and friendship with them," is to bring them under the protection of our
aws.

This subject has been much mooted throughout the United States for the last
three or four years. In the controversies which have been carried on between the state
of Georgia and the Cherokee nation, the feelings of a great proportion of our population
has been warmly enlisted in behalf of the latter, and, on all occasions, my sympathy for
he Indians has been great.

I have remembered that, comparatively, but a few years since, they were the undisputed lords of this immense continent; that, unmolested by the white man and ignorant of
his existence, they pursued their game through the interminable forests which spread them-
elves in every direction; that indulging in a freedom unrestrained as the air, they coursed
heir immense and trackless wilds, changing their situation and country as fancy dictated,
or as the powerful inducement of a greater abundance of game operated upon them. But
he European has landed upon their coasts! Before his perseverance and industry, the
owering forests have fallen; the wild deer have fled from his presence; the Indians too
have receded with the game, until their once extensive domains are reduced to small townships, and even there the chase can be pursued no longer, the game has totally disappeared. I look around for their numerous hunters and warriors, they are only to be found
n the chronicles of past times; in numbers, the race has rapidly diminished, many of the
most powerful tribes are extinct; and the rest seem to be fast tending to the same end;
and I feel a deep anxiety that some plan should be devised, to avert this, their too
probable destiny.

Such reflections excite a warm interest in behalf of the Indian, and we listen to his
complaints fully perpared to believe that he has been injured.

Similar feelings have been general throughout the Union, and, doubtless, they have
often controlled the intellect, and commanded the judgment, when forming an opinion
upon the rights of the states over these rude nations.

But when we contemplate the change which has been wrought in this one savage
wilderness, by the arts, the industry, and the superior knowledge of the new population;
when we visit our thronged cities, smiling fields, and happy habitations; when we contemplate our numerous bays and harbors, once the resort only of the wild fowl and the
inhabitants of the deep; now studded with ships and vessels of all sizes and nations,
pouring upon these lands the rich and extensive commerce of a whole world; when, instead
of a roving tribe of hunters, we behold a powerful nation of agriculturists, as free in
every desirable liberty, as their savage predecessors; when our happy political institutions
and the religion of the Bible, have displaced their barbarous laws, and wretched super-
stitions; can we wish these effects of civilization, religion, and the arts, to disappear,
and the dark forests and roaming Indian again to possess the land? Are we not compelled
to admit that the superintending providence of the Being who first formed the earth, is to
be seen in this mighty change?

35

Such is my conviction: and much as I may sympathise with the savage, when giving the opinion that the law awards the superiority to his civilized neighbor, I am cheered by the belief that the decision of the law, in this, as in other cases, will be promotive of the best interests of the whole country.

My opinion is, that the judgment should be affirmed.

Caldwell's conviction was upheld. For many people it would seem that justice was done since Caldwell had killed a Creek Indian. But the holding of the case is illustrative of the problems that arise when there is a conflict between federal and state jurisdictions over Indian lands and peoples. And the precedent has been a dangerous one. In South Dakota today, for example, there are rarely any indictments issued against whites who kill Indians. The state of South Dakota has continually hewed to the position of the state of Alabama—that in certain instances it has criminal jurisdiction but somehow these instances usually result in failure to indict or punish white men who otherwise would face severe penalties in federal court.

More important than simple state jurisdiction is the justification used by the state by which the agriculturalist is favored over the hunter. Certainly this is not law but mere ramblings of abstract religious ideology clothed in legal jargon. Does, by the same reasoning, the urban dweller take precedent over the farmer and the ecologist take precedent over the urban dweller in disregard of property rights or treaty and constitutional promises?

The ideology of the case also raises some severe questions as to title to the continent. Is the United States any more justified in its claim to the land than the Indian militants of Alcatraz who claim also by Discovery? Do they not have the same claim to lands? Can one people simply "discover" someone else's land and take it by force or trickery? The decisions of the Indian Claims Commission appear to be resolving the question of land purchase. However, not every Indian tribe has been admitted to the Indian Claims Commission. The surviving remnants of Indian tribes in the eastern United States have been denied access to the Indian Claims Commission. If the Indian Claims Commission is the moral answer to the doctrine of Discovery then it would seem that the Indian Claims Commission should be reopened to all tribes regardless of their contemporary status as federal and state tribes. Only this development would provide an adequate answer to the use of the doctrine of Discovery in its contemporary setting.

Indian activists at Alcatraz and elsewhere have thus opened up a valid philosophical question that begs resolution. To be consistent the United States government should re-examine its position as successor to the European invaders. If it intends to purchase the whole continent, however belatedly, it should do so. If not it should cede Alcatraz and other disputed lands. And if Discovery is adequate justification for the invasion of other nations—provided that the economic system of the people invading is acknowledged as superior to that of the nation being invaded—the Indians of All Tribes at Alcatraz again hold a superior philosophical edge: they want the island as an ecological study center—a priority now acknowledged as having first importance in the economy of life resources.

II

THE CHANGING CONCEPT OF THE TRIBE

There are two classic cases in Indian law which attempt to define the status of Indian tribes—*Worcester v. Georgia* and *Cherokee Nation v. Georgia*. John Marshall's opinions acknowledge the sovereign, albeit dependent, nature of the Indian tribe. The problem has been that while Marshall's definitions have been accepted by every court in the land, nevertheless they have been studiously avoided in actual practice.

It would be fair to say that definitions of the nature of Indian tribes have revolved around tangible issues such as taxation, fishing rights, religious freedom, land cessions, and self-government. But as case law has developed, no corresponding theory of tribal rights has evolved. Thus while Indian tribes have been found to be vested with all the rights they originally possessed, modified by treaties and agreements, little has been done to make these rights concrete. Congress can still radically change the status of an Indian tribe by legislation. Indian rights, considered from a tribal governing aspect, have never vested in the tribe itself. John Marshall compared the relationship of the Indian tribe to the United States as that of ward and guardian. But he did not say that it *was* that of ward-guardian, only that it was in some ways analogous.

The following selections are illustrative of some of the problems inherent in the continually changing status of tribal governments. In spite of rather gloomy views held by administrators of the Bureau of Indian Affairs and assertions of learned professors that tribal sovereignty is finished, the concept continues to survive in a number of ways. The next step must be to re-define Marshall's phraseology in contemporary terms maintaining as much flexibility in the creation of new forms of tribal operations so that the Indian tribe can enter the economy capable of competing with the corporate giants of modern society. To do this successfully there must be a drastic limitation on the ability of Congress to change the status of the Indian tribe at its whim and a redefinition of the scope of administration of Indian affairs by the federal government. The following selections contain in themselves ideas and concepts that may someday return to haunt the halls of Congress and the dormitories of the Interior Department.

The Indian Removal Act
4 Stat. 411 (1830)

Contrary to the assertions of popular American history, the Indian tribes were not conquered. With the wars costing close to a million dollars for every Indian killed it became financially impossible for the United States to exterminate the tribes. Early in the game Congress provided an act by which the tribes were induced to move from their original territories to new lands upon which they would be guaranteed rights of self-government and maintenance of their traditional ways of life.

The Indian Removal Act was the first general law passed giving authority to the executive branch to negotiate with the tribes to remove westward to avoid conflict with the advancing tide of white settlement. The basic policies adopted during the 1830's, when the act became law, were generally followed throughout the last century. Treaties signed with the far western and plains tribes in the 1850's and 1860's reflect the basic philosophy of the Removal Act.

There is a real question raised by this law. Can it be regarded as a vesting of tribal rights in the constitutional sense? Does it mean that once removed Indian tribes thus gained a new status on the basis of their negotiations which cannot be denied them by arbitrary acts of Congress?

If we consider the Indian Removal Act as a basic contract of re-establishment of Indian communities as politically defined communities would it not seem that the act still contains a great many provisions by which contemporary problems can be resolved? Could not land exchanges be effected under this act in comparable ways as was the original land exchanged? Would it not be possible for an Indian tribe to open negotiations today under the provisions of this act of at least using this basic philosophy? If so, could lands be exchanged for apartment buildings in cities, forests traded for factories, deserts swapped for river-fronts?

Be it enacted by the Senate and House of Representatives of the United States of America, in Congress assembled, That it shall and may be lawful for the President of the United States to cause so much of any territory belonging to the United States, west of the river Mississippi, not included in any state or organized territory, and to which the Indian title has been extinguished, as he may judge necessary, to be divided into a suitable number of districts, for the reception of such tribes or nations of Indians as may choose to exchange the lands where they now reside, and remove there; and to cause each of said districts to be so described by natural or artificial marks, as to be easily distinguished from every other.

SECTION 2. *And be it further enacted,* That it shall and may be lawful for the President to exchange any or all of such districts, so to be laid off and described, with any tribe or nation of Indians now residing within the limits of any of the states or territories and with which the United States have existing treaties, for the whole or any part or portion of the territory claimed and occupied by such tribe or nation, within the bounds of any one or more of the states or territories, where the land claimed and occupied by the Indians, is owned by the United States, or the United States are bound to the state within which it lies to extinguish the Indian claim thereto.

SECTION 3. *And be it further enacted,* That in the making of any such exchange or exchanges, it shall and may be lawful for the President solemnly to assure the tribe or nation with which the exchange is made, that the United States will forever secure and guaranty to them, and their heirs or successors, the country so exchanged with them; and if they prefer it, that the United States will cause a patent or grant to be made and executed to them for the same: *Provided always,* That such lands shall revert to the United States, if the Indians become extinct, or abandon the same.

SECTION 4. *And be it further enacted,* That if, upon any of the lands now occupied by the Indians, and to be exchanged for, there should be such improvements as add value to the land claimed by any individual or individuals of such tribes or nations, it shall and may be lawful for the President to cause such value to be ascertained by appraisement or otherwise, and to cause such ascertained value to be paid to the person or persons rightfully claiming such improvements. And upon the payment of such valuation, the improvements so valued and paid for, shall pass to the United States, and possession shall not afterwards be permitted to any of the same tribe.

SECTION 5. *And be it further enacted,* That upon the making of any such exchange as is contemplated by this act, it shall and may be lawful for the President to cause such aid and assistance to be furnished to the emigrants as may be necessary and proper to enable them to remove to, and settle in, the country for which they may have exchanged; and also, to give them such aid and assistance as may be necessary for their support and subsistence for the first year after their removal.

SECTION 6. *And be it further enacted,* That it shall and may be lawful for the President to cause such tribe or nation to be protected, at their new residence, against all interruption or disturbance from any other tribe or nation of Indians, or from any other person or persons whatever.

SECTION 7. *And be it further enacted,* That it shall and may be lawful for the President to have the same superintendence and care over any tribe or nation in the country to which they may remove, as contemplated by this act, that he is now authorized to have over them at their present places of residence: *Provided,* That nothing in this act contained shall be construed as authorizing or directing the violation of any existing treaty between the United States and any of the Indian tribes.

SECTION 8. *And be it further enacted,* That for the purpose of giving effect to the provisions of this act, the sum of five hundred thousand dollars is hereby appropriated, to be paid out of any money in the treasury, not otherwise appropriated.

APPROVED, May 28, 1830.

The Kansas Indians
5 Wall 737 (1866)

There has always been a question as to the status of individual Indians. At what point do they become so assimilated and conform so much to the social norms of white society that it can be said that they are no longer Indians? Many of the arguments used against the continuation of the treaty rights and privileges that American Indians enjoy are based upon the assumption that they must adhere to the ways of their ancestors as recorded by scholars. Thus any Indian *not* living in a tent, making his livelihood by the hunt, donned in finest feathers, beads and braids is derided as not being a "real" Indian. The stereotype lives on long after the tribe itself has created a new way of life.

What is important to note is that Indian treaty and statutory rights, Indian title to land, the exemption from taxes on Indian lands and income derived from lands and the special services in health and education that many reservations receive are *vested* rights. That is, they are rights for which the different tribes bargained for a century ago in return for the land cessions they were asked to make.

Under a strict enforcement of the contractual nature of the treaty the United States should by rights give back most of the land area in this nation for its flagrant breach of its treaty-contractual obligations.

Assimilation is therefore irrelevant to the legal rights enjoyed by an Indian tribe. A whole tribe could don space suits and survey the universe. This would not legally affect their rights as members of a tribe with which the United States holds treaty obligations and commitments. When this aspect is understood by non-Indians it places a different light on the emotional posture that Indian people attach to their treaty rights.

This question of assimilation was raised comparatively early in the history of the United States. After the Shawnees, Miamis and Weas had moved to Kansas from their ancestral homes in the Ohio valley they settled down and made the necessary adjustments to life on the western plains. In many ways they lived no differently than did the white settlers of Kansas. They farmed, owned homes, attended social functions, read newspapers, and generally mingled with their white neighbors. In nearly every aspect, then, they lived like the typical citizen of Kansas.

Since they were so well-merged with the other citizens of Kansas the state decided that they no longer had any special rights as members of their respective tribes. It decided, therefore, that despite the disclaimer clause in the Kansas constitution by which the state acknowledged the extant Indian rights, that it could levy taxes and execute judgments against the lands of the tribal members. A number of cases were taken to court and later consolidated as "The Kansas Indians" in the Supreme Court of the United States. At issue was the right of the states to determine who was and who was not an Indian and whether or not a tribe existed or had to exist in a way of life radically differently than other citizens. Do treaties simply fade away by acculturation of the members of the tribe?

With a resounding NO the Supreme Court outlined the legal position and Constitutional rights of Indian tribes. It once again placed the primary responsibility for Indians with the federal government and shaped up the blurring edges to the doctrine of tribal sovereignty and existence. For that reason "The Kansas Indians" has been a major case supporting the rights of Indian tribes to maintain themselves as a distinct community over and above the changing legal doctrines of states' rights.

By article II of the Treaty of December 1825, a tract of country in Kansas was ceded to the Shawnees of Missouri and Ohio.

By the Treaty of 1831 the Ohio Shawnees ceded their country in Ohio to the United States. By the 2nd article and the same treaty, 100,000 acres of the land in Kansas, provided for in the former treaty, was given to them in fee, to be patented, etc. By article X of this Treaty, these lands were not to be ceded except to the United States, and were never to be included within the bounds of any State or Territory, nor subject to its laws.

By the terms of article XV of the Treaty of 1817 the lands granted to the Shawnees, ceded by the Treaty of 1831, in exchange for their Kansas land, were not to be liable for taxes as long as they continued the property of the Indians.

The Ohio Shawnees removed to Kansas and were located on this land, and were resident there on May 30th, 1854 when the Organic Act was passed by Congress.

The rights of the Indians were preserved as they then existed, and in this case the Tribe and its Territory were expressly excepted out of the boundaries and jurisdiction of the Territory, and were to remain precisely the same as though the Act had never been passed—not subject to any jurisdiction but that of their own laws and customs.

July 29, 1854, a Constitution was formed for the State of Kansas, in which by section 1 of schedule it was provided that all rights of individuals should continue as if no State had been formed or change in the government made.

January 29, 1861, an Act for the admission of the State was passed by Congress by which the same provisions were made with reference to the Indians as are contained in the Organic Act, above named. They and their Territory, lands and property were excepted out of the boundaries of the State "Until they should signify their assent to the President of the United States to be included therein."

But by the Treaty approved November 2, 1854, dated May 20, 1854, 10 Stat., pp. 1053, 1063, the tract of land ceded to the Shawnees by the Treaty of 1825 was receded to the United States by article I thereof, and by the second article, 200,000 acres of the same were receded to the Shawnees, p. 1059, same Vol., 2nd amendment, but in the last clause of the first paragraph of the 2nd article, these 200,000 acres are described as reserved by the Shawnees. From this ceded or reserved tract, two hundred acres were to be selected to each individual, except as to the bands of Black-Bob and Long-Tail, who were to have their lands with such others as might wish to join them, assigned to them in common in a compact body. The lands assigned to individuals were to be patented under such limitations and restrictions as Congress might impose. Art. IX., 10 Stat., 1057.

Congress afterwards directed lands assigned in severalty to be patented, subject to such restrictions as the Secretary of the Interior might impose. 11 Stat., 430.

Patents were issued in pursuance thereof, as set out in the record.

Holding their lands thus partly in common and partly in severalty, at the date of the admission of Kansas into the Union, the Act of January 29, 1861, provided that nothing contained in this said Constitution respecting the boundaries of said State shall be construed to impair the rights of person or property now pertaining to the Indians of said Territory, so long as such rights shall remain unextinguished by Treaty with such Indians.

Again; it is provided in the same Act, "that no territory should be included which, by Treaty with such Indian tribes, was not (without the consent of such tribe) to be included within the territorial limits or jurisdiction of any State or Territory; but all such territory shall be excepted out of the boundaries and constitute no part of the State of Kansas, until said tribe shall signify their assent to the President of the United States, to be included in said State."

No treaty has been made by this tribe in which such assent has been given by it.

No such assent is shown to have been given to the President. Their *status* is precisely the same as it was when Kansas was admitted, and these lands and persons were excepted from its boundaries.

The sole question presented by this record is, whether the lands belonging to the united tribe of Shawnee Indians, residing in Kansas, are taxable.

The authorities of the County of Johnson asserting the right, and the highest court of the State having sustained it, the question is properly here for consideration. The solution of it depends on the construction of treaties, the relations of the general government to the Indian tribes, and the laws of Congress. In order to proper understanding of the rights of these Indians, it is necessary to give a short history of some of the treaties that have been made with them.

In 1825 the Shawnee tribe was divided—part being in Missouri and part in Ohio. The Missouri Shawnees were in possession of valuable lands near Cape Girardeau, and in that year ceded them, by treaty, Shawnees' Treaty, Nov. 7, 1825 (7 Stat. at L., 284), to the United States, and, in consideration of the cession, received for their use, and those of the same nation in Ohio, who chose to join them, a tract of country in Kansas, embracing fifty square miles. In pursuance of the favorite policy of the government to persuade all the Indian tribes east of the Mississippi to migrate and settle on territory, to be secured to them, west of that river, in 1831, Shawn. Treat. Aug. 8, 1831 (7 Stat. at L., 355), a convention was concluded with the Ohio Shawnees—they being willing to remove west, in order to obtain "a more permanent and advantageous home for themselves and their posterity." In exchange for valuable lands and improvements in Ohio, they obtained by patent, in fee simple to them and their heirs forever, so long as they exist as a nation, and remain upon the same, one hundred thousand acres of land, to be located under the direction of the President of the United States, within the tract granted in 1825 to the Missouri Shawnees.

This Treaty contained words of promise that the same care, superintendence, and protection which had been extended over them in Ohio should be assured to them in the country to which they were to remove, and also a guaranty that their lands should never be within the bounds of any State or Territory, nor themselves subject to the laws thereof. In obedience to the obligations of this Treaty, they removed and united with their brethren who had preceded them from Missouri, but were soon met by the advancing tide of civilization. In view of the rapid increase of population in the Kansas country, and the small number of Shawnees—the tribe does not now contain over 1,200 souls—it was deemed advisable to lessen their territorial limits.

Accordingly, another Treaty was concluded with them on the 10th day of May, 1854. Shawn. Treat (10 Stat. at L., 1053). By this Treaty, the united Shawnee Nation ceded to the United States all the large domain granted to them by the Treaty of 1825. In consideration for this cession, two hundred thousand acres of these same lands were receded to them, and they also obtained annuities and other property. This Treaty was peculiar in some of its provisions. It did not contemplate that the Indians should enjoy the whole tract, as the quantity for each individual was limited to two hundred acres. The unselected lands were to be sold by the government, and the proceeds appropriated to the uses of the Indians. It also recognized that part of the lands selected by the Indians could be held in common, and part in severalty. If held in common, they were to be assigned in a compact body; if in severalty, the privilege was conceded of selecting anywhere in the tract outside of the common lands.

The Indians who held separate estates were to have patents issued to them, with such guards and restrictions as Congress should deem advisable for their protection. Congress afterwards (11 Stat. at L., 430) directed the lands to be patented, subject to such restrictions as the Minister of the Interior might impose; and these lands are now held by these Indians, under patents, without power of alienation, except by consent of the Secretary of the Interior. This Treaty was silent about the guaranties of the Treaty of 1831; but the Shawnees expressly acknowledged their dependence on the government of the United States, as formerly they had done, and invoked its protection and care. Prior to the ratification of this Treaty (although not before it was signed) the Organic Act for the Territory of Kansas was passed, and on the 29th of January, 1861, Kansas was admitted into the Union; but the rights of the Indians, the powers of Congress over them, their lands and property, and the stipulations of treaties, were fully preserved, and in the same words, both in the Organic Act and the Act for the Admission of Kansas.

The Ohio Shawnees, when they ceded their lands in Ohio, did it in pursuance of an Act of Congress of May 28, 1830, ch. 148 (4 Stat., 411), which assured them the country to which they were translated should be secured and guarantied to them and their heirs

45

forever. The well-defined policy of the government demanded the removal of the Indians from organized States, and it was supposed at the time the country selected for them was so remote as never to be needed for settlement. This policy was deemed advantageous to their interests, as it separated them from the corrupting influences of bad white men, and secured for them a permanent home. It is plain to be seen that the covenants with the Shawnees in the Treaty of 1861, that they should not be subject to the laws of organized States or Territories, nor their lands included within their boundaries, unless with their own consent, signified to the President, must have materially influenced their decision to part with their Ohio possessions and join their brethren in Kansas. They, therefore, removed under the assured protection of the government, to enjoy, as they expected, in perpetuity, free from encroachments, a home adapted to their habits and customs. But these expectations were not to be realized, for the spirit of American enterprise, in a few years, reached their country, and the same white population that pressed upon them in Ohio and Missouri followed them there.

The present and future wants of this population created the necessity for the Treaty of 1854, and the segregation of lands allowed by it, in connection with the power to sell these unsettled tracts, invited what followed—a mixed occupancy of the same territory by the red and white men—the very matter which dictated the removal of the Indians from the older States.

It is insisted, as the guaranties of the Treaty of 1831 are not, in express words, reaffirmed in the Treaty of 1854, they are, therefore, abrogated, and that the division of the Indian Territory into separate estates, so changes the *status* of the Indians that the property of those who hold in severalty is liable to state taxation. It is conceded that those who hold in common cannot be taxed. If such are the effects of this Treaty, they were evidently not in contemplation of one of the parties to it, and it could never have been intended by the government to make a distinction in favor of the Indians who held in common, and against those who held in severalty. If the Indians thus holding had less rights than their more favored brethren, who enjoyed their possession in common, and in compact form, would not good faith have required that it should have been so stated in the Treaty? The general pledge of protection substantially accorded in this Treaty, as in all the other treaties with this tribe, forbids the idea that government intended to withdraw its protection from one part of the tribe and extend it to the other.

But, it is not necessary to import the guarantees of the Treaty of 1831 into that of 1854, in order to save the property of the entire tribe from state taxation. If the necessities of the case required us to do so, we should hesitate to declare that, in the understanding of the parties, the promises under which the Treaty of 1831 was made, and the guaranties contained in it, were all abandoned when the Treaty of 1854 was concluded. If the tribal organization of the Shawnees is preserved intact, and recognized by the Political Department of the Government as existing, then they are a "people distinct from others," capable of making treaties, separated from the jurisdiction of Kansas, and to be governed exclusively by the government of the Union. If under the control of Congress, from necessity, there can be no divided authority. If they have outlived many things, they have not outlived the protection afforded by the Constitution, treaties and laws of Congress. It may be that they cannot exist much longer as a distinct people in the presence of the civilization of Kansas, "but until they are clothed with the rights and bound to all the duties of citizens" they enjoy the privilege of total immunity from state taxation. There can be no question of state sovereignty in the case, as Kansas accepted her admission into the family of States on condition that the Indian rights should remain unimpaired and the general government at liberty to make any regulation respecting them, their lands, property, or other rights, which it would have been competent to make if Kansas had not been admitted into the Union. The Treaty of 1854 left the Shawnee people a united tribe, with a declaration of the dependence on the national government for protection and the vindication of their rights. Ever since this their tribal organization has remained as it was before. They have elective chiefs and an elective council; meeting at stated periods; keeping a record of their proceedings; with powers regulated by custom, by which they punish offenses, adjust differences, and exercise a general oversight over the affairs of the nation. This people have their own customs and laws by which they are governed. Because some of those customs have been abandoned, owing to the proximity of their white neighbors, may be an evidence of the superior influence of our race, but does not tend to prove that their tribal organization is not preserved. There is no evidence in the record to show that the Indians with separate estates have not the same rights in the tribe as those whose estates are held in common. Their machinery of government, though simple, is adapted to their intelligence and wants, and effective, with faithful agents to watch over them. If broken into, it is the natural result of Shawnees and whites owning adjoining plantations, and living and trafficking together as neighbors and friends. But the action of the Political Department of the Government settles beyond controversy, that the Shawnees are as yet a distinct people, with a perfect tribal organization. Within a very recent period their head men negotiated a treaty with the United States, which, for some reason not explained in the record, was either not sent to the Senate, or, if sent, not ratified, and they are under the charge of an agent who constantly resides with them. While the general government has a superintending care over their interests, and continues to treat with them as a nation, the State of Kansas is estopped from denying their title to it. She accepted this *status* when she accepted the Act admitting her into the Union. Conferring rights and privileges on these Indians cannot affect their situation, which can only be changed by treaty stipulation, or a voluntary abandonment of their tribal organization. As long as the United States recognizes their national character they are under the protection of treaties and the laws of Congress, and their property is withdrawn from the operation of state laws.

It follows, from what has been said, that the Supreme Court of Kansas erred in not perpetuating the injunction and granting relief prayed for.

Miami Removal and Allotment Act
17 Stat. 631 (1873)

A great deal is always said about the evils of allotment and the continual statutory enactments in which the Indian tribal land estate was whittled down to practically nothing. Yet few people have examined any of the statutory agreements by which the lands were taken.

The selection below regards the Miami tribe, then resident in Kansas, and the provisions by which their lands were allotted and citizenship granted to their individual members. It is noteworthy that the case of *Elk v. Wilkins* later had to deal with the status of Indian individuals who voluntarily left tribal relations and assumed United States citizenship.

Most of the other acts allotting tribal lands follow this pattern. It is important, therefore, to recognize the many specific provisions which the United States thought necessary to include as well as the continual enticement of tribal members to dismember the tribe. To the credit of the Miami tribe it has survived acts such as these and is alive and well in eastern Oklahoma today.

Be it enacted by the Senate and House of Representatives of the United States of America in Congress assembled, That if the Miami tribe of Indians in Kansas shall signify to the President of the United States their desire to sell the lands reserved for the future homes of the said Indians by the first article of the treaty of June fifth, eighteen hundred and fifty-four, and which remain unallotted, together with the school-section mentioned in said article, said lands shall be disposed of in the following manner, to wit: The said secretary shall appoint three disinterested and competent persons, who shall, after being duly sworn to perform such service faithfully and impartially, personally examine and appraise said lands by legal subdivisions of one hundred and sixty acres or less, separately, and make return thereof to the Commissioner of Indian Affairs: *Provided,* That the Secretary of the Interior may, in his discretion, set aside any appraisements that may be made under the provisions of this act, and cause a new appraisement to be made: *And provided further,* That in making said appraisement, the land and any improvements made by the United States and Indians shall be included, and the improvements made by white settlers shall be excluded in determining an estimate of the value thereof.

SECTION 2. That each bona-fide settler occupying any portion of said lands at the date of the passage of this act, and having made valuable improvements thereon, or the heirs at law of such, who is a citizen of the United States, or who has declared his intention to become such, shall be entitled, at any time within one year from the return of said appraisement, to purchase, for cash, the land so occupied and improved by him, not to exceed one hundred and sixty acres in each case, at the appraised value thereof, under such rules and regulations as the Secretary of the Interior may prescribe. And on failure to make payment within one year from date of said approval of appraisement the right of such settler to purchase as aforesaid shall cease, and it shall be the duty of the Secretary of the Interior to sell the same, either at public sale or on sealed bids, for cash, to the highest bidder, at not less than the appraised value, nor less than one dollar and twenty-five cents per acre, after due notice by public advertisement. And all lands referred to in this and the foregoing sections not so occupied and improved by settlers at the date of the approval of this act shall be appraised by said appraisers, including all improvements thereon of every character, and sold by direction of the Secretary of the Interior to the highest bidder, for cash, after due advertisement, either at public sale or on sealed bids, at not less than the appraised value, nor less than one dollar and twenty-five cents per acre as aforesaid, in quantities not exceeding one hundred and sixty acres aforesaid.

SECTION 3. That if any adult member of said tribe shall desire to become a citizen of the United States, shall prove by at least two competent witnesses, to the satisfaction of the circuit court of the United States for the State of Kansas, that he or she is sufficiently intelligent and prudent to manage his or her own affairs, and has, for the period of five years, been able to maintain himself or herself and family, and has adopted the habits of civilized life, and shall take an oath or allegiance to the United States, as provided by law for the naturalization of aliens, he or she shall be declared by said court to be a citizen of the United States, which shall be entered of record and a certificate thereof given to said party. On the presentation of said certificate to the Secretary of the Interior, with satisfactory proof of identity, he may, at the request of such person or persons, cause the lands severally held by them and their minor children to be conveyed to them by patent in fee-simple, without the power of alienation, and may, at his discretion, cause to be paid to them, from time to time, their proportion of all the moneys and effects of said tribe held for them by the United States, or which may be received as the net proceeds of the sale of lands under the provisions of this act; after which said Indians and their minor children shall cease to be members of any Indian tribe; but the lands so patented to them shall not be subject to levy, taxation, or sale during the natural lives of said Indians or of their minor children.

SECTION 4. That the Secretary of the Interior shall, in ninety days from the passage of this act, cause to be taken a census of all the Miami Indians entitled to a share in the reserved lands and the moneys set apart by the treaty between the United States and the Miami Indians, dated June the fifth, eighteen hundred and fifty-four, for that part of the tribe known as the Western Miamies, including in said census those persons of Miami blood or descent for whom provision was made by the third section of the act of June twelfth, eighteen hundred and fifty-eight, if in the opinion of the Secretary of the Interior the said Indians are entitled to be so included under treaty stipulations; but in such census none shall be included unless justly entitled according to the provisions of said treaty; and with said census there shall also be made two lists, one containing the names of all the Indians so entitled who may elect to become citizens of the United States, and their minor children (heads of families choosing) the other the names of all who elect to remain under the care of the United States, and to unite with the Wea, Peoria, Kaskaskia, and Piankeshaw Indians in the Indian Territory, according to the provisions of a contract dated January the fifteenth, eighteen hundred and seventy-two, between the Western Miami Indians, of Kansas, of one part, and said Wea, Peoria, Kaskaskia, and Piankeshaw Indians, of the other part, and their minor children; which census and lists shall be filed in the office of the Secretary of the Interior, and which census and lists, when properly taken and filed as aforesaid, shall be approved by the Secretary of the Interior, and thenceforward, those whose names are on the citizens' list shall be treated and regarded, in all respects, as citizens of the United States: *Provided,* That they become citizens and comply with the provisions of the third, and fourth sections of this act relating to the naturalization, *And provided further,* That the Secretary of the Interior is hereby directed to ascertain what amount if any is due the Miami tribe of Indians referred to in the corrected lists under the treaty of eighteen hundred and fifty-four, on account of certain annuities which were distributed to and among those persons of Miami blood and descent who were included in the act of eighteen hundred and fifty-eight, and by virtue of the same were authorized and did receive their proportion respectively in said annuities, and to cause that amount to be deducted out of the consolidated fund as herein provided for and paid to said Miami Indians referred to in said corrected lists made by virtue of the said treaty of eighteen hundred and fifty-four.

SECTION 5. And the proceeds of the sales of the said unallotted lands, including said school-section, and all moneys, securities, annuities, and effects held by the United States for said Miami Indians of Kansas, after making the foregoing deductions for citizen Indians and their minor children, shall belong to and be the exclusive property of the last-named Indians, to be known as their consolidated fund.

SECTION 6. That the Secretary of the Interior is hereby authorized and directed to examine a contract made by and between the said Western Miami Indians of Kansas, and the confederated Wea, Peoria, Kaskaskia, and Piankeshaw Indians, made on the fifteenth day of January, anno Domini, eighteen hundred and seventy-two, and to approve the same with such modifications as justice and equity may require; and, for the purpose of carrying into effect said arrangement may withdraw from said consolidated fund, and pay to the confederated Wea, Peoria, Kaskaskia, and Piankeshaw Indians, a sum sufficient to pay said Wea, Peoria, Kaskaskia, and Piankeshaw Indians, according to said contract of the fifteenth of January aforesaid, for an interest in the lands of the last-named confederated tribe, for all of said Miamis, electing as aforesaid, to unite with said confederated tribe; and after making such payment, there shall be set apart and capitalized with the funds of said Wea, Peoria, Kaskaskia, and Piankeshaw Indians, a sum sufficient to warrant and justify all said Miamis so entitled, and so electing, to unite with said Wea, Peoria, Kaskaskia, and Piankeshaw Indians, in drawing thereafter like annuities with said Wea, Peoria, Kaskaskia, and Piankeshaw Indians, without prejudice to the rights and interests of said last-named Indians; and the remainder of such consolidated fund shall then be paid, (under like direction) per capita, to all those so entitled and so electing to unite with said Wea, Peoria, Kaskaskia, and Piankeshaw Indians, to aid them in moving to, and improving their new homes in the Territory; and after their union with said confederated Wea, Peoria, Kaskaskia, and Piankeshaw Indians, the united tribe shall be called the United Peorias and Miamis, and thereafter shall draw equal and like annuities, according to the provisions of said contract of the fifteenth of January, anno Domini, eighteen hundred and seventy-two, and such modifications as may be agreed to by said contracting parties, with the approval of said Secretary, as herein provided.

SECTION 7. That the provisions of this act shall not in any way affect the rights or claims of those individual Miamis or persons of Miami blood or descent who are named in the corrected list referred to in the Senate amendment to the fourth article of the treaty of June fifth, eighteen hundred and fifty-four, or their descendants.

Approved, March 3, 1873

The government allowed different tribes to contract with each other for sale and exchange of lands as you can see from the selection above. Thus tribes consolidated, split apart, changed residences, and exchanged citizenships with one another. These provisions were not included in the subsequent enactments such as the Indian Reorganization Act. Their exclusion reflects the interpretation of bureaucrats in the government who have come to look upon Indian lands as their own, with Indians as mere appendages to the property.

With the loss of this important principle the government and the tribes lost considerable flexibility in solving their problems. If this principle were revived and used today it would prove an important tool in the solution of pressing problems. A number of tribes have proposed buying out tribes that wished to terminate their reservations. With this tool of inter-tribal land purchases and contract consolidations, estate could be accomplished and new mergers of smaller tribes could be accomplished, thus creating new tribal entities of sufficient economic strength and population to succeed in development projects.

Point Elliot Treaty
Article V, 12 Stat. 927 (1854)

Phraseology is tricky. A phrase may mean something in one context and not mean anything in another. Currently in the struggle for fishing rights in the state of Washington a key treaty phrase has been the right to fish "in common with other citizens". The state of Washington has interpreted these words so narrowly as to preclude any Indian fishing rights whatsoever. Every state court has at one time or another violated a common doctrine of treaty interpretation that the phrases of Indian treaties shall be interpreted as the Indians would have understood them at the time the treaty was signed.

. . . The right of taking fish at usual and accustomed grounds and stations is further secured to said Indians in common with all citizens of the Territory, and of erecting temporary houses for the purposes of curing, together with the privilege of hunting and gathering roots and berries on open and unclaimed lands. *Provided, however,* That they shall not take shellfish from any beds staked or cultivated by citizens.

Shoshone-Bannock Agreement of 1888

The following excerpt indicates that the phrase, "in common with other citizens," was used with reference to an agreement with the Shoshone and Bannock Indians of Fort Hall in order to settle whites on the Indian lands. It thus gives the whites equal rights to water with the Indians even though federal doctrines have affirmed that the Indians are entitled to water rising on or flowing through the reservation.

It remains to be seen whether or not there will be an equitable settlement of the fishing rights problem in Washington. The Indians would certainly win if the court interpreted the phrase consistently with its meaning in this agreement since the whites have certainly had their right to water upheld.

An Act to accept and ratify an agreement made with the Shoshone and Bannock Indians, for the surrender and relinquishment . . . of a portion of the Fort Hall Reservation . . . , for the purposes of a town-site, and for the grant of a right of way through said reservation to the Utah and Northern Railway Company.

SECTION 10. That the citizens of the town hereinbefore provided for shall have the free and undisturbed use in common with the said Indians of the waters of any river, creek, stream, or spring flowing through the Fort Hall Reservation in the vicinity of said town, with right of access at all times thereto, and the right to construct, operate, and maintain all such ditches, canals, works, or other aqueducts, drain, and sewerage pipes, and other appliances on the reservation, as may be necessary to provide said town with proper water and sewerage facilities.

(September 1, 1888)

Great Sioux Agreement
25 Stat. 888 (1889)

Some years after the great plains wars, pressure grew to allot the Great Sioux reservation which extended over almost all of western South Dakota. Thousands of hungry whites, demanded that the vast reservation be allotted and the surplus lands be opened to white settlement. Thus it was that General Crook, "Three Stars" was sent out to negotiate the Great Sioux Agreement of 1889. With Crook sitting at the table the Sioux were reminded that if they didn't agree to cede their lands the Army would come in and exterminate them. In spite of such pressures by the United States government less than ten per cent of the adult males signed the paper agreeing to the cession.

Claiming total accord, the negotiators rushed to Washington and pushed the agreement through Congress as a statute. The huge territory was broken into a number of smaller reservations with separate agencies, each declared as executive order reservations thus depriving them of treaty-reservation status which holds a superior right to self-government. For whereas treaty-right reservations have all rights inherent in the original Indian tribe, executive order reservations only have rights implied in their establishment by the executive branch.

The agreement of 1889 must be regarded as a basic document of the Sioux Nation and it may have within it the seeds of Sioux revival. It amends the treaty of 1868 only slightly. Yet, as the next selection will show, it can be regarded as a major step, as yet unrecognized, in the continuing process of treaty negotiations between the Sioux Nation and the United States.

Be it enacted by the Senate and House of Representatives of the United States of America in Congress assembled, That the following tract of land, being a part of the Great Reservation of the Sioux Nation, in the Territory of Dakota, is hereby set apart for a permanent reservation for the Indians receiving rations and annuities at the Pine Ridge Agency, in the Territory of Dakota, namely: Beginning at the intersection of the one hundred and third meridian of longitude with the northern boundary of the State of Nebraska; thence north along said meridian to the South Fork of Cheyenne River, and down said stream to the mouth of Battle Creek; thence due east to White River; thence down White River to the mouth of Black Pipe Creek on White River; thence due south to said north line of the State of Nebraska; thence west on said north line to the place of beginning. Also, the following tract of land situated in the State of Nebraska, namely:. Beginning at a point on the boundary-line between the State of Nebraska and the Territory of Dakota where the range line between ranges forty-four and forty-five west of the sixth principal meridian, in the Territory of Dakota, intersects said boundary-line; thence east along said boundary-line five miles; thence due south five miles; thence due west ten miles; thence due north to said boundary-line; thence due east along said boundary-line to the place of the beginning: *Provided,* That the said tract of land in the State of Nebraska shall be reserved by Executive order, only so long as it may be needed for the use and protection of the Indians receiving rations and annuities at the Pine Ridge Agency.

SECTION 2. That the following tract of land, being a part of the said Great Reservation of the Sioux Nation, in the Territory of Dakota, is hereby set apart for a permanent reservation for the Indians receiving rations and annuities at the Rosebud Agency, in said Territory of Dakota, namely: Commencing in the middle of the main channel of the Missouri River at the intersection of the south line of Brule County; thence down said middle of the main channel of said river to the intersection of the ninety-ninth degree of west longitude from Greenwich; thence due south to the forty-third parallel of latitude; thence west along said parallel to a point due south from the mouth of Black Pipe Creek; thence due north to the mouth of Black Pipe Creek; thence down White River to a point intersecting the west line of Gregory County extended north; thence south on said extended west line of Gregory County to the intersection of the south line of Brule County extended west; thence due east on said south line of Brule County extended to the point of beginning in the Missouri River, including entirely within said reservation all islands, if any, in said river.

SECTION 3. That the following tract of land, being a part of the said Great Reservation of the Sioux Nation, in the Territory of Dakota, is hereby set apart for a permanent reservation for the Indians receiving rations and annuities at the Standing Rock Agency, in the said Territory of Dakota, namely: Beginning at a point in the center of the main channel of the Missouri River, opposite the mouth of Cannon Ball River; thence down said center of the main channel to a point ten miles north of the mouth of the Moreau River, including also within said reservation all islands, if any, in said river; thence due west to the one hundred and second degree of west longitude from Greenwich; thence north along said meridian to its intersection with the South Branch of Cannon Ball River, also known as Cedar Creek; thence down said South Branch of Cannon Ball River to its intersection with the main Cannon Ball River, and down said main Cannon Ball River to the center of the main channel of the Missouri River at the place of beginning.

SECTION 4. That the following tract of land, being a part of the said Great Reservation of the Sioux Nation, in the Territory of Dakota, is hereby set apart for a permanent reservation for the Indians receiving rations and annuities at the Cheyenne River Agency, in the said Territory of Dakota, namely: Beginning at a point in the center of the main channel of the Missouri River, ten miles north of the mouth of the Moreau River, said point being the southeastern corner of the Standing Rock Reservation; thence down said center of the main channel of the Missouri River, including also entirely within said reservation all islands, if any, in said river, to a point opposite the mouth of the Cheyenne River; thence west to said Cheyenne River, and up the same to its intersection with the one hundred and second meridian of longitude; thence north along said meridian to its intersection with a line due west from a point in the Missouri River ten miles north of the mouth of the Moreau River; thence due east to the place of beginning.

SECTION 5. That the following tract of land, being a part of the said Great Reservation of the Sioux Nation, in the Territory of Dakota, is hereby set apart for a permanent reservation for the Indians receiving rations and annuities at the Lower Brule Agency, in said Territory of Dakota, namely: Beginning on the Missouri River at Old Fort George; thence running south on said western boundary to the forty-fourth degree of latitude; thence on said forty-fourth degree of latitude to western boundary of township number seventy-two; thence south on said township western line to an intersecting line running due west from Fort Lookout; thence eastwardly on said line to the center of the main channel of the Missouri River at Fort Lookout; thence north in the center of the main channel of the said river to the original starting point.

SECTION 6. That the following tract of land, being a part of the Great Reservation of the Sioux Nation, in the Territory of Dakota, is hereby set apart for a permanent reservation for the Indians receiving rations and annuities at the Crow Creek Agency, in said Territory of Dakota, namely: The whole of township one hundred and six, range seventy; township one hundred and seven, range seventy-one; township one hundred and eight, range seventy-one; township one hundred and eight, range seventy-two; township one hundred and nine, range seventy-two, and the south half of township one hundred and nine, range seventy-one, and all except sections one, two, three, four, nine, ten, eleven, and twelve of township one hundred and seven, range seventy, and such parts as lie on the east or left bank of the Missouri River, of the following townships, namely: Township one hundred and six, range seventy-one; township one hundred and seven, range seventy-two; township one hundred and eight, range seventy-three; township one hundred and eight, range seventy-four; township one hundred and eight, range seventy-five; township one hundred and eight, range seventy-six; township one hundred and nine, range seventy-three; township one hundred and nine, range seventy-four; south half of township one hundred and nine, range seventy-five, and township one hundred and seven, range seventy-three; also the west half of township one hundred and six, range sixty-nine, and sections sixteen, seventeen, eighteen, nineteen, twenty, twenty-one, twenty-eight, twenty-nine, thirty, thirty-one, thirty-two, and thirty-three, of township one hundred and seven, range sixty-nine.

SECTION 7. That each member of the Santee Sioux tribe of Indians now occupying a reservation in the State of Nebraska not having already taken allotments shall be entitled to allotments upon said reserve in Nebraska as follows: To each head of a family, one-quarter of a section; to each single person over eighteen years, one-eighth of a section; to each orphan child under eighteen years, one eighth of a section; to each other person under eighteen years of age now living, one-sixteenth of a section; with title thereto, in accordance with the provisions of article six of the treaty concluded April twenty-ninth, eighteen hundred and sixty-eight, and the agreement with said Santee Sioux approved February twenty-eighth, eighteen hundred and seventy-seven, and rights under the same in all other respects conforming to this act. And said Santee Sioux shall be entitled to all other benefits under this act in the same manner and with the same conditions as if they were residents upon said Sioux Reservation, receiving rations at one of the agencies herein named: *Provided,* That all allotments heretofore made to said Santee Sioux in Nebraska are hereby ratified and confirmed; and each member of the Flandreau band of Sioux Indians is hereby authorized to take allotments on the Great Sioux Reservation, or in lieu therefor shall be paid at the rate of one dollar per acre for the land to which they would be entitled, to be paid out of the proceeds of lands relinquished under this act, which shall be used under the direction of the Secretary of the Interior; and said Flandreau band of Sioux Indians is in all other respects entitled to the benefits of this act the same as if receiving rations and annuities at any of the agencies aforesaid.

SECTION 8. That the President is hereby authorized and required, whenever in his opinion any reservation of such Indians, or any part thereof, is advantageous for agricultural or grazing purposes, and the progress in civilization of the Indians receiving rations on either or any of said reservations shall be such as to encourage the belief that an allotment in severalty to such Indians, or any of them, would be for the best interest of said Indians, to cause said reservation, or so much thereof as is necessary, to be surveyed or re-surveyed, and to allot the lands in said reservation in severalty to the Indians located thereon as aforesaid, in quantities as follows: To each head of a family, three hundred and twenty acres; to each single person over eighteen years of age, one-fourth of a section; to each orphan child under eighteen years of age, one-fourth of a section; and to each other person under eighteen years now living, or who may be born prior to the date of the order of the President directing an allotment of the lands embraced in any reservation, one eighth of a section. In case there is not sufficient land in either of said reservations to allot lands to each individual of the classes above named in quantities as above provided the lands embraced in such reservation or reservations shall be alloted to each individual of each of said classes *pro rata* in accordance with the provisions of this act: *Provided,* That where the lands on any reservation are mainly valuable for grazing purposes, an additional allotment of such grazing lands, in quantities as above provided, shall be made to each individual; or in case any two or more Indians who may be entitled to allotments shall so agree, the President may assign the grazing lands to which they may be entitled to them in one tract, and to be held and used in common.

SECTION 9. That all allotments set apart under the provisions of this act shall be selected by the Indians, heads of families selecting for their minor children, and the agents shall select for each orphan child, and in such manner as to embrace the improvements of the Indians making the selection. Where the improvements of two or more Indians have been made on the same legal subdivision of land, unless they shall otherwise agree, a provisional line may be run dividing said lands between them, and the amount to which each is entitled shall be equalized in the assignment of the remainder of the land to which they are entitled under this act: *Provided,* That if anyone entitled to an allotment shall fail to make a selection within five years after the President shall direct that allotments may be made on a particular reservation, the Secretary of the Interior may direct the agent of such tribe or band, if such there be, and if there be no agent, then a special agent appointed for that purpose, to make a selection for such Indian, which selection shall be alloted as in cases where selections are made by the Indians, and patents shall issue in like manner: *Provided,* That these sections as to the allotments shall not be compulsory without the consent of the majority of the adult members of the tribe, except that the allotments shall be made as provided for the orphans.

SECTION 10. That the allotments provided for in this act shall be made by special agents appointed by the President for such purpose, and the agents in charge of the respective reservations on which the allotments are directed to be made, under such rules and regulations as the Secretary of the Interior may from time to time prescribe, and shall be certified by such agents to the Commissioner of Indian Affairs, in duplicate, one copy to be retained in the Indian Office and the other to be transmitted to the Secretary of the Interior for his action, and to be deposited in the General Land Office.

SECTION 11. That upon approval of the allotments provided for in this act by the Secretary of the Interior, he shall cause patents to issue therefor in the name of the allottee, which patents shall be of the legal effect, and declare that the United States does and will hold the lands thus allotted for the period of twenty-five years, in trust for the sole use and benefit of the Indian to whom such allotment shall have been made, or, in case of his decease, of his heirs according to the laws of the State or Territory where such land is located, and that at the expiration of said period the United States will convey the same by patent to said Indian, or his heirs, as aforesaid, in fee, discharged of said trust and free of all charge or incumbrance whatsoever, and patents shall issue accordingly. And each and every allottee under this act shall be entitled to all rights and privileges and be subject to all the provisions of section six of the act approved February eighth, eighteen hundred and eighty-seven, entitled "An act to provide for the allotment of lands in severalty to Indians on the various reservations, and to extend the protection of the laws of the United States and the Territories over the Indians and for other purposes." *Provided,* That the President of the United States may in any case, in his discretion, extend the period by a term not exceeding ten years; and if any lease or conveyance shall be made of the lands set apart and allotted as herein provided, or any contract made touching the same, before the expiration of the time above mentioned, such lease or conveyance or contract shall be absolutely null and void: *Provided further,* That the law of descent and partition in force in the State or Territory where the lands may be situated shall apply thereto after patents therefor have been executed and delivered. Each of the patents aforesaid shall be recorded in the General Land Office, and afterward delivered, free of charge, to the allottee entitled thereto.

SECTION 12. That any time after lands have been allotted to all the Indians of any tribe as herein provided, or sooner, if in the opinion of the President it shall be for the best interests of said tribe, it shall be lawful for the Secretary of the Interior to negotiate with such Indian tribe for the purchase and release by said tribe, in conformity with the treaty or statute under which said reservation is held of such portions of its reservation not allotted as such tribe shall, from time to time, consent to sell, on such terms and conditions as shall be considered just and equitable between the United States and said tribe of Indians, which purchase shall not be complete until ratified by Congress: *Provided, however,* That all lands adapted to agriculture, with or without irrigation, so sold or released to the United States by any Indian tribe shall be held by the United States for the sole purpose of securing homes to actual settlers, and shall be disposed of by the United States to actual and bona-fide settlers only in tracts not exceeding one hundred and sixty acres to any one person, on such terms as Congress shall provide, subject to grants which Congress may make in aid of education: *And provided further,* That no patents shall issue therefor except to the person so taking the same as and for a homestead, or his heirs, and after the expiration of five years' occupancy thereof as such homestead; and any conveyance of said lands so taken as a homestead, or any contract touching the same, or lien thereon, created prior to the date of such patent shall be null and void. And the sums agreed to be paid by the United States as purchase money for any portion of any such reservation shall be held in the Treasury of the United States for the sole use of the tribe or tribes of Indians to whom such reservation belonged; and the same, with interest thereon at five per sentum per annum, shall be at all times subject to appropriation by Congress for the education and civilization of such tribe or tribes of Indians, or the members thereof. The patents aforesaid shall be recorded in the General Land Office, and afterward, delivered, free of charge, to the allottee entitled thereto.

SECTION 13. That any Indian receiving and entitled to rations and annuities at either of the agencies mentioned in this act at the time the same shall take effect, but residing upon any portion of said Great Reservation not included in either of the separate reservations herein established, may, at his option, within one year from the time when this act shall take effect, and within one year after he has been notified of his said right of option in such manner as the Secretary of the Interior shall by recording his election with the proper agent at the agency to which he belongs, have the allotment to which he would be otherwise entitled on one of said separate reservations upon the land where such Indian may then reside, such allotment in all other respects to conform to the allotments hereinbefore provided. Each member of the Ponca tribe of Indians now occupying a part of the old Ponca Reservation, within the limits of the said Great Sioux Reservation, shall be entitled to allotments upon said old Ponca Reservation as follows: To each head of a family, three hundred and twenty acres; to each single person over eighteen years of age, one-fourth of a section; to each orphan child under eighteen years of age, one-fourth of a section; and to each other person under eighteen years of age now living, one-eighth of a section, with title thereto and rights under the same in all other respects conforming to this act. And said Poncas shall be entitled to all other benefits under this act in the same manner and with the same conditions as if they were a part of the Sioux Nation receiving rations at one of the agencies herein named. When allotments to the Ponca tribe of Indians and to such other Indians as allotments are provided for by this act shall have been made upon that portion of said reservation which is described in the act entitled "An act to extend the northern boundary of the State of Nebraska" approved March twenty-eighth, eighteen hundred and eighty-two, the President shall, in pursuance of said act, declare that the Indian title is extinguished to all lands described in said act not so allotted hereunder and thereupon all of said land not so allotted and included in said act of March twenty-eighth, eighteen hundred and eighty-two, shall be open to settlements as provided in this act: *Provided,* That the allotments to Ponca and other Indians authorized by this act to be made upon the land described in the said act entitled "An act to extend the northern boundary of the State of Nebraska," shall be made within six months from the time this act shall take effect.

SECTION 14. That in cases where the use of water for irrigation is necessary to render the lands within any Indian reservation created by this act available for agricultural purposes, the Secretary of the Interior be, and he is hereby, authorized to prescribe such rules and regulations as he may deem necessary to secure a just and equal distribution thereof among the Indians residing upon any such Indian reservation created by this act; and no other appropriation or grant of water by any riparian proprietor shall be authorized or permitted to the damage of any other riparian proprietor.

SECTION 15. That if any Indian has, under and in conformity with the provisions of the treaty with the Great Sioux Nation concluded April twenty-ninth, eighteen hundred and sixty-eight, and proclaimed by the President February twenty-fourth, eighteen hundred and sixty-nine, or any existing law, taken allotments of land within or without the limits of any of the separate reservations established by this act, such allotments are hereby ratified and made valid, and such Indian is entitled to a patent therefor in conformity with the provisions of said treaty and existing law and of the provisions of this act in relation to patents for individual allotments.

SECTION 16. That the acceptance of this act by the Indians in manner and form as required by the said treaty concluded between the different bands of the Sioux Nation of Indians and the United States, April twenty-ninth, eighteen hundred and sixty-eight, and proclaimed by the President February twenty-fourth, eighteen hundred and sixty-nine, as hereinafter provided, shall be taken and held to be a release of all title on the part of the Indians receiving rations and annuities on each of the said separate reservations, to the lands described in each of the other separate reservations so created, and shall be held to confirm in the Indians entitled to receive rations at each of said separate reservations, respectively, to their separate and exclusive use and benefit, all the title and interest of every name and nature secured therein to the different bands of the Sioux Nation by said treaty of April twenty-ninth, eighteen hundred and sixty-eight. This release shall not affect the title of any individual Indian to his separate allotment on land not included in any of said separate reservations provided for in this act, which title is hereby confirmed, nor any agreement heretofore made with the Chicago, Milwaukee and Saint Paul Railroad Company or the Dakota Central Railroad Company for a right of way through said reservation; and for any lands acquired by any such agreement to be used in connection therewith, except as hereinafter provided; but the Chicago, Milwaukee and Saint Paul Railroad Company and the Dakota Central Railroad Company shall, respectively, have the right to take and use, prior to any white person, and to any corporation, the right of way provided for in said agreements, with not to exceed twenty acres of land in addition to the right of way, for stations for every ten miles of road; and said companies shall also, respectively, have the right to take and use for right of way, side-track, depot and station privileges, machine-shop, freight-house, round house, and yard facilities, prior to any white person, and to any corporation or association, so much of the two separate sections of land embraced in said agreements; also, the former company so much of the one hundred and eighty-eight acres, and the latter company so much of the seventy-five acres, on the east side of the Missouri River, likewise embraced in said agreements, as the Secretary of the Interior shall decide to have been agreed upon and paid for by said railroad, and to be reasonably necessary upon each side of said river for approaches to the bridge of each said companies to be constructed across the river, for right of way, side-track, depot and station privileges, machine-shop, freight-house, round house, and yard facilities, and no more: *Provided,* That the said railway companies shall have made the payments according to the terms of said agreements for each mile of right of way and each acre of land for railway purposes, which said companies take and use under the provisions of this act, and shall satisfy the Secretary of the Interior to that effect: *Provided further,* That no part of the lands herein authorized to be taken shall be sold or conveyed by way of sale of, or mortgage of the railway itself. Nor shall any of said lands be used directly or indirectly for town site purposes, it being the intention hereof that said lands shall be held for general railway uses and purposes only, including stock yards, warehouses, elevators, terminal and other facilities of and for said railways: but nothing herein contained shall be construed to prevent any such railroad company from building upon such lands houses for the accommodation or residence of their employees, or leasing grounds contiguous to its tracks for warehouse or elevator purposes connected with said railways: *And further provided,* That said payments shall be made and said conditions performed within six months after this act shall take effect: *And provided further,* That said railway companies and each of them shall, within nine months after this act takes effect, definitely locate their respective lines of road, including all station grounds and terminals across and upon the lands of said reservation designated in said agreements, and shall also, within the said period of nine months, file with the Secretary of the Interior a map of such definite location, specifying clearly the line of the road the several station grounds and the amount of land required for railway purposes, as herein specified, of the said separate sections of land and said tracts of one hundred and eighty-eight acres and seventy-five acres, and the Secretary of the Interior shall, within three months after the filing of such map, designate the particular portions of said sections and of said tracts of land which the said railway companies respectively may take and hold under the provisions of this act for railway purposes. And the said railway companies, and each of them, shall, within three years after this act takes effect, construct, complete, and put in operation their said lines of road; and in case the said lines of road are not definitely located and maps of location filed within the periods hereinbefore provided, or in case the said lines of road are not constructed, completed, and put in operation within the time herein provided, then, and in either case, the lands granted for right of way, station grounds, or other railway purposes, as in this act provided, shall, without any further act or ceremony, by declared by proclamation of the President forfeited, and shall, without entry or further action on the part of the United States, revert to the United States and be subject to entry under the other provisions of this act; and whenever such forfeiture occurs the Secretary of the Interior shall ascertain the fact and give due notice thereof to the local land officers, and thereupon the lands so forfeited shall be open to homestead entry under the provisions of this act.

SECTION 17. That it is hereby enacted that the seventh article of the said treaty of April twenty-ninth, eighteen hundred and sixty-eight, securing to said Indians the benefits of education, subject to such modifications as Congress shall deem most effective to secure to said Indians equivalent benefits of such education, shall continue in force for twenty years from and after the time this act shall take effect; and the Secretary of the Interior is hereby authorized and directed to purchase from time to time, for the use of said Indians, such and so many American breeding cows of good quality, not exceeding twenty-five thousand in number, as in his judgment can be under regulations furnished by him, cared for and preserved, with their increase, by said Indians: *Provided,* That each head of family or single person over the age of eighteen years, who shall have or may hereafter take his or her allotment of land in severalty, shall be provided with two milch cows, one pair of oxens, with yoke and chain, or two mares and one set of harness in lieu of said oxen, yoke and chain, as the Secretary of the Interior may deem advisable, and they shall also receive one plow, one wagon, one harrow, one hoe, one axe, and one pitchfork, all suitable to the work they may have to do, and also fifty dollars in cash; to be expended under the direction of the Secretary of the Interior in aiding such Indians to erect a house and other buildings suitable for residence or the improvement of his allotment; no sales, barters, or bargains shall be made by any person other than said Indians with each other, of any of the personal property hereinbefore provided for, and any violation of this provision shall be deemed a misdemeanor and punished by fine not exceeding one hundred dollars, or imprisonment not exceeding one year or both in the discretion of the court; That for two years the necessary seeds shall be provided to plant five acres of ground into different crops, if so much can be used, and provided that in the purchase of such seed preference shall be given to Indians who may have raised the same for sale, and so much money as shall be necessary for this purpose is hereby appropriated out of any money in the Treasury not otherwise appropriated; and in addition thereto there shall be set apart, out of any money in the Treasury not otherwise appropriated, the sum of three millions of dollars, which said sum shall be deposited in the Treasury of the United States to the credit of the Sioux Nation of Indians as a permanent fund, the interest of which, at five per centum per annum, shall be appropriated, under the direction of the Secretary of the Interior, to the use of the Indians receiving rations and annuities upon the reservations created by this act, in proportion to the numbers that shall so receive rations and annuities at the time this act takes effect as follows: One-half of said interest shall be so expended for the promotion of industrial and other suitable education among said Indians, and the other half thereof in such manner and for such purposes, including reasonable cash payments per capita as, in the judgment of said Secretary, shall, from time to time, most contribute to the advancement of said Indians in civilization and self-support; and the Santee Sioux, the Flandreau Sioux, and the Ponca Indians shall be included in the benefits of said permanent fund, as provided in sections seven and thirteen of this act: *Provided,* That after the Government has been reimbursed for the money expended for said Indians under the provisions of this act, the Secretary of the Interior may, in his discretion, expend, in addition to the interest of the permanent fund, not to exceed ten per centum per annum of the principal of said fund in the employment of farmers and in the purchase of agricultural pursuits, and he shall report to Congress in detail each year his doings hereunder. And at the end of fifty years from the passage of this act, said fund shall be expended for the purpose of promoting education, civilization, and self-support among said Indians or otherwise distributed among them as Congress shall from time to time thereafter determine.

SECTION 18. That if any land in said Great Sioux Reservation is now occupied and used by any religious society for the purpose of missionary or educational work among Indians, whether situated outside of or within the lines of any reservation constituted by this act, or if any such land is now occupied upon the Santee Sioux Reservation, in Nebraska, the exclusive occupation and use of said land, not exceeding one hundred and sixty acres in any one tract, is hereby, with the approval of the Secretary of the Interior, granted to any such society so long as the same shall be occupied and used by such society for educational and missionary work among said Indians; and the Secretary of the Interior is hereby authorized and directed to give to such religious society patent of such tract of land to the legal effect aforesaid; and for the purpose of such educational or missionary work any such society may purchase, upon any of the reservations herein created, any land not exceeding in any one tract one hundred and sixty acres, not interfering with the title in severalty of any Indian, and with the approval of and upon such terms, not exceeding one dollar and twenty-five cents an acre, as shall be prescribed by the Secretary of the Interior. And the Santee Normal Training School may, in like manner, purchase for such educational or missionary work on the Santee Reservation, in addition to the foregoing, in such location and quantity, not exceeding three hundred and twenty acres, as shall be approved by the Secretary of the Interior.

SECTION 19. That all the provisions of the said treaty with the different bands of the Sioux Nation of Indians concluded April twenty-ninth, eighteen hundred and sixty-eight, and the agreement with the same approved February twenty-eighth, eighteen hundred and seventy-seven, not in conflict with the provisions and requirements of this act, are hereby continued in force according to their tenor and limitation, anything in this act notwithstanding.

SECTION 20. That the Secretary of the Interior shall cause to be erected not less than thirty school-houses, and more, if found necessary, on the different reservations, at such points as he shall think for the best interests of the Indians, but at such distance only as will enable as many as possible attending schools to return home nights, as white children do attending district schools: *And provided,* That any white children residing in the neighborhood are entitled to attend the said school on such terms as the Secretary of the Interior may prescribe.

SECTION 21. That all lands in the Great Sioux Reservation outside of the separate reservations herein described are hereby restored to the public domain, except American Island, Farm Island, and Niobrara Island, and shall be disposed of by the United States to actual settlers only, under the provisions of the homestead law (except section two thousand three hundred and one thereof) and under the law relating to town-sites; *Provided,* That each settler, under and in accordance with the provisions of said homestead acts, shall pay to the United States, for the land so taken by him, in addition to the fees provided by law, the sum of one dollar and twenty-five cents per acre for all lands disposed of within the first three years after the taking effect of this act, and the sum of seventy-five cents per acre for all lands disposed of within the next two years following thereafter, and fifty cents per acre for the residue of the lands then undisposed of, and shall be entitled to a patent therefor according to said homestead laws, and after the full payment of said sums: but the rights of honorably discharged Union soldiers and sailors in the late civil war as defined and described in sections twenty-three hundred and four and twenty-three hundred and five of the Revised Statutes of the United States, shall not be abridged, except as to said sums; *Provided,* That all lands herein opened to settlement under this act remaining undisposed of at the end of ten years from the taking effect of this act shall be taken and accepted by the United States and paid for by said United States at fifty cents per acre, which amount shall be added and credited to said Indians as part of their permanent fund, and said lands shall thereafter be a part of the public domain of the United States to be disposed of under the homestead laws of the United States, and the provisions of this act; and any conveyance of said lands so taken as a homestead, or any contract touching the same, or lien thereon, created prior to the date of final entry, shall be null and void: *Provided,* That there shall be reserved public highways four rods wide around every section of land allotted, or opened to settlement by this act, the section lines being the center of said highways; but no deduction shall be made in the amount to be paid for each quarter-section of land by reason of such reservation. But if the said highway shall be vacated by any competent authority the title to the respective strips shall inure to the then owner of the tract of which it formed a part of the original survey. *And provided further,* That nothing in this act contained shall be so construed as to affect the right of Congress or of the government of Dakota to establish public highways, or to grant to railroad companies the right of way through said lands, or to exclude the said lands, or any thereof, from the operation of the general laws of the United States now in force granting to railway companies the right of way and depot grounds over and upon the public lands, American Island, an island in the Missouri River, near Chamberlain, in the Territory of Dakota, and now a part of the Sioux Reservation, is hereby donated to the said city of Chamberlain:

Provided further, That said city of Chamberlain shall formally accept the same within one year from the passage of this act, upon the express condition that the same shall be preserved and used for all time entire as a public park, and for no other purpose, to which all persons shall have free access; and said city shall have authority to adopt all proper rules and regulations for the improvement and care of said park; and upon the failure of any said conditions the said island shall revert to the United States, to be disposed of by future legislation only. Farm Island, an island in the Missouri River near Pierre, in the Territory of Dakota, and now a part of the Sioux Reservation, is hereby donated to the said city of Pierre: *Provided further,* That said city of Pierre shall formally accept the same within one year from the passage of this act, upon the express condition that the same shall be preserved and used for all time entire as a public park, and for no other purpose, to which all persons shall have free access; and said city shall have authority to adopt all proper rules and regulations for the improvement and care of said park; and upon the failure of any of said conditions the said island shall revert to the United States, to be disposed of by future legislation only. Niobrara Island, an island in the Niobrara River, near Niobrara, and now a part of the Sioux Reservation, is hereby donated to the said city of Niobrara: *Provided further,* That the said city of Niobrara, shall formally accept the same within one year from the passage of this act, upon the express condition that the same shall be preserved and used for all time entire as a public park, and for no other purpose, to which all persons shall have free access; and said city shall have authority to adopt all proper rules and regulations for the improvement and care of said park; and upon failure of any of the said conditions the said island shall revert to the United States, to be disposed of by future legislation only; *And provided further,* That if any full or mixed blood Indian of the Sioux Nation shall have located upon Farm Island, American Island, or Niobrara Island before the date of the passage of this act, it shall be the duty of the Secretary of the Interior, within three months from the time this act shall have taken effect, to cause all improvements made by any such Indian so located upon either of said islands, and all damage that may accrue to him by a removal therefrom, to be appraised, and upon the payment of the sum so determined, within six months after notice thereof by the city to which the island is herein donated to such Indian, said Indian shall be required to remove from said island, and shall be entitled to select instead of such location his allotment according to the provisions of this act upon any of the reservations herein established, or upon any land opened to settlement by this act not already located upon.

SECTION 22. That all money accruing from the disposal of lands in conformity with this act shall be paid into the Treasury of the United States and be applied solely as follows: First, to the reimbursement of the United States for all necessary actual expenditures contemplated and provided for under the provisions of this act, and the creation of the permanent fund hereinbefore provided; and after such reimbursement to the increase of said permanent fund for the purposes hereinbefore provided.

SECTION 23. That all persons who, between the twenty-seventh day of February, eighteen hundred and eighty-five, and the seventeenth day of April, eighteen hundred and eighty-five, in good faith, entered upon or made settlements with intent to enter the same under the homestead or pre-emption laws of the United States upon any part of the Great Sioux Reservation lying east of the Missouri River, and known as the Crow Creek and Winnebago Reservation, which, by the President's proclamation of date February twenty-seventh, eighteen hundred and eighty-five, was declared to be open to settlement, and not included in the new reservation established by section six of this act, and who, being otherwise legally entitled to make such entries, located or attempted to locate thereon homestead, pre-emption, or town site claims, by actual settlement and improvement of any portion of such lands, shall, for a period of ninety days after the proclamation of the President required to be made by this act, have a right to re-enter upon said claims and procure title thereto under the homestead or pre-emption laws of the United States, and complete the same as required therein, and their said claims shall, for such time, have a preference over later entries; and when they shall have in other respects shown themselves entitled and shall have complied with the law regulating such entries, and, as to homesteads, with the special provisions of this act, they shall be entitled to have said lands, and patents therefor shall be issued as in like cases: *Provided,* That pre-emption claimants shall reside on their lands the same length of time before procuring title as homestead claimants under this act. The price to be paid for town-site entries shall be such as is required by law in other cases, and shall be paid into the general fund provided for by this act.

SECTION 24. That sections sixteen and thirty-six of each township of the lands open to settlement under the provisions of this act, whether surveyed or unsurveyed, are hereby reserved for the use and benefit of the public schools, as provided by the act organizing the Territory of Dakota; and whether surveyed or unsurveyed said sections shall not be subject to claim, settlement, or entry under the provision of this act or any of the land laws of the United States: *Provided, however,* That the United States shall pay to said Indians, out of any moneys in the Treasury not otherwise appropriated, the sum of one dollar and twenty-five cents per acre for all lands reserved under the provisions of this section.

SECTION 25. That there is hereby appropriated the sum of one hundred thousand dollars, out of money in the Treasury not otherwise appropriated, or so much thereof as may be necessary, to be applied and used towards surveying the lands herein described as being opened for settlement, said sum to be immediately available; which sum shall not be deducted from the proceeds of lands disposed of under this act.

SECTION 26. That all expenses for the surveying, platting, and disposal of the lands opened to settlement under this act shall be borne by the United States, and not deducted from the proceeds of said lands.

SECTION 27. That the sum of twenty-eight thousand two hundred dollars, or so much thereof as may be necessary, be, and hereby is, appropriated out of any money in the Treasury not otherwise appropriated, to enable the Secretary of the Interior to pay to such individual Indians of the Red Cloud and Red Leaf bands of Sioux as he shall ascertain to have been deprived by the authority of the United States of ponies in the year eighteen hundred and seventy-six, at the rate of forty dollars for each pony; and he is hereby authorized to employ such agent or agents as he may deem necessary in ascertaining such facts as will enable him to carry out this provision, and to pay them therefor such sums as shall be deemed by him fair and just compensation: *Provided,* That the sum paid to each individual Indian under this provision shall be taken and accepted by such Indian in full compensation for all loss sustained by such Indian in consequence of the taking from him of ponies as aforesaid: *And provided further,* That if any Indian entitled to such compensation shall have deceased, the sum to which such Indian would be entitled shall be paid to his heirs-at-law, according to the laws of the Territory of Dakota.

SECTION 28. That this act shall take effect, only, upon the acceptance thereof and consent thereto by the different bands of the Sioux Nation of Indians, in manner and form prescribed by the twelfth article of the treaty between the United States and said Sioux Indians concluded April twenty-ninth, eighteen hundred and sixty-eight, which said acceptance and consent, shall be made known by proclamation by the President of the United States, upon satisfactory proof presented to him, that the same has been obtained in the manner and form required, by said twelfth article of said treaty; which proof shall be presented to him within one year from the passage of this act; and upon failure of such proof and proclamation this act becomes no effect and null and void.

SECTION 29. That there is hereby appropriated, out of any money in the Treasury not otherwise appropriated, the sum of twenty-five thousand dollars, or so much thereof as may be necessary which sum shall be expended, under the direction of the Secretary of the

Interior, for procuring assent of the Sioux Indians to this act provided in section twenty-seven.

SECTION 30. That all acts and parts of acts inconsistent with the provisions of this act are hereby repealed.

Approved, March 2, 1889.

Waldron v. United States
143 Fed. Repts. 413 (1905)

Some years after the Great Sioux Agreement in 1889 a case was brought in federal court attempting to define exactly what rights were given under that agreement. While the agreement had been passed as a statute by the United States Congress and the days of the treaty-making powers with all Indian tribes had long since vanished, the court came up with a remarkable conclusion—the act of March 3, 1889 was in fact a TREATY.

This obscure case may someday reach out of the past to haunt the United States. For if statutes can be interpreted at will by the United States as treaties may not the Indians also do the same? If so would it not appear that, as in any treaty-making situation, the tribes have the right to reject the overtures of the United States? Would it not also follow that regardless of the intention of the United States Congress in passing statutes none can be effective with respect to Indian tribes unless they are consented to by Indian tribes since they are in the nature of a treaty and not a statute?

What then about the myriads of laws passed since 1871? Are they valid when passed without the consent of the tribe? Is not a law passed which has the nature of a treaty a violation of the tribe's constitutional rights? What now, *Lone Wolf v. Hitchcock?*

Through commissioners appointed by the United States the provisions of the act of March 2, 1889, were accepted by the Sioux Nations of Indians and the President of the United States by proclamation fixed February 10, 1890 as the date on which said act should take effect. From the decisions of the General Land Office it appears that the right of complainant to have the land allotted to her was denied solely for the reason that complainant was not an Indian, within the meaning of that term as used in section 13 of the act of Congress of March 2, 1889. As the court finds in this case that complainant is an Indian, within the meaning of said act, it is proper that the law affecting this question be referred to in connection with the facts in the case. In the first place, it is necessary to keep in mind that the act of Congress of March 2, 1889, does not stand, for the purposes of construction and interpretation, as ordinary laws of Congress, so far as the Indians are concerned, for while it appears in form as an independent legislative act of the government, it was and is a treaty or contract made by the United States and the Sioux Nation of Indians. The act was to have no force or effect unless the provisions thereof were accepted by the Sioux Nations of Indians in the manner provided by Article 12 of the treaty of 1868.

The Indians were an ignorant and uncivilized race. They knew little or nothing of the terms of the law which they were to accept except what they were told by the commissioners who negotiated its acceptance. A man who can read cannot be heard to say that he understood a contract to mean something different than its terms imply; but a man who cannot read, and signs a contract on the faith of what the other party to the contract tells him, stands in a very different position. The commissioners of the United States stated to the Indians before obtaining their signatures that the law included mixed-bloods as well as full-bloods. It must be presumed that Congress knew when the law was submitted for acceptance that there were numerous mixed-bloods living upon the reservation about to be divided and drawing rations at the different agencies, and it cannot be presumed that these mixed-bloods were intended to be deprived of their rights to tribal property be a law that, without their signature, would not have become effective for any purpose. These observations are made for the purpose of showing that the law must be looked at as a contract and construed with reference to the understanding the Indians had of the law at the time they accepted its provisions. Mixed-bloods were accepted as going to make up the number of Indians necessary to accept the law. . .

When this very case was before the Secretary of the Interior the advice of the then Attorney General of the United States, Mr. Olney, was asked as to the status of complainant as an Indian. Under date of February 9, 1894, in a letter addressed to the Secretary of the Interior, Mr. Olney used the following language:

> It will be noticed that the act under consideration was dependent for its validity upon the consent of the Indians. In other words, it was substantially a treaty with the Sioux Nation; acts of this form having taken the place of the ancient Indian treaty since the latter was prohibited by the act of Congress in 1871. By the agreement confirmed in this act the Sioux Nation gave up a large amount of territory, and the rights conferred on the nation or on individuals were in consideration thereof.

The Indian Reorganization Act (Wheeler-Howard Act)
48 Stat. 984 (1934)

One of the most progressive eras in Indian history was the New Deal of Franklin D. Roosevelt. Under his Commissioner of Indian Affairs, John Collier (an anthropologist incidentally) recognition of the basic strength of the tribal structure was made official government policy. Early in the Roosevelt years the Congress passed the Wheeler-Howard Act allowing the tribes self-government for the first time since they had settled on the reservations.

Because this act is the foundation for the modern tribal council it has been included as a selection in this chapter. You will note that the Sioux Benefit as described in section 17 of the Great Sioux Agreement of 1889 was reaffirmed in section 14 of this new law by the crafty Sioux lobbyists. Of the Sioux tribe today only the Cheyenne River Sioux have maintained their "Sioux benefit" while the other tribes have liquidated it.

The only provision detrimental to Indians in the act is the provision that having once voted against the law no tribe could subsequently adopt a constitution under its provisions. Some tribes who voted against the Indian Reorganization Act during the Depression would certainly adopt it today if they had the opportunity. A major step for the future would be to reopen the provisions of the law to tribes who had previously voted against it and to open it to urban Indian centers and scattered tribes under state supervision east of the Mississippi.

Be it enacted by the Senate and House of Representatives of the United States of America in Congress assembled, That hereafter no land of any Indian reservation, created or set apart by treaty or agreement with the Indians, Act of Congress, Executive order, purchase, or otherwise, shall be allotted in severalty to any Indian.

SECTION 2. The existing periods of trust placed upon any Indian lands and any restriction on alienation thereof are hereby extended and continued until otherwise directed by Congress.

SECTION 3. The Secretary of the Interior, if he shall find it to be in the public interest, is hereby authorized to restore to tribal ownership the remaining surplus lands of any Indian reservation heretofore opened, or authorized to be opened, to sale, or any other form of disposal by Presidential proclamation, or by any of the public land laws of the United States: *Provided, however,* That valid rights or claims of any persons to any lands so withdrawn existing on the date of the withdrawal shall not be affected by this Act: *Provided further,* That this section shall not apply to lands within any reclamation project heretofore authorized in any Indian reservation: *Provided further,* That the order of the Department of the Interior signed, dated, and approved by Honorable Ray Lyman Wilbur, as Secretary of the Interior, on October 28, 1932, temporarily withdrawing lands of the Papago Indian Reservation in Arizona from all forms of mineral entry or claim under the public land mining laws, is hereby revoked and rescinded, and the lands of the said Papago Indian Reservation are hereby restored to exploration and location, under the existing mining laws of the United States, in accordance with the express terms and provisions declared and set forth in the Executive orders establishing said Papago Indian Reservation: *Provided further,* That a yearly rental not to exceed five cents per acre shall be paid to the Papago Tribe for loss of the use or occupancy of any land withdrawn by the requirements of mining operations, and payments derived from damages or rentals shall be deposited in the Treasury of the United States to the credit of the Papago Tribe: *Provided further,* That in the event any person or persons, partnership, corporation, or association, desires a mineral patent, according to the mining laws of the United States, he or they shall first deposit in the Treasury of the United States to the credit of the Papago Tribe the sum of $1.00 per acre in lieu of annual rental, as hereinbefore provided, to compensate for the loss or occupancy of the lands withdrawn by the requirements of mining operations: *Provided further,* That patentee shall also pay into the Treasury of the United States to the credit of the Papago Tribe damages for the loss of improvements not heretofore paid in such a sum as may be determined by the Secretary of the Interior, but not to exceed the cost thereof; the payment of $1.00 per acre for surface use to be refunded to patentee in the event that patent is not acquired.

Nothing herein contained shall restrict the granting or use of permits for easements or rights-of-way; or ingress or egress over the lands for all proper and lawful purposes; and nothing contained herein, except as expressly provided, shall be construed as authority for the Secretary of the Interior, or any other person, to issue or promulgate a rule or regulation in conflict with the Executive order of February 1, 1917, creating the Papago Indian Reservation in Arizona or the Act of February 21, 1931.

SECTION 4. Except as herein provided, no sale, devise, gift, exchange or transfer of restricted Indian lands or of shares in the assets of any Indian tribe or corporation organized hereunder, shall be made or approved: *Provided, however,* That such lands or interests may, with the approval of the Secretary of the Interior, be sold, devised, or otherwise transferred to the Indian tribe in which the lands or shares are located or from which the shares were derived or to a successor corporation; and in all instances such lands or interests shall descend or be devised, in accordance with the then existing laws of the State, or Federal laws where applicable, in which said lands are located or in which the subject matter of the corporation is located, to any member of such tribe or of such corporation or any heirs of such member: *Provided further,* That the Secretary of the Interior may authorize voluntary exchanges of lands of equal value and the voluntary exchange of shares of equal value whenever such exchange, in his judgment, is expedient and beneficial for or compatible with the proper consolidation of Indian lands and for the benefit of cooperative organizations.

SECTION 5. The Secretary of the Interior is hereby authorized, in his discretion, to acquire through purchase, relinquishment, gift, exchange, or assignment, any interest in lands, water rights or surface rights to lands, within or without existing reservations, including trust or otherwise restricted allotments whether the allottee be living or deceased, for the purpose of providing land for Indians.

For the Acquisition of such lands, interests in lands, water rights, and surface rights, and for expenses incident to such acquisition, there is hereby authorized to be appropriated, out of any funds in the Treasury not otherwise appropriated, a sum not to exceed $2,000,000 in any one fiscal year: *Provided,* That no part of such funds shall be used to acquire additional land outside of the exterior boundaries of Navajo Indian Reservation for the Navajo Indians in Arizona and New Mexico, in the event that the proposed Navajo boundary extension measures now pending in Congress and embodied in the bills (S. 2499 and H.R. 8927) to define the exterior boundaries of the Navajo Indian Reservation in Arizona, and for other purposes, and the bills (S. 2531 and H.R. 8982) to define the exterior boundaries of the Navajo Indian Reservation in New Mexico and for other purposes, or similar legislation, become law.

The unexpended balances of any appropriations made pursuant to this section shall remain available until expended.

Title to any lands or rights acquired pursuant to this Act shall be taken in the name of the United States in trust for the Indian tribe or individual Indian for which the land is acquired, and such lands or rights shall be exempt from State and local taxation.

SECTION 6. The Secretary of the Interior is directed to make rules and regulations for the operation and management of Indian forestry units on the principle of sustained-yield management, to restrict the number of livestock grazed on Indian range units to the estimated carrying capacity of such ranges, and to promulgate such other rules and regulations as may be necessary to protect the range from deterioration, to prevent soil erosion, to assure full utilization of the range, and like purposes.

SECTION 7. The Secretary of the Interior is hereby authorized to proclaim new Indian reservations on lands acquired pursuant to any authority conferred by this Act, or to add such lands to existing reservations: *Provided,* That lands added to existing reservations shall be designated for the exclusive use of Indians entitled by enrollment or by tribal membership to residence at such reservations.

SECTION 8. Nothing contained in this Act shall be construed to relate to Indian holdings of allotments or homesteads upon the public domain outside of the geographic boundaries of any Indian reservation now existing or established hereafter.

SECTION 9. There is hereby authorized to be appropriated, out of any funds in the Treasury not otherwise appropriated, such sums as may be necessary, but not to exceed $250,000 in any fiscal year to be expended at the order of the Secretary of the Interior, in defraying the expenses of organizing Indian chartered corporations or other organizations created under this Act.

SECTION 10. There is hereby authorized to be appropriated, out of any funds in the Treasury not otherwise appropriated, the sum of $10,000,000 to be established as a revolving fund from which the Secretary of the Interior, under such rules and regulations as he may prescribe, may make loans to Indian chartered corporations for the purpose of promoting the economic development of such tribes and of their members, and may defray the expenses of administering such loans. Repayment of amounts loaned under this authorization shall be credited to the revolving fund and shall be available for the purposes for which the fund is established. A report shall be made annually to Congress of transactions under this authorization.

SECTION 11. There is hereby authorized to be appropriated, out of any funds in the United States Treasury not otherwise appropriated, a sum not to exceed $250,000 annually, together with any unexpended balances of previous appropriations made pursuant to this section, for loans to Indians for the payment of tuition and other expenses in recognized vocational and trade schools: *Provided,* That not more than $50,000 of such sum shall be available for loans to Indian students in high schools and colleges. Such loans shall be reimbursable under rules established by the Commissioner of Indian Affairs.

SECTION 12. The Secretary of the Interior is directed to establish standards of health, age, character, experience, knowledge, and ability for Indians who may be appointed, without regard to civil-service laws, to the various positions maintained, now and hereafter, by the Indian Office, in the administration of functions or services affecting any Indian tribe. Such qualified Indians shall hereafter have the preference to appointment to vacancies in any such positions.

SECTION 13. The provisions of this Act shall not apply to any of the Territories, colonies, or insular possessions of the United States, except that sections 9, 10, 11, 12, and 16, shall apply to the Territory of Alaska: *Provided,* That sections 2, 4, 7, 16, 17, and 18 of this Act shall not apply to the following-named Indian tribes, the members of such Indian tribes, together with members of other tribes affiliated with such named tribes located in the State of Oklahoma, as follows: Cheyenne, Arapaho, Apache, Comanche, Kiowa, Caddo, Delaware, Wichita, Osage, Kaw, Otoe, Tonkawa, Pawnee, Ponca, Shawnee, Ottawa, Quapaw, Seneca, Wyandotte, Iowa, Sac and Fox, Kickapoo, Pottawatomi, Cherokee, Chickasaw, Choctaw, Creek, and Seminole. Section 4 of this Act shall not apply to the Indians of the Klamath Reservation in Oregon.

SECTION 14. The Secretary of the Interior is hereby directed to continue the allowance of the articles enumerated in section 17 of the Act of March 2, 1889, or their commuted cash value under the Act of June 10, 1896, to all Sioux Indians who would be eligible, but for the provisions of this Act, to receive allotments of lands in severalty under section 19 of the Act of May 29, 1908, or under any prior Act, and who have the prescribed status of the head of a family or single person over the age of eighteen years, and his approval shall be final and conclusive, claims therefor to be paid as formerly from the permanent appropriation made by said section 17 and carried on the books of the Treasury for this purpose. No person shall receive in his own right more than one allowance of the benefits, and application must be made and approved during the lifetime of the allottee or the right shall lapse. Such benefits shall continue to be paid upon such reservation until such time as the lands available therein for allotment at the time of the passage of this Act would have been exhausted by the award to each person receiving such benefits of an allotment of eighty acres of such land.

SECTION 15. Nothing in this Act shall be construed to impair or prejudice any claim or suit of any Indian tribe against the United States. It is hereby declared to be the intent of Congress that no expenditures for the benefit of Indians made out of appropriations authorized by this Act shall be considered as offsets in any suit brought to recover upon any claim of such Indians against the United States.

SECTION 16. Any Indian tribe, or tribes, residing on the same reservation, shall have the right to organize for its common welfare, and may adopt an appropriate constitution and bylaws, which shall become effective when ratified by a majority vote of the adult members of the tribe, or of the adult Indians residing on such reservation, as the case may be, at a special election authorized and called by the Secretary of the Interior under such rules and regulations as he may prescribe. Such constitution and bylaws when ratified as aforesaid and approved by the Secretary of the Interior shall be revocable by an election open to the same voters and conducted in the same manner as hereinabove provided. Amendments to the constitution and bylaws may be ratified and approved by the Secretary in the same manner as the original constitution and bylaws.

In addition to all powers vested in any Indian tribe or tribal council by existing law, the constitution adopted by said tribe shall also vest in such tribe or its tribal council the following rights and powers: To employ legal counsel, the choice of counsel and fixing of fees to be subject to the approval of the Secretary of the Interior; to prevent the sale, disposition, lease, or encumbrance of tribal lands, interests in lands, or other tribal assets without the consent of the tribe; and to negotiate with the Federal, State, and local Governments. The Secretary of the Interior shall advise such tribe or its tribal council of all appropriation estimates or Federal projects for the benefit of the tribe prior to the submission of such estimates to the Bureau of the Budget and the Congress.

SECTION 17. The Secretary of the Interior may, upon petition by at least one third of the adult Indians, issue a charter of incorporation to such tribe: *Provided,* That such charter shall not become operative until ratified at a special election by a majority vote of the adult Indians living on the reservation. Such charter may convey to the incorporated tribe the power to purchase, take by gift, or bequest, or otherwise, own, hold, manage, operate, and dispose of property of every description, real and personal, including the power to purchase restricted Indian lands and to issue in exchange therefor interests in corporate property, and such further powers as may be incidental to the conduct of corporate business, not inconsistent with law, but no authority shall be granted to sell, mortgage, or lease for a period exceeding ten years any of the land included in the limits of the reservation. Any charter so issued shall not be revoked or surrendered except by Act of Congress.

SECTION 18. This Act shall not apply to any reservation wherein a majority of the adult Indians, voting at a special election duly called by the Secretary of the Interior, shall vote against its application. It shall be the duty of the Secretary of the Interior, within one year after the passage and approval of this Act, to call such an election, which election shall be held by secret ballot upon thirty days' notice.

SECTION 19. The term "Indian" as used in this Act shall include all persons of Indian descent who are members of any recognized Indian tribe now under Federal jurisdiction, and all persons who are descendants of such members who were, on June 1, 1934, residing within the present boundaries of any Indian reservation, and shall further include all other persons of one half or more Indian blood. For the purposes of this Act, Eskimos and other aboriginal peoples of Alaska shall be considered Indians. The term "tribe" wherever used in this Act shall be construed to refer to any Indian tribe, organized band, pueblo, or the Indians residing on one reservation. The words "adult Indians" wherever used in this Act shall be construed to refer to Indians who have attained the age of twenty-one years.

Approved, June 18, 1934.

United States as Guardian of the Hualapai Indians of Arizona
v. Santa Fe Pacific Railroad Company
314 U.S. 326 (1941)

At rare times the courts have recognized the legal position of the American Indian. On those rare occurences it would appear that not even heaven and earth can shake a decision from the logic of its supporting aboriginal rights.

There are many cases involving railroads and Indian lands. The majority of them just give the railroad a blank check to hunt Indians, let alone make any effort to support treaty rights. Recently the Seneca Reservation in New York, already rent lengthwise by the Kinzua Dam, was overcome by a certain party's desire to make the state more accessible to motorists. Thus a superhighway was built crosswise across the territory, thereby destroying the reservation in toto.

But aboriginal rights have prevailed on a few occasions and the Hualapai case is such a happy occurrence. Handling the case for the Indians and the government were Felix Cohen and William Brophy, two of the ablest lawyers in the history of Indian law. With brilliance surpassed nowhere in the annals of Indian cases, Cohen and Brophy forged a contemporary definition of aboriginal title that stands today as a useful tool for tribal rights. The case contains a fascinating account of the establishment of the reservation and defines exactly what is the status of executive order reservations in light of the aboriginal title which the Supreme Court for over a century has defined as "sacred as fee".

This case, therefore, stands as a landmark case in the continual definition of the rights of Indian people.

This is a suit brought by the United States, in its own right and as guardian of the Indians of the Walapai (Hualapai) Tribe of Arizona to enjoin respondent [the Santa Fe Railroad] from interfering with the possession and occupancy by the Indians of certain lands in northwestern Arizona. Respondent claims full title to the lands in question under the grant to its predecessor, the Atlantic and Pacific Railroad Co., provided for in the Act of July 27, 1866. The bill sought to establish that respondent's rights under the grant of 1866 are subject to the Indians' right of occupancy both inside and outside their present reservation which was established by the Executive Order of President Arthur, January 4, 1883. The bill consists of two causes of action—the first relating to lands inside, and the second, to lands outside, that reservation. The bill prayed, *inter alia,* that title be quieted and that respondent "account for all rents, issues and profits derived from the leasing, renting or use of the lands subject to said right of occupancy" by the Indians. Respondent moved to dismiss on the ground that the facts alleged were "insufficient to constitute a valid cause of action in equity". The District Court granted that motion. The Circuit Court of Appeals affirmed. We granted the petition for certiorari because of the importance of the problems raised in the administration of the Indian laws and the land grants.

Sec. 2 of the Act of July 27, 1866, the Act under which respondent's title to the lands in question derived, provided: "The United States shall extinguish, as rapidly as may be consistent with public policy and the welfare of the Indians, and only by their voluntary cession, the Indian title to all lands falling under the operation of this act and acquired in the donation to the road named in the act."

Basic to the present causes of action is the theory that the lands in question were the ancestral home of the Walapais, that such occupancy constituted "Indian title" within the meaning of § 2 of the 1866 Act, which the United States agreed to extinguish, and that in absence of such extinguishment the grant to the railroad "conveyed the fee subject to this right of occupancy". The Circuit Court of Appeals concluded that the United States had never recognized such possessory rights of Indians within the Mexican Cession and that in absence of such recognition the Walapais had no such right good against grantees of the United States.

Occupancy necessary to establish aboriginal possession is a question of fact to be determined as any other question of fact. If it were established as a fact that the lands in question were, or were included in, the ancestral home of the Walapais in the sense that they constituted definable territory occupied exclusively by the Walapais (as distinguished from lands wandered over by many tribes), then the Walapais had "Indian title" which, unless extinguished, survived the railroad grant of 1866.

"Unquestionably it has been the policy of the Federal Government from the beginning to respect the Indian right of occupancy, which could only be interfered with or determined by the United States". This policy was first recognized in *Johnson v. McIntosh* and has been repeatedly reaffirmed. As stated in *Mitchel v. United States,* Indian "right of occupancy is considered as sacred as the fee simple of the whites." Whatever may have been the rights of the Walapais under Spanish law, the *Cramer* case assumed that lands within the Mexican Cession were not excepted from the policy to respect Indian right of occupancy. Though the *Cramer* case involved the problem of individual Indian occupancy, this Court stated that such occupancy was not to be treated differently from "the original nomadic tribal occupancy". Perhaps the assumption that aboriginal possession would be respected in the Mexican Cession was, like the generalizations in *Johnson v. McIntosh,* not necessary for the narrow holding of the case. But such generalizations have been so often and so long repeated as respects land under the prior sovereignty of the various European nations, including Spain, that, like other rules governing titles to property they should now be considered no longer open. Furthermore, treaties negotiated with Indian tribes, wholly or partially within the Mexican Cession, for delimitation of their occupancy rights or for the settlement and adjustment of their boundaries, constitute clear recognition that no different policy as respects aboriginal possession obtained in this area than in other areas. Certainly it would take plain and unambiguous action to deprive the Walapais of the benefits of that policy. For it was founded on the desire to maintain just and peaceful relations with Indians. The reasons for its application to other tribes are no less apparent in case of the Walapais, a savage tribe which in early days caused the military no end of trouble.

Nor is it true, as respondent urges, that a tribal claim to any particular lands must be based upon a treaty, statute, or other formal government action. As stated in the *Cramer* case, "The fact that such right of occupancy finds no recognition in any statute or other formal governmental action is not conclusive."

Extinguishment of Indian title is based on aboriginal possession is of course a different matter. The power of Congress in that regard is supreme. The manner, method and time of such extinguishment raise political, not justiciable, issues. As stated by Chief Justice Marshall in *Johnson v. McIntosh,* "the exclusive right of the United States to extinguish" Indian title has never been doubted. And whether it be done by treaty, by the sword, by purchase, by the exercise of complete dominion adverse to the right of occupancy, or otherwise, its justness is not open to inquiry in the courts.

If the right of occupancy of the Walapais was not extinguished prior to the date of definite location of the railroad in 1872, then the respondent's predecessor took the fee subject to the encumbrance of Indian title. For on that date the title of respondent's predecessor attached as of July 27, 1866.

Certainly, prior to 1865 any right of occupancy of the Walapais to the lands in question was not extinguished; nor was the policy of respecting such Indian title changed. The Indian Trade and Intercourse Act of June 30, 1834 was extended over "the Indian tribes in the Territories of New Mexico and Utah" by §7 of the Act of February 27, 1851. The Act, which derived from the Act of July 22, 1790 made it an offense to drive stock to range or feed "on any land belonging to any Indian or Indian tribe, without the consent of such tribe" (§9); gave the superintendent of Indian Affairs authority "to remove from the Indian country all persons found therein contrary to law" (§10); made it unlawful to settle on "any lands belonging, secured, or granted by treaty with the United States to any Indian tribe" (§11); and made invalid any conveyance of lands "from any Indian nation or tribe of Indians" (§12). The Act of 1851 obviously did not create any Indian right of occupancy which did not previously exist. But it plainly indicates that in 1851 Congress desired to continue in these territories the unquestioned general policy of the Federal Government to recognize such right of occupancy. As stated by Chief Justice Marshall in *Worcester v. Georgia,* the Indian trade and intercourse acts "manifestly consider the several Indian nations as distinct political communities, having territorial boundaries, within which their authority is exclusive, and having a right to all the lands within those boundaries, which is not only acknowledged, but guarantied by the United States."

The court below laid considerable stress upon the Act of July 22, 1854, as indicating that Congress recognized no rights of the Indians in Arizona and New Mexico other than those existing under Mexican law or created by reservations after the Mexican Cession. But we do not agree that, so far as the respondent's rights are concerned, that Act instituted a policy of non-recognition of Indian title nor do we think that it effected any extinguishment of that title.

The Act of 1854 established the office of Surveyor General of New Mexico. It donated land to certain qualified citizens (§2) with the exception, *inter alia,* of "military or other reservations" (§4). Unlike the Pre-emption Act of September 4, 1841, the 1854 Act did not extend only to "the public lands to which the Indian title had been at the time of such settlement extinguished." It did provide, however, that "any of the lands not taken" under it should "be subject to the operation" of the Pre-emption Act (§7). Moreover, the 1854 Act provided as respects the Territories of Nebraska and Kansas that the grants should extend only to lands "to which the Indian title has been or shall be extinguished" (§12).

From that it is argued that since Congress recognized Indian title in Nebraska and

Kansas and under the Pre-emption Act but did not recognize it as respects the lands in this area, a shift of policy in the Mexican Cession was indicated. The issue here, however, is not between a settler claiming under the 1854 Act and the Walapais. Whether in such a case the 1854 Act should be construed as extinguishing any Indian title to land taken under it we need not decide. Respondent does not claim under that Act and hence can derive no rights from it.

Some stress is likewise placed on §8 of the Act of July 22, 1854, and on the Act of July 15, 1870. The former required the Surveyor General for New Mexico "to ascertain the origin, nature, character, and extent of all claims to lands under the laws, usages, and customs of Spain and Mexico"; and to make a report "on all such claims as originated before the cession of the territory to the United States by the treaty of Guadalupe Hidalgo . . . denoting the various grades of title, with his decision as to the validity or invalidity of each of the same under the laws, usages, and customs of the country before its cession to the United States." Such report was to be "laid before Congress for such action thereon as may be deemed just and proper, with a view to confirm *bona fide* grants and give full effect" to the treaty. It was also provided that "until the final action of Congress on such claims, all lands covered thereby shall be reserved from sale or other disposal by the government, and shall not be subject to the donations granted by the previous provisions of this act." The 1870 Act directed the Surveyor General for Arizona (which was separated as a Territory from New Mexico in 1863) "to ascertain and report upon the origin, nature, character, and extent of the claims to lands in said Territory under the laws, usages, and customs of Spain and Mexico." His report was to be "laid before Congress for such action thereon as shall be deemed just and proper."

These Acts did not extinguish any Indian title based on aboriginal occupancy which the Walapais may have had. In that respect they were quite different from the Act of March 3, 1851 passed to ascertain and settle certain land claims in California. Under §13 of that Act "all lands the claims to which shall not have been presented" to the commissioners, appointed to receive and act upon all petitions for confirmation of land claims, "within two years after the date of this act, shall be deemed, held, and considered as part of the public domain of the United States." This Court passed on that Act in *Barker v. Harvey*. The plaintiff there claimed under two Mexican grants. The defendants were Indians who claimed a right of permanent occupancy; but they had not presented their claims to the commissioners within the time specified by §13. This Court held that as a result of that failure their claims were barred. That is to say, the Act of 1851 was interpreted as containing machinery for extinguishment of claims, including those based on Indian right of occupancy. Since Congress had provided a method for extinguishment, its appropriateness raised only a political, not a justiciable, issue. The Acts of 1854 and 1870, unlike the Act of 1851, merely called for a report to Congress on certain land claims. If there was an extinguishment of the rights of the Walapais, it resulted not from action of the Surveyor General but from action of Congress based on his reports. We are not advised that Congress took any such action. In its absence we must conclude that these Acts were concerned not with the problem of ascertaining the boundaries of Indian country but with the problem of quieting titles originating under Spanish or Mexican grants. For it should be noticed that §8 of the 1854 Act contemplated confirmation by Congress of *"bona fide* grants."

This brings us to the Act of March 3, 1865, which provided: "All that part of the public domain in the Territory of Arizona, lying west of a direct line from Half-Way Bend to Corner Rock on the Colorado River, containing about seventy-five thousand acres of land, shall be set apart for an Indian reservation for the Indians of said river and its tributaries." It is plain that the Indians referred to included the Walapais. The suggestion for removing various Indian tribes in this area to a reservation apparently originated with a former Indian agent, Superintendent Poston, who was a Territorial Representative in Congress in 1865. His explanation on the floor of the House of the bill, which resulted in the creation of the 1865 reservation, indicates that he had called a council of the confederated tribes of the Colorado, including the Walapais, and had told them that "they should abandon" their lands and confine themselves to the place on the Colorado River which was later proposed for a reservation. He entered into no agreement with them nor did he propose a treaty. He merely stated that if elected to Congress he would try to get Congress to provide for them. As stated by the Commissioner of Indian Affairs in 1864, "Assuming that the Indians have a right of some kind to the soil, Mr. Poston's arrangement proposes a compromise with these Indians, by which on their confining themselves to their reservation, and yielding all claims to lands beyond it, they shall, in lieu of an annuity in money or supplies, be furnished by government with an irrigating canal, at a cost estimated at something near $100,000, which, by insuring them their annual crops, will enable them to support themselves, independently of other aid by the government."

We search the public records in vain for any clear and plain indication that Congress in creating the Colorado River reservation was doing more than making an offer to the Indians, including the Walapais, which it was hoped would be accepted as a compromise of a troublesome question. We find no indication that Congress by creating that reservation intended to extinguish all of the rights which the Walapais had in their ancestral home. That Congress could have effected such an extinguishment is not doubted. But an extinquishment cannot be lightly implied in view of the avowed solicitude of the Federal Government for the welfare of its Indian wards. As stated in *Choate v. Trapp*, the rule of construction recognized without exception for over a century has been that "doubtful expressions, instead of being resolved in favor of the United States, are to be resolved in favor of a weak and defenseless people, who are wards of the nation, and dependent wholly upon its protection and good faith." Nor was there any plain intent or agreement on the part of the Walapais to abandon their ancestral lands if Congress would create a reservation. Furthermore, the Walapais did not accept the offer which Congress had tendered. In 1874 they were, however, forcibly removed to the Colorado River reservation on order from the Indian Department. But they left it in a body the next year. And it was decided "to allow them to remain in their old range during good behavior." They did thereafter remain in their old country and engaged in no hostilities against the whites. No further attempt was made to force them onto the Colorado River reservation, even though Congress had made various appropriations to defray the costs of locating the Arizona Indians in permanent abodes, including the Colorado River reservation. On these facts we conclude that the creation of the Colorado River reservation was, so far as the Walapais were concerned, nothing more than an abortive attempt to solve a perplexing problem. Their forcible removal in 1874 was not pursuant to any mandate of Congress. It was a high-handed endeavor to wrest from these Indians lands which Congress had never declared forfeited. No forfeiture can be predicated on an unauthorized attempt to effect a forcible settlement on the reservation, unless we are to be insensitive to the high standards for fair dealing in light of which laws dealing with Indian rights have long been read. Certainly, a forced abandonment of their ancestral home was not a "voluntary cession" within the meaning of §2 of the Act of July 27, 1866.

The situation was, however, quite different in 1881. Between 1875 and that date there were rather continuous suggestions for settling the Walapais on some reservation. In 1881 the matter came to a head. A majority of the tribe, "in council assembled," asked an officer of the United States Army in that region "to aid them and represent to the proper authorities" the following proposal: "They say that in the country, over which they used to roam so free, the white men have appropriated all the water; that large numbers of cattle have been introduced and have rapidly increased during the past year or two; that in many places the water is fenced in and locked up; and they are driven from all waters. They say that the Railroad is now coming, which will require more water, and will bring more men who will take up all the small springs remaining. They urge that the following reservation be set aside for them while there is still time; that the land can never be of any great use to the Whites; that there are no mineral deposits upon it, as it has been thoroughly prospected; that there is little or no arable land; that the water is in such small quantities, and the country is so rocky and void of grass, that it would not be available for stock raising, I am credibly informed, and from my observations believe, the above facts to be true. I, therefore, earnestly recommend that the hereafter described Reservation be, at as early a date as practicable, set aside for them."

Pursuant to that recommendation, the military reservation was constituted on July 8, 1881, subject to the approval of the President. The Executive Order creating the Walapai Indian Reservation was signed by President Arthur on January 4, 1883. There was an indication that the Indians were satisfied with the proposed reservation. A few of them thereafter lived on the reservation; many of them did not. While suggestions recurred for the creation of a new and different reservation, this one was not abandoned. For a long time it remained unsurveyed. Cattlemen used it for grazing, and for some years the Walapais received little benefit from it. But in view of all the circumstances, we conclude that its creation at the request of the Walapais and its acceptance by them amounted to a relinquishment of any tribal claims to lands which they might have had outside that reservation and that that relinquishment was tantamount to an extinguishment by "voluntary cession" within the meaning of §2 of the Act of July 27, 1866. The lands were fast being populated. The Walapais saw their old domain being pre-empted. They wanted a reservation while there was still time to get one. That solution had long seemed desirable in view of recurring tensions between the settlers and the Walapais. In view of the long standing attempt to settle the Walapais' problem by placing them on a reservation, their acceptance of this reservation must be regarded in law as the equivalent of a release of any tribal rights which they may have had in lands outside the reservation. They were in substance acquiescing in the penetration of white settlers on condition that permanent provision was made for them too. In view of this historical setting, it cannot be fairly implied that tribal rights of the Walapais in lands outside the reservation were preserved. That would make the creation of the 1883 reservation, as an attempted solution of the violent problems created when two civilizations met in this area, illusory indeed. We must give it the definitiveness which the exigencies of that situation seem to demand. Hence, acquiescence in that arrangement must be deemed to have been a relinquishment of tribal rights in lands outside the reservation and notoriously claimed by others.

On January 23, 1941, the date of the filing of this petition for certiorari, respondent quitclaimed to the United States, under §321 (b), Pt. III of the Interstate Commerce Act (Transportation Act of 1940) all lands claimed by it under the Act of July 27, 1866, within the Walapai Indian Reservation. Since the decree below must stand as to the second cause of action and since by virtue of the quitclaim deeds the United States has received all the lands to which the first cause of action relates, the decree will not be reversed. It is apparent, however, that it must be modified so as to permit the accounting as respects lands in the first cause of action. It does not appear whether those lands were included in the ancestral home of the Walapais in the sense that they were in whole or in part occupied exclusively by them or whether they were lands wandered over by many tribes. As we have said, occupancy necessary to establish aboriginal possession is a question of fact. The United States is entitled to an accounting as respects any or all of the lands in the first cause of action which the Walapais did in fact occupy exclusively from time immemorial. Such an accounting is not precluded by the Act of February 20, 1925 which authorized the Secretary of the Interior "to accept reconveyances to the Government of privately owned and State school lands and relinquishments of any valid filings, under the homestead laws, or of other valid claims with the Walapai Indian Reservation." The implication is that there may be some land within the reservation that is not subject to Indian occupancy. But that Act certainly cannot be taken as an extinguishment of any and all Indian title that did exist or as a repeal by implication of §2 of the Act of July 27, 1866, requiring such extinguishment by "voluntary cession." It was passed so that lands "retained for Indian purposes may be consolidated and held in a solid area so far as may be possible." Such statements by the Secretary of the Interior as that "title to the odd-numbered sections" was in the respondent do not estop the United States from maintaining this suit. For they could not deprive the Indians of their rights any more than could the unauthorized leases in *Cramer v. United States, supra.*

Hence, an accounting as respects such lands in the reservation which can be proved to have been occupied by the Walapais from time immemorial can be had. To the extent that the decree below precludes such proof and accounting, it will be modified. And as so modified, it is

Affirmed.

Native American Church v. Navajo Tribal Council
272 F. 2d 131 (1959)

Native American Church v. Navajo Tribal Council could easily be placed in the chapter on Indian Civil Rights since it deals with the religious freedom of the individual Indian in relation to his tribal government. But the case has greater implication today for its characterization of the status of an Indian tribe—higher than a state! With the continual conflict between states and Indian tribes over hunting and fishing rights, taxation, law and order jurisdiction, and economic development this case should occupy a prominent position in the struggle to define more precisely the nature and powers of Indian tribal governments.

HUXMAN, CIRCUIT JUDGE

This action was filed in the United States Court for the District of New Mexico by the Native American Church of North America, a corporation, William Peter Tsosie, Shorty Duncan, and Frank Hanna, Jr., a minor, by and through Frank Hanna, Sr., his next friend, against the Navajo Tribal Council, Paul Jones, individually and as Chairman of said Tribal Council, Joe Duncan, and Sam Garnez. The action was brought by plaintiffs on their own behalf and in behalf of all others similarly situated. In its first cause of action, the church sought to enjoin the enforcement of an ordinance adopted by the Navajo Tribal Council making it an offense to introduce into the Navajo country, sell, use, or have in possession within the Navajo country, the bean known as peyote, and imposing both imprisonment and a fine for its violation.

The first cause of action alleged that from time immemorial, the church and its predecessors have used the vegetable substance, commonly known as peyote, in connection with and as a part of its religious ceremonies. It was alleged that the ordinance was void because it violated the church's rights and the rights of its members under the First, Fourth, and Fifth Amendments to the United States Constitution. The prayer was that the court enjoin enforcement of the ordinance. In a second cause of action, damages were sought from Sam Garnez and Joe Duncan. As to Garnez, it was alleged that he entered Shorty Duncan's house where religious ceremonies were being conducted, without a search warrant, searched the premises and the persons there present, and arrested Duncan and others, without a warrant, and thus deprived them of their liberty and right of worship without due process of law. As to Joe Duncan, it was alleged that he, acting as a judge of the Navajo court, denied Duncan the opportunity to secure counsel or to demand a jury trial, found him guilty of violating the ordinance and assessed penalties. Judgment for damages of $5,000 was asked. The trial court sustained a motion by the defendants to dismiss plaintiff's first cause of action. The second cause of action is not in issue in this appeal.

The court predicated its judgment of dismissal on four grounds. First, that the ordinance was a valid exercise of police powers and was, therefore, not repugnant to the Constitution; second, that the Navajo Tribal Council cannot be sued without the consent of the Congress of the United States, which consent had not been given; third, that since the seat of the Government of the Navajo Tribe is in Window Rock, Arizona, the court was without jurisdiction over matters concerning the validity of the acts of the Navajo Tribal Council; and, fourth, that the face of the complaint shows a misjoinder of parties defendant and causes of action. In our view, not all of these grounds need to be discussed or considered in arriving at a decision of the case.

Much has been written with respect to the status of Indian tribes under our Government, and with respect to the jurisdiction of Federal or State courts over controversies between non-members and a tribe, or between members of a tribe, or controversies between Indian members of a tribe and the tribe as an entity. The early case of *Worcester v. Georgia,* is the leading case on the subject. The opinion of Chief Justice Marshall developed the subject at great length. The gist of the opinion is that Indian nations and tribes are distinct political entities, having territorial boundaries within which their authority is exclusive; that within their borders they have their own Government, laws of the State in which they are located or to the laws of the United States, except where Federal laws are made applicable to them by Congressional enactment, and that Federal courts are without jurisdiction unless jurisdiction is expressly conferred by Congressional enactment. In *United States v. Kagama,* the court sums up their status in the following language:

> They were, and always have been, regarded as having a semi-independent position when they preserved their tribal relations; not as possessed of the full attributes of sovereignty, but as a separate people, with the power of regulating their internal and social relations, and thus far not brought under the laws of the Union or of the state within whose limits they resided.

These declarations by the Supreme Court have been adhered to in a long line of cases.

(1) The status of Indian nations or tribes, preserving their political entity under the decisions of the Supreme Court, has been summed up in Felix S. Cohen's *Handbook of Federal Indian Law,* at page 122, as follows:

> "The whole course of judicial decision on the nature of Indian tribal powers is marked by adherence to three fundamental principles: (1) An Indian tribe possesses, in the first instance, all the powers of any sovereign state. (2) Conquest renders the tribe subject to legislative power of the United States and, in substance, terminates the external powers of sovereignty of the tribe, *e.g.,* its power to enter into treaties with foreign nations, but does not by itself affect the internal sovereignty of the tribe, *i.e.,* its powers of local self-government. (3)

76

These powers are subject to qualification by treaties and by express legislation of Congress, but save as thus expressly qualified, full powers of internal sovereignty are vested in the Indian tribes and in their duly constituted organs of government."

This subject was again before the Supreme Court in the late case of *Williams v. Lee.* This case involved a suit by a non-Indian against an Indian member of the Navajo tribe for goods sold to him. This action was brought in the State courts. The court reviewed the status of Indian tribes. It adhered to the principles of the Worcester case. Concerning that case, the court said, "Over the years this Court has modified these principles in cases where essential tribal relations were not involved and where the rights of Indians would not be jeopardized, but the basic policy of Worcester has remained." And speaking of the Navajo nation and the treaty with them, the court said "Implicit in these treaty terms, as it was in the treaties with the Cherokees involved in *Worcester v. Georgia,* was the understanding that the internal affairs over the Indians remained exclusively within the jurisdiction of whatever tribal government existed." No law is cited and none has been found which undertakes to subject the Navajo tribe to the laws of the United States with respect to their internal affairs, such as police powers and ordinances passed for the purposes of regulating the conduct of the members of the tribe on the reservation. It follows that the Federal courts are without jurisdiction over matters involving purely penal ordinances passed by the Navajo legislative body for the regulation of life on the reservation.

But it is contended that the First Amendment to the United States Constitution applies to Indian nations and tribes as it does to the United States and to the States. It is, accordingly, argued that the ordinanace in question violates the Indians' rights of religious free-dom and freedom of worship guaranteed by the First Amendment. No case is cited and none has been found where the impact of the First Amendment, with respect to religious freedom and freedom of worship by members of the Indian tribes, has been before the court. In *Talton V. Mayes,* the court held that the Fifth Amendment did not apply to local legislation by the Cherokee nation. In *Barta v. Oglala Sioux Tribe of Pine Ridge Reservation,* the court held that neither the Fifth nor the Fourteenth Amendments had any application to action, legislative in character, of Indian tribes imposing a tax on the use of Indian trust land, and in *Toledo v. Pueblo De Jemez, D.C.,* the court held that deprivation of religious liberties by Tribal government could not be redressed by action under the Civil Rights Act. Cohen's *Handbook of Federal Indian Law, 1942,* at page 124, states that restraints upon Congress or upon the Federal courts or upon the States, by the Constitution, do not apply to Indian tribal laws and courts. And, at page 181, it is stated that, "The provisions of the Federal Constitution protecting personal liberty or property rights, do not apply to tribal action."

(2-4) The First Amendment applies only to Congress. It limits the powers of Congress to interfere with religious freedom or religious worship. It is made applicable to the States only by the Fourteenth Amendment. Thus construed, the First Amendment places limitations upon the action of Congress and of the States. But as declared in the decisions hereinbefore discussed, Indian tribes are not states. They have a status higher than that of states. They are subordinate and dependent nations possessed of all powers as such only to the extent that they have expressly been required to surrender them by the supreme law of the land, but it is nonetheless a part of the laws of the United States. Under the philosophy of the decisions, it, as any other law, is binding upon Indian nations only where it expressly binds them, or is made binding by treaty or some act of Congress. No provision in the Constitution makes the First Amendment applicable to Indian nations nor is there any law of Congress doing so. It follows that neither, under the Constitution or the laws of Congress, do the Federal courts have jurisdiction of tribal laws or regulations, even though they may have an impact to some extent on forms of religious worship.

Affirmed.

Menominee Tribe v. United States

In 1954, at the instigation of Senator Arthur Watkins of Utah, the Menominee tribe of Wisconsin was terminated from federal supervision. This capricious act violated a longstanding treaty and created a desperate pocket of poverty, simply because of an erroneous abstract social theory held by the Senator.

Throughout the hearings the tribe asked Watkins to clarify its rights with respect to hunting and fishing privileges. But there was never any effort either to make restitution if they were being taken away or to clarify that they were not being taken away.

Years after the termination had gone into effect there was still a considerable doubt in the minds of the tribe and the state officials as to the Menominees' rights. Finally a case was brought into the Court of Claims that conflicted with the decision of the state courts in Wisconsin and the way was cleared to petition the Supreme Court for a decision on the subject.

The court found that the termination act had not been a "backhanded" way of breaking the treaty of 1854 with respect to hunting and fishing rights. But it found more than that. It found that the Menominee Tribe *still existed*. The jurisdiction was simply transferred to the state of Wisconsin from the federal government. Since the case was only decided two years ago it would appear that this decision is the first and major stepping stone to a complete overthrow of the termination legislation and to the reversal of federal termination policy. For, if nothing else, this case means that an Indian tribe cannot be destroyed by an arbitrary act of Congress.

Because this case will prove so important in the future for a definition of tribal existence it has been included in the materials of this chapter with the salutation that "we shall hear of this case in the future".

MR. JUSTICE DOUGLAS delivered the opinion of the Court.

The Menominee Tribe of Indians was granted a reservation in Wisconsin by the Treaty of the Wolf River in 1854. 10 Stat. 1064. By this treaty the Menominees retroceded certain lands they had acquired under an earlier treaty and the United States confirmed to them the Wolf River Reservation "for a home, to be held as Indian lands are held." Nothing was said in the 1854 treaty about hunting and fishing rights. Yet we agree with the Court of Claims that the language "to be held as Indian lands are held" includes the right to fish and to hunt. The record shows that the lands covered by the Wolf River Treaty of 1854 were selected precisely because they had an abundance of game. The essence of the Treaty of Wolf River was that the Indians were authorized to maintain on the new lands ceded to them as a reservation their way of life which included hunting and fishing.

What the precise nature and extent of those hunting and fishing rights were we need not at this time determine. For the issue tendered by the present decision of the Court of Claims, 179 Ct.Cl. 496, is whether those rights, whatever their precise extent, have been extinguished.

That issue arose because, beginning in 1962, Wisconsin took the position that the Menominees were subject to her hunting and fishing regulations. Wisconsin prosecuted three Menominees for violating those regulations and the Wisconsin Supreme Court held that the state regulations were valid, as the hunting and fishing rights of the Menominees had been abrogated by Congress in the Menominee Termination Act of 1954.

Thereupon the tribe brought suit in the Court of Claims against the United States to recover just compensation for the loss of those hunting and fishing rights. The Court of Claims by a divided vote held that the tribe possessed hunting and fishing rights under the Wolf River Treaty; but it held, contrary to the Wisconsin Supreme Court, that those rights were not abrogated by the Termination Act of 1954. We granted the petition for a writ of certiorari in order to resolve that conflict between the two courts. On oral argument both petitioner and respondent urged that the judgment of the Court of Claims be affirmed. The State of Wisconsin appeared as *amicus curiae* and argued that that judgment be reversed.

In 1953 Congress by concurrent resolution instructed the Secretary of the Interior to recommend legislation for the withdrawal of federal supervision over certain American Indian tribes, including the Menominees. Several bills were offered, one for the Menominee Tribe that expressly preserved hunting and fishing rights. But the one that became the Termination Act of 1954, viz. H.R. 2828, did not mention hunting and fishing rights. Moreover, counsel for the Menominees spoke against the bill, arguing that its silence would by implication abolish those hunting and fishing rights. It is therefore argued that they were abolished by the Termination Act.

The purpose of the 1954 Act was by its terms "to provide for orderly termination of federal supervision over the property and members" of the tribe. Under its provisions, the tribe was to formulate a plan for future control of tribal property and service functions theretofore conducted by the United States. On or before April 30, 1961, the Secretary was to transfer to a tribal corporation or to a trustee chosen by him all property real and personal held in trust for the tribe by the United States.

The Menominees submitted a plan, looking toward the creation of a county in Wisconsin out of the former reservation and the creation by the Indians of a Wisconsin corporation to hold other property of the tribe and its members. The Secretary of the Interior approved the plan with modifications; The Menominee Indian Tribe of Wisconsin, Inc., was incorporated; and numerous ancillary laws were passed by Wisconsin integrating the former reservation into its county system of government. The Termination Act provided that after the transfer by the Secretary of title to the property of the tribe, all federal supervision was to end and "the laws of the several States shall apply to the tribe and its members in the same manner as they apply to other citizens or persons within their jurisdiction."

It is therefore argued with force that the Termination Act of 1954, which became fully effective in 1961, submitted the hunting and fishing rights of the Indians to state regulation and control. We reach, however, the opposite conclusion. The same Congress that passed the Termination Act also passed Public Law 280, 67 Stat. 588, as amended, 18 U.S.C. §1162. The latter came out of the same committees of the Senate and the House as did the Termination Act; and it was amended in a way that is critical here only two months after the Termination Act became the law. As amended, Public Law 280 granted designated States, including Wisconsin, jurisdiction "over offenses committed by or against Indians in the areas of Indian country" named in the Act, which in the case of Wisconsin was described as "All Indian country within the State". But Public Law 280 went on to say that "Nothing in this section . . . shall deprive any Indian or any Indian tribe, band, or community of any right, privilege, or immunity afforded under Federal treaty, agreement, or statute *with respect to hunting, trapping, or fishing,* or the control, licensing, or regulation thereof". (Italics added) That provision on its face contains no limitation; it protects any hunting, trapping, or fishing right granted by a federal treaty. Public Law 280, as amended, became the law in 1954, nearly seven years *before* the Termination Act became fully effective in 1961. In 1954, when Public Law 280 became effective, the Menominee Reservation was still "Indian country" within the meaning of Public Law 280.

Public Law 280 must therefore be considered *in pari materia* with the Termination Act. The two Acts read together mean to us that, although federal supervision of the tribe was to cease and all tribal property was to be transferred to new hands, the hunting and fishing rights granted or preserved by the Wolf River Treaty of 1854 survived the Termination Act of 1954.

This construction is in accord with the overall legislative plan. The Termination Act by its terms provided for the "orderly termination of Federal *supervision* over the property and members" of the tribe. 25 U.S.C. §891. (Emphasis added.) The Federal Government ceded to the State of Wisconsin its power of supervision over the tribe and the reservation lands, as evident from the provision of the Termination Act that the laws of Wisconsin "shall apply to the tribe and its members as they apply to other citizens or persons within (its) jurisdiction."

The provision of the Termination Act that "all statutes of the United States which affect Indians because of their status as Indians shall no longer be applicable to members of the tribe" plainly refers to the termination of federal supervision. The use of the word "statutes" is potent evidence that no *treaty* was in mind.

We decline to construe the Termination Act as a backhanded way of abrogating the hunting and fishing rights of these Indians. While the power to abrogate those rights exists (see *Lone Wolf v. Hitchcock*) "the intention to abrogate or modify a treaty is not to be lightly imputed to the Congress".

Our conclusion is buttressed by the remarks of the legislator chiefly responsible for guiding the Termination Act to enactment, Senator Watkins, who stated upon the occasion of the signing of the bill that it "in no way violates any treaty obligation with this tribe."

We find it difficult to believe that Congress, without explicit statement, would subject the United States to a claim for compensation by destroying property rights conferred by treaty, particularly when Congress was purporting by the Termination Act to settle the Government's financial obligations toward the Indians.

Accordingly the judgment of the Court of Claims is affirmed.

The struggle to define the nature of tribal existence is just beginning. It would appear that an Indian tribe cannot be destroyed—legally. *The Kansas Indians* and *Menominee* case both indicate that it is the voluntary act of the tribe, not the act of any state or Congress that finally terminates tribal existence. And if, as the *Navajo* case would seem to indicate, a tribe has greater status than a state, what is the real nature of that status? To that question must be directed the energies and thinking of a whole generation of people. With local governments becoming less able to handle their own affairs, with regional development schemes now on the planning boards—with commissions such as the Four Corners Development Commission in Colorado, Arizona, Utah and New Mexico, and the now-ancient Tennessee Valley Authority all claiming status superior in some aspects to the traditional states—the development of an Indian tribal rights theory may be the crucial movement for all American society in the years ahead. It is important, therefore, to Indian and non-Indian alike to meditate on the possibilities which the concept of the Indian tribe in its sovereign aspect holds for American society in the constitutional framework.

III

DIVERSITY OF CITIZENSHIP AND CIVIL RIGHTS

The definition of Indian civil rights under the Constitution has always been a problem. Since Indians were originally members of tribes that had superior treaty-making powers with the European nations, many early agreements between the whites and the more powerful Indian tribes gave equal jurisdiction to each side. Thus Indians could punish a white found within their boundaries while individual Indians committing crimes within white territory were punished according to the law of the state or colony within which the crime was committed.

As time went on their equality proved to be unsatisfactory to the United States. It was becoming more powerful while the tribes were becoming less independent. Thus treaties during the early years of the 19th century had provisions for the tribes to turn over white offenders for punishment by the state or federal government. This development was paralleled by provisions to provide for individual Indians who wished to leave tribal society and live with the whites. In general these treaties allowed them to take homesteads in the ceded territory and submit to state or territorial law.

With the Removal policy, the severance of tribal relations became a major avenue of achieving American citizenship and receiving a land allotment. Nearly every treaty signed until the 1840's provided that individual Indians could forswear their rights to treaty annuities and assets of the tribe in return for farming land allotments in the states from which their tribes were moving. Eventually there was no place to move. So beginning with the Omaha Treaty of 1854, allotment was forced on many Indians as a quick method of eliminating tribal governing powers.

From 1854 until the early 1900's taking allotments and leaving reservation or tribal society was rewarded by citizenship and the right to sell their lands. Certain portions in the general land laws gave citizenship to those members of Indian tribes who left the reservation and took allotments on the public domain. After allotment there was a general period of twenty-five years during which restrictions were imposed forbidding the individual Indian to sell his land. When the restrictions were lifted all those Indians not obviously incompetent were considered full citizens of the United States.

The theory did not, however, work out in practice—just as the passage of the Civil Rights Amendments after the Civil War did not actually give rights of citizenship to members of the black community. One of the key cases regarding the civil rights of Indians residing off the reservation was heard in 1884 in Nebraska. John Elk, an Indian of unknown tribe, had fulfilled every conceivable responsibility or citizenship. He lived in Omaha, worked at a job, paid taxes and one day attempted to vote.

John Elk's desire to vote became the spectacular early Indian civil rights case of *Elk v. Wilkins.* The court was anxious to deny Elk citizenship. To do so it had to twist a series of treaties, statutes, and their citizenship provisions beyond recognition. But it found, nevertheless, that an Indian could not of his own power become a citizen of the United States—even if federal law appeared to say that he could. The Indians who had followed the directions of the United States and severed their tribal ties thus became men without a country.

The opposite situation was true with respect to the rights of Indians remaining within their tribal societies. The United States continually intruded its conception of domestic relations into the traditional customary laws of the Indian tribes. Thus *Ex Parte Crow Dog* was an effort to make the Sioux tribe subservient to the Bill of Rights and to place the Sioux under federal penalties for infractions of laws which white society considered serious. No recognition was given to Indian customs which were allegedly to govern. On the other hand, in *Talton v. Mayes* the Cherokee Nation was upheld as a valid nation against which the procedures and ideas of the Constitution could not be superimposed.

But the doctrine of tribal sovereignty to police its own members was perverted by the courts. The application of Anglo-Saxon concepts of procedure to Indian tribes became the overriding issue. This problem was not resolved until 1968 when the Civil Rights Bill of that year contained several provisions restricting the powers of Indian tribes with respect to their own membership: first, by applying the Bill of Rights, it forced traditional tribes to grant freedom of religion; then it more clearly defined appeal procedures from tribal court to federal court.

In the meantime Indians had received citizenship in the United States government. First as individuals receiving allotments Indians were required to go through a ceremony to emphasize their change in legal status—though few were prepared to know or understand the significance of this ritual. Then in 1924 Congress passed a blanket citizenship act bringing all Indians into full citizenship.

The dual nature of the citizenship-civil rights problem is illustrated in this chapter's selections. It may be that the period of greatest litigation is still ahead. The Pueblos of New Mexico, for example, are challenging the right of Congress to impose its foreign law; the Iroquois steadfastly refuse to accept American citizenship. Thus the diversity of the status of the individual is hardly settled, particularly for many people in the Indian community who will, after all, be the plaintiffs in any future litigation.

Elk v. Wilkins
112 U.S. 94 (1884)

From the earliest days of the republic it was the policy of the government to assimilate individual Indians. Almost every treaty signed with Indian tribes had provisions by which individual Indians who wanted to assume American citizenship could take land allotments away from the tribe and become citizens. But the promise of equality before the law was a cruel delusion at best. In the south there was such wholesale fraud that some of the treaties provided for reimbursement of individual Indians who had been defrauded of their treaty reservation allotments.

As the tribes reached the great plains, the tendency to allot and grant citizenship became more pronounced. In treaty after treaty articles were inserted which purported to grant full citizenship to Indians willing to leave the tribe and live among the whites. Some treaties had provisions whereby smaller tribes were given citizenship in larger ones as a price of receiving a small portion of their own lands. Thus the Cherokee Nation, for example, grew tremendously as smaller remnants of the Shawnees and Delawares were absorbed by them.

By the middle 1880's there were thousands of Indians who had left the tribe and moved into the growing towns. In most cases they had complied with the provisions of their treaties and expected to participate fully in the new life as white men. The following selection shows that the whites were not about to give voting rights to Indians regardless of their status. The court in *Elk v. Wilkins* used every conceivable means of disqualifying Elk from exercising the voting franchise. Never has there been such a torturous interpretation of treaties and statutes. In effect the court barred Indians from voting until the Indian Citizenship Act of 1924—despite the fact that hundreds of Indian Agents directing activities on the reservations were engaged in convincing the Indians that American citizenship was a goal to be sought.

Indians soon got the message that equality was merely a guise under which their lands could be put up for sale while they were systematically denied any privileges of citizenship. Thus when Senators and Congressmen speak today about giving "full citizenship" and "freeing" the Indians it is an immediate tip-off that they've hatched some new scheme to deprive the tribes of further lands.

With the enactment of the Civil Rights voting bills in the middle 1960's, a number of Indian reservations suddenly became target areas for federal voting registrars—particularly on the Navajo reservation. Some whites in Arizona feared retaliation by the Indians if they were allowed to vote. It didn't happen, however, and Arizona conservatives were calmed when they realized that a substantial number of Navajos were Republicans.

But the case of *Elk v. Wilkins* stands as a high water mark of legal deprivation of constitutional rights. Contained in the decision are a number of ideas which may return to plague the federal government. The Iroquois have continually maintained that they are not citizens of the United States and that the Indian Citizenship Act was illegally extended over them. Now other tribes are beginning to examine their peculiar status and to consider the advantages of dual citizenship. It may be that the *Elk* case will provide the basis of a new ideology of separatism for the nationalists of all minority groups.

This is an action brought by an Indian, in the Circuit Court of the United States for the District of Nebraska, against the registrar of one of the wards of the city of Omaha, for refusing to register him as a qualified voter therein. The petition was as follows:

"John Elk, plaintiff, complains of Charles Wilkins, defendant, and avers that the matter in dispute herein exceeds the sum of five hundred dollars, to wit, the sum of six thousand dollars, and that the matter in dispute herein arises under the Constitution and laws of the United States; and for cause of action against the defendant, avers that he, the plaintiff, is an Indian, and was born within the United States; that more than one year prior to the grievances hereinafter complained of he had severed his tribal relation to the Indian tribes, and had fully and completely surrendered himself to the jurisdiction of the United States, and still so continues subject to the jurisdiction of the United States; and avers that, under and by virtue of the Fourteenth Amendment to the Constitution of the United States, he is a citizen of the United States, and entitled to the right and privilege of citizens of the United States.

"That on the sixth day of April, 1880, there was held in the city of Omaha, (a city of the first class, incorporated under the general laws of the State of Nebraska providing for the incorporation of cities of the first class,) a general election for the election of members of the city council and other officers for said city.

"That the defendant, Charles Wilkins, held the office of and acted as registrar in the fifth ward of said city, and that as said registrar it was the duty of such defendant to register the names of all persons entitled to exercise the elective franchise in said ward of said city at said general election.

"That this plaintiff was a citizen of and had been a *bona fide* resident of the State of Nebraska for more than six months prior to said sixth day of April, 1880, and had been a *bona fide* resident of Douglas County, wherein the city of Omaha is situate, for more than forty days, and in the fifth ward of said city more than ten days prior to the said sixth day of April, and was such citizen and resident at the time of said election, and at the time of his attempted registration, as hereinafter set forth, and was in every way qualified, under the laws of the State of Nebraska and of the city of Omaha, to be registered as a voter and to cast a vote at said election, and complied with the laws of the city and State in that behalf.

"That on or about the fifth day of April, 1880, and prior to said election, this plaintiff presented himself to said Charles Wilkins, as such registrar, at his office, for the purpose of having his name registered as a qualified voter, as provided by law, and complied with all the provisions of the statutes in that regard, and claimed that, under the Fourteenth and Fifteenth Amendments to the Constitution of the United States, he was a citizen of the United States, and was entitled to exercise the elective franchise, regardless of his race and color; and that said Wilkins, designedly, corruptly, wilfully and maliciously, did then and there refuse to register this plaintiff, for the sole reason that the plaintiff was an Indian, and therefore not a citizen of the United States, and not, therefore, entitled to vote, and on account of his race and color, and with the wilful, malicious, corrupt and unlawful design to deprive this plaintiff of his right to vote at said election, and of his rights, and all other Indians of their rights, under said Fourteenth and Fifteenth Amendments to the Constitution of the United States, on account of his and their race and color."

MR. JUSTICE GRAY delivered the opinion of the court.

The Plaintiff, in support of his action, relies on the first clause of the first section of the Fourteenth Amendment of the Constitution of the United States, by which "all persons born or naturalized in the United States, and subject to the jurisdiction thereof, are citizens of the United States and of the State wherein they reside;" and on the Fifteenth Article of Amendment, which provides that "the right of citizens of the United States to vote shall not be denied or abridged by the United States or by any State on account of race, color, or previous condition of servitude."

This being a suit at common law, in which the matter in dispute exceeds $500, arising under the Constitution of the United States, the Circuit Court had jurisdiction of it under the Act of March 3, 1875, even if the parties were citizens of the same State. The judgment of that court, dismissing the action for costs, must have proceeded upon the merits, for, if the dismissal had been for want of jurisdiction, no costs could have been awarded. The only point argued by the defendant in this court is whether the petition sets forth facts enough to constitute cause of action.

The decision of this point, as both parties assume in their briefs, depends upon the question whether the legal conclusion, that under and by virtue of the Fourteenth Amendment of the Constitution the plaintiff is a citizen of the United States, is supported by the facts alleged in the petition and admitted by the demurrer, to wit: The plaintiff is an Indian, and was born in the United States, and has severed his tribal relation to the Indian tribes, and fully and completely surrendered himself to the jurisdiction of the United States, and still continues to be subject to the jurisdiction of the United States, and is a *bona fide* resident of the State of Nebraska and city of Omaha.

The petition, while it does not show of what Indian tribe the plaintiff was a member, yet by the allegations that he "is an Indian, and was born within the United States," and that "he had severed his tribal relation to the Indian tribes", clearly implies that he was born a member of one of the Indian tribes within the limits of the United States, which still exists and is recognized as a tribe by the government of the United States. Though the plaintiff alleges that he "had fully and completely surrendered himself to the jurisdiction of the United States," he does not allege that the United States accepted his surrender, or that he has ever been naturalized, or taxed, or in any way recognized or treated as a citizen, by the State or by the United States. Nor is it contended by his counsel that there is any statute or treaty that makes him a citizen.

The question then is, whether an Indian, born a member of one of the Indian tribes within the United States, is, merely by reason of his birth within the United States, and of his afterwards voluntarily separating himself from his tribe and taking up his residence among white citizens, a citizen of the United States, within the meaning of the first section of the Fourteenth Amendment of the Constitution.

Under the Constitution of the United States, as originally established, "Indians not taxed" were excluded from the persons according to whose numbers representatives and direct taxes were apportioned among the several States; and Congress had and exercised the power to regulate commerce with the Indian tribes, and the members thereof, whether within or without the boundaries of one of the States of the Union. The Indian tribes, being within the territorial limits of the United States, were not, strictly speaking, foreign States; but they were alien nations, distinct political communities, with whom the United States might and habitually did deal, as they thought fit, either through treaties made by the President and Senate, or through acts of Congress in the ordinary forms of legislation. The members of those tribes owed immediate allegiance to their several tribes, and were not part of the people of the United States. They were in a dependent condition, a state of pupilage, resembling that of a ward to his guardian. Indians and their property, exempt from taxation by treaty or statute of the United States, could not be taxed by any State. General acts of Congress did not apply to Indians, unless so expressed as to clearly manifest an intention to include them.

The alien and dependent condition of the members of the Indian tribes could not be put off at their own will, without the action or assent of the United States. They were never deemed citizens of the United States, except under explicit provisions of treaty or statute to that effect, either declaring a certain tribe, or such members of it as chose to remain behind on the removal of the tribe westward, to be citizens, or authorizing individuals of particular tribes to become citizens on application to a court of the United States for naturalization, and satisfactory proof of fitness for civilized life.

The distinction between citizenship by birth and citizenship by naturalization is clearly marked in the provisions of the Constitution, by which "no person, except a natural born citizen, or a citizen of the United States at the time of the adoption of this Constitution, shall be eligible to the office of President;" and "the Congress shall have power to establish an uniform rule of naturalization."

By the Thirteenth Amendment of the Constitution slavery was prohibited. The main object of the opening sentence of the Fourteenth Amendment was to settle the question, upon which there had been a difference of opinion throughout the country and in this court, as to the citizenship of free negroes; and to put it beyond doubt that all persons, white or black, and whether formerly slaves or not, born or naturalized in the United States, and owing no allegiance to any alien power, should be citizens of the United States and of the State in which they reside.

This section contemplates two sources of citizenship, and two sources only: birth and naturalization. The persons declared to be citizens are "all persons born or naturalized in the United States, and subject to the jurisdiction thereof." The evident meaning of these last words, is, not merely subject in some respect or degree to the jurisdiction of the United States, but completely subject to their political jurisdiction, and owing them direct and immediate allegiance. And the words relate to the time of birth in one case as they do the the time of naturalization in the other. Persons not thus subject to the jurisdiction of the United States at the time of birth cannot become so afterwards, except by being naturalized, whether individually, as by proceedings under the naturalization acts, or collectively, as by the force of a treaty by which foreign territory is acquired.

Indians born within the territorial limits of the United States, members of, and owing immediate allegiance to, one of the Indian tribes (an alien, though dependent, power), although in a geographical sense born in the United States, are no more "born in the United States and subject to the jurisdiction thereof," within the meaning of the first section of the Fourteenth Amendment, than the children of subjects of any foreign government born within the domain of that government, or the children born within the United States, of ambassadors or other public ministers of foreign nations.

This view is confirmed by the second section of the Fourteenth Amendment, which provides that "representatives shall be apportioned among the several States according to their respective numbers, counting the whole number of persons in each State, excluding Indians not taxed." Slavery having been abolished, and the persons formerly held as slaves made citizens, this clause fixing the apportionment of representatives has abrogated so much of the corresponding clause of the original Constitution as counted only three-fifths of such persons. But Indians not taxed are still excluded from the count, for the reason that they are not citizens. Their absolute exclusion from the basis of representation, in which all other persons are now included, is wholly inconsistent with their being considered citizens.

So the further provision of the second section for a proportionate reduction of the basis of the representation of any State in which the right to vote for presidential electors, representatives in Congress, or executive or judicial officers or members of the legislatures of a State, is denied, except for participation in rebellion or other crime, to "any of the male inhabitants of such State, being twenty-one years of age and citizens of the United States," cannot apply to a denial of the elective franchise to Indians not taxed, who form no part of the people entitled to representation.

It is also worthy of remark, that the language used, about the same time, by the very Congress which framed the Fourteenth Amendment, in the first section of the Civil Rights Act of April 9, 1866, declaring who shall be citizens of the United States, is "all persons born in the United States, and not subject to any foreign power, excluding Indians not taxed."

Such Indians, then, not being citizens by birth, can only become citizens in the second way mentioned in the Fourteenth Amendment, by being "naturalized in the United States," by or under some treaty or statute.

The action of the political departments of the government, not only after the proposal of the Amendment by Congress to the States in June, 1866, but since the proclamation in July, 1868, of its ratification by the requisite number of States, accords with this construction.

While the Amendment was pending before the legislatures of the several States, treaties containing provisions for the naturalization of members of Indian tribes as citizens of the United States were made on July 4, 1866, with the Delawares, in 1867 with various tribes in Kansas, and with the Pottawatomies, and in April, 1868, with the Sioux.

The treaty of 1867 with the Kansas Indians strikingly illustrates the principle that no one can become a citizen of a nation without its consent, and directly contradicts the supposition that a member of an Indian tribe can at will be alternately a citizen of the United States and a member of the tribe.

That treaty not only provided for the naturalization of members of the Ottawa, Miami, Peoria, and other tribes, and their families, upon their making declaration, before the District Court of the United States, of their intention to become citizens; but, after reciting that some of the Wyandotts, who had become citizens under the treaty of 1855, were "unfitted for the responsibilities of citizenship," and enaction that a register of the whole people of this tribe, resident in Kansas or elsewhere, should be taken, under the direction of the Secretary of the Interior, showing the names of "all who declare their desire to be and remain Indians and in a tribal condition," and of incompetents and orphans as described in the treaty of 1855, and that such persons, and those only, should thereafter constitute the tribe; it provided that "no one who has heretofore consented to become a citizen, nor the wife or children of any such person, shall be allowed to become members of the tribe, except by the free consent of the tribe after its new organization, and unless the agent shall certify that such party is, through poverty or incapacity, unfit to continue in the exercise of the responsibilities of citizenship of the United States, and likely to become a public charge."

Since the ratification of the Fourteenth Amendment, Congress has passed several acts for naturalizing Indians of certain tribes, which would have been superflous if they were, or might become, without any action of the government, citizens of the United States.

By the act of July 15, 1870, for instance, it was provided that if at any time thereafter any of the Winnebago Indians in the State of Minnesota should desire to become citizens of the United States, they should make application to the District Court of the United States for the State of Minnesota, and in open court make the same proof and take the same oath of allegiance as is provided by law for the naturalization of aliens, and should also make proof to the satisfaction of the court that they were sufficiently intelligent and prudent to control their own affairs and interests, that they had adopted the habits of civilized life, and had for at least five years before been able to support themselves and their families; and thereupon they should be declared by the court to be citizens of the United States, the declaration entered of record, and a certificate thereof given to the applicant; and the Secretary of the Interior, upon presentation of that certificate, might issue to them patents in fee simple, with power of alienation, of the lands already held by them in severalty, and might cause to be paid to them their portion of the money and effects of the tribe held in trust under any treaty or law of the United States; and thereupon such persons should cease to be members of that tribe, and the lands so patented to them should be subject to levy, taxation, and sale, in like manner with the property of other citizens. By the act of March 3, 1865 similar provision was made for the naturalization of any adult members of the Miami tribe of Kansas, and their minor children. And the act of March 3, 1865 making corresponding provision for the naturalization of any of the chiefs, warriors, or heads of families of the Stockbridge Indians, is re-enacted in section 2312 of the Revised Statutes.

The recent statutes concerning homesteads are quite inconsistent with the theory that Indians do or can make themselves independent citizens by living apart from their tribe. The act of March 3, 1875 allowed to "any Indian born in the United States, who is head of a family, or who has arrived at the age of twenty-one years, and who has abandoned, or may hereafter abandon, his tribal relations," the benefit of the homestead acts, but only upon condition of his "making satisfactory proof of such abandonment, under rules to be prescribed by the Secretary of the Interior;" and further provided that his title in the homestead should be absolutedly inalienable for five years from the date of the patent, and that he should be entitled to share in all annuities, tribal funds, lands and other property, as if he maintained his tribal relations. And the act of March 3, 1884, while it allows Indians "located on public lands" to "avail themselves of the homestead laws as fully and to the same extent as may now be done by citizens of the United States," provides that the form and legal effect of the patent shall be that the United States does and will hold the land for twenty-five years, in trust for the Indian making the entry, and his widow and heirs, and will then convey it in fee to him or them.

The national legislation has tended more and more towards the education and civilization of the Indians, and fitting them to be citizens. But the question whether any Indian tribes, or members thereof, have become so far advanced in civilization, that they should be let out of the state of pupilage, and admitted to the privileges and responsibilities of citizenship, is a question to be decided by the nation whose wards they are and whose citizens they seek to become, and not by each Indian for himself.

There is nothing in the statutes or decisions, referred to by counsel, to control the conclusion to which we have been brought by a consideration of the language of the Fourteenth Amendment, and of the condition of the Indians at the time of its proposal and ratification.

The passages cited as favorable to the plaintiff from the opinions delivered in *Ex parte Kenyon*, in *Ex parte Reynolds*, and in *United States v. Crook*, were *obiter dicta*. The Case of Reynolds was an indictment in the Circuit Court of the United States for the Western District of Arkansas for a murder in the Indian country, of which that court had jurisdiction if either the accused or the dead man was not an Indian, and was decided by Judge Parker in favor of the jurisdiction, upon the ground that both were white men, and that, conceding the one to be an Indian by marriage, the other never was an Indian in any sense. Each of the other two cases was a writ of *habeus corpus;* and any person, whether a citizen or not, unlawfully restrained of his liberty, is entitled to that writ. In Kenyon's case, Judge Parker held that the court in which the prisoner had been convicted had no jurisdiction of the subject matter, because the place of the commission of the act was beyond the territorial limits of its jurisdiction, and, as was truly said, "this alone would be conclusive of this case." In *United States v. Crook,* the Ponca Indians were discharged by Judge Dundy because the military officers who held them were taking them to the Indian Territory by force and without any lawful authority; and in the case at bar, as the record before us shows, that learned judge concurred in the judgment below for the defendant. The law upon the question before us has been well stated by Judge Deady in the District Court of the United States for the District of Oregon. In giving judgment against the plaintiff in a case resembling the case at bar, he said: "Being born a member of 'an independent political community'—the Chinook—he was not born subject to the jurisdiction of the United States— not born in its allegiance." And in a later case he said: "But an Indian cannot make himself a citizen of the United States without the consent and co-operation of the government. The fact that he has abandoned his nomadic life or tribal relations, and adopted the habits and manners of civilized people, may be a good reason why he should be made a citizen of the United States, but does not of itself make him one. To be a citizen of the United States is a political privilege which no one, not born to, can assume without its consent in some form. The Indians in Oregon, not being born subject to the jurisdiction of the United States, were not born citizens thereof, and I am not aware of any law or treaty by which any of them have been made so since."

Upon the question whether any action of a State can confer rights of citizenship on Indians of a tribe still recognized by the United States as retaining its tribal existence, we need not, and do not, express an opinion, because the State of Nebraska is not shown to have taken any action affecting the condition of this plaintiff.

The plaintiff, not being a citizen of the United States under the Fourteenth Amendment of the Constitution, has been deprived of no right secured by the Fifteenth Amendment, and cannot maintain this action.

Judgment affirmed.

Ritual on Admission of Indians to Full American Citizenship

In the early reservation days a ceremony was established by which Indians were given their citizenship. In many cases they had agreed to accept their lands in fee simple under the Allotment Act. In other cases they had fulfilled certain requirements by which it was felt that they should have the privileges of citizenship. For the most part the ceremony was designed to wean them away from the life they had once known decades earlier as rovers and hunters on plain and forest.

In no case was there any effort to determine if the individual Indian really understood the nature of citizenship. He did not have to take courses in the English language, pass tests as to the meaning of the United States Constitution or form of government. Nor did he have to know who was the Senator, Governor, or Congressman of his state. Citizenship was relatively simple—the Indian merely had to agree to take his allotment in fee simple—in a situation where white settlers, county assessors, state tax agents, or banks could get their hands on it should they be able to fool him on some minor point of law. *That* was all that was required for Indian citizenship.

In the citizenship ceremony each individual was required to foreswear his Indian name. Thus was the simplistic idea that once having received citizenship and taken a white name, the Indian was an Indian no more. The ritual should be an adequate example of the utter failure of white society to comprehend the nature and meaning of culture.

Representative of Department speaking:

The President of the United States has sent me to speak a solemn and serious word to you, a word that means more to some of you than any other that you have ever heard. He has been told that there are some among you who should no longer be controlled by the Bureau of Indian Affairs, but should be given their patents in fee and thus become free American citizens. It is his decision that this shall be done, and that those so honored by the people of the United States shall have the meaning of this new and great privilege pointed out by symbol and by word, so that no man or woman shall not know its meaning. The President has sent me papers naming those men and women, and I shall call out their names one by one, and they will come before me.

For men: (Read name.) —— (white name). What was your Indian name? (Gives name.)

—— (Indian name). I hand you a bow and an arrow. Take this bow and shoot the arrow. (He shoots.)

—— (Indian name). You have shot your last arrow. That means that you are no longer to live the life of an Indian. You are from this day forward to live the life of the white man. But you may keep that arrow, it will be to you a symbol of your noble race and of the pride you feel that you come from the first of all Americans.

—— (white name). Take in your hand this plow. (He takes the handles of the plow.)

This act means that you have chosen to live the life of the white man—and the white man lives by work. From the earth we all must get our living, and the earth will not yield unless man pours upon it the sweat of his brow. Only by work do we gain a right to the land or to the enjoyment of life.

—— (white name). I give you a purse. This purse will always say to you that the money you gain from your labor must be wisely kept. The wise man saves his money so that when the sun does not smile and the grass does not grow, he will not starve.

I give into your hands the flag of your country. This is the only flag you have ever had or ever will have. It is the flag of freedom, the flag of free men, the flag of a hundred million free men and women of whom you are now one. That flag has a request to make of you,——(white name); that you take it into your hands and repeat these words:

"For as much as the President has said that I am worthy to be a citizen of the United States, I now promise to this flag that I will give my hands, my head, and my heart to the doing of all that will make me a true American citizen."

And now beneath this flag I place upon your breast the emblem of your citizenship. Wear this badge of honor always; and may the eagle that is on it never see you do aught of which the flag will not be proud.

(The audience rises and shouts: "—— (white name) is an American citizen.")

For women: Allie Fox Duncan (white name). Take in your hand this work bag and purse. (She takes the work bag and purse.)

This means that you have chosen the life of the white woman—and the white woman loves her home. The family and the home are the foundation of our civilization. Upon the character and industry of the mother and home maker largely depends the future of our Nation. The purse will always say to you that the money you gain from your labor must be wisely kept. The wise woman saves her money, so that when the sun does not smile and the grass does not grow, she and her children will not starve.

I give into your hands the flag of your country. This is the only flag you have ever had or will ever have. It is the flag of freedom, the flag of free men, a hundred million free men and women of whom you are now one. That flag has a request to make of you, —— (white name), that you take it into your hands and repeat these words:

"For as much as the President has said that I am worthy to be a citizen of the United States, I now promise to this flag that I will give my hands, my head, and my heart to the doing of all that will make me a true American citizen."

And now beneath this flag I place upon your breast the emblem of your citizenship. Wear this badge of honor always; and may the eagle that is on it never see you do aught of which the flag will not be proud.

(The audience rises and shouts: "Allie Fox Duncan (white name) is an American citizen.")

Indian Citizenship Act
June 2, 1924

After the Removal Treaties between the United States and the Five Civilized Tribes, individual Indians received their citizenship in a number of ways. In *Elk v. Wilkins,* as we have seen, an Indian had fulfilled every requirement of the allotment procedure and still had not been recognized as a citizen. In other treaties and statutes, particularly those attached to various land laws, individual Indians had also achieved a citizenship status. Yet there was still not a consistent general statute by which individual Indians could prove their citizenship without a multitude of papers carried on their person for emergency situations.

The response of the young Indians to service in World War I was so overwhelming that it even shamed Congress. After the end of the First World War there was considerable pressure to pass a general citizenship statute for Indians. Finally in 1924 a simple one-paragraph law was passed giving blanket citizenship. But it was not until 1948 that the state of Arizona recognized the law and in the middle 1950's the Indians of Utah had to go to court to prove their right to vote.

Even today the 1924 Citizenship Act is suspect, particularly among the Iroquois who maintain that citizenship cannot be forced upon them by the United States without their consent. They refuse to vote and pay taxes and deny any citizenship but their own, even to the point of issuing their own passports to be used in traveling across the United States-Canadian border.

There has never been any significant test case brought on this statute in relation to the due process clause against the arbitrary actions of the Federal government. Thus the law has as yet been unused except for voting in national and state elections.

Be it enacted by the Senate and House of Representatives of the United States of America in Congress assembled, That all non-citizen Indians born within the territorial limits of the United States be, and they are hereby, declared to be citizens of the United States: *Provided,* That the granting of such Citizenship shall not in any manner impair or otherwise affect the right of any Indian to tribal or other property.

Approved, June 2, 1924.

Davis v. Sitka School Board
3 Alaska 481 (1908)

Sometimes there appears to be no way in which Indian people can qualify or the ordinary rights given to other American citizens. In Alaska there has been ension between native and white settlers for close to a century. Part of the difficulty has been the refusal of the federal government to adequately compensate he Alaska natives for their lands. Since the territory was purchased from Russia, he United States felt no need to pay the natives for the land it was using. Even hough treaties were still being signed with other Indian tribes as late as the 1870's, the natives of Alaska were no military threat to the white settlers and hence there was no need to sign a treaty with them.

Another reason for the tension has been that the natives have not been brought into full citizenship rights. The following selection indicates to what lengths the courts of this country will go to deny Indians their rights. Had the Davis's lived in any of the western states, the Indian agent would have used them as his brightest prospects for the civilized life. In Alaska, however, the mere trace of Indian blood was sufficient, once and for all, to bar the person from full participation in the normal life of the community.

The portions of the statute by virtue of which the Sitka school was established, and which bear on the present controversy are in sections 5 and 7 of the act of 1905. Section 5 provides that:

> The school district established outside of the towns shall contain not less than twenty white children between the ages of six and twenty years. The petition shall be signed by not less than twelve persons of adult age who are citizens of the United States, or who have declared their intention to become such.

Section 7 is as follows:

> SECTION 7. That the schools specified and provided for in this act shall be devoted to the education of white children and children of mixed blood who lead a civilized life. The education of the Eskimos and Indians in the district of Alaska shall remain under the direction and control of the Secretary of the Interior, and schools for and among the Eskimos and Indians of Alaska shall be provided for by an annual appropriation, and the Eskimo and Indian children of Alaska shall have the same right to be admitted to any Indian boarding school as the Indian children in the states or territories of the United States.

A clear distinction is here made between the school for the native—i.e., the Eskimo and the Indian, whether civilized or otherwise—and the school for the white child, or the child with the white man's blood in its veins, though it be mixed with that of another race. But of the child of mixed blood there is made the further requirement, to wit, that he shall live a civilized life. But why this further qualification? Why not admit any child of mixed blood? From the very inception of the United States, the care and education of the Indian has been one of the problems that has vexed the government. The Indian in his native state has everywhere been found to be savage, an uncivilized being, when measured by the white man's standard. At first, Indians were dealt with as independent tribes, though in later years this attitude was changed. But, whatever the method adopted by the government in its dealings with the aboriginal inhabitants of this continent, it has always regarded him as of a benighted race, in a state of pupilage, a ward of the nation, needing care, control, protection, and education, and until comparatively recent years incapable of citizenship. And even then when it was thought that under certain conditions some of that race might at last have become capable of intelligently exercising the duties of citizenship, the action or assent of the guardian, the United States, as was said in *U.S. v. Boyd,* "was absolutely essential to enable the Indian to renounce the independent condition in which he had been since the adoption of the Constitution."

Nor is the status of the Alaskan native materially different from that of the red man of the States. In an early case (*In re Sah Quah*), in which the status of the Alaskan Indian was considered, Judge Dawson said:

> The United States has at no time recognized any tribal independence or relations among these Indians [Alaskan], has never treated with them in any capacity; but from every act of Congress in relation to the people of this territory it is clearly inferable that they have been and now are regarded as dependent subjects, amenable to the penal laws of the United States, and subject to the jurisdiction of its courts. They are practically in a state of pupilage, and sustain a relation to the United States similar to that of a ward to a guardian.

It will be seen from the language of the third article of the treaty of March 30, 1867, between Russia and the United States, by which the territory of Alaska became American soil, that the Alaskan natives were classed with the Indians of the states as "uncivilized." It was there stipulated that:

> The uncivilized tribes will be subject to such laws and regulations as the United States may from time to time adopt in regard to the aboriginal tribes of that country.

The aboriginal tribes of Alaska and their descendants are, then, the wards of the nation as truly as are those inhabiting the states with which the government since its organization has had to deal.

But in what relation do those of the mixed blood stand to the native, and what in the law constitutes a person of mixed blood? It is said in the opinion in *Sloan v. United States,* that:

> As ordinarily understood by white people, a person of white and Indian parentage is deemed to be of mixed blood, without regard to the source of the Indian blood. In other words, in common parlance the child of a white father and Indian mother, as well as a child of an Indian father and a white mother, are equally of mixed blood, and therefore, when in a convention of Indians half or mixed bloods are included, no distinction can be drawn between those who derive it from the father."

In other words, "mixed blood" means "mixed Indian blood," regardless of whether it comes from the father or mother, and whether it be half or quarter.

In the case at bar I am of the opinion that the test to be applied should be as to whether or not the persons in question have turned aside from old association, former habits of life, and easier modes of existence; in other words, have exchanged the old barbaric, uncivilized environment for one changed, new, and so different as to indicate an advanced and improved condition of mind, which desires and reaches out for something altogether distinct from and unlike the old life. This is far from a completely satisfactory test; but it will, I apprehend, meet the exigencies of the occasion and aid in a just determination of the cause.

Having determined upon a test, inadequate though it may be, let us examine the facts as they appear from the testimony, and apply that test to them. The plaintiffs, six in number, must, since they are minor children of four different families, be considered with relation to their families and surroundings—*i.e.,* first, Dora and Tillie Davis; second, John and Lottie Littlefield; third, Lizzie Allard; and fourth, Peter Allard.

But before considering that subject, it may be well to ascertain what is disclosed by the testimony relative to the institution of this proceeding through Walton, the guardian ad litem, who is the stepfather of the Davis children. It appears that the parents of none of the other children were consulted as to this proceeding, nor was Walton himself advised concerning the legal proceedings and steps taken by counsel for securing the admission of his stepchildren to the Sitka school. This fact of itself has, I think, a strong bearing on the attitude of the parents toward the proceedings, as well as their condition and habits of live. It is readily understood that Mr. Kelley, of plaintiffs' counsel, and others who interested themselves on behalf of these children, because of their peculiar field of labor among the native Alaskans, are entirely in earnest in their efforts to advance the conditions of the native children and of the children of the mixed blood. And it is evident from the testimony that the efforts to obtain the admission of these plaintiffs to the school were not so much, if at all, those of the parents as those of Mr. Kelly and his co-laborers among the natives. It appears in every instance that the parents were quite content with the schooling obtained by their children in the native school during such part of the year as it was open. Nothing was done by the parents and guardian of the children in furtherance of securing their admission to the Sitka school until after the native school had closed, or before the possibility of attending the Sitka school had been suggested to the parents, and, at least in the case of Lizzie Allard, before such steps had been urged upon the relatives by those having no legal responsibility for or authority over the children. No animadversion is here intended, however, upon those who made these suggestions.

The testimony also discloses the fact that, in the enumeration of the children eligible for the Sitka school made to obtain data for the petition for the establishment of the school, these plaintiffs were by the enumerator included as children of mixed blood who live a civilized life. This fact is advanced as a reason why the plaintiffs should not be excluded from the school. It is unnecessary to consider this contention, since it is too plain to require argument or citation of authorities that, if the plaintiffs lacked the requisite qualifications to entitle them to admission to the school, an erroneous enumeration will not supply the deficiency.

Whether or not the essentials are possessed by these plaintiffs must be ascertained from the testimony, and, in examining this question, the status of each of the four groups of plaintiffs must be considered separately.

The first group consists of Dora and Tillie Davis. They are aged, respectively, eight and seven years, and are the children of Fred Davis, a full-blood Indian, now deceased, and a woman whom some of the witnesses declare is a full-blood native, while others testify that she has white blood in her veins. None seem to know her ancestry. From the testimony, and from an inspection of her photograph, I am inclined to believe her to be of mixed blood. Davis and his wife were legally married at Sitka, on December 14, 1896. Dora and Tillie Davis, then, were born in lawful wedlock and are of the mixed blood. The mother married again. Her second husband is Rudolph Walton, a full-blood native, and the guardian ad litem of all the plaintiffs in this case. Walton owns a house in the native village, lying on the outskirts of the town of Sitka. The children live there with their mother and stepfather. Their associates and playmates are presumably the native children who live in the Indian village. So far as these plaintiffs are concerned, there is nothing to indicate any difference between them and the other children of the Sitka native village, except the testimony of Walton and others as to Walton's business. Walton conducts a store on the edge of the town of Sitka, in which he manufactures and sells Indian curios, and for which business he pays the business license tax required by the laws of Alaska. He rents a box in the post office, and has worked out his road tax in the Sitka road district, when warned out by the overseer. He and his family have adopted the white man's style of dress. All who testified concerning Walton himself speak of him as an industrious, law-abiding, intelligent native. He seems, so far as business matters are concerned, to have endeavored to conduct his business according to civilized methods, even to the installation of an expensive cash register in his store. He speaks, reads, and writes the English language. But the testimony fails to disclose a corresponding progress in the domestic and social relations of his family. It does appear that he and his family reside in a house separate and apart from the other natives, and that he clothes and supports his family; but nothing further than that appears. What is the manner of their life? What are their domestic habits? Who are their associates and intimates? These matters do not appear. True, the Waltons are members of the Presbyterian Church; but many natives, for whom the claim of civilization would not be made, are members of churches of the various denominations which are striving to better the conditions in this country. Civilization, though, of course, the term must be considered relative, includes, I apprehend, more than a prosperous business, a trade, a house, white man's clothes, and membership in a church. The burden of establishing that the plaintiffs live the civilized life is upon them, and I fail to find in the testimony evidence of a condition that inclines me to the opinion that the Davis children have that requisite.

The second group is composed of the Littlefield children, John and Lottie, both minors. The testimony in their case is clear and unequivocal that they are children of the mixed blood. They too, were born in wedlock; their parents having been married at Sitka, by the Presbyterian missionary, July 1, 1891. John Littlefield, the father, is a white man and a citizen of the United States. The mother is a native. Littlefield, by occupation a laborer, was for some time prior to and at the time of the commencement of this proceeding employed at Killisnoo in connection with the fishing industry there conducted. The Littlefield family, like the Waltons, have in the native village at Sitka a separate house, in which they live when there; but it appears that during the fishing season Littlefield lives at Killisnoo, and that his wife and children live there with him, when they are not off with the other natives on hunting and fishing trips. Littlefield, I take it, supports his family. How well or how ill does not appear. Certain it is that the children are unrestrained, and live the life of their native associates, rather than a civilized life.

Lizzie Allard is the next plaintiff whose status is to be considered. She is seven years old, and undoubtedly a child of mixed blood born in lawful wedlock. Her parents are George Allard, an ex-soldier and a citizen of the United States, and a full-blood Indian woman. The mother has been dead for some time. Since her death the child has lived with and has been cared for by her maternal grandmother, "whose white name is Mary Susie." The child's father has contributed but little, practically nothing, to her support during the years since her mother's death. What he did before that does not appear. He is a miner, living here and there at whatever mining camp he can find employment.

Like the Waltons and Littlefields, Lizzie and her grandmother live alone in the grandmother's house in the native village at Sitka. It appears that the child has her own bed, and that upon a sewing machine, also the property of the grandmother, which graces their domicile, Lizzie's clothes are made. Her father, in response to the question, "You say she lives the life of white people?" testifies, "They have butter," and let it go at that, except that later she said she "had her little bead work." It also appears that the child attends the Russian Indian school, the Russian church, and sings in the choir of that church. Rev. Father Kashaveroff, director of the Russian church and mission at Sitka, testified that

Lizzie was of a respectable character, so far as he knew, and that she "acts very nicely." He also testified to a conversation with the child's grandmother, after the Russian school had closed for that year, in which the grandmother told him that she had been urged to put Lizzie in the American school, and that she did not want her to go there.

Lizzie's playmates are children of mixed blood and Indian children living in the Indian village. Practically all her associations are with the natives. During the sealing season, both Lizzie and her grandmother take part in the fishing and hunting expeditions of the native bands, living as do their companions. The grandmother speaks no English. Her testimony in this proceeding was given entirely through an interpreter.

Peter Allard is the last of the plaintiffs. He is the son of William (or "Wasca") Allard, mixed blood, and a native woman. They were regularly married. Their residence is also in the native village, where the mother owns a house. The father is a laborer, finding a varied and intermittent employment about the town of Sitka. His associates are natives, and from his testimony I conclude that he prefers the life and associations to be found in the Indian village, with and occasional sortie into the whiteman's world, to a prolonged or permanent residence elsewhere. Nor is this to be considered as altogether strange, or as discrediting him, since he was born and grew to manhood among these people. His friends of a life-time are there, and some inducement, which to him appears to be great and enticing, must be held out to him before he will turn his back on all those old friends and associations. And this is true of man generally, no matter what his race, color, or blood may be. It appears that his wife is a good housekeeper, so far as their means and station in life will allow her to be; that the pots and kettles and frying pans are not left upon the floor, after the native fashion, but are hung up, and that curtains drape the windows of their house. This indicates progress; but does it satisfy the test? It is urged that Allard and his wife have been entertained by white men of culture and refinement; but that cannot be considered as a criterion of civilization. To me it is an evidence of the kindliness and of the interest and effort of the hosts in behalf of a people among and for whom they have labored long and assiduously, not an evidence of the civilization of the guests. These isolated instances do not make a condition of life. As we have seen, something more is required to meet the test. Those who from choice make their homes among an uncivilized or semi-civilized people and find there their sole social enjoyments and personal pleasures and associations cannot, in my opinion, be classed with those who live a civilized life.

Can it be said, after applying the test to conditions surrounding these plaintiffs and in which they live, that the test is satisfied in a single instance? I am compelled, after a most careful scrutiny of the evidence, to conclude that it is not. In the case of none of the plaintiffs do the conditions disclosed by the evidence lead me to the opinion that his or her family lives a civilized life, and, as in each instance the life of the family is the life of the plaintiff, the same opinion is held with regard to the plaintiffs themselves, though in fairness be it said that Walton himself is far in advance of the others. What his family life may be is not disclosed.

It was urged by the defendants that the right to invoke the aid of the court in this proceeding was a separate and independent right in each plaintiff; that they could not join in the same writ. This contention is undoubtedly well-founded. But, in view of the importance to the community of the interpretation of the statute, it appeared advisable to consider the matter on its merits, rather than to dismiss the proceeding on a technical point.

I am of the opinion that the defendants acted within their powers in refusing these plaintiffs admission. A consideration of those powers is, I take it, unnecessary at this time, since the main issue in the controversy appears to have been as to whether or not plaintiffs lead a civilized life.

That issue being determined adversely to the plaintiffs, the proceeding should be dismissed.

Ex Parte Crow Dog
109 U.S. 556 (1883)

Throughout most of the treaties the tribes had been given "free and undisturbed use" of their lands. In many previous cases this phrase had been interpreted to mean that the United States could not interfere with the domestic relations of the tribe when practiced according to custom.

In the various Sioux Treaties the phrase had occurred many times. But the Sioux did not have formal courts as did the Five Civilized Tribes of Oklahoma. Thus while the judgments of the Cherokee, Chickasaw, Creek, Choctaw and Seminole courts were upheld in capital offenses, there was no precedent in Sioux country for the situation of one tribal member killing another.

A longstanding feud had developed between Spotted Tail, chief of the Brule Sioux at the Rosebud Agency and Crow Dog, one of the tribal members. Laying in wait for Spotted Tail, Crow Dog killed him one day while the chief was out riding on the reservation. Although the usual tribal amenities were observed when the public discovered that the murderer was not to be executed, a great outcry against the savagery of the Sioux arose.

The result was immediate Congressional reaction. In the next session a rider was placed on an appropriation bill establishing seven major crimes that, when committed by one Indian against another, would become federal crimes transcending Indian jurisdiction.

By thus assuming power over certain aspects of tribal life, the United States government broke the ancient customs of the Sioux tribe and imposed a foreign standard of justice. Breakdown of tribal customs was fairly rapid after that, leading to the present situation where federal law is considered an outside force of the white man and not a means of establishing tribal law and order.

In 1968 the United States government extended the Bill of Rights over tribal governments in their relations with the individual tribal members. This law created within the traditional Pueblos of New Mexico the same situation as had the *Crow Dog* case nearly half a century earlier.

Ex Parte Crow Dog is thus an important case in two aspects. First it marks the beginning of the intrusion of the United States Government into the internal domestic affairs of the Sioux Nation. Second, it is the first major case in which there is an effort made to define the relationship between a tribal form of government and an individual member. Additionally the opinion contains important interpretations of the Sioux Treaties as understood by the United States Government in 1883, six years before the Great Sioux Agreement which divided the reservation into the smaller constituent reservations that we find in South Dakota at the present time.

MR. JUSTICE MATTHEWS delivered the opinion of the court.

The petitioner is in the custody of the marshal of the United States for the Territory of Dakota, imprisoned in the jail of Lawrence County, in the First Judicial District of that Territory, under sentence of death, adjudged against him by the district court for that district, to be carried into execution January 14th, 1884. That judgment was rendered upon a conviction for the murder of an Indian of the Brule Sioux band of the Sioux nation of Indians, by the name of Sin-ta-ge-le-Scka, or in English, Spotted Tail, the prisoner also being an Indian, of the same band and nation, and the homicide having occurred as alleged in the indictment, in the Indian country, within a place and district of country under the exclusive jurisdiction of the United States and within the said judicial district. The judgment was affirmed, on a writ of error, by the Supreme Court of the Territory. It is claimed on behalf of the prisoner that the crime charged against him, and of which he stands convicted, is not an offence under the laws of the United States; that the district court had no jurisdiction to try him, and that its judgment and sentence are void. He therefore prays for a writ of *habeas corpus,* that he may be delivered from an imprisonment which he asserts to be illegal.

The indictment is framed upon section 5339 of the Revised Statutes. That section is found in title LXX., on the subject of crimes against the United States, and in chapter three, which treats of crimes arising within the maritime and territorial jurisdiction of the United States. It provides that "every person who commits murder . . . within any fort, arsenal, dock-yard, magazine, or any other place or district of country under the exclusive jurisdiction of the United States . . . shall suffer death."

Title XXVIII. of the Revised Statutes relates to Indians, and the sub-title of chapter four is, Government of Indian Country. It embraces many provisions regulating the subject of intercourse and trade with the Indians in the Indian country, and imposes penalties and punishments for various violations of them. Section 2142 provides for the punishment of assaults with deadly weapons and intent, by Indians upon white persons, and by white persons upon Indians; section 2143, for the case of arson, in like cases; and section 2144 provides that "the general laws of the United States defining and prescribing punishments for forgery and depredations upon the mails shall extend to the Indian country."

The next two sections are as follows:

"SEC. 2145. Except as to crimes, the punishment of which is expressly provided for in this title, the general laws of the United States as to the punishment of crimes committed in any place within the sole and exclusive jurisdiction of the United States, except the District of Columbia, shall extend to the Indian country.

"SEC. 2146. The preceding section shall not be construed to extend to [crimes committed by one Indian against the person or property of another Indian, nor to] any Indian committing any offence in the Indian country who has been punished by the local law of the tribe, or to any case where by treaty stipulations the exclusive jurisdiction over such offences is or may be secured to the Indian tribes respectively."

That part of section 2146 placed within brackets was in the act of 27th March, 1854, ch. 26, § 3, was omitted by the revisers in the original revision, and restored by the act of 18th February, 1875, c. 80, and now appears in the second edition of the Revised Statutes. It is assumed for the purposes of this opinion that the omission in the original revision was inadvertent, and that the restoration evinces no other intent on the part of Congress than that the provision should be considered as in force, without interruption, and not a new enactment of it for any other purpose than to correct the error of the revision.

The district courts of the Territory of Dakota are invested with the same jurisdiction in all cases arising under the laws of the United States. The reservation of the Sioux Indians, lying within the exterior boundaries of the Territory of Dakota, was defined by Art. II. of the treaty concluded April 29th, 1868, and by § 1839 Rev. Stat. it is excepted out of and constitutes no part of that Territory. The object of this exception is stated to be to exclude the jurisdiction of any State or Territorial government over Indians, within its exterior lines, without their consent, where their rights have been reserved and remain unextinguished by treaty. But the district courts of the Territory having, by law, the jurisdiction of district and circuit courts of the United States, may, in that character, take cognizance of offences against the laws of the United States, although committed within an Indian reservation, when the latter is situate within the space which is constituted by the authority of the Territorial government the judicial district of such court. If the land reserved for the exclusive occupancy of Indians lies outside the exterior boundaries of any organized Territorial government, it would require an act of Congress to attach it to a judicial district; of which there are many instances, the latest being the act of January 6th, 1883, by which a part of the Indian Territory was attached to the District of Kansas and a part to the Northern District of Texas. In the present case the Sioux reservation is within the geographical limits of the Territory of Dakota, and being excepted out of it only in respect to the Territorial government, the district court of that Territory, within the geographical boundaries of whose district it lies, may exercise jurisdiction under the laws of the United States over offences made punishable by them committed within its limits.

The district court has two distinct jurisdictions. As a Territorial court it administers the local law of the Territorial government; as invested by act of Congress with jurisdiction to administer the laws of the United States, it has all the authority of circuit and district courts; so that, in the former character, it may try a prisoner for murder committed in the Territory proper, under the local law, which requires the jury to determine whether the punishment shall be death or imprisonment for life, Laws of Dakota, 1833, ch. 9; and, in the other character, try another for a murder committed within the Indian reservation, under a law of the United States, which imposes, in case of conviction, the penalty of death.

Section 2145 of the Revised Statutes extends the general laws of the United States as to the punishment of crimes committed in any place within their sole and exclusive jurisdiction, except the District of Columbia, to the Indian country, and it becomes necessary, therefore, to inquire whether the locality of the homicide, for which the prisoner was convicted of murder, is within that description.

The first section of the Indian Intercourse Act of June 30th, 1834, defines the Indian country as follows:

"That all that part of the United States west of the Mississippi, and not within the States of Missouri and Louisiana, or the Territory of Arkansas, and, also, that part of the United States east of the Mississippi River, and not within any State to which the Indian tribe has not been extinguished, for the purposes of this act, be taken and be deemed to be the Indian country."

Since the passage of that act great changes have taken place by the acquisition of new territory, by the creation of new States, and by the organization of Territorial governments; and the Revised Statutes, while retaining the substance of many important provisions of the act of 1834, with amendments and additions since made regulating intercourse with the Indian tribes, have, nevertheless, ommitted all definition of what new must be taken to be "the Indian country." Nevertheless, although the section of the act of 1834 containing the definition of that date has been repealed, it is not to be regarded as if it had never been adopted, but may be referred to in connection with the provisions of its original context which remain in force, and may be considered in connection with the changes which have taken place in our situation, with a view of determining from time to time what must be regarded as Indian country where it is spoken of in the statutes. It is an admitted rule in the interpretation of statutes that clauses which have been repealed may still be considered in construing the provisions that remain in force. This rule was applied in reference to the very question now under consideration in *Bates v. Clark,* decided at the October term, 1877. It was said in that case by Mr. Justice Miller, delivering the opinion of the court, that "it follows from this that all the country described by the act of 1834 as Indian country remains Indian country so long as the Indians retain their original title to the soil, and ceases to be Indian country whenever they lose that title, in the absence of any different provision by treaty or by act of Congress." In our opinion that definition now applies to all the country to which the Indian title has not been extinguished within the limits of the United States, even when not within a reservation expressly set apart for the exclusive occupancy of Indians, although much of it has been acquired since the passage of the act of 1834, and notwithstanding the formal definition in that act has been dropped from the statutes, excluding, however, any territory embraced within the exterior geographical limits of a State, not excepted from its jurisdiction by treaty or by statute, at the time of its admission into the Union, but saving, even in respect to territory not thus excepted and actually in the exclusive occupancy of Indians, the authority of Congress over it, under the constitutional power to regulate commerce with the Indian tribes, and under any treaty made in pursuance of it.

This definition, though not now expressed in the Revised Statutes, is implied in all those provisions, most of which were originally connected with it when first enacted, and which still refer to it. It would be otherwise impossible to explain these references, or give effect to many of the most important provisions of existing legislation for the government of Indian country.

It follows that the *locus in quo* of the alleged offence is within Indian country, over which, territorially, the District Court of the First Judicial District of Dakota, sitting with the authority of a Circuit Court of the United States, had jurisdiction.

But if § 2145 Rev. Stat. extends the act of Congress, § 5339, punishing murder, to the locality of the prisoner's offence, § 2146 expressly excepts from its operation "crimes committed by one Indian against the person or property of another Indian;" an exception which includes the case of the prisoner, and which, if it is effective and in force, makes his conviction illegal and void. This brings us at once to the main question of jurisdiction, deemed by Congress to be of such importance to the prisoner and the public, as to justify a special appropriation for the payment of the expenses incurred on his behalf in presenting it for decision in this proceeding to this court.

The argument in support of the jurisdiction and conviction is, that the exception contained in § 2146 Rev. Stat. is repealed by the operation and legal effect of the treaty with the different tribes of the Sioux Indians of April 29th, 1868, and an act of Congress, approved February 28th, 1877, to ratify an agreement with certain bands of the Sioux Indians.

The following provisions of the treaty of 1868 are relied on:

"ARTICLE I. From this day forward all war between the parties to this agreement shall forever cease. The government of the United States desires peace, and its honor is hereby pledged to keep it. The Indians desire peace, and they now pledge their honor to maintain it.

"If bad men among the whites, or among other people subject to the authority of the United States, shall commit any wrong upon the person or property of the Indians, the United States will, upon proof made to the agent and forwarded to the commissioner of Indian affairs at Washington City, proceed at once to cause the offender to be arrested and punished according to the laws of the United States, and also reimburse the injured person for the loss sustained.

"If bad men among the Indians shall commit a wrong or depredation upon the person or property of any one, white, black, or Indian, subject to the authority of the United States and at peace therewith, the Indians herein named solemnly agree that they will upon proof made to their agent and notice by him, deliver up the wrong-doer to the United States, to be tried and punished according to its laws; and in case they wilfully refuse so to do, the person injured shall be reimbursed for his loss from the annuities or other moneys due or to become due to them under this or other treaties made with the United States. And the President, on advising with the Commissioner of Indian Affairs, shall prescribe such rules and regulations for ascertaining damages under the provisions of this article as in his judgment may be proper. But no one sustaining loss while violating the provisions of this treaty or the laws of the United States, shall be reimbursed therefor."

The second article defines the reservation which, it is stipulated, is

"set apart for the absolute and undisturbed use and occupation of the Indians herein named, and for such other friendly tribes or individual Indians as from time to time they may be willing, with the consent of the United States, to admit amongst them; and the United States now solemnly agrees that no persons except those herein designated and authorized so to do, and except such officers, agents, and employees of the government as may be authorized to enter upon Indian reservations in discharge of duties enjoined by law, shall ever be permitted to pass over, settle upon, or reside in the territory described in this article."

"ARTICLE V. The United States agrees that the agent for said Indians shall in future make his home at the agency building; that he shall reside among them and keep an office open at all times for the purpose of prompt and diligent inquiry into such matters of complaint by and against the Indians as may be presented for investigation under their treaty stipulations, as also for the faithful discharge of other duties enjoined upon him by law. In all cases of depredation on person or property he shall cause evidence to be taken in writing and forwarded, together with his findings, to the Commissioner of Indian Affairs, whose decision, subject to the revision of the Secretary of the Interior, shall be binding on the parties to this treaty."

Other provisions of this treaty are intended to encourage the settlement of individuals and families upon separate agricultural reservations, and the education of children in schools to be established. The condition of the tribe in point of civilization is illustrated by stipulations on the part of the Indians, that they will not interfere with the construction of railroads on the plains or over their reservation, nor attack persons at home or travelling, nor disturb wagon trains, mules, or cattle belonging to the people of the United States, nor capture nor carry off white women or children from the settlements, nor kill nor scalp white men, nor attempt to do them harm.

By the Indian Appropriation Act of August 15th, 1876, Congress appropriated one million dollars for the subsistence of the Sioux Indians, in accordance with the treaty of 1868, and "for purposes of their civilization," but coupled it with certain conditions relative to a cession of a portion of the reservation, and with the proviso, "that no further appropriation for said Sioux Indians for subsistence shall hereafter be made until some stipulation, agreement or arrangement shall have been entered into by said Indians with the President of the United States, which is calculated and designed to enable said Indians to become self-supporting."

In pursuance of that provision the agreement was made, which was ratified in part by the act of Congress of February 28th, 1877. The enactment of this agreement by statute, instead of its ratification as a treaty, was in pursuance of the policy which had been declared for the first time in a proviso to the Indian Appropriation Act of March 3d, 1871, and permanently adopted in section 2079 of the Revised Statutes, that thereafter "no Indian nation or tribe within the territory of the United States, shall be acknowledged or recognized as an independent nation, tribe, or power with whom the United States may contract by treaty," but without invalidating or impairing the obligation of subsisting treaties.

The instrument in which the agreement was embodied was signed by the commissioners, on the part of the United States, and by the representative chiefs and head men of the various Sioux tribes, but with certain exceptions on the part of some of the latter, and consisted of eleven articles.

The first defines the boundaries of the reservation; the second provides for wagon roads through it to the country lying west of it, and for the free navigation of the Mississippi; the third for the places where annuities shall be received.

Article 4 was as follows:

"The government of the United States and the said Indians being mutually desirous that the latter should be located in a country where they may eventually become self-supporting and acquire the arts of civilized life, it is therefore agreed that the said Indians shall select a delegation of five or more chiefs and principal men from each band, who shall, without delay, visit the Indian Territory, under the guidance and protection of suitable persons, to be appointed for that purpose by the Department of the Interior, with a view to selecting therein a permanent home for the said Indians. If such delegation shall make a selection which shall be satisfactory to themselves, the people whom they represent, and to the United States, then the said Indians agree that they will remove to the country so selected within one year from this date. And the said Indians do further agree in all things to submit themselves to such beneficent plans as the government may provide for them in the selection of a country suitable for a permanent home where they may live like white men."

The fifth article recites that, in consideration of the foregoing cession of territory and rights, the United States agrees "to provide all necessary aid to assist the said Indians in the work of civilization; to furnish to them schools, and instruction in mechanical and agricultural arts, as provided for by the treaty of 1868;" to provide subsistence, &c.

Article 8 is as follows:

"The provisions of the said treaty of 1868, except as herein modified, shall continue in full force, and with the provisions of this agreement, shall apply to any country which may hereafter be occupied by the said Indians as a home; and Congress shall, by appropriate legislation, secure to them an orderly government; they shall be subject to the laws of the United States, and each individual shall be protected in his rights of property, person, and life.

"ARTICLE 9. The Indians, parties to this agreement do hereby solemnly pledge themselves, individually and collectively, to observe each and all of the stipulations herein contained; to select allotments of land as soon as possible after their removal to their permanent home, and to use their best efforts to learn to cultivate the same. And they do solemnly pledge themselves that they will, at all times, maintain peace with the citizens and government of the United States; that they will observe the laws thereof, and loyally endeavor to fulfil all the obligations assumed by them under the treaty of 1868 and the present agreement, and to this end will, whenever requested by the President of the United

States, select so many suitable men from each band to co-operate with him in maintaining order and peace on the reservation as the President may deem necessary, who shall receive such compensation for their services as Congress may provide."

By the 11th and last article it was provided that the term reservation, as therein used, should be held to apply to any country which should be selected under the authority of the United States as their future home.

The 4th article and part of the 6th article of the agreement, which referred to the removal of the Indians to the Indian Territory, were omitted from its ratification, not having been agreed to by the Indians.

If this legislation has the effect contended for, to support the conviction in the present case, it also makes punishable, when committed within the Indian country by one Indian against the person or property of another Indian, the following offences, defined by the general laws of the United States as to crimes committed in places within their exclusive jurisdiction, viz.: manslaughter, § 5341; attempt to commit murder or manslaughter, § 5342; rape, § 5345; mayhem, § 5348; bigamy, § 5352; larceny, § 5356; and receiving stolen goods, § 5357.

That this legislation could constitutionally be extended to embrace Indians in the Indian country, by the mere force of a treaty, whenever it operates of itself, without the aid of any legislative provision, was decided by this court in the case of *The United States v. 43 Gallons of Whiskey*. It becomes necessary, therefore, to examine the particular provisions that are supposed to work this result.

The first of these is contained in the first article of the treaty of 1868, that "if bad men among the Indians shall commit a wrong or depredation upon the person or property of any one, white, black, or Indian, subject to the authority of the United States and at peace therewith, the Indians herein named solemnly agree that they will, upon proof made to their agent and notice by him, deliver up the wrong-doer to the United States, to be tried and punished according to its laws."

But it is quite clear from the context that this does not cover the present case of an alleged wrong committed by one Indian upon the person of another of the same tribe. The provision must be construed with its counterpart, just preceding it, which provides for the punishment by the United States of any bad men among the whites, or among other people subject to their authority, who shall commit any wrong upon the person or property of the Indians. Here are two parties, among whom, respectively, there may be individuals guilty of a wrong against one of the other—one is the party of whites and their allies, the other is the tribe of Indians with whom the treaty is made. In each case the guilty party is to be tried and punished by the United States, and in case the offender is one of the Indians who are parties to the treaty, the agreement is that he shall be delivered up. In case of refusal, deduction is to be made from the annuities payable to the tribe, for compensation to the injured person, a provision which points quite distinctly to the conclusion that the injured person cannot himself be one of the same tribe. Similar provisions for the extradition of criminals are to be found in most of the treaties with the Indian tribes, as far back, at least, as that concluded at Hopewell with the Cherokees, November 28th, 1785.

The second of these provisions, that are supposed to justify the jurisdiction asserted in the present case, is the eighth article of the agreement, embodied in the act of 1877, in which it is declared:

"And Congress shall, by appropriate legislation, secure to them an orderly government; they shall be subject to the laws of the United States, and each individual shall be protected in his rights of property, person, and life."

It is equally clear, in our opinion, that these words can have no such effect as that claimed for them. The pledge to secure to these people, with whom the United States was contracting as a distinct political body, an orderly government, by appropriate legislation thereafter to be framed and enacted, necessarily implies, having regard to all the circumstances attending the transaction, that among the arts of civilized life, which it was the very purpose of all these arrangements to introduce and naturalize among them, was the highest and best of all, that of self-government, the regulation by themselves of their own domestic affairs, the maintenance of order and peace among their own members by the administration of their own laws and customs. They were nevertheless to be subject to the laws of the United States, not in the sense of citizens, but as they had always been, as wards subject to a guardian; not as individuals, constituted members of the political community of the United States, with a voice in the selection of representatives and the framing of the laws, but as a dependent community who were in a state of pupilage, advancing from the condition of a savage tribe to that of a people who, through the discipline of labor and by education, it was hoped might become a self-supporting and self-governed society. The laws to which they were declared to be subject were the laws then existing, and which applied to them as Indians, and, of course, included the very statute under consideration, which excepted from the operation of the general laws of the United States, otherwise applicable, the very case of the prisoner. Declaring them subject to the laws made them so, if it effected any change in their situation, only in respect to laws in force and existing, and did not effect any change in the laws themselves. The phrase cannot, we think, have any more extensive meaning than an acknowledgment of their allegiance as Indians to the laws of the United States, made or to be made in the exercise of legislative authority over them as such. The corresponding obligation of protection on the part of the government is immediately connected with it, in the declaration that each individual shall be protected in his rights of property, person, and life; and that obligation was to be fulfilled by the enforcement of the laws then existing appropriate to these objects, and by that future appropriate legislation which was promised to secure to them an orderly government. The expressions contained in these clauses must be taken in connection with the entire scheme of the agreement as framed, including those parts not finally adopted, as throwing light on the meaning of the remainder; and looking at the purpose so clearly disclosed in that, of the removal of the whole body of the Sioux nation to the Indian Territory proper, which was not consented to, it is manifest that the provisions had reference to their establishment as a people upon a defined reservation as a permanent home, who were to be urged, as far as it could successfully be done, into the practice of agriculture, and whose children were to be taught the arts and industry of civilized life, and that it was no part of the design to treat the individuals as separately responsible and amenable, in all their personal and domestic relations with each other, to the general laws of the United States, outside of those which were enacted expressly with reference to them as members of an Indian tribe.

It must be remembered that the question before us is whether the express letter of § 2146 of the Revised Statutes, which excludes from the jurisdiction of the United States the case of a crime committed in the Indian country by one Indian against the person or property of another Indian, has been repealed. If not, it is in force and applies to the present case. The treaty of 1868 and the agreement and act of Congress of 1877, it is further admitted, do not repeal it by any express words. What we have said is sufficient at least to show that they do not work a repeal by necessary implication. A meaning can be given to the legislation in question, which the words will bear, which is not unreasonable, which is not inconsistent with its scope and apparent purposes, whereby the whole may be made to stand. Implied repeals are not favored. The implication must be necessary. There must be a positive repugnancy between the provisions of the new laws and those of the old.

The language of the exception is special and express; the words relied on as a repeal are general and inconclusive. The rule is, *generalia specialibus non derogant.* "The general principle to be applied," said Bovill, C.J., in *Thorpe v. Adams,* "to the construction of acts of Parliament is that a general act is not to be construed to repeal a previous particular act, unless there is some express reference to the previous legislation on the subject, or unless there is a necessary inconsistency in the two acts standing together." "And the reason is," said Wood, V.C., in *Fitzgerald v. Champenys,* "that the legislature having had its attention directed to a special subject, and having observed all the circumstances of the case and provided for them, does not intend by a general enactment afterwards to derogate from its own act when it makes no special mention of its intention so to do."

The nature and circumstances of this case strongly reinforce this rule of interpretation in its present application. It is a case involving the judgment of a court of special and limited jurisdiction, not to be assumed without clear warrant of law. It is a case of life and death. It is a case where, against an express exception in the law itself, that law, by argument and inference only, is sought to be extended over aliens and strangers; over the members of a community separated by race, by tradition, by the instincts of a free though savage life, from the authority and power which seeks to impose upon them the restraints of an external and unknown code, and to subject them to the responsibilities of civil conduct, according to rules and penalties of which they could have no previous warning; which judges them by a standard made by others and not for them, which takes no account of the conditions which should except them from its exactions, and makes no allowance for their inability to understand it. It tries them, not by their peers, nor by the customs of their people, nor the law of their land, but by superiors of a different race, according to the law of a social state of which they have an imperfect conception, and which is opposed to the traditions of their history, to the habits of their lives, to the strongest prejudices of their savage nature; one which measures the red man's revenge by the maxims of the white man's morality. It is a case, too, of first impression, so far as we are advised, for, if the question has been mooted heretofore in any courts of the United States, the jurisdiction has never before been practically asserted as in the present instance. The provisions now contained in § 2145 and § 2146 of the Revised Statutes were first enacted in § 25 of the Indian Intercourse Act of 1834. Prior to that, by the act of 1796, and the act of 1802, offences committed by Indians against white persons and by white persons against Indians were specifically enumerated and defined, and those by Indians against each other were left to be dealt with by each tribe for itself, according to its local customs. The policy of the government in that respect has been uniform. As was said by Mr. Justice Miller, delivering the opinion of the court in *United States v. Joseph:*

> "The tribes for whom the act of 1834 was made were those semi-independent tribes whom our government has always recognized as exempt from our laws, whether within or without the limits of an organized State or Territory, and, in regard to their domestic government, left to their own rules and traditions, in whom we have recognized the capacity to make treaties, and with whom the governments, State and national, deal, with a few exceptions only, in their national or tribal character, and not as individuals."

To give to the clauses in the treaty of 1868 and the agreement of 1877 effect, so as to uphold the jurisdiction exercised in this case, would be to reverse in this instance the general policy of the government towards the Indians, as declared in many statutes and treaties, and recognized in many decisions of this court, from the beginning to the present time. To justify such a departure, in such a case, requires a clear expression of the intention of Congress, and that we have not been able to find.

It results that the First District Court of Dakota was without jurisdiction to find or try the indictment against the prisoner, that the conviction and sentence are void, and the his imprisonment is illegal.

The writs of habeas corpus and certiorari prayed for will accordingly be issued.

So the Sioux actually won this case, but Congress was so enraged at their initial failure to superimpose the Angle-Saxon concepts of vengeful justice, that they promptly initiated legislation which would deny the tribes jurisdiction over any major crimes committed by Indians against Indians.

Act of March 3, 1885
Section 9

With the addition of section 9 to the Act of March 3d, 1885, the United States extended the jurisdiction of its courts to seven offenses committed between Indians on reservations. In doing so the white idea of vengeance replaced the Indian idea of compensation as the ideology behind punishment for a capital offense. Considered in all its aspects this was a backward move for American jurisprudence.

. . . That immediately upon and after the date of the passage of this act all Indians, committing against the person or property of another Indian or other person any of the following crimes, namely, murder, manslaughter, rape, assault with intent to kill, arson, burglary, and larceny within any Territory of the United States, and either within or without an Indian reservation, shall be subject therefor to the laws of such Territory relating to said crimes, and shall be tried therefor in the same courts and in the same manner and shall be subject to the same penalties as are all other persons charged with the commission of said crimes, respectively; and the said courts are hereby given jurisdiction in all such cases; and all such Indians committing any of the above crimes against the person or property of another Indian or other person within the boundaries of any State of the United States, and within the limits of any Indian reservation, shall be subject to the same laws, tried in the same courts and in the same manner, and subject to the same penalties as are all other persons committing any of the above crimes within the exclusive jurisdiction of the United States.

Talton v. Mayes
163 U.S. 376 (1896)

It is unfortunate for the Sioux Nation that it never achieved the status of the Cherokee—civilized. Nearly a decade after the case of *Crow Dog*—at a time when

109

the other tribes had been placed under the Seven Major Crimes Act—the so-called Five Civilized Tribes still had well-operated and valid court systems of their own. The courts of the Five Civilized Tribes were probably the best operated on this continent. It was therefore, a case of two systems of law running concurrently on parallel tracks rather than any interference from one to the other.

In spite of various treaty violations, the Five Civilized Tribes had been able to maintain their governments with a great deal of integrity from the time they arrived in Oklahoma until the early years of the twentieth century. There was, therefore, no intrusion by the federal government into the workings of the Cherokee Republic. *Talton v. Mayes* was rather an attempt to weld the two systems, Cherokee and American, into one consistent pattern of jurisprudence.

In a great decision, which still has relevance to every Indian tribe that operates its own tribal courts, the Supreme Court found that the Bill of Rights did not apply to the relationship between the Cherokee Nation and its citizens *because the Cherokee Nation had enjoyed self-government before the Constitution had been adopted!* AS DID EVERY OTHER TRIBE!!!

Thus there remains an unanswered question of Constitutional law—can Congress legally extend the Bill of Rights to affect the rights of Indian tribes over their tribal members? Since 1968 it has been assumed by many people that the Civil Rights Bill of that year settled the question forever. BUT, it has not yet been settled and may yet emerge as yet another hot issue of the 1970's in Indian country.

On February 15, 1893, a petition for *habeas corpus* was filed in the District Court of the United States for the Western District of Arkansas, setting forth that the plaintiff therein (who is the appellant here) was, on the 31st day of December, 1892, convicted, on a charge of murder, in a special Supreme Court of the Cherokee nation, Cooweeskoowee District, and sentenced to be hanged on February 28, 1893, and that petitioner was then held, awaiting the time of execution, in the national jail at Tahlequah, Indian Territory, by Wash. Mayes, high sheriff of the Cherokee nation. It was further alleged that the petitioner was deprived of his liberty without due process of law; that he was in confinement in contravention to the Constitution and laws of the United States, and also in violation of the constitution and laws of the Cherokee nation. These contentions rested upon the averment that the indictment under which he had been tried and convicted was void because returned by a body consisting of five grand jurors, which was not only an insufficient number to constitute a grand jury under the Constitution and laws of the United States, but also was wholly inadequate to compose such jury under the laws of the Cherokee nation, which, it was alleged, provided for a grand jury of thirteen, of which number a majority was necessary to find an indictment. The petitioner, moreover, averred that he had not been tried by a fair and impartial jury, and that many gross irregularities and errors to his prejudice had been committed on the trial. The district judge issued the writ, which was duly served upon the high sheriff, who produced the body of the petitioner and made return setting up the conviction and sentence as justifying the detention of the prisoner. Incorporated in the return was a transcript of the proceedings in the Cherokee court had upon the indictment and trial of the petitioner. In the copy of the indictment contained in the original transcript, filed in this court, it was recited that the indictment was found by the grand jury on the 1st day of December, 1892, while the offence therein stated was alleged to have been committed "on or about the 3d day of December, 1892." The evidence contained in the transcript, however, showed that the offence was committed on November 3, 1892, and in a supplement to the transcript, filed in this court, it appears that said date was given in the indictment. No motion or demurrer or other attack upon the sufficiency of the indictment was made upon the trial in the Cherokee court based upon the ground that the offence was stated in the indictment to have been committed on a date subsequent to the finding of the indictment, nor is there any specification of error of that character contained in the petition for the allowance of the writ of *habeas corpus.* After hearing, the district judge discharged the writ and remanded the petitioner to the custody of the sheriff, and from this judgment the appeal now under consideration was allowed.

Prior to May, 1892, a law enacted by the legislature of the Cherokee nation made it the duty of the judges of the Circuit and District Courts of the nation, fourteen days before the commencement of the first regular term of said courts, to furnish to the sheriff a list of the names of five persons, who should be summoned by the sheriff to act as grand jurors for that district during the year. The first regular term of the courts named commenced on the second Monday in May. On November 28, 1892, a law was enacted providing for the summoning and empanelling of a grand jury of thirteen, the names of the persons to compose such jury to be furnished to the sheriff, as under the previous law, fourteen days before the commencement of the regular term of the Circuit and District Courts. There was no express repeal of the provisions of the prior law. Under the terms of the act of November 28, 1892, a grand jury could not have been empanelled before the term beginning on the second Monday of May, 1893. The indictment in question was returned in December, 1892, by a grand jury consisting of five persons, which grand jury had been empanelled under the prior law, to serve during the year 1892.

The right of the appellant to the relief which he seeks must exist, if at all, by virtue of section 753 of the Revised Statutes of the United States, which is as follows:

"The writ of *habeas corpus* shall in no case extend to a prisoner in jail, unless where he is in custody under or by color of the authority of the United States, or is committed for trial before some court thereof; or is in custody for an act done or omitted in pursuance of a law of the United States, or of an order, process or decree of a court or judge thereof; or is in custody in violation of the Constitution or of a law or treaty of the United States; or, being a subject or citizen of a foreign State, and domiciled therein, is in custody for an act done or omitted under any alleged right, title, authority, privilege, protection or exemption claimed under the commission, or order, or sanction of any foreign State, or under color thereof, the validity and effect whereof depend upon the law of nations; or unless it is necessary to bring the prisoner into court to testify."

Appellant and the person he was charged with having murdered were both Cherokee Indians, and the crime was committed within the Cherokee territory.

To bring himself within the statute, the appellant asserts, 1st, that the grand jury, consisting only of five persons, was not a grand jury within the contemplation of the Fifth Amendment to the Constitution, which it is asserted is operative upon the Cherokee nation in the exercise of its legislative authority as to purely local matters; 2d, that the indictment by a grand jury thus constituted was not due process of law within the intendment of the Fourteenth Amendment; 3d, even if the law of the Cherokee nation providing for a grand jury of five was valid under the Constitution of the United States such law had been repealed, and was not therefore in existence at the time the indictment was found. A decision as to the merits of these contentions involves a consideration of the relation of

111

the Cherokee nation to the United States, and of the operation of the constitutional provisions relied on upon the purely local legislation of that nation.

By treaties and statutes of the United States the right of the Cherokee nation to exist as an autonomous body, subject always to the paramount authority of the United States, has been recognized. And from this fact there has consequently been conceded to exist in that nation power to make laws defining offences and providing for the trial and punishment of those who violate them when the offences are committed by one member of the tribe against another one of its members within the territory of the nation.

Thus, by the fifth article of the treaty of 1835, 7 Stat. 478, 481, it is provided:

"The United States hereby covenant and agree that the lands ceded to the Cherokee nation in the foregoing article shall, in no future time without their consent, be included within the territorial limits or jurisdiction of any State or Territory. But they shall secure to the Cherokee nation the right by their national councils to make and carry into effect all such laws as they may deem necessary for the government and protection of the persons and property within their own country belonging to their people or such persons as have connected themselves with them: Provided always that they shall not be inconsistent with the Constitution of the United States and such acts of Congress as have been or may be passed regulating trade and intercourse with the Indians; and also, that they shall not be considered as extending to such citizens and army of the United States as may travel or reside in the Indian country by permission according to the laws and regulations established by the government of the same." This guarantee of self government was reaffirmed in the treaty of 1868, 14 Stat. 799, 803, the thirteenth article of which reads as follows:

"Article XIII. The Cherokees also agree that a court or courts may be established by the United States in said territory, with such jurisdiction and organized in such manner as may be prescribed by law: Provided, That the judicial tribunals of the nation shall be allowed to retain exclusive jurisdiction in all civil and criminal cases arising within their country in which members of the nation, by nativity or adoption, shall be the only parties, or where the cause of action shall be the only parties, or where the cause of action shall arise in the Cherokee nation, except as otherwise provided in this treaty."

So, also, in "An act to provide a temporary government for the Territory of Oklahoma, to enlarge the jurisdiction of the United States court in the Indian Territory, and for other purposes." Approved May 2, 1890, C. 182, 26 Stat. 81, it was provided, in section 30, as follows:

"That the judicial tribunals of the Indian nations shall retain exclusive jurisdiction in all civil and criminal cases arising in the country in which members of the nation by nativity or by adoption shall be the only parties; and as to all such cases the laws of the State of Arkansas extended over and put in force in said Indian Territory by this act shall not apply."

And section 31 of the last mentioned act closes with the following paragraph:

"The Constitution of the United States and all general laws of the United States except in the District of Columbia, and all laws relating to national banking associations, shall have the same force and effect in the Indian Territory as elsewhere in the United States; but nothing in this act shall be so construed as to deprive any of the courts of the civilized nations of exclusive jurisdiction over all cases arising wherein members of said nations, whether by treaty, blood or adoption, are the sole parties, nor so as to interfere with the right and powers of said civilized nations to punish said members for violation of the statutes and laws enacted by their national councils where such laws are not contrary to the treaties and laws of the United States."

The question, therefore, is, does the Fifth Amendment to the Constitution apply to the local legislation of the Cherokee nation so as to require all prosecutions for offences committed against the laws of that nation to be initiated by a grand jury organized in accordance with the provisions of that amendment. The solution of this question involves an inquiry as to the nature and origin of the power of local government exercised by the Cherokee nation and recognized to exist in it by the treaties and statutes above referred to. Since the case of *Barron v. Baltimore,* 7 Pet. 243, it has been settled that the Fifth Amendment to the Constitution of the United States is a limitation only upon the powers of the National Government which the Constitution called into being. To quote the language of Chief Justice Marshall, this amendment is limitative of the "powers granted in the instrument itself and not of distinct governments framed by different persons and for different purposes. If these propositions be correct, the Fifth Amendment must be understood as restraining the power of the General Government, not as applicable to the States." The cases in this court which have sanctioned this view are too well recognized to render it necessary to do more than merely refer to them.

The case in this regard therefore depends upon whether the powers of local government exercised by the Cherokee nation are Federal powers created by and springing from the Constitution of the United States, and hence controlled by the Fifth Amendment to that Constitution, or whether they are local powers not created by the Constitution, although subject to its general provisions and the paramount authority of Congress. The repeated adjudications of this court have long since answered the former question in the negative. In *Cherokee Nation v. Georgia,* 5 Pet. 1, which involved the right of the Cherokee nation to maintain an original bill in this court as a foreign State, which was ruled adversely to that right, speaking through Mr. Chief Justice Marshall, this court said (p. 16):

"Is the Cherokee nation a foreign State in the sense in which that term is used in the Constitution?

"The counsel for the plaintiffs have maintained the affirmative of this proposition with great earnestness and ability. So much of the argument as was intended to prove the character of the Cherokees as a State, as a distinct political society, separated from others, capable of managing its own affairs and governing itself, has, in the opinion of a majority of the judges, been completely successful. They have been uniformly treated as a State from the settlement of our country. The numerous treaties made with them by the United States recognize them as a people capable of maintaining the relations of peace and war, of being responsible in their political character for any violation of their engagements or for any aggression committed on the citizens of the United States by any individual of their community. Laws have been enacted in the spirit of these treaties. The acts of our government plainly recognize the Cherokee nation as a State, and the courts are bound by those acts."

It cannot be doubted, as said in *Worcester v. The State of Georgia,* 6 Pet. 515, 559, that prior to the formation of the Constitution treaties were made with the Cherokee tribes by which their autonomous existence was recognized. And in that case Chief Justice Marshall also said (p. 559):

"The Indian nations had always been considered as distinct, independent political communities, retaining ther original natural rights. . . The very term 'nation,' so generally applied to them, means a 'people distinct from others.' The Constitution, by declaring treaties already made, as well as those to be made, to be the supreme law of the land, has adopted and sanctioned the previous treaties with the Indian nations, and consequently admits their rank among those powers who are capable of making treaties."

In reviewing the whole subject in *Kagama v. United States,* 118 U.S. 375, this court said (p. 381):

"With the Indians themselves these relations are equally difficult to define. They were, and always have been, regarded as having a semi-independent position when they preserved their tribal relations; not as States, not as nations, not as possessed of the full attributes of sovereignty, but as a separate people with the power of regulating their internal and social relations, and thus far not brought under the laws of the Union, or of th State within whose limits they resided."

True it is that in many adjudications of this court the fact has been fully recognized that although possessed of these attributes of local self government, when exercising thei tribal functions, all such rights are subject to the supreme legislative authority of th United States. *Cherokee Nation v. Kansas Railway Co.,* 135 U.S. 641, where the cases ar fully reviewed. But the existence of the right in Congress to regulate the manner in whicl the local powers of the Cherokee nation shall be exercised does not render such loca powers Federal powers arising from and created by the Constitution of the United States It follows that as the powers of local self-government enjoyed by the Cherokee natioi existed prior to the Constitution, they are not operated upon by the Fifth Amendment which, as we have said, had for its sole object to control the powers conferred by th Constitution of the National Government. The fact that the Indian tribes are subject to th dominant authority of Congress, and that their powers of local self government are alse operated upon and restrained by the general provisions of the Constitution of the Unite States, completely answers the argument of inconvenience which was pressed in the dis cussion at bar. The claim that the finding of an indictment by a grand jury of less thaı thirteen violates the due process clause of the Fourteenth Amendment is conclusivel answered by *Hurtado v. California,* 110 U.S. 516, and *McNulty v. California,* 149 U.S. 645 The question whether a statute of the Cherokee nation which was not repugnant to th Constitution of the United States or in conflict with any treaty or law of the nation, and th determination of what was the existing law of the Cherokee nation as to the constitution o the grand jury, were solely matters within the jurisdiction of the courts of that nation, anc the decision of such a question in itself necessarily involves no infraction of the Constitu tion of the United States. Such has been the decision of this court with reference t similar contentions arising upon an indictment and conviction in a state court. *In re Dun can,* 139 U.S. 449. The ruling in that case is equally applicable to the contentions in thi particular arising from the record before us.

The counsel for the appellant has very properly abandoned any claim to relief because of alleged errors occurring subsequent to the finding of the indictment. As to the poin raised in reference to the date of the commission of the offence as stated in the indictment, the record as corrected shows that the error in question did not exist. It is, therefore, unnecessary to notice the argument based upon the assumption that the indictmen charged the offence to have been committed subsequent to the finding of the true bill.

The judgment is *Affirmed.*

Toledo v. Pueblo de Jemez
119 F. Supp. 429 (1954)

Until the Civil Rights Act of 1968, it was assumed that Indian tribes were exempt from the procedural safeguards of the Constitution. For tribes such as the Pueblos of New Mexico this assertion buttressed their traditional forms of government. Being essentially theocratic and as yet unbroken by white pressures, the Pueblos were able to maintain themselves as islands of traditional Indian

ociety. One of the key cases in protecting their rights of self-government was
he next selection, *Toledo v. Pueblo de Jemez*. In this case the court neatly side-
teps the issue of constitutional rights as applied to the internal functioning of
he Pueblo by finding that they have a government superior to and antedating
he establishment of the state of New Mexico.

Besides being a crucial case in the development of the rights of self-
government the case eloquently illustrates the effect of missionizing by the
Christian denominations. "Now," as an Indian once said, "they will teach us to
argue about God." Instead of allowing the Pueblo Indians to maintain themselves
as a self-sufficient community, religious bodies have insisted that they be allowed
o proselytize. As converts have been made controversies have arisen that need
not have been experienced. The end result has frequently been the destruction
of the internal strengths of various Indian communities and the eventual dissolu-
ion of the people themselves.

Six Jemez Pueblo Indians, all of whom are members of various Protestant denominations, filed a complaint for a declaratory judgment for themselves and in a representative
capacity, against the Pueblo de Jemez, a community of Pueblo Indians, in New Mexico,
and the Governor of that Pueblo, charging that the Pueblo through its governing body and
its Governor has subjected them to indignities, threats and reprisals because of their Protestant faith. All of the plaintiffs and those whom they represent are citizens of the United
States.

Specifically, the plaintiffs complain that the Pueblo has refused them the right to bury
their dead in the community cemetery; denied them the right to build a church of their
own on Pueblo land; prohibited them from using their homes for church purposes; refused
to permit Protestant missionaries freely to enter the Pueblo at reasonable times; deprived
some of them of the right to use a communal threshing machine which threatened the loss
of their wheat crop. They also allege that the officials of the Pueblo threatened them with
loss of their birthrights, homes and personal property unless they accept the Catholic religion. All this was done, it is alleged, despite the fact that the Pueblo had validly adopted
an ordinance recognizing that every member of the Pueblo should have freedom to worship as his conscience dictates and that no member of the Pueblo should be molested in
person or property by the Pueblo on account of his or her mode of religious worship.

It is worthy of emphasis that the plaintiffs carefully acknowledge and allege specifically that the dispute is not between the Catholic and Protestant Churches or faiths as such
but is one between the civil authorities of the Pueblo and the plaintiffs who adhere to
various Protestant denominations.

The complaint is founded solely on alleged violations of the Civil Rights Act, Title 8,
U.S.C.A. § 43, which reads:

> "Every person who, under color of any statute, ordinance, regulation, cus-
> tom, or usage, or any State or Territory, subjects, or causes to be subjected, any
> citizen of the United States or other person within the jurisdiction thereof to the
> deprivation of any rights, privileges, or immunities secured by the Constitution
> and laws, shall be liable to the party injured in an action at law, suit in equity, or
> other proper proceeding for redress."

"The district courts shall have original jurisdiction of any civil action authorized by law to be commenced by any person:

* * *

"(3) To redress the deprivation, under color of any State law, statute, ordinance, regulation, custom or usage, of any right, privilege or immunity secured by the Constitution of the United States or by any Act of Congress providing for equal rights of citizens or of all persons within the jurisdiction of the United States."

The defendants filed motions to dismiss the complaint on the ground that this court has no jurisdiction for the reason that none of the actions complained of by the plaintiffs was taken under color of any statute, ordinance, regulation, custom or usage of any State or Territory.

Other grounds were contained in the motions to dismiss, but the one set out explicitly is the only one to which consideration need be given.

There is, therefore, presented a serious charge of invasion of religious liberty by a Pueblo Indian tribal government. The question for decision is not whether the tribal government has the right to interfere with the religious beliefs and practices of its members but whether or not the objectionable actions of the Pueblo come within the scope of the Civil Rights Act and whether this court has jurisdiction of this case as it is presented by the complaint.

There are some general allegations in the complaint that the actions of the defendants amounted to a violation of the First Amendment to the Constitution of the United States the guarantees of which it is said are among the privileges and immunities protected from state action by the Fourteenth Amendment. Likewise, in general terms, there are references to the Treaty of Guadalupe Hidalgo, and to the Kearney Code of Laws of New Mexico. However, the heart of the whole case rests upon the question of whether or not the defendants acted under color of a law, statute, ordinance, regulation, custom or usage of New Mexico.

(1) United States District Courts have only special or limited jurisdiction. They have only the jurisdiction that Congress has given them by statute. With jurisdiction so stringently narrowed, it is not every case that may be brought in this court no matter how serious a problem is presented nor how great the necessity for remedial action. Always this court must act within the scope of its jurisdiction. Otherwise, its action is of no validity.

(2) For an action to succeed under the Civil Rights Statute which plaintiffs rely on, at least two conditions must exist. First, a person must be subjected to the deprivation of some right, privilege or immunity secured him by the Constitution and laws of the United States. Second, the action complained of must have been done under the color of a statute, ordinance, regulation, custom or usage of a state or territory. To bring themselves with the second condition the plaintiffs contend that by an 1847 Law of New Mexico, now carried as Section 54-1601, N.M. Stat. 1941, Ann., all of the Pueblos of New Mexico, including the defendant, were constituted bodies politic and corporate with the right to sue and be sued in certain types of cases and that this is sufficient in and of itself to permit the court to conclude that the action of the defendants was under color of state law. However, the New Mexico Statute does not purport to vest any governmental powers, rights or duties in the Pueblos of New Mexico which are dependent Indian communities, Indian Tribes, under the guardianship of the United States. 25 U.S.C.A. § 331 note, is a statutory recognition of the guardianship of the United States over Pueblos or Pueblo Indians. Not to be ignored in this connection is Section 2 of Article 21 of the Constitution of New Mexico which provides that New Mexico disclaims all right to land within its boundaries owned or held by any Indian or Indian tribe, the right or title to which shall have been acquired through the United States or any prior sovereignty. Until the title of the Indian or Indian tribes has been extin-

guished said lands remain under the absolute jurisdiction and control of Congress. It is Congress and not the State of New Mexico that legislates for the Pueblos of New Mexico.

(3) At least since the Sandoval decision in 1913, it has been clear that the Pueblos do not derive their governmental powers from the State of New Mexico. It has, indeed, been held that the powers of an Indian tribe do not spring from the United States although they are subject to the paramount authority of Congress. *(Talton v. Mayes.)* Their right to govern themselves has been recognized in such statutes as the Indian Reorganization Act.

(4) Consequently, there is no basis for holding that the conduct of the defendants of which the plaintiffs complain was done under color of state law, statute, ordinance, regulation, custom or usage.

In these circumstances the Court must conclude that since the defendants did not act under color of state law, statute, ordinance, regulation, custom or usage no violation of the Civil Rights Act has been alleged and the Court, therefore, has no jurisdiction of the case under Section 1343 (3) of Title 28 U.S.C.A.

The complaint, therefore, will be dismissed.

Colliflower v. Garland
342 F. 2d. 369 (1965)

For nearly seventy years Indian tribes had certain protections against outside interferences. *Talton v. Mayes* and subsequent cases exempted them from the doctrines of criminal law and the developments of constitutional theories. But since the Indian societies were changing and the old customs were dying, a nebulous situation arose. Indian people were guaranteed the usual procedural safeguards when in the courts of the white men. But there was a vacuum in Indian society. Gradually, the safeguards which had automatically operated as customs were no longer available to individual Indians in their dealings with tribal governments.

A case arose on the Fort Belknap reservation in Montana that severely taxed the theory of tribal self-government. Mrs. Madeline Colliflower sued for a writ of habeas corpus to gain release from commitment by a tribal court. Existing case law was strongly against any appeal to normal federal courts yet the discrimination by the Indian court against tribal member called for extraordinary measures. This case is delightful. One can see the court walk softly where no one had dare tread since *Talton v. Mayes.* The intent of the court is obvious—to free Mrs. Colliflower. And the court finally does it.

The *Colliflower* case has been superceded by the 1968 Civil Rights Act, which gives direct appeal from tribal courts to the federal court system. But the case has more important aspects. Until the late 1930's Indian tax-exemption was supported by the theory that Indian tribes and lands were federal instrumentalities and therefore exempted from any forms of taxation by states and other branches of the federal government. Now in this case, as you will see, the main justification appears to be that the tribal court, supported by federal appropriations, is a federal instrumentality and by that reasoning an extension of the federal court system.

Is it fair to characterize tribal courts as federal instrumentalities for the purposes of controlling tribal governments while denying tribal economic ventures the same status—thereby jeopardizing their tax-exemptions? It is this inconsistency that plagues Indian tribes when they are asked to develop plans for economic development, educate their children in the ways of the white man and participate in the "American mainstream".

If this case revives the doctrine of federal instrumentalities, then Indian people should understand that and make their plans accordingly. And the Internal Revenue Service and state taxing authorities should recognize the justice in the Indian position and stop their continual harrassment of Indian tribes. *Colliflower* may prove to be embarassing to units of both state and federal governments that are intent upon eroding the sovereignty of the tribal governments.

Madeline Colliflower is an Indian, a member of the Gros Ventre Indian tribe, which is a part of the Fort Belknap Indian community, located on the Fort Belknap reservation in Blaine County, Montana. Under date of June 20, 1963 Joe Plumage, Chief Policeman, filed a criminal complaint in the "Court of Indian Offenses, Fort Belknap Jurisdiction, United States Indian Service", under the title *"Fort Belknap Indian Community v. Madeline Colliflower"* in which he charged Mrs. Colliflower with "disobedience to lawful orders of the Court in violation of sec. 36, Chapter 5, Law and Order Code of the Fort Belknap Indian Community," in that on June 13, 1963, within the Fort Belknap Indian Reservation, she "did disobey a lawful order of the Court by failing to remove her cattle from land leased by another person, after being ordered to do so by the Court, and against the peace and dignity of the Fort Belknap Indian Community." On the same day Cranston Hawley, Judge of the Court, issued a warrant directed "to any Police or Police Officer of the United States Indian Service," reciting the filing of the complaint, and ordering the arrest of Mrs. Colliflower, and that she be brought before a judge of the court to show why she should not be held for trial.

There is also a transcript of the proceedings of the "Law and Order Court" on June 25, 1963. The court was presided over by Chief Judge Cranston Hawley, and there were present the Chief of Police, Joe Plumage, an "Area Special Officer," Mr. Willett, an "Agency Special Officer", Mr. Reddog, an "Agency Special Officer, Crow Agency," Mr. Joe Gray, and the defendant. The judge read the complaint to the defendant, and, following some discussion as to who was the lessee of the land in question, the judge stated: "I put out another order just after that to have your cattle removed, which was done, and the cattle were put back in the unit the same evening. Isn't that correct?" To this Mrs. Colliflower replied: "Yes." The judge then inquired as to her plea and she pled not guilty. He then found her guilty and sentenced her to a fine of $25 or five days in jail. Mrs. Colliflower, following a further colloquy, elected to take the jail sentence because she could not pay the fine. In her petition, Mrs. Colliflower alleged that pursuant to the judgment of the court, she was committed to the custody of the sheriff of Blaine County, who is appellee. She claimed in the district court, and she claims in this court, that her confinement is illegal and in violation of her constitutional rights, because she was not afforded the right to counsel, was not afforded any trial, was not afforded any trial, was not confronted by any witnesses against her, and because the action of the court was taken summarily and arbitrarily, and without just cause. Her reliance is upon the due process clauses of Amendment Article 5 of the Constitution of the United States, and of the Fourteenth Amendment to the Constitution. The district court did not pass upon the merits of these questions because it decided that it did not have jurisdiction to issue a writ of habeas corpus for the purpose of determining the legality of the detention of an Indian who was committed by a tribal court, and it is the correctness of that decision that presents the sole question that is before us.

The solution of this question requires the recitation of some history. On September 17, 1851 a treaty was signed by the Blackfoot and Gros Ventre Indians and other tribes and the United States. It has been said that this treaty, which is known as the treaty of Fort Laramie, was not fully ratified. The treaty was actually ratified on May 24, 1852 and the Court of Claims, in two cases, *Moore v. United States,* and *Roy v. United States,* has held that the treaty is binding on the United States. The treaty deals largely with the territories of the tribes and an annuity to be paid to the Indians. It contains no reference to self-government by the Indians or to tribal courts.

On October 17, 1855, a second treaty was made with the Blackfoot nation composed of Piegans, Bloods, Blackfeet and Gros Ventres. To this treaty the Flatheads and the Nez Perces were also parties. This treaty again is primarily concerned with the definition of boundaries, the prevention of disputes among the tribes, and the establishment of peace. There is no specific reference in the treaty to Indian self-government, although Article II contains certain provisions designed to secure peace. It can fairly be said, however, that the treaty, like many other Indian treaties made by the United States, is a recognition of the Blackfoot nation as a nation. There is at least one other treaty, not ratified.

Congress put a stop to the making of treaties with Indians by the Act of March 3, 1871. This enactment, however, contains a proviso that it is not to be construed to invalidate or impair the obligation of any treaty theretofore lawfully made and ratified with any Indian tribe or nation. Thus it would appear that these treaties are still in effect.

By an executive order of July 5, 1873, a Blackfoot Indian reservation, very large in size, was established in what is now the State of Montana. On April 15, 1874 Congress established a reservation for the various Blackfoot tribes. This was a smaller territory than that established by the executive order. There were subsequent executive orders modifying the boundaries of the reservation. By Act of May 1, 1888 Congress ratified an agreement with the Indians whereby the Blackfoot reservation was divided into three parts, one of which is the Fort Belknap Reservation. A description of this reservation appears in Fletcher, Indian Education and Civilization, 1888.

The first reference to tribal courts such as that at Fort Belknap which has been brought to our attention is contained in the annual report of Commissioner of Indian Affairs to the Secretary of the Interior, 1885:

"Under date of April 10, 1883, the then Secretary of the Interior gave his official approval to certain rules prepared in this office for the establishment of a court of Indian Offenses at each of the Indian agencies, except the agency for the five civilized tribes in the Indian Territory. It was found that the longer continuance of certain old heathen and barbarous customs, such as the sun-dance, scalp-dance, polygamy, etc. were operating as a serious hindrance to the efforts of the Government for the civilization of the Indians. * * *

"There is no special law authorizing the establishment of such a court, but authority is exercised under the general provisions of law giving this Depart-

119

ment supervision of the Indians. The policy of the government for many years past has been to destroy the tribal relations as fast as possible and to use every endeavor to bring the Indians under the influence of law."

Congress took cognizance of these courts in 1888, in an Appropriation Act. This act, in addition to appropriations of $1,000 for the pay of an Indian Agent at Ft. Belknap and of sums for "subsistence and civilization" of the Gros Ventres, appropriates money for the employment of Indian police and for compensation of judges of Indian courts. In the Commissioner's Annual Report for 1889, the following statement appears:

"Prior to the last fiscal year there was no fund for maintaining these courts, nor any law recognizing their existence, although this office had made repeated and urgent recommendations that provision be made for the pay of judges of the courts * * * the Appropriation Act of June 29, 1888, contains the following item: 'For compensation of judges of Indian Courts, at such rate as may be fixed from time to time by the Secretary of the Interior, five thousand dollars, or so much thereof as may be necessary.'

"Under this legislation it is practicable to make important changes and improvements in the organizations of the courts of Indian offenses and the methods adopted therein. * * * "

The 1889 report also states:

"Since 1882, what is known as a 'court of Indian offenses' has been established and maintained upon a number of Indian Reservations. It has been a tentative and somewhat crude attempt to break up superstitious practices, brutalizing dances, plural marriages, and kindred evils, and to provide an Indian tribunal which, under the guidance of the agent, could take cognizance of crimes, misdemeanors, and disputes among Indians, and by which they could be taught to respect law and obtain some rudimentary knowledge of legal processes. Notwithstanding their imperfections and primitive character these so-called Courts have been a great benefit to the Indians and of material assistance to the agents."

There appears to be no mention of the creation of a tribal court at Fort Belknap earlier than 1899. A contemporary judicial view of these tribal courts appears in *United States v. Clapox*, as follows:

"These 'courts of Indian offenses' are not the constitutional courts provided for in section 1, article 3, Const., which Congress only has the power to "ordain and establish", but mere educational and disciplinary instrumentalities, by which the government of the United States is endeavoring to improve and elevate the condition of these dependent tribes to whom it sustains the relation of guardian. In fact, the reservation itself is in the nature of a school, and the Indians are gathered there, under the charge of an agent for the purpose of acquiring the habits, ideas, and aspirations which distinguish the civilized from the uncivilized man."

In 1934 the congress passed the Wheeler-Howard Indian Reorganization Act. This statute permits an Indian tribe to organize for its common welfare and adopt an appropriate constitution and by-laws which are to become effective when ratified by the members of the tribe and approved by the Secretary of the Interior. The statute further provides:

"In addition to all powers vested in any Indian tribe or tribal council by law, the constitution adopted by said tribe shall also vest in such tribe or its tribal council the following rights and powers: To employ legal counsel and fixing of fees to be subject to the approval of the Secretary of the Interior; to prevent the sale, disposition, lease, or encumbrance of tribal lands, interests in lands, or other tribal assets without the consent of the tribe; and to negotiate with the Federal, State and local Governments."

According to House Report No. 2503, 82nd Congress 1953, Table I, page 48, the Gros Ventres are governed by an administrative body and an administrative board subcommittee organized under the foregoing Act. Their constitution and by-laws were approved by the Secretary of the Interior on December 13, 1935, and the Charter became effective on August 25, 1937. Table XII, page 105, of the foregoing report shows that there is a tribal court and a court of Indian offenses. The latter we take to be the "Law and Order Court" that is here involved, or its predecessor.

While there is apparently still no Act of Congress providing for the establishment of tribal courts, the congress, as well as the executive, has assumed considerable responsibility for these courts. Thus, the Bureau of Indian Affairs is now authorized to direct, supervise, and expend such moneys as Congress may from time to time appropriate for the benefit, care and assistance of the Indians for various purposes, including the employment of Indian police and Indian judges. 25 U.S.C., section 200 requires that whenever an Indian is incarcerated, a report or record of the offense is to be immediately submitted to the superintendent of the reservation and made a part of the records of the agency office. Mrs. Colliflower's confinement in the Blaine County jail is pursuant to a written contract entered into on June 6, 1957 between the United States, through the area director for the Bureau of Indian Affairs, and the County. By this contract the United States agrees to pay $2.75 per day for each prisoner.

Moreover, we are told by tribal counsel, who represents the appellee sheriff in this proceeding, that the Code of Indian tribal offenses which has been adopted by the Fort Belknap Indian community is taken almost verbatim from the regulations of the Bureau of Indian Affairs which are now codified in Title 25, Chapter 21, sub-chapter B of the Code of Federal Regulations. These regulations appear to have been first promulgated in substantially their present form on November 27, 1935. They establish or define a complete judicial system, and a code of offenses, and are prefaced as follows:

"The regulations in this part relative to Courts of Indian Offenses shall apply to all Indian reservations on which such courts are maintained.

"It is the purpose of the regulations in this part to provide adequate machinery of law enforcement for those Indian tribes in which traditional agencies for the enforcement of tribal law and custom have broken down and for which no adequate substitute has been provided under Federal or State law.

"No Court of Indian Offenses will be established on reservations where justice is effectively administered under State laws and by State law enforcement agencies.

"The regulations in this part shall continue to apply to tribes organized under the Act of June 18, 1934 until a Law and Order code has been adopted by the tribe in accordance with its constitution and by-laws and has become effective."

Among other things, they provide that judges are appointed by the Commissioner of Indian Affairs, subject to confirmation by two-thirds vote of the tribal council, for removal of a judge by the commissioner, for cause upon recommendation of the tribal council, for Rules of Court approved by the tribal council and by the superintendent of the reservation, and for participation in their affairs, in various ways, by the superintendent. We are not told when the Fort Belknap Indian community adopted its own law and order code, but we are told, in appellee's brief, that "with only a couple of differences not material here, the Belknap Law and Order Code was taken bodily from 25 CFR 11."

(1) The status of Indian tribes as separate nations or entities having some degree of sovereignty has long been recognized by the Supreme Court. The leading decision is the famous opinion of Chief Justice Marshall in *Worcester v. State of Georgia*. That case upheld, against the pretensions of the State of Georgia, the treaty rights of the Cherokee Nation. In so doing, Chief Justice Marshall said:

"The Indian nations had always been considered as distinct, independent, political communities, retaining their original natural rights, as the undisputed possessors of the soil, from time immemorial. * * *

"The Cherokee nations, then, is a distinct community, occupying its own territory, with boundaries accurately described, in which the laws of Georgia can have no force, and which the citizens of Georgia have no right to enter, but with the assent of the Cherokees themselves, or in conformity with treaties, and with the acts of Congress. The whole intercourse between the United States and this Nation, is, by our Constitution and laws, vested in the government of the United States. The act of the State of Georgia, under which the plaintiff in error was prosecuted, is, consequently void, and the judgment a nullity."

We know that in the more than one hundred and thirty years that have since passed, the "independence" of the Indian tribes and their resemblance to nations, have decreased, and their dependency has increased. As the United States has expanded, it has repeatedly broken its treaties, has taken the Indians' land by force, has repeatedly imposed new and more restrictive treaties upon them, has confined them in ever smaller reservations, often far from their original homes, and has reduced them to the status of dependent wards of the government.

The status of the Indian tribes at the time of the creation of the Fort Belknap tribal court is well described in *United States v. Kagama,* in which the Court upheld the "Seven Major Crimes" Act. There the Court said:

" * * * They (the Indian tribes) were, and always have been regarded as having a semi-independent position when they preserved their tribal relations; not as states, not as nations, not as possessed of the full attributes of sovereignty, but as a separate people, with the power of regulating their internal and social relations, and thus far not brought under the laws of the Union or of the state within whose limits they resided.

" * * * These Indian tribes are wards of the nation. They are communities dependent on the United States,—dependent largely for their daily food; dependent for their political rights. They owe no allegiance to the states, and receive from them no protection. Because of the local ill feeling, the people of the states where they are found are often their deadliest enemies. From their very weakness and helplessness, so largely due to the course of dealing of the federal government with them, and the treaties in which it has been promised, there arises the duty of protection, and with it the power. This has always been recognized by the executive, and by Congress, and by this court, whenever the question has arisen."

"The power of the general government over these remnants of a race once powerful, now weak and diminished in numbers, is necessary to their protection, as well as to the safety of those among whom they dwell. It must exist in that government, because it never has existed anywhere else; because the theatre of its exercise is within the geographical limits of the United States; because it has never been denied; and because it alone can enforce its laws on all the tribes."

It was long held that reservation Indians are not citizens *(Elk v. Wilkins).* However, in 1924, the Congress amended the Nationality Act to provide that a person born in the United States to a member of an Indian tribe shall be a national and citizen of the United States at birth.

In more recent times it has been the policy of the government to encourage the Indians to become independent participating citizens, while at the same time preserving the territories and the rights of those tribes which elect to continue to function as such. The recent history and present policy are stated in the opinion of Mr. Justice Frankfurter in *Organized Village of Kake v. Egan* as follows:

"As the United States spread westward, it became evident that there was no place where the Indians could be forever isolated. In recognition of this fact the United States began to consider the Indians less as foreign nations and more as a part of our country. *　*　*"

"The general notion drawn from Chief Justice Marshall's opinion in *Worcester v. State of Georgia;* The Kansas Indians; The New York Indians, that an Indian reservation is a distinct nation within whose boundaries state law cannot penetrate, has yielded to closer analysis when confronted, in the course of subsequent developments, with adverse concrete situations. By 1880 the Court no longer viewed reservations as distinct nations. On the contrary, it was said that a reservation was in many cases a part of the surrounding State or Territory, and subject to its jurisdiction except as forbidden by federal law.

"The policy of assimilation was reversed abruptly in 1934. A great many allotees of reservation lands had sold them and disposed of the proceeds. Further allotments were prohibited in order to safeguard remaining Indian properties. The Secretary of the Interior was authorized to create new reservations and to add lands to existing ones. Tribes were permitted to become chartered federal corporations with powers to manage their affairs, and to organize and adopt constitutions for their own self-government.

"Concurrently the influence of state law increased rather than decreased decreased *　*　*"

The basic position of appellee, which was accepted by the trial court, is that the Indian tribal courts, to the extent that they still have jurisdiction of Indian offenses, are not courts of the states or of the nation, but of separate sovereignties, to which the Constitution does not apply, and over which the federal courts have no jurisdiction.

(2,3) These tribal courts do still have a very considerable jurisdiction, and such jurisdiction is still, to a considerable extent, exclusive. This is the normal rule as to criminal offenses and as to suits against Indians arising out of matters occurring on the reservation. The notion of sovereignty still bars the way of one who wishes to sue an Indian tribe. There is, however, a strong tread toward applying general congressional legislation to Indians.

(4) It is also true that an Indian tribe has the power, absent some treaty provision or act of Congress to the contrary, to enact its own laws for the government of its people, and to establish courts to enforce them. It has been said that the adoption by a tribe of the law and order code makes the code tribal law, not federal law. And the fact that all Indians are now citizens does not affect the jurisdiction of tribal courts.

(5,6) All of these cases, and many others, however, recognize the basic proposition stated in *Winton v. Amos*: "It is thoroughly established that Congress has plenary authority over the Indians and all their tribal relations." And it is now the law, whatever may once have been the rule, that Indian reservations are a part of the territory of the United States. See *United States v. Kagama* where the court said:

"But these Indians are within the geographical limits of the United States. The soil and the people within these limits are under the political control of the government of the United States, or of the states of the Union."

It has been said that the Constitution applies to the Indians, in the conduct of tribal affairs, only when it expressly binds them, or is made binding by treaty or act of Congress. We doubt the present validity of this proposition, as so broadly stated, but we confine our decision to the question actually before us. No case has been cited to us that holds that the courts of the United States do not have jurisdiction to issue writs of habeas corpus to inquire into the legality of the imprisonment of an Indian pursuant to an order or judgment of an Indian court. One case has squarely held that the Thirteenth Amendment prohibiting slavery "within the United States, or any place subject to their jurisdiction" does apply to

Indians, and this in a habeas corpus case. That case, however, did not involve a person convicted in an Indian court, it relied on the very broad language of the Thirteenth Amendment, and it dealt with Alaska Indians, whose status is somewhat different. Most heavily relied upon by appellee and most closely in point, is *Talton v. Mayes.* There, an Indian of the Cherokee nation, convicted of murder in a Cherokee court sought a writ of habeas corpus in a federal court. He asserted that his conviction was void because he had been indicted by a five-man grand jury, as provided by tribal law, and was thus deprived of his right to a grand jury as prescribed by the Sixth Amendment to the Constitution. Denial of the writ was affirmed. The court did not hold that the district court was without jurisdiction. It decided the question on the merits. It relied in large part on the treaty with the Cherokee, which expressly preserved the exclusive jurisdiction of their courts. It said that the offense was against the Cherokee Nation, not the United States, whose laws do not apply, that the Fifth Amendment applies only to the United States, and that the powers exercised by the Cherokee were not federal powers. But it also said:

> "True it is that in many adjudications of this court the fact has been fully recognized that, although possessed of these attributes of local self-government, when exercising their tribal functions, all such rights are subject to the supreme legislative authority of the United States. *Cherokee Nation v. Southern Kansas Railway Co,* where the cases are fully reviewed. But the existence of the right in Congress to regulate the manner in which the local powers of the Cherokee Nation shall be exercised does not render such local powers federal powers arising from and created by the Constitution of the United States. It follows that, as the powers of local self-government enjoyed by the Cherokee Nation existed prior to the Constitution, they are not operated upon by the Fifth Amendment, which, as we have said, had for its sole object to control the powers conferred by the Constitution on the national government. The fact that the Indian tribes are subject to the dominant authority of Congress, and that their powers of local self-government are also operated upon and restrained by the general provisions of the Constitution of the United States, completely answers the argument of inconvenience which was pressed in the discussion at bar. The claim that the finding of an indictment by a grand jury of less than 13 violates the due process clause of the Fourteenth Amendment is conclusively answered by *Hurtado v. People of the State of California.*"

Here, reliance is upon the due process clause, not the indictment clause. The language of the case supports appellee; the holding, however, is narrower. We note particularly that the Cherokee treaty provided that the laws of the Cherokee "shall not be inconsistent with the Constitution of the United States," and the court's reference to "the general provisions of the Constitution," which, it apparently thought, do apply. Whether the court was of this opinion because of the language of the treaty, or otherwise, does not appear.

None of the other cases upon which tribal counsel relies in support of the order appealed from is as closely in point. *Worcester v. State of Georgia* sustains the treaty rights of the Cherokee nation against the pretentions of the state of Georgia. It does not deal at all with whether a federal court may issue a writ of habeas corpus at the behest of an Indian imprisoned under orders of a tribal court. *Ex parte Crow Dog* recognized the jurisdiction of the Indian courts. It dealt directly with the jurisdiction of a federal court, which was held not to have jurisdiction of the offense in question because that offense was under the exclusive jurisdiction of an Indian court. *Iron Crow v. Oglala Sioux Tribe* held that an Indian court had jurisdiction of a charge of adultery committed by Indians on the Pine Ridge Reservation. It did not touch upon the question of whether the Constitution applies to the procedure of Indian courts. The court said: "The facts which were the basis for the verdict of guilty in the proceedings before the Tribal Court and the fairness of the procedures of the Tribal Court are not disputed or involved in this case." All that the court held was that the Indian court did have jurisdiction of the offense, which is not disputed here. *Native American Church v. Navajo Tribal Council* refused to enjoin the enforcement of a Navajo tribal council ordinance against the use on the reservation of the drug peyote. The court rested its decision on the proposition that the federal Constitution is binding the Indian nations only where it expressly binds them or is made binding on them by treaty or some act of Congress. It held, therefore, that the Native American Church, which claimed that the use of peyote was a part of its religious practice, could not invoke the First Amendment to enjoin enforcement of the ordinance. The Eighth Circuit used the same reasoning in upholding the validity of an Indian tax against an attack based upon the Fifth and Fourteenth Amendments to the Constitution *(Barta v. Oglala Sioux Tribe)*. These cases do not decide whether, if an Indian were convicted in an Indian court, the federal court could inquire into the propriety of the conviction in a proceeding in habeas corpus.

(7) In spite of the theory that for some purposes an Indian tribe is an independent sovereignty, we think that, in the light of their history, it is pure fiction to say the the Indian courts functioning in the Fort Belknap Indian community are not in part, at least, arms of the federal government. Originally they were created by the federal executive and imposed upon the Indian community, and to this day the federal government still maintains a partial control over them. In *Iron Crow v. Oglala Sioux Tribe* the court held that comparable Indian courts "have been authorized by federal legislative action" and that "federal legislative action and rules promulgated thereunder support the authority of the Tribal Courts."

(8) Under these circumstances, we think that these courts function in part as a federal agency and in part as a tribal agency, and that consequently it is competent for a federal court in a habeas corpus proceeding to inquire into the legality of the detention of an Indian pursuant to an order of an Indian court. We confine our decision to the courts of the Fort Belknap reservation. The history of other Indian courts may call for a different ruling, a question which is not before us.

(9) The writ of habeas corpus lies on behalf of anyone who is "in custody under or by color of the authority of the United States" or "in violation of the Constitution of the United States. We think that this covers Mrs. Colliflower's case.

It may well be that one hundred years ago it would have been held that a federal court lacked jurisdiction to issue a writ of habeas corpus at the instance of an Indian imprisoned in a tribal jail, pursuant to the judgment of a tribal court. We think, whoever, that the status of the Indians today is such, and particularly that the history and status of the tribal court at the Fort Belknap Reservation is such, that we should uphold the jurisdiction of a federal court in this habeas corpus proceeding.

We do not pass upon the merits of Mrs. Colliflower's claims, because the district court did not reach them. It does not follow from our decision that the tribal court must comply with every constitutional restriction that is applicable to federal or state courts. Nor does it follow that the Fourteenth Amendment applies to tribal courts at all; some of the cases cited above indicate that it does not. And the vestige of "sovereignty" that the tribe retains and exercises through its Tribal Council and Tribal Courts may call for application of the principles applied in such cases as *Territory of Hawaii v. Mankichi, Downes v. Bidwell* and *Talton v. Mayes.*

The order is reversed and the matter is remanded for further proceedings.

IV

CLAIM AND COUNTERCLAIM

In 1969, James Forman issued his famous Manifesto demanding reparations for the black community. This Manifesto caused such a stir that the activists of major minority communities veered sharply left and began demanding reparations for centuries of atrocity and deprivation.

Indian history is strangely experienced in reparations, claims and counter-claims. Even the earliest treaties made provisions for reparations and compensation for incidents on both sides. Thus some of the treaties contained off-sets that the Indian tribes had to give to various whites against whom they had fought prior to the signing of the treaty. In some cases a tribe was made to return horses and cattle stolen in the course of the war. In other cases the federal government assumed responsibility for the acts of whites who had intruded on tribal hunting lands.

Because there are so many incidents today as Indian militants attempt to raise the whole question of reparations, this chapter has been included in an effort to sketch out the highlights of the past. The records of the various claims commissions are a gold mine of information on the frictions between red and white during the last century. A number of important claims are still unresolved. Simple justice demands that they be settled as quickly as possible. In the light of the My Lai massacre and the tremendous controversy surrounding the war in Southeast Asia it would be well for everyone to remember that the domestic past is no better than the contemporary foreign scene. A deep feeling of injustice still runs as an undercurrent through Indian country. Promises that the United States will accept responsibility for the Sand Creek massacre are not yet kept. These promises are now over a century old.

Once the Indian wars ended the government was beseiged with claims for hostile acts against the settlers by warring bands. The United States, it was argued, had insisted on treating with the Indians as equals and had guaranteed a peace that had not, in many cases, continued. The property losses from hostile acts of the tribes therefore had to be reimbursed.

Not one to pay out of its own pocket, Congress promptly passed the Indian Depredations Act so that the tribes could be sued directly for treaty violations. This during an era when tribes themselves were barred from going to court against the United States for violations of those same treaties.

In effect the United States held the arms of the Indian tribes while every white who could have conceivably lost a stray dog while the Sioux or Cheyenne were fleeing a hundred miles in the distance calmly picked their pockets. The nature of the act violated the tenets of every equitable case of law. If a judgment were rendered against the tribe the claimant could wait until the tribe had funds and then cash in his claim. If bankruptcy law ever read like that the western world would never have left the shores of Europe.

When the news of today's important claims by Indian tribes creates concern among the average person he should remember that the Indian Claims are just, that the whites got their money years and years ago and that in many cases they got better than 100 cents on the dollar while even today Indians get less than half of an inflated dollar and never the true value of the taking.

The Indian Depredations Act
26 Stat. 851 (1891)

Be it enacted, That in addition to the jurisdiction which now is, or may hereafter be, conferred upon the Court of Claims, said Court shall have and possess jurisdiction and authority to inquire into and finally adjudicate, in the manner provided in this act, all claims of the following classes, namely:

First. All claims for property of citizens of the United States taken or destroyed by Indians belonging to any band, tribe, or nation, in amity with the United States, without just cause or provocation on the part of the owner or agent in charge, and not returned or paid for.

Second. Such jurisdiction shall also extend to all cases which have been examined and allowed by the Interior Department.

And also to such cases as were authorized to be examined under the act of Congress making appropriations for the current and contingent expenses of the Indian Department, and for fulfilling treaty stipulations with various Indian tribes for the year ending June thirtieth, eighteen hundred and eighty-six, and for other purposes, approved March third, eighteen hundred and eighty-five, and under subsequent acts, subject, however to the limitations hereinafter provided.

Third. All just offsets and counterclaims to any claim of either of the preceding classes which may be before such court for determination.

SECTION 2. That all questions of limitations as to time and manner of presenting claims are hereby waived, and no claim shall be excluded from the jurisdiction of the court because not heretofore presented to the Secretary of the Interior or other officer or department of the Government: *Provided,* That no claim accruing prior to July first, eighteen hundred and sixty-five, shall be considered by the court unless the claim shall be allowed or has been or is pending, prior to the passage of this act, before the Secretary of the Interior or the Congress of the United States, or before any superintendent, agent, sub-agent or commissioner, authorized under any act of Congress to enquire into such claims; but no case shall be considered pending unless evidence has been presented therein: *And provided further,* That all claims existing at the time of the taking effect of this act shall be presented to the court by petition, as hereinafter provided, within three years after the passage hereof, or shall be thereafter forever barred: *And provided further,* That no suit or proceeding shall be allowed under this act for any depredation which shall be committed after the passage thereof.

SECTION 3. That all claims shall be presented to the court by petition setting forth in ordinary and concise language, without unnecessary repetition, the facts upon which such claims are based, the persons, classes of persons, tribe or tribes, or band of Indians by whom the alleged illegal acts were committed, as near as may be, the property lost or destroyed, and the value thereof, and any other facts connected with the transactions and material to the proper adjudication of the case involved. The petition shall be verified by the affidavit of the claimant, his agent, administrator, or attorney, and shall be filed with the clerk of said court. It shall set forth the full name and residence of the claimant, the damages sought to be recovered, praying the court for a judgment upon the facts and the law.

SECTION 4. The service of the petition shall be made upon the Attorney-General of the United States in such manner as may be provided by the rules or orders of said court. It shall be the duty of the Attorney-General of the United States to appear and defend the interests of the Government and of the Indians in the suit, and within sixty days after the service of the petition upon him, unless the time shall be extended by order of the court made in the case, to file a plea, answer or demurrer on the part of the Government and the Indians, and to file a notice of any counterclaim, set-off, claim of damages, demand, or defense whatsoever of the Government or of the Indians in the premises: *Provided,* That should the Attorney-General neglect or refuse to file the plea, answer, demurrer or defense as required, the claimant may proceed with the case under such rules as the court may adopt in the premises; but the claimant shall not have judgment for his claim, or for any part thereof, unless he shall establish the same by proof satisfactory to the court: *Provided,* That any Indian or Indians interested in the proceedings may appear and defend, by an attorney employed by such Indian or Indians with the approval of the Commissioner of Indian Affairs, if he or they shall choose so to do.

In considering the merits of claims presented to the court, any testimony, affidavits, reports of special agents or other officers, and such other papers as are now on file in the departments or in the courts, relating to any such claims, shall be considered by the court as competent evidence and such weight given thereto as in its judgment is right and proper: *Provided,* That all unpaid claims which have heretofore been examined, approved, and allowed by the Secretary of the Interior, or under his direction, in pursuance of the act of Congress making appropriations for the current and contingent expenses of the Indian Department, and for fulfilling treaty stipulations with various Indian tribes, for the year ending June thirtieth, eighteen hundred and eighty-six, and for other purposes, approved March third, eighteen hundred and eighty-five, and subsequent Indian appropriation acts, shall have priority of consideration by such court.

And judgments for the amounts therein found due shall be rendered, unless either the claimant or the United States shall elect to re-open the case and try the same before the court, in which event the testimony in the case given by the witnesses and the documentary evidence, including reports of Department agents therein, may be read as depositions and proofs: *Provided,* That the party electing to re-open the case shall assume the burden of proof.

SECTION 5. That the said court shall make rules and regulations for taking testimony in the causes herein provided for, by depositions or otherwise, and such testimony shall be taken in the county where the witness resides, when the same can be conveniently done.

And no person shall be excluded as a witness because he is party to or interested in said suit, and any claimant or party in interest may be examined as a witness on the part of the Government.

That the court shall determine in each case the value of the property taken or destroyed at the time and place of the loss or destruction, and, if possible, the tribe of Indians or other persons by whom the wrong was committed, and shall render judgment in favor of the claimant or claimants against the United States, and against the tribe of Indians committing the wrong, when such can be identified.

SECTION 6. That the amount of any judgment so rendered against any tribe of Indians shall be charged against the tribe by which, or by members of which, the court shall find that the depredation was committed, and shall be deducted and paid in the following manner:

First, from annuities due said tribe from the United States;

Second, if no annuities are due or available, then from any other funds due said tribe from the United States, arising from the sale of their lands or otherwise;

Third, if no such funds are due or available, then from any appropriation for the benefit of said tribe, other than appropriations for their current and necessary support, subsistence and education;

And, Fourth, if no such annuity, fund, or appropriation is due or available, then the amount of the judgment shall be paid from the Treasury of the United States: *Provided,* That any amount so paid from the Treasury of the United States shall remain a charge against such tribe, and shall be deducted from any annuity fund or appropriation hereinbefore designated which may hereafter become due from the United States to such tribe.

SECTION 7. That all judgments of said court shall be a final determination of the causes decided and of the rights and obligations of the parties thereto, and shall not thereafter be questioned unless a new trial or rehearing shall be granted by said court, or the judgment reversed or modified upon appeals as hereafter provided.

SECTION 8. That immediately after the beginnning of each session of Congress the Attorney-General of the United States shall transmit to the Congress of the United States a list of all final judgments rendered in pursuance of this act, in favor of claimants and against the United States, and not paid as hereinbefore provided, which shall thereupon be appropriated for in the proper appropriation bill.

SECTION 9. That all sales, transfers, or assignments of any such claims beretofore or hereafter made, except such as have occurred in the due administration of decedent's estates, and all contracts heretofore made for fees and allowances to claimants' attorneys are hereby declared void.

And all warrants issued by the Secretary of the Treasury, in payment of such judgments, shall be made payable and delivered only to the claimant or his lawful heirs, executors or administrators or transferee under administrative proceedings, except so much thereof as shall be allowed the claimant's attorneys by the court for prosecuting said claim, which may be paid direct to such attorneys, and the allowances to the claimant's attorneys shall be regulated and fixed by the court at the time of rendering judgment in each case and entered of record as part of the findings thereof; But in no case shall the allowance exceed fifteen per cent of the judgment recovered, except in the case of claims of less amount than five hundred dollars, or where unusual services have been rendered or expenses incurred by the claimant's attorney, in which case not to exceed twenty per cent, of such judgment shall be allowed by the court.

SECTION 10. That the claimant, or the United States, or the tribe of Indians, or other party thereto interested in any proceeding brought under the provisions of this act, shall have the same rights of appeal as are or may be reserved in the Statutes of the United States in other cases, and upon the conditions and limitations therein contained. The mode of procedure in claiming and perfecting an appeal shall conform, in all respects, as near as may be, to the statutes and rules of court governing appeals in other cases.

SECTION 11. That all papers, reports, evidence, records, and proceedings now on file or of record in any of the departments, or the office of the Secretary of the Senate, or the office of the Clerk of the House of Representatives, or certified copies of the same, relating to any claims authorized to be prosecuted under this act, shall be furnished to the court upon its order, or at the request of the Attorney-General.

SECTION 12. To facilitate the speedy disposition of the cases herein provided for, in said Court of Claims, there shall be appointed, in the manner prescribed by law for the appointment of Assistant Attorney-Generals, one additional Assistant Attorney-General of the United States, who shall receive a salary of twenty-five hundred dollars per annum.

SECTION 13. That the investigations and examinations, under the provisions of the acts of Congress heretofore in force, of Indian depredation claims, shall cease upon the taking effect of this act, and the unexpended balance of the appropriation therefor shall be covered into the Treasury, except so much thereof as may be necessary for disposing of the unfinished business pertaining to the claims now under investigation in the Interior

Department, pending transfer of said claims and business to the Court or courts herein provided for, and for making such transfers and a record of the same, and for the proper care and custody of the papers and records relating thereto.

(March 3, 1891)

Jaeger v. The United States and the Yuma Indians
29 Ct. Cl. 278 (1894)

Jaeger was, to say the least, a sharp man with a pencil. The Indian Depredations Act was created to compensate white settlers who had lost property because of the acts of war committed by a tribe which had a peace treaty with the United States. But once the Indian Depredations Act was passed the Secretary of the Interior was flooded with claims against all the respective tribes. Of all the cases that finally got to court the *Jaeger* case was the most humorous since it was only the merest coincidence that any Yumas were even in the neighborhood.

If only the Indian Claims Commission or the Court of Claims would let us get cases like this into consideration we could really have a good time and perhaps make some money as well.

In August, 1872, a ferry boat belonging to the claimant broke from her moorings and floated down the Colorado River. In the vicinity of and nearly opposite to a point on the west bank of the Colorado called Pilot Knob, a few miles below the town of Arizona City, she was made fast to the bank by the claimant, who then left her in charge of two of the Indian defendants, they being his hired employees. While in their charge the river fell and she stranded. The boat then caught fire from fires on the bank and was destroyed. Her value was $3,000.

The fires above referred to were those of Yumas Indians, dwelling in a village adjacent to and near by the place where the boat stranded. The fires were not kindled from any malicious intent or design to destroy the boat. The conflagration of the boat was accidental. It does not appear how near to the boat the Indian village was situated, nor what was the purpose and character of the fires, *i.e.,* whether they were ordinary fires for cooking food or fires for burning grass or brushwood; nor whether they were kindled before or after the boat stranded; nor that the Indians who kindled them had been notified of the stranding of the boat and that she could not be removed; nor that they were guilty of negligence.

It appears by the testimony of the claimant that the character of the defendant Indians, the Yumas, at the time of the alleged depredation, was as follows:

"Those Indians would do most anything like white persons to look out for me there, and as good Indians; and I put them in charge of the boat, and they looked out for me just the same as white men would."

"And you arranged and employed some of the Indians to take charge of your boat and put it in their charge?"

"Certainly."

"Did you agree to pay them anything for it?"

"I did pay them long ago."

"You hired them to do it?"

"Yes; I did."

The Commissioner of Indian Affairs, in his report for 1872, says:

"These Indians number about 2,000, and inhabit the country near the mouth of the Colorado River and in the vicinity of Arizona City, and subsist by planting and by cutting wood for steamers plying on the river."

General Howard, in a report to the Secretary of the Interior in 1872 says:

"This tribe is scattered all along the Colorado River from its mouth to the vicinity of Fort Yuma."

It does not appear that the Yumas have ever entered into treaty relations with the United States; that they have ever been recognized as having "a tribal character" or as having a "capacity to make treaties"; that they have ever had a tribal organization capable of entering into a treaty; that they are anything more than a race of quiet, inoffensive, self-supporting, industrious persons. The only action of the Government toward them, proposed or executed, so far as has been shown to the court, was in supplying them with a few agricultural implements, "to enable them to plant and raise crops during the present year," 1872. The counsel for the claimant avers that these Indians are classed by the Commissioner of Indian Affairs in 1872 under the head of "Cape Verde Agency (special) as Apache Yumas." But the Supreme Court has said of a similar body of Indians: "We have no hesitation in saying that their status is not, in the face of the facts we have stated, to be determined solely by the circumstance that some officer of the Government has appointed for them an agent, even if we could take judicial notice of the existence of that fact, suggested to us in argument."

Such being the character of the tribe, we turn now to the character of the transaction. The evidence consists of the claimant's own deposition, of the *ex parte* affidavits of four persons who witnessed the burning of the boat from the deck of a steamer which was passing down the river, of a letter from an Indian agent who was a passenger on a steamer, and of the *ex parte* affidavits of the two Indians who were in charge of claimant's boat. The four affidavits narrate that the deponents saw "that said boat was on fire and rapidly being destroyed, and was destroyed thereby;" and each concludes with substantially the same averment, that "this affiant further states that some incendiary must have set this boat on fire, and he verily believes some member or members of the Yuma tribe of Indians did the deed, as that part of the country where the boat was is inhabited almost exclusively by said tribe."

The Indian agent says: "I witnessed the destruction of the boat from the steamer while coming up the river in August, 1872, and noticed its proximity to an Indian camp; but, the owner being the oldest white settler and always friendly to the Indians, I could not believe it was destroyed willfully by them. They admit now, however, that it was the result of carelessness. I consider the claim a just and reasonable one."

"Ackawamar on oath says that he belongs to the Yuma tribe of Indians," "that about two years ago, the river being high, the boat broke loose and came down the river and was caught near the Indian camp." "I know that the boat was burnt up by the Indians building fires alongside where she stranded as the water fell, and before they could get her away the Yumas burnt her, but I cannot say which ones." "Joseyo on oath says that he belongs to the Yuma tribe of Indians." "About two years ago, in high water, the boat broke away and drifted down river to an Indian camp near Pilot Knob, where it was caught, and before they could get her away she stranded. The Yumas built fires near her and about her, and she was burnt up. I don't think they intended to burn her, but when she got on fire they got frightened and ran off and let her burn." These two Indian deponents were the employees of the claimant and in charge of the boat.

It is manifest that this evidence does not establish a malicious intent, and does not show such a condition of negligence as would establish a liability at common law for the destruction of the boat. The Indians were on their own ground, and had a right to build fires there. It does not appear that they knew the boat was stranded, and it does not even appear with certainty that the fires were not kindled before the stranding of the boat. The admission of some unknown, nondesignated Indians to the conclusion of law that the burning "was the result of carelessness" can not be considered.

Without passing upon the questions whether these Indians were citizens by virtue of the treaty of Guadalupe Hidalgo, and whether the accidental and unintentional destruction of property by Indians can be deemed a depredation within the intent of the statute, or the destruction of property by American Indians in Mexican territory (which is also a question in the case), the court is of the opinion that the evidence is insufficient under the statute or at common law to establish a liability either against the Indian defendants or the United States.

The judgment of the court is that the petition be dismissed.

Re Claims of the Six Nations (New York)
Petition

The oldest and best claims against the United States belong to the Iroquois Confederacy. For centuries before the founding of the American Republic the Iroquois were staunch allies of the English, providing the edge in determining which nation, England or France, should rule the new world. During the days of the American Revolution—a time when the Iroquois could easily have snuffed out the tiny revolt—they maintained a strong friendship with the revolutionaries and split the League rather than commit themselves to total opposition.

Later in the days of Little Turtle and the struggle for the Ohio Valley—when Iroquois intervention might easily have defeated the American armies and sealed western settlement for a century—the Iroquois again maintained friendship with George Washington and saved the small nation. In a series of international treaties the Iroquois received rights superior to those of other tribes and were accorded equal status as a nation among other, i.e. European, nations.

The treatment of the Iroquois has been the darkest in the history of international dealings. Treaty after treaty has been broken or nullified by the United States and Canada. Even today, only a decade after the shameful breaking of the Pickering Treaty of 1794, Canada is trying to break the Jay Treaty provisions, thereby preventing the Indian workers from coming to work the high steel in the United States. The Canadian government is trying to turn the Indian reserves of Quebec into garbage dumps and industrial areas, pushing the Iroquois residents into the slums of Montreal.

In the 1920's a Congressional investigating committee was surveying the subject of Indian claims against the United States. The Iroquois filed a statement covering their claims. It stands today as a moral indictment against the United States for its treatment of this tribe.

To the INDIAN INVESTIGATING COMMITTEE OF THE UNITED STATES SENATE:
We, the Hodinonshonni, the league of the Iroquois, otherwise known as the Six Nations Confederacy, who were the first to establish on this continent law and order and a government respected by the tribes of Indians, America, and by foreign nations; we, who were the original authors of that form of government which has given the largest degree of freedom to mankind, thereby making possible western civilization; we, who through the most critical times of a struggling foreign people gave to them the heart's right hand, and bread and life, and by these things secured and determined the liberty of the land and made possible the great Republic of the United States; we, who put our trust in time-old honor between men and between nations and our whole faith in the national honor and integrity of the people we had helped to become a nation made a solemn covenant with the United States of America.

We, the Hodinonshonni, your petitioners, respectfully submit to your honorable investigating commission that by the treaty of Fort Stanwix, 1784, the Six Nations were secured in the possession of approximately 18,000,000 acres of land in western New York and Pennsylvania, bounded by the survey known as the Sir William Johnson line of property handed down to us from the treaty with Great Britain of 1768.

That by the treaty of 1784 the Six Nations were secured in their independent self-government.

That by this treaty the Six Nations were guaranteed protection from the United States Government.

That by this treaty the Six Nations ceded to the United States the whole of the Ohio Valley.

That by this treaty the United States and the Six Nations were to remain faithful friends.

That, according to our traditional honor, we the Hodinonshonni, have kept the faith to the present day.

And we desire to remind the United States of America, of the great circumstances out of which this treaty grew.

The terms came out of the pre-war promises of the Revolution by Gen. George Washington. At that time both the British and the colonial forces coveted the alliance of the league of the Iroquois.

Both sides knew whichever side could ally itself with the confederacy would have the balance of power. A treaty council was asked for by Sir William Johnson, and was granted by the confederacy. Sir William told them that the English asked for an alliance, and their support against the Colonies; that the English Government would pay them five pounds gold for every fighting man, and offered them a treaty guaranteeing them security in their title to their territory, and protection, against all encroachments "as long as water runs and grass grows." Also should the British be whipped, they would deed them as much land in Canada as they then possessed in New York and would guarantee them their sovereignty as a nation there.

Gen. George Washington, two months later, asked for a national council of the Iroquois, and it was granted. He told them the Colonies were poor, but they were fighting for liberty, the one thing dearest to every Indian heart. He said he could not offer them gold, but asked for an alliance between them and the Continental Congress soon to be formed. And should the British be whipped, the new Government of the United States would renew the alliance, both recognizing the sovereignty of one another. The United States would guarantee them in their title to their lands forever.

At first the Six Nations firmly held to their policy of neutrality. Had not Gen. Joseph Brant, a powerful Mohawk leader, been persuaded to lead away a following of the confederacy to the British side, the Revolutionary War would not have been so prolonged. Still the Six Nations remained neutral, but the British now sent primitive expeditions into the Six Nations country. The Oneidas, always the friends of General Washington, now put all the fighting men of the Oneidas, the Tuscaroras, and those of their adopted peoples, the Stockbridges and Brothertowns behind General Washington and gave his starving army adequate provisions and so quickly determined the outcome of the Revolution.

As the President of the new United States, the Father of his Country kept the faith of his Iroquois allies and personally directed the Fort Stanwix treaty of 1784.

It was made with the most vigilant observance of all the formalities due an international document. It was the result of conferences between duly authorized representatives of both nations.

It was duly ratified by the United States Senate and promulgated to the world.

It remains today the most dignified treaty in the whole history of this country's Indian relations.

It was made with a civilized power already recognized as such by France, Holland, and England, and a government which was a better established political unit than the white government for many years.

For a hundred and forty-four years your petitioners have lived and seen the embarrassments of the United States Government toward the Six Nations, promoted by the State of New York. When the confederacy first protested the President of the United States answered them in these words: "Be assured that the United States of America will never see you defrauded, but will protect you in all your just rights." And the protests of President Washington to Governor Clinton of New York is a matter of history.

Beginning with 1786, contrary to the constitutional provision prohibiting the States to enter into treaty relations with Indian nations, the State of New York began a series of treaties with separate nations of the confederacy for cessions of their coveted territory. Ruin and fraud were the order of these transactions.

Parties interested in the cessions of land were made members of the personnel of the New York treaty commissions.

Parties representing the Six Nations had no power constitutionally on the Indian side to sell, without the consent of the people of each nation, and without the consent and ratification of the general council of the Six Nations Confederacy. The loss of Six Nations citizenship to the Delaware Indians is an example of the punishment due any Six Nations people who violated this provision of the Iroquois constitution.

Finally, by the treaty of 1784, the Six Nations had no power to sell land without the consent of the guardian, the United States Government.

Under the articles of confederation, "Treaties shall constitute the supreme law of the land."

Your petitioners pray that your honorable commission will investigate the facts and the charges herein set forth to the end that a sacred covenant between the league of the Iroquois and the United States of America may not become a scrap of paper at the hands of a powerful nation through a sinister organ whose power to destroy the Indian peoples of the land has come to be ground for a world appeal; that the "reign of terror" in bureaucracy may be ended and the day of better understanding between the red man and the white man may be made possible.

Your petitioners charge:

1. That Governor Clinton and delegation from New York did all in their power to keep the Senate from ratifying the treaty of 1784.

2. That the officials of the State of New York from 1784 through the years willfully defied President Washington and his successors; defied the Congress of the United States, the Supreme Court, and the United States Constitution.

3. That though both the Congress of the United States and the Legislature of New York have passed stringent liquor laws making it a crime to give or sell liquor to an Indian, that liquor was the main argument used by New York State commissioners in procuring the so-called Indian treaties.

4. That every foot of land bought from the Mohawks, Oneidas, Cayugas, and Onondagus was illegally obtained in absolute contravention to the laws of Congress, to the United States Constitution, and to the treaties.

5. That President Washington vigorously protested to Governor Clinton that these so-called State treaties were made and the land taken away in utter contempt of Federal authority.

6. That from the day the treaty of 1784 was ratified and promulgated, the State of New York through officials, through local chambers of commerce, and through paid hirelings, both white and Indian traders, have used every means in their power to discredit and disorganize the Six Nations and that they succeeded since 1786 in destroying to a great extent their solidarity and integrity.

7. That prior to 1876 the State of New York had no help or abetting from the Federal Government in the interference with the Six Nations' affairs, but since then a system has been built up under the Interior Department, the Indian Bureau. This bureau has joined hands with New York to further break down the Six Nations as a nation.

8. That the State of New York has taken these lands illegally procured from nations of the Six Nations and has issued State patents to its citizens for same.

9. That the United States Government has issued no patents for any of this land and that the patents issued by the State are null and void and have no force of effect.

10. That a great deal of this land, especially city real estate, has no title but is strictly on lease.

11. That the title of the land along the rivers and streams now controlled by the Power Trust and its connections is vested in the Six Nations and that the Six Nations' claim to riparian rights are as well founded as any other peoples'.

12. That the Six Nations Confederacy vigorously protested to the Federal Government through the years so that no statute of limitations can run against them; that the law of laches does not apply to people who have no power to sue.

13. That prior to 1867, when the Indian Bureau was organized, the State of New York claimed no jurisdiction over the Six Nations, yet throughout the last 60 years New York has assumed considerable jurisdiction over the Six Nations' people and their affairs. It has appointed agents over each reserve, who inefficiently take charge of business affairs without a protest from the Federal Government, and we charge that the agents have been partial, and have at all times sought to create discord among the Indians.

14. That any act performed by these so-called State agents, except the distribution of State annuity, is illegal and without warrant of Federal law; that dual control over our people is illegal, a nuisance, and must be stopped.

The Boylan case has brought the American people face to face with the crime which has been perpetrated on the Six Nations Indians. It has brought the State of New York and the United States Government to a point when they must face this issue and make a settlement with the confederacy for the wrongs of degrading, pauperizing, and well-nigh annihilating a once powerful nation, which was the hope of the American Indian on the Western Continent. An Indian by the name of Margaret Honyost had mortgaged 32 acres in Oneida, N.Y. In a few years she was foreclosed and forced to move. An action was started by the United States district attorney to declare the foreclosure illegal. The said action went to the Federal Circuit Court of Northern New York, with Judge George W. Ray presiding. After a long hearing Judge Ray handed down a decision, stating that the title to the land had never left the Six Nations. That the Iroquois Confederacy was still a nation and had never given up its right of self-government. And in effect, therefore, no one but the Six Nations government could mortgage or sell one foot of the property guaranteed under the treaty of 1784. The effect of this decision was that the 32 acres then in the hands of an innocent purchaser reverted back to the Six Nations by court order and so stands today.

An appeal was taken by the white man to the Federal court of appeals, and there Judge Ray's decision was sustained.

This case brought up the question of jurisdiction between the Federal and State Governments over the Six Nations. As a result of the discussion, the State appointed a commission to investigate the status of the Six Nations. The report of the chairman of that commission follows:

First. The Six Nations Indians consummated a treaty with the United States Government through its regular channels, the same being approved and ratified by Gen. George Washington, at Fort Stanwix in the State of New York in 1784, by which they were ceded certain territory within the State of New York.

Second. That the ceding and setting over to the Indians of this territory was in accordance with and at the conclusion of a treaty consummated by the Indians as a nation and by the United States as a nation.

Third. Further, that the passing of the title of the ceded territory to the Indians of the State was a legal and proper transaction, and that the Indians as a nation became possessed of the ceded territory the same as any other nation would become possessed.

Fourth. That the said Indians of the State of New York as a nation are still the owners of the fee-simple title to the territory ceded to them by the treaty of 1784.

We charge that since the Six Nations began a rehabilitation program and a litigation against the St. Lawrence River Power Co. and the State of New York, that the Indian Bureau has carried on a constant propaganda against them in its usual sinister way to break up their solidarity and progress, and that through it the United States Government is made to appear as an ally of the political and other enemies of the Six Nations.

That among its efforts, it caused postal authorities to investigate the officers and organizers of the Six Nations, and that when the postal investigators found no fraud against them that the bureau next conspired with one Duncan Scott, commissioner of Indian affairs at Ottawa, to have the Six Nations' officers and representatives arrested and tried in Canada on charges of fraud.

That the Indian Bureau put its inspectors on their trail to try to find evidence to convict them in Canada.

That during the trial at Montreal the bureau sent its chief clerk to testify against the indicted people. That under cross-examination he admitted that the bureau had been carrying on a propaganda against the Six Nations; that he was the man authorized to do it; and that public money had been spent in this effort.

The trial at Montreal before Judge Wilson, of the King's bench lasted 10 days. During the trial no evidence was produced before the court along the line of the charges of fraud above made; but the Six Nations were compelled to try their whole case, leaving the court to define the Six Nations' position. The Six Nations did not want a "whitewash." They wanted a clear-cut decision of Six Nations' status as well as a verdict as to the honor and integrity of their representatives.

Justice Wilson, one of Canada's greatest jurists handed down the following:

"I am not surprised that the Six Nations should look for more and more independence. They have their own government; there is not doubt of that. They say they are self-governing. So they are, to the same extent that a municipality is self-governing or that the legislature of the Province of Quebec is self-governing."

The jury decided in eight minutes that the Six Nations' representatives were conducting the affairs of their nation as they should be conducted. We are informed that this trial cost the prosecution over $17,000. We have our suspicions that the bureau at Washington gave its share in money as it did in other things to procure conviction.

We charge that the conspiracy between the Indian Bureau of Washington and the Indian bureau at Ottawa has brought about the enactment by the Canadian Parliament of a law to arrest any Indian who contributes money to prosecute any claim without the consent of the commissioner of Indian affairs in Canada; that this law is intended to persecute the Mohawk constituency of the Six Nations, who by the Jay treaty were wrongfully left on the Canadian side against their protest and the protest of the Six Nations, and the specific agreement finally with the commissioners of the Jay treaty that the boundary line between Canada and the United States was to be lifted into the sky over the Mohawk Indian land.

We charge that Barnhart Island, which belongs to the Mohawks, is in the United States boundaries, and that the State of New York has assumed title to it, and has transferred it to the St. Lawrence River Power Co. That the lease for Barnhart Island has expired long ago and that no lease money has been paid for over 60 years.

Your petitioners desire to remind the United States of America that the Six Nations are not under the Bureau of Indian Affairs, and that the Indian Bureau's acts of wanton contempt, interference, and persecution against the independence and integrity of the official personnel of the confederacy is ground for war between nations, were not the protectorate reduced to a state of pauperism and helplessness by acts of fraud and harassments allowed through the years by the guardian Government. Believing intensely in the justice of our cause, we petition your honorable commission to investigate how many means, how many people, and how much money has been used in the Indian Bureau's propaganda against the Six Nations, more particularly between the dates of February 15, 1922, and October 18, 1927.

The Seneca Nation in 1849 changed its form of government with a separate understanding between it and the United States Government, and that in the absence of machinery provided by the Federal Government in their relations with the Six Nations the Seneca Nation left the Indian form of government, adopting, to a certain extent, the white form. Under this form and under the eye of the Indian Bureau, a most corrupt government has reigned ever since among the Seneca Nation. Elected councilors, in the place of chiefs, largely mixed bloods, have carried on a system of looting quite equal to their white example. No report as to the oil, gas, and land lease revenues are made to the Seneca Nation. No increase in the per capita distribution of royalties to the Seneca people has been made for years despite the increase in the revenues. The Seneca declaration of the change in 1849 was not acknowledged before a notary until 1923, long after the original signers were dead.

The Onondaga Indians own a reservation of four miles square. Most of it is hills, there being a small part in bottom lands which alone can be used for crops.

We charge that the city of Syracuse covets this reservation and that immediately it has a plan to take away the bottom lands for dam sites, and that the Indian Bureau has promised its assistance in getting the land; that a prominent New York politician offered the Onondagas $15 per acre for land worth $250 and told the Onondagas that if they would not accept it the Indian Bureau would help him get it anyway.

A litigation was started June 6, 1925, in an ejectment action against the St. Lawrence River Power Co. by James Deer, a St. Regis Mohawk, under the auspices of the Six Nations. This suit was filed in the Federal District Court of Northern New York by the New York law firm of Wise, Whitney & Parker. Some months later the State of New York came in as party defendant on its own volition.

On September 29, 1925, the St. Lawrence River Power Co. filed a motion to dismiss the complaint on the ground that no Federal question was involved and that the plaintiff being an Indian had no legal authority to sue, although being a citizen of the United States. It was at this stage of the proceedings that the State of New York interpleaded as a party defendant.

The motion to dismiss was argued November 21, 1925, by Col. Jennings C. Wise for the plaintiff and by Hon. Charles Evans Hughes for the defendant.

At no time in the pleadings did defendant's council undertake to set up a title to land in question for the obvious reason that the so-called treaty of 1824 by which the St. Regis band had been divested of possession was wholly without effect at law, being null and void, under the Constitution of the United States, and the Federal statutes enacted pursuant thereto including the treaties of 1784 and 1797.

It was specifically stated under the articles of confederation that the United States took protectorate over the Indian nations and a proclamation was issued that Indian nations should be independent of any State.

Article 1, section 8, of the United States Constitution conferred upon Congress the right to regulate commerce with Indian nations.

Article 1, section 10, of the Constitution forbids any State from entering into any treaty or alliance with an Indian nation.

Article 2, section 2, of the Constitution conferred upon the President of the United States the exclusive power by and with the consent of the Senate to make any treaty.

July 22, 1790, at President Washington's request, Congress passed an act (1 Stat. 137) expressly forbidding the States, no matter what their pre-emption rights might be, from entering into a treaty with any Indian tribe or nation.

In 1823, 1831, and 1832, John Marshall, Supreme Court Justice, handed down three decisions, laying down three great fundamental principles. Indian rights were guaranteed by solemn treaty between Great Britain and the United States and protection by the Constitution was expressly declared.

Judge Cooper, of the Federal District Court of Northern New York, took the case under advisement and no decision was handed down until October 18, 1927.

Immediately a formal request was made on the United States through the Secretary of the Interior to intervene on behalf of its wards. The request was referred by the Secretary of the Interior to the Attorney General. The Six Nations attorneys took the matter up with the Department of Justice, and pointing out to Assistant Attorney General Parmenter that intervention was necessary, not alone to protect the prima facie title of the United States, but the right of occupancy of its citizen wards as well.

Pending final action the Department of Justice at once notified the United States district attorney for the Northern District of New York to prepare himself to intervene without delay should the Attorney General decide so to do.

Immediately Deputy Attorney General Manley, of New York, arrived on the scene and, with powerful support, succeeded in heading off intervention.

At least three times representatives of the St. Lawrence River Power Co. have approached Six Nations' representatives asking if there was no way by which matters could be settled out of court. July 6, 1927, a day was tentatively fixed for a settlement conference between the Six Nations' representatives and those of the St. Lawrence River Power Co. The Six Nations' representatives were asked to come to the conference prepared to state the amount they would accept and to be able to show how the title was to be quieted. There was no Federal intervention obtainable.

We wish now to call the commission's attention to the memorial submitted by Hon. Charles E. Hughes, then Secretary of State, in answer to the memorial submitted by Great Britain in the case of the Cayuga Indians, before the British American Claims Commission in 1926.

The right of domain which vested in a nation ultimate fee to the land carried with it the exclusive right of acquiring from the various Indian tribes inhabiting it their right to the soil, which were considered as limited to a right of occupancy of the land respectively used by such tribes as their hunting grounds. This limited occupancy might be lost by the Indian tribes through abandonment, or forfeited through engaging in war against the sovereign, or the title in some instances might be extinguished by purchase from the Indians by persons authorized by the sovereign. This dominant right in a sovereign to extinguish the Indians' right to use or occupy land of which the ultimate fee is in the sovereign is called the right of pre-emption. It precludes not only other powers but also the subjects of the sovereign, without his express authority from acquiring the Indian right of use or occupancy of lands.

It is this example which the United States since they became by their independence the sovereigns of the territory, have adopted and organized into a political system. Under that system the Indians are so far independent that they live under their own customs and not under the laws of the United States; that their rights upon the lands where they inhabit are secured to them by boundaries defined in amicable treaties between the United States and themselves, and that whenever these boundaries are varied it is also by amicable and voluntary treaties by which they receive from the United States ample compensation for every right they have to the lands ceded by them.

The Six Nations believe this treatise by Judge Hughes to be the greatest summary of the treaties, the United States Constitution, and the laws of Congress in regard to the purchase of Indian lands ever penned by man.

As Secretary of State, knowing the Constitution and the laws of Congress as no other man living, we can well understand the forceful position he took. And we can well understand that he never dreamed that a great Nation like the United States could have allowed any other method but this one to be pursued. He has stated the only legal and tenable way of securing land title from the Indians.

In conclusion, we pray your honorable commission to consider that the United States of America gladly received our assistance to its nationhood in the trying days between 1776 and 1783. That we gave that assistance on the assurance that we could trust the national honor and integrity of the United States. That beyond the beautiful traditions between the two nations of that time, the Six Nations are secured doubly in the protection guaranteed to them by the supreme law of the land and by the cession of billions of acres of the Ohio Valley.

That though the Six Nations have suffered heavily in the looting of their lands, their more recent persecution by the arm of the United States Government through the Indian

Bureau is calculated to break them; that inasmuch as Federal intervention which is their just due from the United States Government is at the same time being withheld without adequate reason, your petitioners charge there is a collusion between the United States Government and the politicians of the State of New York to keep them defrauded and broken.

Indian Claims Commission Act
60 Stat. 1049 (1946)

Indian claims are not new. In the 1860's Indian tribes began to appear in the federal courts asking for redress of wrongs suffered. Consequently Congress passed a law providing that Indian tribes did not have standing to sue. Thus as the claims mounted, there was no recourse for the tribes but to seek special legislation giving them standing to press their cases in the federal courts. Many tribes were effectively barred from asserting their claims at a time when they had the original signers of treaties among them and could use their chiefs as expert witnesses.

Finally the process got so tedious that the Indian Claims Commission Act was passed enabling all tribes to come directly before the commission in search of justice. The problem was that the scope of the Indian Claims Commission was severely limited. No one decision appeared to relate to another in any consistent theory of reparations or claims. The tribes were paid in modern dollars whereas they had been deprived of lands at a time when the dollar meant something. Thus a land sale at $3 an acre in 1830 was not the same as a land sale in 1950. No interest was allowed even though in some cases the federal government had squandered tribal funds on projects that did not even remotely benefit Indians— and with tribal moneys.

The ultimate insult was the appointment of former Senator Arthur Watkins, a mortal enemy of Indian people, as Chief Commissioner of the Indian Claims Commission. Watkins did his best to deprive the tribes of any recovery at all. At one Congressional hearing on an extension of the Indian Claims Commission Watkins was asked why the cases were going so slowly—some had been in court for twenty years with no apparent settlement in view. Watkins replied that he needed new legal tools to use "against the Indians". And this type of justice has passed as impartial when Indian claims have been litigated.

To create an Indian Claims Commission, to provide for the powers, duties, and functions, thereof, and for other purposes.

Be it enacted by the Senate and House of Representatives of the United States of America in Congress assembled, That there is hereby created and established an Indian Claims Commission, hereafter referred to as the Commission.

SECTION 2. The Commission shall hear and determine the following claims against the United States on behalf of any Indian tribe, band, or other identifiable group of American Indians residing within the territorial limits of the United States or Alaska: (1) claims in law or equity arising under the Constitution, laws, treaties of the United States, and Executive orders of the President; (2) all other claims in law or equity, including those sounding in tort, with respect to which the claimant would have been entitled to sue in a court of the United States if the United States was subject to suit; (3) claims which would result if the treaties, contracts, and agreements between the claimant and the United States were revised on the ground of fraud, duress, unconscionable consideration, mutual or unilateral mistake, whether of law or fact, or any other ground cognizable by a court of equity; (4) claims arising from the taking by the United States, whether as the result of a treaty of cession or otherwise, of lands owned or occupied by the claimant without the payment for such lands of compensation agreed to by the claimant; and (5) claims based upon fair and honorable dealings that are not recognized by any existing rule of law or equity. No claim accruing after the date of the approval of this Act shall be considered by the Commission.

All claims hereunder may be heard and determined by the Commission notwithstanding any statute of limitations or laches, but all other defenses shall be available to the United States.

In determining the quantum of relief the Commission shall make appropriate deductions for all payments made by the United States on the claim, and for all other offsets, counterclaims, and demands that would be allowable in a suit brought in the Court of Claims under section 145 of the Judicial Code, as amended; the Commission may also inquire into and consider all money or property given to or funds expended gratuitously for the benefit of the claimant and if it finds that the nature of the claim and the entire course of dealings and accounts between the United States and the claimant in good conscience warrants such action, may set off all or part of such expenditures against any award made to the claimant, except that it is hereby declared to be the policy of Congress that monies spent for the removal of the claimant from one place to another at the request of the United States, or for agency or other administrative, educational, health or highway purposes, or for expenditures made prior to the date of the law, treaty or Executive Order under which the claim arose, or for expenditures made pursuant to the Act of June 18, 1934, save expenditures made under section 5 of that Act, or for expenditures under any emergency appropriation or allotment made subsequent to March 4, 1933, and generally applicable throughout the United States for relief in stricken agricultural areas, relief from distress caused by unemployment and conditions resulting therefrom, the prosecution of public work and public projects for the relief of unemployment or to increase employment, and for relief (including the Civil Works Program) shall not be a proper offset against any award.

SECTION 3. (a) The Commission shall consist of a Chief Commissioner and two Associate Commissioners, who shall be appointed by the President, by and with the advice and consent of the Senate, and each of whom shall receive a salary of $10,000 per year. At all times at least two members of the Commission shall be members of the bar of the Supreme Court of the United States in good standing: *Provided further,* That not more than two of the members shall be of the same political party. Each of them shall take an oath to support the Constitution of the United States and to discharge faithfully the duties of his office.

(b) The Commissioners shall hold office during their good behavior until the dissolu-

143

tion of the Commission as hereinafter provided. Vacancies shall be filled in the same manner as the original appointments. Members of the Commission may be removed by the President for cause after notice and opportunity to be heard.

(c) No Commissioner shall engage in any other business, vocation, or employment during his term of office nor shall be, during his term of office or for a period of two years thereafter, represent any Indian tribe, band, or group in any matter whatsoever, or have any financial interest in the outcome of any tribal claim. Any person violating the provisions of this subdivision shall be fined not more than $10,000 or imprisoned not more than two years, or both.

(d) Two members shall constitute a quorum, and the agreement of two members shall be necessary to any and all determinations for the transaction of the business of the Commission, and, if there be a quorum, no vacancy shall impair or affect the business of the Commission, or its determinations.

SECTION 4. The Commission shall appoint a clerk and such other employees as shall be requisite to conduct the business of the Commission. All such employees shall take oath for the faithful discharge of their duties and shall be under the direction of the Commission in the performance thereof.

SECTION 5. The principal office of the Commission shall be in the District of Columbia.

SECTION 6. All necessary expenses of the Commission shall be paid on the presentation of itemized vouchers therefor approved by the Chief Commissioner or other member or officer designated by the Commission.

SECTION 7. The time of the meetings of the Commission shall be prescribed by the Commission.

SECTION 8. A full written record shall be kept of all hearings and proceedings of the Commission and shall be open to public inspection.

SECTION 9. The Commission shall have power to establish its own rules of procedure.

SECTION 10. Any claim within the provisions of this Act may be presented to the Commission by any member of an Indian tribe, band, or other identifiable group of Indians as the representative of all its members; but wherever any tribal organization exists, recognized by the Secretary of the Interior as having authority to represent such tribe, band, or group, such organization shall be accorded the exclusive privilege of representing such Indians, unless fraud, collusion, or laches on the part of such organization be shown to the satisfaction of the Commission.

SECTION 11. Any suit pending in the Court of Claims or the Supreme Court of the United States or which shall be filed in the Court of Claims under existing legislation, shall not be transferred to the Commission: *Provided,* That the provisions of section 2 of this Act, with respect to the deduction of payments, offsets, counterclaims and demands, shall supersede the provisions of the particular jurisdictional Act under which any pending or authorized suit in the Court of Claims has been or will be authorized; *Provided further,* That the Court of Claims in any suit pending before it at the time of the approval of this Act shall have exclusive jurisdiction to hear and determine any claim based upon fair and honorable dealings arising out of the subject matter of any such suit.

SECTION 12. The Commission shall receive claims for a period of five years after the date of the approval of this Act and no claim existing before such date but not presented within such period may thereafter be submitted to any court or administrative agency for consideration, nor will such claim thereafter be entertained by the Congress.

SECTION 13 (a) As soon as practicable the Commission shall send a written explanation of the provisions of this Act to the recognized head of each Indian tribe and band, and to any other identifiable groups of American Indians existing as distinct entities, residing within the territorial limits of the United States and Alaska, and to the superintendents of all Indian agencies, who shall promulgate the same, and shall request that a detailed statement of all claims be sent to the Commission, together with the names of aged or invalid Indians from whom depositions should be taken immediately and a summary of their proposed testimonies.

(b) The Commission shall establish an Investigation Division to investigate all claims referred to it by the Commission for the purpose of discovering the facts relating thereto. The Division shall make a complete and thorough search for all evidence affecting each claim, utilizing all documents and records in the possession of the Court of Claims and the several Government departments, and shall submit such evidence to the Commission. The Division shall make available to the Indians concerned and to any interested Federal agency any data in its possession relating to the rights and claims of any Indian.

SECTION 14. The Commission shall have the power to call upon any of the departments of the Government for any information it may deem necessary, and shall have the use of all records, hearings, and reports made by the committees of each House of Congress, when deemed necessary in the prosecution of its business.

At any hearing held hereunder, any official letter, paper, document, map, or record in the possession of any officer or department, or court of the United States or committee of Congress (or a certified copy thereof), may be used in evidence insofar as relevant and material, including any deposition or other testimony of record in any suit or proceeding in any court of the United States to which an Indian or Indian tribe or group was a party, and the appropriate department of the Government of the United States shall give to the attorneys for all tribes or groups full and free access to such letters, papers, documents, maps, or records as may be useful to said attorneys in the preparation of any claim instituted hereunder, and shall afford facilities for the examination of the same and, upon written request by said attorneys, shall furnish certified copies thereof.

SECTION 15. Each such tribe, band, or other identifiable group of Indians may retain to represent its interests in the presentation of claims before the Commission an attorney or attorneys at law, of its own selection, whose practice before the Commission shall be regulated by its adopted procedure. The fees of such attorney or attorneys for all services rendered in prosecuting the claim in question, whether before the Commission or otherwise, shall, unless the amount of such fees is stipulated in the approved contract between the attorney or attorneys and the claimant, be fixed by the Commission at such amount as the Commission, in accordance with standards obtaining for prosecuting similar contingent claims in courts of law, finds to be adequate compensation for services rendered and results obtained, considering the contingent nature of the case, plus all reasonable expenses incurred in the prosecution of the claim; but the amount so fixed by the Commission, exclusive of reimbursements for actual expenses, shall not exceed 10 per centum of the amount recovered in any case. The attorney or attorneys for any such tribe, band, or group as shall have been organized pursuant to section 16 of the Act of June 18, 1934, shall be selected pursuant to the constitution and bylaws of such tribe, band, or group. The employment of attorneys for all other claimants shall be subject to the provisions of sections 2103 to 2106, inclusive, of the Revised Statutes (25 U.S.C., sec. 81-84).

The Attorney General or his assistants shall represent the United States in all claims presented to the Commission, and shall have authority, with the approval of the Commission, to compromise any claim presented to the Commission. Any such compromise shall be submitted by the Commission to the Congress as a part of its report as provided in section 21 hereof in the same manner as final determinations of the Commission, and shall be subject to the provisions of section 22 hereof.

SECTION 16. No Senator or Member of or Delegate to Congress shall, during his continuance in office, practice before the Commission.

SECTION 17. The Commission shall give reasonable notice to the interested parties and an opportunity for them to be heard and to present evidence before making any final determination upon any claim. Hearings may be held in any part of the United States or in the Territory of Alaska.

SECTION 18. Any member of the Commission or any employee of the Commission, designated in writing for the purpose by the Chief Commissioner, may administer oaths and examine witnesses. Any member of the Commission may require by subpoena (1) the attendance and testimony of witnesses, and the production of all necessary books, papers, documents, correspondence, and other evidence, from any place in the United States or Alaska at any designated place of hearing; or (2) the taking of depositions before any designated individual competent to administer oaths under the laws of the United States or of any State or Territory. In the case of a deposition, the testimony shall be reduced to writing by the individual taking the deposition or under his direction and shall be sub-scribed by the deponent. In taking testimony, opportunity shall be given for cross-examination, under such regulations as the Commission may prescribe. Witnesses subpoenaed to testify or whose depositions are taken pursuant to this Act, and the officers or persons taking the same, shall severally be entitled to the same fees and mileage as are paid for like services in the courts of the United States.

SECTION 19. The final determination of the Commission shall be in writing, shall be filed with its clerk, and shall include (1) its findings of the facts upon which its conclusions are based; (2) a statement (a) whether there are any just grounds for relief of the claimant and, if so, the amount thereof; (b) whether there are any allowable offsets, counterclaims, or other deductions, and, if so, the amount thereof; and (3) a statement of its reasons for its findings and conclusions.

SECTION 20. (a) In considering any claim the Commission at any time may certify to the Court of Claims any definite and distinct questions of law concerning which in-structions are desired for the proper disposition of the claim; and thereupon the Court of Claims may give appropriate instructions on the questions certified and transmit the same to the Commission for its guidance in the further consideration of the claim.

(b) When the final determination of the Commission has been filed with the clerk of said Commission the clerk shall give notice of the filing of such determination to the parties to the proceeding in manner and form as directed by the Commission. At any time within three months from the date of the filing of the determination of the Commission with the clerk either party may appeal from the determination of the Commission to the Court of Claims, which Court shall have exclusive jurisdiction to affirm, modify, or set aside such final determination. On said appeal the Court shall determine whether the findings of fact of the Commission are supported by substantial evidence, in which event they shall be conclusive, and also whether the conclusions of law, including any conclusions respecting "fair and honorable dealings", where applicable, stated by the Commission as a basis for its final determination, are valid and supported by the Commission's findings of fact. In making the foregoing determinations, the Court shall review the whole record or such portions thereof as may be cited by any party, and due account shall be taken of the rule of prejudicial error. The Court may at any time remand the cause to the Commis-sion for such further proceedings as it may direct, not inconsistent with the foregoing provisions of this section.

(c) Determinations of questions of law by the Court of Claims under this section shall be subject to review by the Supreme Court of the United States in the manner prescribed by section 3 of the Act of February 13, 1925, as amended.

SECTION 21. In each claim, after the proceedings have been finally concluded, the Commission shall promptly submit its report to Congress.

The report to Congress shall contain (1) the final determination of the Commission;

(2) a transcript of the proceedings or judgment upon review, if any, with the instructions of the Court of Claims; and (3) a statement of how each Commissioner voted upon the final determination of the claim.

SECTION 22. (a) When the report of the Commission determining any claimant to be entitled to recover has been filed with Congress, such report shall have the effect of a final judgment of the Court of Claims, and there is hereby authorized to be appropriated such sums as are necessary to pay the final determination of the Commission.

The payment of any claim, after its determination in accordance with this Act, shall be a full discharge of the United States of all claims and demands touching any of the matters involved in the controversy.

(b) A final determination against a claimant made and reported in accordance with this Act shall forever bar any further claim or demand against the United States arising out of the matter involved in the controversy.

SECTION 23. The existence of the Commission shall terminate at the end of ten years after the first meeting of the Commission or at such earlier time after the expiration of the five-year period of limitation set forth in section 12 hereof as the Commission shall have made its final report to Congress on all claims filed with it. Upon its dissolution the records of the Commission shall be delivered to the Archivist of the United States.

SECTION 24. The jurisdiction of the Court of Claims is hereby extended to any claim against the United States accruing after the date of the approval of this Act in favor of any Indian tribe, band, or other identifiable group of American Indians residing within the territorial limits of the United States or Alaska whenever such claim is one arising under the Constitution, laws, treaties of the United States, or Executive orders of the President, or is one which otherwise would be cognizable in the Court of Claims if the claimant were not an Indian tribe, band, or group. In any suit brought under the jurisdiction conferred by this section the claimant shall be entitled to recover in the same manner, to the same extent, and subject to the same conditions and limitations, and the United States shall be entitled to the same defenses, both at law and in equity, and to the same offsets, counterclaims, and demands, as in cases brought in the Court of Claims under section 145 of the Judicial Code, as amended: *Provided, however,* That nothing contained in this section shall be construed as altering the fiduciary or other relations between the United States and the several Indian tribes, bands, or groups.

SECTION 25. All provisions of law inconsistent with this Act are hereby repealed to the extent of such inconsistency, except that existing provisions of law authorizing suits in the Court of Claims by particular tribes, bands, or groups of Indians and governing the conduct or determination of such suits shall continue to apply to any case heretofore or hereafter instituted thereunder save as provided by section 11 hereof as to the deduction of payments, offsets, counterclaims, and demands.

SECTION 26. If any provision of this Act, or the application thereof, is held invalid, the remainder of the Act, or other applications of such provisions, shall not be affected.

Approved August 13, 1946.

Sioux Tribe of Indians v. United States
146 F. Supp. 229 (1956)

The United States has frequently skipped back and forth between the pages of legal fictions in order to justify its actions. Nowhere is this aspect so well-illustrated as in the disgraceful material below. Using a number of illogical and irreconcilable theories of ward-dependent nation, plenary powers of Congress and treaty abrogation the court skips along spinning off inconsistencies like a new sun exploding comets as it tips its way out of the dawn of creation.

The ruling, which affects the Sioux rights to the Black Hills, is inconsistent with every known case of law that has ever dealt with treaty or tribal rights. Yet it remains law until someone sorts out the inconsistencies and forces the Supreme Court to take a definitive position.

The court cannot disclaim any relationship between the Sioux Nation and Congress while maintaining that Congress has plenary powers over the Indians. Meanwhile if the commissioners solicited the signature of ten per cent of the Sioux for the cession of the Black Hills then it would appear there was some reason for doing so other than to get autographs of famous Indian chiefs. Yet the court concludes that this was all irrelevant. Without acknowledging their existence, Congress is able to regulate them. Besides, the court feels treaties are not contracts (see *Waldron*) nor are Indians wards, nor did the whole procedure violate the treaties which need not have been made anyway.

In short, this case is a testimonial to the proposition that the United States will say anything to get out of paying for the Black Hills, a territory first thought valueless, then discovered to be rich in gold, timber and other resources and ultimately robbed from the Great Sioux Nation.

The facts of the case date back to September 17, 1851, at which time the Fort Laramie Treaty, 11 Stat. 749, was signed between the United States Government and the Sioux Tribe of Indians describing the territorial limits of the Sioux or Dahcotah Nation. As the result of subsequent gold discoveries and the resultant tide of white travelers across the Indian lands to reach the gold fields lying farther west, many conflicts between the whites and the Indians arose and resulted in the Powder River War following which the Treaty of April 29, 1868 was signed between the Sioux and the United States. This treaty was ratified February 16, 1869, and proclaimed on February 24, 1869. The treaty, in addition to other land, set apart the above referred to 7,345,157 acres for the absolute and undisturbed use and occupation of the appellant Indians as their permanent reservation and further provided in article 2 that "the United States now solemnly agrees that no persons except those herein designated and authorized so to do, and except such officers, agents, and employees of the government as may be authorized to enter upon Indian reservations in discharge of duties enjoined by law, shall ever be permitted to pass over, settle upon, or reside in the territory described in this article".

The treaty also set forth requirements for any future cession of land as follows:

Article XII. No treaty for the cession of any portion or part of the reservation herein described which may be held in common shall be of any validity or force as against the said Indians, unless executed and signed by at least three fourths of all the adult male Indians, occupying or interested in the same; and no cession by the tribe shall be understood or construed in such manner as to deprive, without his consent, any individual member of the tribe of his rights to any tract of land selected by him, as provided in Article VI. of this treaty.

At the time of the signing of the treaty it was known both to the Indians and the defendant that there was gold in the land though it was not known to what extent.

In the early 1870's many white settlers began invading the Indian lands and the United States, living up to its treaty commitments with the Indians, expelled these white people by military force. When, as the result of the Custer expedition in 1874, it became more generally known that there was gold in the Black Hills in paying quantities, the Hills were invaded by large numbers of white settlers and prospectors.

It became apparent to the President of the United States that it was imperative to have this land ceded to the United States not only for the protection of both the whites and the Indians but for the good of the entire country as well. Subsequent efforts were made by Commissioners appointed by the President to acquire the property by purchase. The Commissioners, however, were unable to get the consent of 75 per cent of the male adults of the tribe as required by the treaty of 1868. Between September 20 and October 27, 1876, however, they did manage to get the signatures of nearly all the chiefs and about 10 per cent of the male adults on an agreement ceding the Black Hills area to the United States Government and providing for certain compensation to be paid the Indians. This agreement was subsequently presented to the Congress and passed into law on February 28, 1877, supra.

It is undeniable that the ceded land was rich in gold and timber and contained huge expanses of arable lands. It is equally undeniable that at this time of history the Sioux Indians were entirely dependent upon the United States Government for their livelihood and had very little or no initiative to support themselves. They were incapable as farmers and indicated no inclination to mine the gold in their land. They were primarily hunters. Their plight was such that if they did not obtain their Government subsistence for one season they would have been reduced to starvation.

The treaty of 1868 contemplated that the Indians, with the assistance agreed to be rendered by the Government, would soon become self-supporting on their reservation. By the treaty of that year the United States agreed to provide the Indians with farming equipment, to furnish educational facilities for not less than 29 years, and to furnish each Indian with certain necessities for 30 years. The Government also agreed to pay the sum of $10 to each Indian while he roamed and hunted and $20 to each Indian who engaged in farming. In addition to these provisions, the defendant agreed to provide subsistence for the Indians for four years, this amounting to a total of $5,295,761.91 for the 4-year period. This provision was completely discharged by the disbursement of $1,314,000 under the Act of February 14, 1873. Nevertheless, Congress continued to appropriate on June 22, 1874, March 3, 1875, and April 6, 1876, large sums of money for the continued subsistence of the Sioux Indians totaling about $2,350,000. The continuing appropriations were felt to be necessary, though not obligatory on the United States, as the Sioux were not yet self-supporting, contrary to the expectations of the 1868 treaty that they would be well on their way in that direction after four years.

It must be kept in mind that all the while these unobligated appropriations and payments were being made, hostilities existed between the Indians and the whites and, concurrently, the United States Commissioners were attempting to get the Indians to cede by treaty the territory in question as well as other lands.

On August 15, 1876 another appropriation was made by the Congress to the Sioux Tribe for $1,000,000 but the act provided that none of it should be paid to the Indians while there existed hostilities between them and the white people. The appropriating act further provided that:

" . . . and hereafter there shall be no appropriation made for the subsistence of said Indians, unless they shall first agree to relinquish all right and claim to any country outside the boundaries of the permanent reservation established by the treaty of eighteen hundred and sixty-eight for said Indians; and also so much of their said permanent reservation as lies west of the one hundred and third meridian of longitude, and shall also grant right of way over said reservation to the country thus ceded for wagon or other roads, ..."

The act went on to say:

"*And provided also,* That no further appropriation for said Sioux Indians for subsistence shall hereafter be made until some stipulation, agreement, or arrangement shall have been entered into by said Indians with the President of the United States, which is calculated and designed to enable said Indians to become self-supporting: ..."

Faced with this, the above referred to chiefs and 10 per cent of the male adults signed the agreement which resulted in the Act of February 28, 1877, supra. The act provided in article V for the consideration to be paid the Sioux for the ceded territory. Under this article the United States agreed to provide "all necessary aid to assist the said Indians in the work of civilization; to furnish to them schools and instruction in mechanical and agricultural arts, as provided for by the treaty of 1868." It also stipulated that the United States would supply each Indian with a designated amount of rations as subsistence until the Indians "are able to support themselves." These subsistence commitments continue to be paid to this day and it is estimated that it will be necessary to continue the payments for many years to come at the rate of many hundreds of thousands of dollars per year as the Sioux are still incapable of supporting themselves without Governmental aid. As further consideration for the land taken, the 1877 act added 917,000 acres of grazing lands to the permanent reservation.

The appellant contends that the United States is guilty of duress in securing the signatures of the Indians that signed the agreement which led to the 1877 act ceding the land in question. As examples of the alleged duress, appellant points (1) to the appropriation act of August 15, 1876, supra, cutting off all future subsistence payments until the terms of that act were met, and (2) to other evidence in the record tending to show reprehensible methods used by the treaty commissioners to get the Indians to sign, such as, getting them drunk and then presenting the documents to them for signature. It argues also that such actions on the part of the United States constitutes unfair and dishonorable dealings.

Secondly, appellant contends that the compensation received for the lands it was forced to cede was unconscionable.

The Government denies that it acted unfairly or dishonorable and urges that the taking of the land in question, even though accomplished contrary to the expressed provisions of the treaty of 1868, was in accordance with established legal principles and was the only thing that could have been done under the circumstances when the Government's duty to all the people, whites and Indians alike, is taken into consideration. It further denies that the withdrawal of subsistence payments until the Sioux ceased hostilities and ceded parts of their land as demanded by the Act of August 15, 1876, supra, was duress as the United States was no longer obligated to make the payments. The treaty of 1868 which initiated the subsistence obligations on the part of the Government provided for them to be made for only a 4-year period. The last required payment was made three years previous to the appropriation act of 1876. The Government, in denying duress and lack of fair and honorable dealings, points also to the fact that for over two years it attempted unsuccessfully to negotiate with the Indians for the purchase of their land or, if not this, for the purchase of a license to mine the lands, and the right to grow stock and cultivate the soil as a necessary incident to the mining operations.

The government, in answer to appellant's allegation of unconscionable consideration, contends that not only was the consideration paid for the land not unconscionable but that based on projected land values in 1877 the Indians have been overpaid. It points out that the United States still makes and will have to continue to make subsistence payments for many years to come.

(1) On the question of unconscionable consideration, which is that consideration which is so much less than the actual value of the property sold that the disparity shocks the conscience, *The Osage Nation of Indians v. United States,* 1951, the appellant urges that the proper value of the lands was not the market value or sales value at the time of taking which amount they concede has already been paid them, but, rather, a sum representing all the royalties which could have been earned from leasing the right to extract minerals, in addition to payment for all the timber lands that are part of the land in question. The basis of this theory of compensation is that because of the alleged legal relationship of guardian and ward existing between the Sioux and the United States, the United States had no power to appropriate the ward's property even on payment of its sales value, but only the power to manage that property for the continuing benefit of the ward and pay over to the ward the proceeds realized by the guardian's best efforts. The appellant insists that since it was known to the defendant that gold and silver in paying quantities were in the lands, the Government should have developed the lands and operated the mines for the benefit of the Indian tribes as a necessary corollary to its fiduciary position as guardian of its ward Indians. The argument is, in effect, that the guardian-ward relationship existing between the United States Government and the Sioux Indians is the same fiduciary relationship that exists between the guardian and ward in private law. This being so, the Government's action in forcing the Indians to cede to it their land was a violation of their fiduciary duty to their wards to manage its property to the benefit of the wards.

The Government disputes this method of determining the proper measure of compensation for the land taken, asserting that the proper measure is found by comparing the consideration provided for in the act requiring the cession to the market value of the property at the time of the involuntary cession.

The Indian Claims Commission decided (1) that the contention of the Government relating to compensation was correct; (2) that the consideration received by the plaintiff was not inadequate or unconscionable; and (3) that the Government made a strenuously sincere effort to reach a fair basis of cession of the gold and silver producing lands to the Government, pointing out that the Indians themselves could not subsist on the gold and silver in the hills, nor extract the minerals or develop commercial mines. The Commission therefore concluded that the Indians were treated fairly and honorably and that the consideration received for the ceded land was not inadequate or unconscionable. *The Sioux Tribe of Indians v. United States,* 2 Ind. Cls. Comm. 646.

This court is in complete agreement with all the findings of fact and conclusions of law of the Commission and, therefore, denies appellants request for reversal.

(2) The appellant's allegation of duress is of no avail under the circumstances of this case because regardless of the reprehensible methods that may have been used by the Commissioners in getting signatures on the 1877 agreement, it was not the agreement that caused the cession of land, but the subsequent act of Congress. The agreement as submitted by the treaty commissioners was ineffectual since it did not meet the requirements of the 1868 treaty for the cession of land. The fact that reprehensible methods were used to get signatures on a document that was binding on no one does not constitute duress. The treaty commissioners' mission was a complete failure. Since their actions did not result in the cession of the land, they cannot be the basis for an allegation of duress.

(3) While it had been the practice and policy of the United States Government during the many years of tension between the whites and the Indians to negotiate with them by

treaty convention and to settle differences, if possible, by treaty, those treaties did not absolutely abrogate the right of the Government to regulate the Indians or, when necessary, to legislate contrary to or inconsistently with a treaty. The primary consideration must be the good of the country and the duty the Government owes to all its citizens, not only the obligation that arose as the result of a previous treaty with the Indians or the duty that was created in the United States by virtue of its superior bargaining position in relation to a weak and defenseless people.

In *Lone Wolf v. Hitchcock,* the Court said:

> "The power exists to abrogate the provisions of an Indian treaty, though presumably such power will be exercised only when circumstances arise which will not only justify the government in disregarding the stipulations of the treaty, but may demand, in the interest of the country and the Indians themselves, that it should do so. When, therefore, treaties were entered into between the United States and a tribe of Indians it was never doubted that the *power* to abrogate existed in Congress, and that in a contingency such power might be availed of from considerations of governmental policy, particularly if consistent with perfect good faith towards the Indians ... "

(4) Treaties with the Indians are no different than any other public laws and are subject to contrary legislation by the Congress when it is felt to be in the interest of the country. By the same token, treaties with foreign countries can be breached by legislation from the Congress if it is deemed to be in the best interests of the country.

The Court further said in *Lone Wolf v. Hitchcock:*

> " ... Until the year 1871 the policy was pursued of dealing with the Indian tribes by means of treaties, and, of course, a moral obligation rested upon Congress to act in good faith in performing the stipulations entered into on its behalf. But, as with treaties made with foreign nations, the legislative power might pass laws in conflict with treaties made with the Indians."

The Supreme Court, in *Choate v. Trapp,* while speaking on this subject, stated as follows:

> " ... the plenary power of Congress over the Indian tribes and tribal property cannot be limited by treaties so as to prevent repeal or amendment by a later statute. The tribes have been regarded as dependent nations, and treaties with them have been looked upon not as contracts, but as public laws which could be abrogated at the will of the United States."

(5,6) The state of the law being thus, the fact that the defendant did not secure the required 75 per cent of the male adult signatures on the 1876 agreement with the Indians is immaterial. The Government was free to legislate in spite of this and, in fact could have legislated without even attempting to negotiate an agreement. The only standard the Government had to observe was that it be in the best interests of the country to enact such contrary legislation, and that the Indians be treated fairly by it in view of the fact that they had been made certain guarantees by the treaty that was about to be abrogated. Fair treatment would include payment by the United States of just compensation for the lands taken. This, of course, would be necessary whether the suit involved Indians or other citizens. As the Court stated in Missouri, *Kansas & Texas Railway Company v. Roberts,* " ... the United States will be governed by such considerations of justice as will control a Christian people in their treatment of an ignorant and dependent race..."

(7) It may be further pointed out that it is a basic principle of Indian law that even when lands are granted to a tribe of Indians by treaty, the fee remains in the United States subject to the Indians right of occupation. While the Indians have a better title than they

had before the treaty guaranteed the land to them, it is not absolute. They cannot alienate the land without the permission of the Government of the United States.

"Though the lands of the Indians were reserved by treaty for their occupation, *the fee was always under the control of the government;* and when transferred, without reference to the possession of the lands, and without designation of any use of them requiring the delivery of their possession, the transfer was subject to their right of occupancy; and the manner, time, and conditions on which that right should be extinguished were matters for the determination of the government, and not for legal contestation in the courts between private parties. This doctrine is applicable, generally, to the rights of Indians to lands occupied by them under similar conditions. . . . *The right of the United States to dispose of the fee of land occupied by them, . . . has always been recognized by this court from the foundation of the government."* Missouri, Kansas & Texas Ry. Co. v. Roberts.

The aforementioned being the controlling principles of law, the court cannot sustain the allegation of duress and must declare that the Governments's action in requiring the cession of the land was, at least, not improper though it is liable to the extent of paying the Indians just compensation for the lands acquired.

(8) The appellant's reliance on its guardian-ward theory of determining the conscionableness of the consideration is not well founded. If the United States was in any legal sense the guardian of the Sioux with respect to the property in question, there might be some merit to appellant's argument. However, we do not find that the legal relationship of guardian and ward did exist between the United States and the Sioux. While it has often been said by this court and the Supreme Court that the general relationship of the Government to the Indians of the United States is *similar* to that of a guardian and ward, it has never been held that such a general relationship amounts to a legal guardian-ward relationship in the absence of some specific language to that effect in a treaty, agreement, or act of Congress. In the absence of such specific language, the general relationship of the United States to the Indians has been that of a strong and powerful sovereign to a comparatively weak and defenseless people and because of that fact, the courts have likened the relationship to that of guardian and ward and held that doubts in treaties and agreements should be resolved in favor of the weak and defenseless party to such treaties and agreements. This issue of the existence of a legal guardian-ward relationship between the Indians and the United States absent a specific provision in a treaty or agreement spelling out such a relationship was before this court in the case of *Gila River Pima-Maricopa Indian Community v. United States,* which stated:

"Whether or not the legal relationship of guardian and ward exists between a particular Indian tribe and the United States depends, we think, upon the express provisions of the particular treaty, agreement, executive order, or statute under which the claim presented arises. It is true that the word 'fiduciary' and the expression 'guardian-ward relationship' have been used by the courts to describe generally the nature of the relationship existing between the Indians and the Government. However, in the absence of some language in a treaty, agreement or statute spelling out such a relationship, the courts seem to have meant merely that the relationship between the Indians and the Government is 'similar to' or 'resembles' such a legal relationship and that doubtful language in the treaty or statute under consideration should be interpreted in favor of the weak and dependent Indians." *Creek Nation v. United States.*

A reference to the Treaty of Fort Laramie, supra, or the treaty of 1868, supra, upon which this claim is based, will show no provision whereby the United States assumes the status of guardian of the Sioux Tribe of Indians in relation to the land in question.

Accordingly, appellant cannot properly base this claim for conscionable consideration on the amount it would have received had the Government been required to manage the appellant's property as a legal guardian for the benefit of its ward.

The appellant does not, and well it cannot, question the power of the Government to take the property in question upon the payment of just compensation. It asserts its guardian-ward argument only as a means of substantiating its theory of compensation on a royalty basis.

(9,10) It is a long established rule that just compensation must be based on the value of the property as of the time of its acquisition by the Government, in this case February 28, 1877; *United States v. Miller,* 1943. In determining just what the value of the land was at the time of acquisition many things must be taken into consideration including the minerals in the ground and the timber standing thereon. *United States v. Shoshone Tribe,* 1938. Not to be forgotten in establishing this valuation are the facilities available for extracting the minerals and the means of transportation available after they have been extracted. Therefore, mere knowledge that gold in paying quantities lay beneath the ground in a given tract of land does not make it valuable if it can be mined only at an exorbitant expense. Thus, the projected value of a piece of gold bearing land in 1877 would not be as great as it is in this present day of rapid transportation and modern mining methods. The appellant seems to agree with these considerations in valuing a piece of property as it conceded that if the property, for the purposes of this suit, is to be valued as of 1877 they have already been overpaid for the property.

(11) Since the appellant admits that as a result of the treaty of 1868 and its provisions for payment for the land it has already been paid in excess of the 1877 value of the land in question, and since the proper method of compensating for property taken is to base it on land values at the time of the acquisition, the appellant's claim is without merit. The Sioux have been justly compensated for the land they were forced to cede to the United States.

On appeal the appellant asserts that the Commission's findings of fact numbered 19, 22, and 23 are in error. The court does not find any error as the findings are substantially supported by the evidence in the record.

Finding 19, relating to duress or undue influence in securing the signatures of the Indians on the agreement which formed the basis for the 1877 act, has been discussed earlier herein. Finding 23, to the effect that the Indians were paid conscionable consideration and dealt with fairly and honorably under all the circumstances in relation to the land in question, has also been discussed earlier herein. Finding 22 is to the effect that the evidence in the record failed to establish that the Government or subsequent private owners of the land in question profited in any way from the gold and silver mined from the land; that the evidence also failed to establish what expense was involved in the mining of gold and silver from the property in question or that a monetary consideration based on a guess as to the prospective value of the mineral deposits in the land would have been as safe a provision for the future subsistence of the Indians as the actual monetary consideration provided for the land in the 1877 act. While this finding may not have been necessary to support the Commission's decision, it is true that the evidence in the record does not establish any of the facts stated, and that circumstance does bolster the Commission's conclusion that the Indians were fairly and honorably treated and that the consideration paid them for their land was not unconscionable in view of all the facts and circumstances.

Appellant also makes seven specifications of errors of law. The first two relate to the guardian-ward relationship which has already been disposed of above. The third and fourth are as follows:

"(3) It was error for the Commission to enter a dismissal of Plaintiffs' petition at a preliminary stage of the proccedings, when the entire matter was before

154

the Commission on a pretrial basis, without proof but based on estimates of mineral and timber production."

"(4) It was error for the Commission to enter a decision dismissing the case without extending to the Plaintiffs' the right to establish, by testimony, the contentions of Plaintiffs."

The proceedings were not dismissed at the pretrial stage. The plaintiff's case had already been rested once and a motion to dismiss for failure of proof was made by defendant, but denied. Plaintiff offered no proof of the value of the land. It was plaintiff's contention that the question of liability should be determined first, and only after that was decided should proof of value be determined. Subsequent briefs by the plaintiff and defendant were permitted by the Commission. In its briefs, and orally before the Commission, plaintiff insisted on its theory of determining the proper compensation for the lands, it being based on a percentage of the value of minerals extracted since the date of acquisition by the United States. The Commission disagreed, and announced to the plaintiff that the correct method would be by proving the value of the land at the date of acquisition by the Government. The plaintiff did not indicate that it would attempt to prove what the value was on that date and did not offer any evidence to that effect. The Commission then made its findings and conclusions denying the plaintiff recovery. If, as argued for in assignment of error number (4), the Commission had allowed the Plaintiff to establish its contentions by testimony respecting value based on later royalty payments, the result would have been nothing but a waste of time. Assuming without deciding that it was error for the Commission not to allow plaintiff to introduce evidence supporting its theory of value, it was harmless error and not prejudicial to the plaintiff's case.

The fifth specification of error of law complains that the Commission disregarded the plaintiff's pleas for relief under categories numbered (2), (3), (4), and (5) of section 2 of the Indian Claims Commission Act, supra. There is no merit in this specification. The Commission in its decision and findings specifically ruled on the conscionableness of the consideration, duress, and fair and honorable dealings, such being the substance of categories numbered (3) and (5). Category (2), we think, involves a claim already decided by this court, *Sioux Tribe of Indians v. United States,* 1943, when this identical case was tried and decided before this court under a special jurisdictional act, authorizing the Court of Claims "to hear and determine all legal and equitable claims, if any, of said tribe against the United States, and to enter judgment thereon." The Court there held that the claimants had no legal right to any compensation other than that which was provided for by the Act of February 28, 1877, and stated that the only claim the Sioux Indians had, if they had one at all, was moral and until the court was given jurisdiction by the Congress to hear a moral claim it could not act. The Commission has been given the jurisdiction to hear moral claims under categories numbered (3) and (5). The appellant in this case can bring suit only under those categories. It has done so and relief has been denied.

(12) Category (4) does not give the appellant in this case a claim. That category was included to cover these situations where the United States had, after mutual agreement as to price, acquired Indian land by treaty of cession or otherwise but did not subsequently pay the price already agreed to by the Indians. It does not, as claimed by appellant, give jurisdiction in a situation where land that was taken from the claimant and was actually paid for but in an amount not agreed to by the claimant as is the situation in the case at hand. Payment of the consideration provided for in the act of cession in this case was never withheld from the Indians, in fact, payments are still being made and will continue to be made.

Specifications of error of law numbered (6) and (7) relate to conscionable consideration and duress and have already been disposed of in other parts of this opinion. The decision of the Indian Claims Commission is affirmed.

The Baker Massacre of the Blackfeet

While Wounded Knee and Sand Creek stand out as days of infamy little is known about other massacres which, while as violent and dastardly, did not attract the national concern necessary to be remembered. During the hearings on conditions in the United States of the Indian people some testimony was introduced into the record of an obscure massacre of the Blackfeet Indians of Montana that was fully as horrible as either Wounded Knee or Sand Creek.

It had, in fact, so many similarities with the two more famous massacres that it is possible that events of the Blackfeet massacre were gradually merged with incidents of general knowledge, so that every time someone would mention the massacre of Bear's Head's people they would be told that the event they were trying to remember was really Wounded Knee or Sand Creek.

In order that the innocent Blackfeet did not die in vain, an excerpt from the testimony covering this event is presented herewith. As surely as Wounded Knee and Sand Creek cry out for reparations so the slaughter of the Blackfeet deserves compensation also.

Still worse was the Baker massacre of Blackfeet on January 23, 1870.

A border ruffian, a white man named Clark, had assaulted a young Indian, beating him severely, and the Indian, in retaliation, had killed Clark and gone off into Canada. Without troubling to find the guilty party, or even the band he belonged to, Brevet Col. E. M. Baker, Major, Second Cavalry, stationed at Fort Shaw, marched out, under orders from Gen. Philip H. Sheridan, to the nearest Indian village, on Marias River; as it happened, they were peaceable, friendly Indians, under Bear's Head. Without warning, the soldiers silently surrounded the sleeping village. But the story is better told by Schultz, who was on the spot later, and heard it all from those who saw:

"In a low tone Colonel Baker spoke a few words to his men, telling them to keep cool, aim to kill, to spare none of the enemy; and then he gave the command to fire. A terrible scene ensued. On the day previous, many of the men of the camp had gone out toward the Sweetgrass Hills on a grand buffalo hunt; so, save for Chief Bear's Head and a few old men, none were there to return the soldiers' fire. Their first volley was aimed low down into the lodges, and many of the sleeping people were killed or wounded in their beds. The rest rushed out, men, children, women, many of the latter with babes in their arms, only to be shot down at the doorways of their lodges.

"Bear's Head, frantically waving a paper which bore testimony to his good character and friendliness to the white men, ran toward the command on the bluff, shouting to them to cease firing, entreating them to save the women and children; down he also went with several bullet holes in his body. Of the more than 400 souls in camp at the time, very few escaped. And when it was all over, when the last wounded woman and child had been put out of misery, the soldiers piled the corpses on overturned lodges, firewood, and household property and set fire to it all.

"Several years afterward I was on the ground. Everywhere scattered about in the long grass and brush, just where the wolves and foxes had left them, gleamed the skulls and bones of those who had been so ruthlessly slaughtered. 'How could they have done it?' I asked myself time and time again. 'What manner of men were these soldiers who deliberately shot down defenseless women and innocent children?' They had not even the excuse of being drunk; nor was their commanding officer intoxicated; nor were they excited or in any danger whatever. Deliberately, coolly, with steady and deadly aim they shot them down, killed the wounded, and then tried to burn the bodies of their victims. But I will say no more about it. Think it over, yourself, and try to find a fit name for men who did this."

According to G. B. Grinnell, 176 innocent persons were butchered on this day of shame; 90 of them women, 55 babies, the rest chiefly very old or very young men, most of the able-bodied hunters being away on a hunt. No punishment of any kind was given the monsters who did it.

There is no Indian massacre of whites to compare with this shocking barbarity, for at least the Indian always had the excuse that war had been declared and he was acting on the defensive. Of a similar character were the massacres at Cos Cob, 1641; Conestoga, 1763; Gnadenwhuetten, 1782; Coquille River 1854; Wounded Knee, 1890; and a hundred more that could be mentioned. And no punishment was ever meted out to the murderers. Why? First, because, apparently, the bureau at Washington approved; second, because "An Indian has no legal status; he is merely a live and particularly troublesome animal in the eye of the law." *(Survey of Conditions of Indians in the United States, Part 26, 1930, pp. 14042-14043.)*

The Sand Creek Massacre

One of the most savage acts in the history of warfare occurred right here in the United States when the troops of Colonel Chivington (a Methodist minister) ruthlessly slaughtered the camp of Black Kettle, chief of the friendly Cheyennes.

The tribe had been promised protection against both the United States troops and marauding hostiles who sought to embroil them in the fight for hunting grounds in eastern Colorado. Flying the American flag as they had been instructed, the camp lay peacefully asleep when it was surrounded by United States cavalry and leveled. Avco-Embassy made a film in 1970 entitled *Soldier Blue* which depicted the Sand Creek Massacre. It showed only some of the atrocities that were committed against the innocent Cheyennes—many had to be left on the cutting room floor to spare the sensibilities of the audience. Many more could not even be filmed!!

Some years later at the signing of the Medicine Lodge Treaty the tribe was guaranteed compensation for Chivington's depredations. But when the treaty came to Congress for ratification, the section admitting the liability of the United States was deleted from the treaty—this in spite of a report of a House of Representatives committee sent to investigate the incident, which clearly established the liability of the United States.

In a number of Congresses bills were introduced to compensate the tribe for the depredations by the United States. None ever passed the full Congress so the liability and the treaty provision remain as mute testaments to the infidelity of the United States government.

On the night of the 28th (of December, 1864) the entire party started from Fort Lyon, and, by a forced march, arrived at the Indian camp, on Sand Creek, shortly after daybreak. This Indian camp consisted of about 100 lodges of Cheyennes, under Black Kettle, and from 8 to 10 lodges of Arapahoes under Left Hand. It is estimated that each lodge contained five or more persons, and that more than one-half were women and children.

Upon observing the approach of the soldiers, Black Kettle, the head chief, ran up to the top of his lodge an American flag, which had been presented to him some years before by Commissioner Greenwood, with a small white flag under it, as he had been advised to do in case he met with any troops on the prairies. Mr. Smith, the interpreter, supposing they might be strange troops, unaware of the character of the Indians encamped there, advanced from his lodge to meet them, but was fired upon and returned to his lodge.

And then the scene of murder and barbarity began — men, women, and children were indiscriminately slaughtered. In a few minutes all the Indians were flying over the plain in terror and confusion. A few who endeavored to hide themselves under the bank of the creek were surrounded and shot down in cold blood, offering little resistance. From the sucking babe to the old warrior, all who were overtaken were deliberately murdered. Not content with killing women and children who were incapable of offering any resistance, the soldiers indulged in acts of barbarity of the most revolting character; such, it is to be hoped, as never before disgraced the acts of men claiming to be civilized. No attempt was made by the officers to restrain the savage cruelty of the men under their command, but they stood by and witnessed these acts without one word of reproof, if they did not incite their commission. For more than two hours the work of murder and barbarity was continued, until more than one hundred dead bodies, three-fourths of them of women and children lay on the plain as evidence of the fiendish malignity and cruelty of the officers who had so sedulously and carefully plotted the massacre, and of the soldiers who had so faithfully acted out the spirit of their officers.

It is difficult to believe that beings in the forms of men, and disgracing the uniform of United States soldiers and officers, could commit or countenance the commission of such acts of cruelty and barbarity as are detailed in the testimony, but which your committee will not specify in their report. It is true that there seems to have existed among the people inhabiting that region of country a hostile feeling towards the Indians. Some of the Indians had committed acts of hostility towards the whites; but no effort seems to have been made by the authorities there to prevent these hostilities, other than by the commission of even worse acts. The hatred of the whites to the Indians would seem to have been inflamed and excited to the utmost; the bodies of persons killed at a great distance—whether by Indians or not, it is not certain—were brought to the capital of the Territory and exposed to the public gaze for the purpose of inflaming still more the already excited feeling of the people. Their cupidity was appealed to, for the governor in a proclamation calls upon all "either individually or in such parties as they may organize", "to kill and destroy as enemies of the country, wherever they may be found, all such hostile Indians" authorizing them to "hold to their own private use and benefit all the property of said hostile Indians that they may capture". What Indians he would ever term friendly it is impossible to tell. His testimony before your committee was characterized by such prevarication and shuffling as has been shown by no witness they have examined during the four years they have been engaged in their investigations; and for the evident purpose of avoiding the admission that he was fully aware that the Indians massacred so brutally at Sand Creek, were then, and had been, actuated by the most friendly feelings towards the whites, and had done all in their power to restrain those less friendly disposed.

The testimony of Major Anthony, who succeeded an officer disposed to treat these Indians with justice and humanity, is sufficient of itself to show how unprovoked and unwarranted was this massacre. He testifies that he found these Indians in the neighborhood of Fort Lyon when he assumed command of that post; that they professed their friendliness to the whites, and their willingness to do whatever he demanded of them; that they delivered their arms up to him; that they went to and encamped upon the place designated by him; that they gave him information from time to time of acts of hostility which were meditated by other and hostile bands, and in every way conducted themselves properly and peaceably, and yet he says it was fear and not principle which prevented his killing them while they were completely in his power. And when Colonel Chivington appeared at Fort Lyon, on his mission of murder and barbarity, Major Anthony made haste to accompany him with men and artillery, although Colonel Chivington had no authority whatever over him.

As to Colonel Chivington, your committee can hardly find fitting terms to describe his conduct. Wearing the uniform of the United States, which should be the emblem of justice and humanity; holding the important position of commander of a military district, and therefore having the honor of the government to that extent in his keeping, he deliberately planned and executed a foul and dastardly massacre which would have disgraced the veriest savage among those who were the victims of his cruelty. Having full knowledge of their friendly character, having himself been instrumental to some extent in placing them in their position of fancied security, he took advantage of their inapprehension and defenceless condition to gratify the worst passions that ever cursed the heart of man. It is thought by some that desire for political preferment prompted him to this cowardly act; that he supposed that by pandering to the inflamed passions of an excited population he could recommend himself to their regard and consideration. Others think it was to avoid the being sent where there was more of danger and hard service to be performed; that he was willing to get up a show of hostility on the part of the Indians by committing himself acts which savages themselves would never premeditate. Whatever may have been his motive, it is to be hoped that the authority of this government will never again be disgraced by acts such as he and those acting with him have been guilty of committing.

There were *hostile* Indians not far distant, against which Colonel Chivington could have led the force under his command. Major Anthony testifies that but three or four days' march from his post were several hundreds of Indians, generally believed to be engaged in acts of hostility towards the whites. And he deliberately testifies that only the fear of them prevented him from killing those who were friendly and entirely within his reach and control. It is true that to reach them required some days of hard marching. It was not to be expected that they could be surprised as easily as those on Sand Creek; and the warriors among them were almost, if not quite, as numerous as the soldiers under the control of Colonel Chivington. Whatever influence this may have had upon Colonel Chivington, the truth is that he surprised and murdered, in cold blood, the unsuspecting men, women, and children on Sand Creek, who had every reason to believe they were under the protection of the United States authorities, and then returned to Denver and boasted of the brave deeds he and the men under his command had performed. (House Report, Massacre of Cheyenne Indians, January 10, 1865.)

TESTIMONY OF UNITED STATES SOLDIERS
The Massacre at Sand Creek, Colorado

John S. Smith, Interpreter

Question: Were the women and children slaughtered indiscriminately, or only so far as they were with the warriors?

Answer: Indiscriminately.

Question: Were there any acts of barbarity perpetrated there that came under your own observation?

Answer: Yes, sir; I saw the bodies of those lying there cut all to pieces, worse mutilated than any I ever saw before, the women all cut to pieces.

Question: How cut?

Answer: With knives; scalped; their brains knocked out; children two or three months old; all ages lying there, from sucking infants up to warriors.

Question: Did you see it done?

Answer: Yes, sir. I saw them fall.

Question: Fall when they were killed?

Answer: Yes, sir.

Question: By whom were they mutilated?

Answer: By the United States troops.

Major Scott J. Anthony

I saw one instance, however. There was one little child, probably three years old, just big enough to walk through the sand. The Indians had gone ahead, and this little child was behind following after them. The little fellow was perfectly naked, travelling on the sand. I saw one man get off his horse, at a distance of about seventy-five yards, and draw up his rifle and fire—he missed the child. Another man came up and said "Let me try the son of a bitch; I can hit him." He got down off his horse, kneeled down and fired at the little child, but he missed him. A third man came up and made a similar remark, and fired, and the little fellow dropped.

James D. Cannan, First Lieutenant.

In going over the battle-ground the next day, I did not see a body of man, woman, or child but was scalped; and in many instances their bodies were mutilated in the most horrible manner, men, women, and children—privates cut out, etc. I heard one man say that he had cut a woman's private parts out and had them for exhibition on a stick; I heard another man say that he had cut the fingers off an Indian to get the rings on the hand. According to the best of my knowledge and belief, these atrocities that were committed were with the knowledge of J.M. Chivington, and I do not know of his taking any measures to prevent them. I heard of one instance of a child a few months old being thrown in the feed-box of a wagon, and after being carried some distance, left on the ground to perish. I also heard of numerous instances in which men had cut out the private parts of females, and stretched them over the saddle-bows, and wore them over their hats, while riding in the ranks.

In a later treaty the United States promised to compensate the Cheyennes and Arapahos for the depredations which Chivington's troops had committed against their people. But when the treaty got to Washington for ratification Congress casually deleted the provision for compensation. For years the Indians were led to believe that they would still be compensated but in fact there was no intention to resolve the incident or compensate the tribes.

Sand Creek is a more blatant example of what happened at Wounded Knee. There is no question but that the United States is liable for the atrocities committed. Whenever Wounded Knee is brought up the Army immediately attempts to justify the massacre as a battle. Some conservative Senators blithely pass the massacre off as a "battle" just as today they speak of My Lai in complimentary terms. But there has never been any question as to the Sand Creek massacre. The United States, after positively acknowledging responsibility, has simply refused to move.

Before there can be any warm feelings that we are all "one people", the United States must make compensation to the Cheyennes and Arapahos for Sand Creek. No Indian can view a western movie without remembering, in the back of his mind, that it wasn't even as fair as it appears on the screen. Indians remember that the United States Army led by a Methodist minister ruthlessly slaughtered nearly five hundred defenseless Indians because of a racial hatred of red men that went far beyond considerations of humanity or decency.

A BILL

Authorizing payment of indemnities to the descendants of Cheyenne and Arapaho Indians who lost relatives or property in the Sand Creek Massacre and were entitled to indemnities under the treaty of October 14, 1865.

Be it enacted by the Senate and House of Representatives of the United States of America in Congress assembled, That there is hereby authorized to be appropriated not more than $1,500,000 for the purpose of making payment to the descendants of all those Cheyenne and Arapaho Indians who were entitled to indemnities under the terms of the treaty of October 14, 1865 (14 Stat. 703), together with interest at 6 per centum from the date such indemnities became due until payment thereof.

Section 2. The Secretary of the Interior shall appoint a board of three appraisers to appraise the value of land which was to have been conveyed to those entitled thereto under the terms of said treaty of October 14, 1865, and to return said appraisal to the Secretary of the Interior within a reasonable time, but not later than three months after the appointment of the board.

Section 3. The Secretary of the Interior shall make and promulgate rules and regulations for the making and paying of claims by the descendants of those entitled to indemnities under such treaty of October 14, 1865. The Sand Creek Descendants Association, a corporation, is hereby authorized to represent claimants to such indemnities and to assist in establishing heirship of all those making such claims, and may be paid such percentage of such claims as may be determined to be reasonable by the Secretary of the Interior.

Section 4. All descendants of those entitled to indemnities under such treaty of October 14, 1865, shall be paid per stirpes for the value of lands and property lost, together with interest thereon as provided in this Act.

Section 5. In determining heirship for the purposes of this Act, the list of names and properties, together with values placed thereon, called "Schedule of Property Lost at Sand Creek by Cheyennes and Arapahos, Annexed to Treaty of October 14, 1865," may be used, but shall not be conclusive as to all such persons and property.

Section 6. All claims under this Act must be filed with the Secretary of the Interior within six years of the date of enactment of this Act.

The Wounded Knee Massacre

In the late 1930's a hearing was held to determine the liability of the United States for the Wounded Knee Massacre where several hundred innocent men, women, and children were ruthlessly slaughtered by soldiers of the Seventh Cavalry and left to die in a three-day blizzard. The Department of the Army, in the face of overwhelming evidence to the contrary, maintained that the incident was a battle. When bodies of Indian women were found with wounds in the back three and four miles from the scene of the slaughter the Army maintained that the incidents were unrelated.

In the same way that the contemporary Army insists on covering up the massacre of innocent Vietnamese peasants, so in the 1930's did representatives of the Army deny all knowledge of genocide—this in the face of survivors sitting across the table. The excerpts that follow describe some of the incidents at Wounded Knee. Needless to say the United States has never sought fit to reimburse the survivors of the massacre or their descendants. In view of the American experience of the last two decades it would be fitting to pass this legislation now, as a belated effort to do what is right.

STATEMENT OF JAMES H. RED CLOUD
(in support of legislation to compensate victims
of the Wounded Knee Massacre)

In compliance with the orders of the United States Government and the Army, where they made these treaties with us we laid down our arms. Then we started up the way. We pledged our people to support the United States Government by laying down our arms. We agreed to adopt the social and every other mode of living and at one time we held the entire country that you own today.

Although those treaties were made prior to that killing, you came in there and murdered and slaughtered our babies.

You made a pledge through the treaty that anybody who committed an offense shall pay the penalty or compensate for same, and that is all we are here to ask for, compensation for the survivors of Wounded Knee.

In 1877 you made agreements that any Indians who shall commit an offense of murder or slaughter shall be punished, and so you took and hung a member of our tribe, Two Sticks. Now, we ask you to live up to your agreement.

You came here and we received you with our hospitality, we extended all courtesy to you, and you returned to us powder and crowded us to the outer parts of our country.

You have taken the wealth and resources of our country and called it your own and we have none; we are starving today.

We are presenting our claim, legitimate claim, not as a racket but legitimate claim for the wrong that has been done us.

You higher Congressmen in both Houses do not know the actual living conditions of the Indians today. Very few Congressmen from the Indian country understand the economic conditions of the American Indians. They are all starving. You are all bucking the American Indian issue.

The majority has ruled; they have depopulated this country from Indians; they have depopulated the horse population; they have taken everything that we had and we are starving. We are in need. We are in dire need. We are, therefore, here trying to get aid through you Congressmen.

TESTIMONY OF THE SURVIVORS

American Horse.

The men were separated as has already been said from the women, and they were surrounded by the soldiers. Then came next the village of the Indians and that was entirely surrounded by the soldiers also. When the firing began, of course the people who were standing immediately around the young man who fired the first shot were killed right together, and then they turned their guns, Hotchkiss guns, and so forth, upon the women who were in the lodges standing there under a flag of truce, and of course as soon as they were fired upon they fled, the men fleeing in one direction and the women running in two different directions. So that there were three general directions in which they took flight.

There was a woman with an infant in her arms who was killed as she almost touched the flag of truce, and the women and children of course were strewn all along the circular village until they were dispatched. Right near the flag of truce a mother was shot down with her infant; the child not knowing that its mother was dead was still nursing, and that was especially a very sad sight. The women as they were fleeing with their babes on their backs were killed together, shot right through, and the women who were very heavy with child were also killed. All the Indians fled in these three directions, and after most all of them had been killed a cry was made that all those who were not killed or wounded should come forth and they would be safe. Little boys who were not wounded came out of their places of refuge, and as soon as they came in sight a number of soldiers surrounded them and butchered them there.

Of course we all feel very sad about this affair. I stood very loyal to the Government all through those troublesome days, and believing so much in the Government and being so loyal to it, my disappointment was very strong, and I have come to Washington with a very great blame on my heart. Of course it would have been alright if only the men were killed; we would feel almost grateful for it. But the fact of the killing of the women and more especially the killing of the young boys and girls who are to go to make up the future strength of the Indian people, is the saddest part of the whole affair and we feel it very sorely.

Dewey Beard.

I would like to tell you gentlemen today that there was no reason at all that the United States troops massacred the Big Foot band. I want to bring out the fact that the United States has done what we call one of the biggest murders, as we call them, and that the United States must be ashamed of it, or something, because they have never offered to re-imburse us or settle in any way.

At that time we stuck up our white flag, and they took our guns away from us. When we were bare-handed they cut loose on us. The children did not know what was going on. We always had been told that when the white flag was stuck up there would be no trouble, and the people believed in that white flag. All at once they cut loose on us, and at that time I was shot in the leg, and up till today I never found out why they did that to me—shot me like that; and some time I would like to find out what was the reason why the American troops should do that; why they should ever injure anybody unless anyone was bothering the law. But still they shot me down.

The United States soldiers murdered the bunch of us, and they have never made an offer of any kind of settlement.

In saying a few words on this massacre, I want to point out a very few of the things that I have seen with my own eyes at that time. At that time my wife and I had a baby of 22 days old, and right at the time when the firing started I missed my wife, and later I found out that she was shot through the breast. The little 22-day-old baby was nursing from the same side where the mother was wounded and the child was choked with blood. A few days afterwards the little boy died.

I saw on that field small children like that lying by the side of their mothers, and I saw four or five of them lying there frozen to death.

After that—they knew I was wounded; I was shot in the leg, and I fell down; they knew I was wounded and helpless, and they came and shot me all over again, in the breast. I was laying off there to one side, right by the camp side, and the soldiers were going through the field, and the men and women were wounded and could not help themselves, and the soldiers came over there and put the bullets through them again.

The massacre at Wounded Knee was a slaughter of innocent frightened Indians who just happened to be in the way when the American soldiers felt like killing someone. It is not difficult to understand the incidents in Southeast Asia if one knows anything about Wounded Knee. The recent report of a government committee stating that My Lai was so out of character that it raised the defense of temporary insanity for the soldiers participating shows an appalling lack of knowledge of American history.

The following was introduced in four consecutive Congresses in the late thirties and early forties. There were hearings, but the House Committee which received the testimony never did anything about the bill. On that committee was Will Rogers, Jr., the famous Cherokee Indian, who also saw no reason to get the bill enacted into law.

Many of the people who survived Wounded Knee are now gone. Various promoters keep offering to build a "Disneyland—plains" on the site of the massacre. Thus not only has the incident been uncompensated but it may be that the ultimate exploitation will be an annual re-enactment of the "battle". It is imperative that someone take a stand and see that the descendants are adequately compensated for this massacre. It is the least that can be done.

A BILL TO LIQUIDATE THE LIABILITY OF THE UNITED STATES FOR THE MASSACRE OF SIOUX INDIAN MEN, WOMEN, AND CHILDREN AT WOUNDED KNEE ON DECEMBER 29, 1890

Be it enacted by the Senate and House of Representatives of the United States of America in Congress assembled, That there is hereby authorized to be appropriated, out of any money in the Treasury not otherwise appropriated, the amounts indicated herein: For each Sioux Indian man, woman, or child who suffered death in the massacre of the Sioux Indians at Wounded Knee Creek on December 29, 1890, the sum of $1,000, which shall be paid to the heirs of such deceased Indian; for each man, woman, or child who suffered wounds or other bodily injury in said massacre the sum of $1,000, which shall be paid to the injured individual, if living, or to his heirs, if deceased:
· *Provided,* The Secretary of the Interior be, and he is hereby directed to investigate and report to Congress by January 4, 1938, and show the names, sex, and approximate age of each Sioux Indian who was killed, wounded, or suffered other injury at the time and place aforesaid and in the said massacre of the Sioux Indians, *Provided further,* That the Secretary of the Interior may, in his discretion, pay the amount found due any living survivor in monthly installments.

This bill was introduced in four consecutive Congresses and never passed in to law.

There have been a great many claims and counterclaims between red and white men. In some cases there has been justice. In a great many cases the courts have found a means of getting the United States off the hook. But the important thing is that a claims commission is now set up that, for better or for worse, can hear the cases which the tribes present and can come to some conclusions as to what happened so long ago.

The problem has been that the Senate Interior Committee has refused to give the tribes their money once it has been awarded. The committee often demands that the Indians give up all their rights to federal services, sell their lands at very low prices to the government, and disband their tribal government—all as the prerequisite to receiving money that has been awarded in a court of law.

In the recorded cases of both the Indian Depredations Commission and the Indian Claims Commission are sufficient concepts, ideas and doctrines to adequately comprehend a new philosophy of law. If these cases can be regarded as the legal commentary on American history as it finally achieved its legal expression then we can look forward to increased activity in the field of claims. The black and Mexican communities may conceivably use some of the ideas contained in the Indian cases, and we may begin to have a deeper, more profound understanding of relationships and responsibilities between minority groups and the Federal government.

V

WHITE DEFENDERS OF INDIAN RIGHTS

Whenever the situation has looked darkest a friend of Indian people has appeared and tried to do his best to stem the tide. During the period of Removal, Sam Houston fought like a tiger to prevent the wholesale theft of the Cherokee lands and their removal west. It was a lonely fight. One man against the combined pressures of landgrabbers and do-gooders of his day. Houston fought and lost, but he wrote a bright chapter in the history of race relations.

We've also had a multitude of do-gooders and muckraking lawyers out to make a reputation as a champion of Indians, churchmen who "really know" what is best for non-caucasians and movie stars that are suddenly thrust into prominence as spokesmen for Indians. All these can be done without. The speeches and writing of this chapter are of those white men who took a stand when it was not popular to take a stand. They had everything to lose and nothing to gain. Only a fine sense of morality and justice impelled them to act. Their only reward was to be derided as stubborn men who made a fuss on behalf of a handful of naked savages.

As Indian people we have a responsibility not simply to recite the sins of the white man but to acknowledge his virtues as well. There must always be a balance maintained lest we fall guilty of the sins which we see in others. Thus this chapter is a tribute to three Senators and a Virginia lawyer with belated thanks for their courage to stand up for Indian people at a time when no one else would do so.

Speech of Senator Teller Against
The Allotment Act (1881)

One man dared to stand against the world during the 1880's and that man was Senator Teller of Colorado. Coming from a state in which the racism against Indians was perhaps worse than anything ever experienced in the West, Teller had everything to lose by even acknowledging that Indians had any rights whatsoever. Remember that Denver was the city that cheered and gave thanksgiving when the scalps of Indian children and the sexual organs of Indian men and women were displayed on the stage of a theatre shortly after the massacre at Sand Creek. Colorado was the state where editorials thundered for years demanding the removal or extinction of the Utes, finally resulting in the alleged "Meeker Massacre".

Thus for Teller to take a stand in support of Indian rights was to take his life virtually in his hands. And he did. For years he made it his business to ensure that some modicum of justice was given to Indian tribes. He violently opposed the allotment of Indian reservations knowing full well that the people would die on desert allotments of 40 and 80 acres without water and food. Well versed in the logic and conclusions of history, Teller continually reminded his fellow Senators that the proposed bill would be the disaster that it turned out to be. He opposed the President, Secretary of the Interior and other members of the executive branch—which meant a drastic loss of patronage powers.

Teller ended his speech with a prophecy that Indians would curse the day when people wanted them to allot their lands. The day has long since come. Today younger Indians are coming to realize that the kindly old missionaries were really land agents who helped rape the tribe of its land base. By the same token Senator Teller of Colorado should receive his just due as a true friend of Indian people.

You propose to divide all this land and to give each Indian his quarter-section, or whatever he may have, and for twenty-five years he is not to sell it, mortgage it, or dispose of it in any shape, and at the end of that time he may sell it. It is safe to predict that when that shall have been done, in thirty years thereafter there will not be an Indian on the continent, or there will be very few at least, that will have any land. That has been the experience wherever we have given land to Indians and guarded it as well as we might and as well as we could; they have eventually got rid of the land and the land has been of no particular benefit to them. I know it will be said, "Why, in twenty-five years they will be all civilized; these people will be church-going farmers, having schools and all the appliances of civilized life in twenty-five years." Mr. President, the other day I went into the Library and I took up the report of old Jedediah Morse, made in 1818 or 1822—I do not remember which—on Indian affairs when Indian affairs were under the control of the War Department. No man can read that report and not come to the conclusion that ten or fifteen years at the furthest would see a solution of all these difficulties, because in that length of time the Indians were to be civilized. Mr. Morse told what progress they were making; he told about the prayer-meetings that the female Indians were holding, and he told about the religious zeal among the Indians all over the country and what strides they were making in civilization. That has been the cry every year since. You may go back fifteen years ago—and I have done it and examined them—and take the reports of the agents for these very Ute Indians, and you would suppose each year that the next year there would be very little use of an agent and the year after none at all. Every agent who goes out, who is sent out, is desirous of making good reports. He goes to the Indians, and he probably does his best, at least many of the agents do, to civilize them, and if he is a man who does not he is more sure to report to his superior, the Commissioner, that his Indians are making great progress and that in a little while they will all be civilized and enlightened Indians.

Now, divide up this land and you will in a few years deprive the Indians of a resting-place on the face of this continent; and no man who has studied this question intelligently, and who has the Indian interest at heart, can talk about dividing this land and giving them tracts in severalty till they shall have made such progress in civilization that they know the benefits and the advantages of land in severalty, and of a fee-simple absolute title; and the whole Presbyterian Church and all other churches all over this country cannot convince me, with an observation of twenty years, and, I believe, a heart that beats as warmly for the Indians as that of any other man living, that that is in the interest of the Indians. It is in the interest of speculators; it is in the interest of the men who are clutching up this land, but not in the interest of the Indians at all; and there is the baneful feature of it that when you have allotted the Indians land on which they cannot make a living the Secretary of the Interior may then proceed to purchase their land, and Congress will, as a matter of course ratify the purchase, and the Indians will become the owners in a few years in fee, and away goes their title, and, as I said before, they are wanderers over the face of this continent, without a place whereon to lay their heads. And yet every man who raises his voice against a bill of this kind is charged with not looking to the interest of the Indians, and I am met by the astonishing argument that because the Secretary of the Interior, and because the Committee on Indian Affairs, (for whose opinion I have due and proper respect,) and because public sentiments say that they should have land in severalty, I am running amuck against all the intelligence and all the virtue of the country, and therefore I must be wrong.

Mr. President, what I complain of in connection with this Indian business is that practical common sense is not applied to it. Sentiment does not do the Indians any good. It does not educate them and feed them for us to pass high-sounding resolutions and to put upon the statute-book enactments that declare they shall be protected in their rights.

Furthermore, it does not accomplish the great purposes of civilization to send a few wild Indians down to Hampton and a few up to Carlisle. The Indians cannot be educated by such methods. We must put the schools in the Indian community; we must bring the influences where a whole Indian tribe or a whole band will be affected and influenced by them. It is folly to suppose that this will civilize them.

If I stand alone in the Senate, I want to put upon the record my prophecy in this matter, that when thirty or forty years shall have passed and these Indians shall have parted with their title, they will curse the hand that was raised professedly in their defense to secure this kind of legislation, and if the people who are clamoring for it understood Indian character, and Indian laws, and Indian morals, and Indian religion, they would not be here clamoring for this at all.

Speech of Senator Morgan Against
The Allotment Act (1881)

Time and again Senator Teller's lonely voice echoed through the Senate chambers against the allotment act. He was joined one day by Senator Morgan, who used a number of constitutional arguments against the idea of allotment. Many of the arguments raised by Senator Morgan should be raised in the courts today. In many senses the constitutional rights of Indian tribes were violated by the allotment act. In view of the position taken by the United States in the British-American Arbitration hearings—when the United States swore to a foreign nation that it treated Indian rights with utmost sanctity—there may be a closed case against further deprivation of Indian rights using some of the same arguments that were voiced here long ago.

So much respect has been paid to the communal idea, the tribal government of these Indians in our treaty relations with them and in our statutory enactments heretofore, that we have not seen proper to disturb anything of that kind; and I venture to say that plenty of instances can be found of treaties solemnly entered into between us and the Indian tribes which will be plainly violated if this law is put in force. Therefore, whether we have the power or not we should not do it in a broad and sweeping enactment of this kind, but we should take up the particular case of a particular tribe and adapt our legislation to them. If we do not pause in our movement, if we are not a little more circumspect in our treatment of the Indians, a little less heroic in our treatment of this subject, we shall have ample leisure to repent either that we have done ourselves gross injustice in the violation or abuse of our treaty obligation, or that we have compelled a poor people who have suffered enough to suffer more or else fight in defense of their rights. We shall have leisure to repent of this law after we have passed it. We shall have ample time to understand that this committee, able as it is, had not the power, as no living set of men to-day have the power, to grasp this great and magnificent problem and to solve it in the form of a bill of such dimensions as this.

The Senator from Texas says that the ninth section of this bill provides that this law shall not be effectual until it has the consent of two-thirds of the male members twenty-one years of age of each of these tribes. Mr. President, there we do either to ourselves or to the Indians a very gross injustice. The Senator from Missouri said he did not concur with some Senators in this body in reference to their views of the effect of the fourteenth amendment upon the Indians, whether it conferred upon them the rights of citizenship or not. That is not the very question that is presented here. It is a question different from that which is now presented. The question we are dealing with is this, shall we, notwithstanding the declaration we have solemnly made and acted upon, that hereafter the tribal relations of the Indians would not justify us treating the tribe in any sense as a foreign people, maintain that tribal relation by statute so far that it shall become necessary that two-thirds of the male members of an Indian tribe shall give its assent to a law of Congress before it becomes a law. I do not know of any body of men in this country, in any State or any Territory, or elsewhere, who by our statutes have heretofore been dignified with this peculiar power of interposing the voice of one-third of the members of a community for the purpose of giving effect to an act of Congress, or else for the purpose of preventing it from going into effect. One-third of an Indian tribe can veto an act of Congress! It requires the assent of two-thirds of the male members—shutting out the women from all participation in it, though they should be widows and the heads of families—the assent of two-thirds of the male members of every tribe of Indians, now numbering two hundred, I believe in the United States, before this act of Congress can have any effect with regard to them!

I set out with the declaration that I thought this act of Congress was based on false principles. Unquestionably it is. We should do one of two things: we should either exercise the ordinary treaty-making power, in which the Senate participates, in dealing with Indian tribes, or we should legislate with regard to them just as we do with regard to all the other people of the United States. There is no middle ground that can be taken, unless we assert that the Indian tribes, owing to their peculiar circumstances, have the right to intercept the action of Congress and prevent its having validity after the President has signed the bill until it shall get the consent of two-thirds of the male members of the tribe. This is very extraordinary legislation, that we should leave standing on the statute-book a law which prohibits us from recognizing the tribal relation so as to treat with them, and yet that we should put into the body of this enactment a provision that the law itself shall not become effectual as a statute until the consent of two-thirds of the Indians of each tribe is obtained.

I confess, Mr. President, that I do not see the principle upon which such a law operates. I cannot understand the logic of the system. It does not address itself to my reason and judgment as a sound and judicious principle of legislation on which the Senate of the United States is authorized to act. On the contrary, I can see mischief in the principle of legislation thus advanced, and I can see a great deal more of mischief in the application of this doctrine to these Indians and to the white people. What do you do? You assemble these bucks in council, you go and make great speeches to them, and you allow them to get up and orate extensively. They talk about the Great Father, and the head of the bureau, and the Indian agents, and the man who sells the goods around there. They perhaps do not mention it, but still in ninety-nine cases out of one hundred it is so, that the principal men when they go into council have got a little extra cash in their pockets, put there for the purpose of putting them in a good humor. They are recognized by this great Government as being a government, so that one-third of the men there can prevent the operation of the law at all.

But suppose you have the law going into effect by the consent of two-thirds of the tribe; you have got your enactment perfect; the law is in operation. What use are you going to make of it? The moment this Indian council, uniting its power with the Congress of the United States, enacts a law for the disposal of a vast territory of rich land—it may be richer than any opened in the great Golconda of the West—yet the moment that is done, the moment the law is applicable, the President is appealed to by the border settlers who are camped upon the border for the purpose of going in, and he forces the location of the lands. The Indians are located in a large domain which is held in common; it may be the very best mining land in all the territory of the reservation, or it may be the best agricultural land. Here is a vast domain that is excluded from the right of private ownership because every man, woman, and child in the Indian nation has received its modicum of land, got its title to it, and the balance is common domain. How are you going to dispose of that? You have dissolved the tribal relation. Then the President, with the assent of Congress, can buy all the balance. At what price? And who are to be the beneficiaries? Where is the trust fund to go after it is realized by a sale of the land?

Mr. President, we understand from the history of the past that it is a mere sacrifice of a fund sacredly set apart for the Indians in perpetuity under the treaties. We are now by compulsion of law undertaking to force the Indians off their lands and to open them to settlement.

There is another feature of it that strikes my attention with great force. While this is supposed to be a good and necessary law in regard to the Indians, reaching up into the northern boundaries of Alaska, where to-day we have no form of government except a ship with its guns bearing on the coast; while this law has this broad extent to the north, and will open up the whole country there to the access of the white man, when you come to the south, to the Indian Territory, it locks it up and seals it. The Indians in the Indian Territory, many of whom we have carried there by compulsion, like the Cheyennes and the Arapahoes and the Poncas and the Wyandottes, and many others, are not to be allowed to participate in this great beneficial measure for the relief of the Indians and for the restoration of them to the light of civilization.

But there is a reason for that. I suppose they see that there is a band of white men hanging along the borders there that want to go in. How is it in Dakota, in Washington Territory, in Idaho, in Oregon, in all that northern country? Are not the white men pushing in there? This bill is intended to make a road for them so that no man can obstruct their entrance and immigration in that country; but when you come to the southern territory of the Indian Nation, this bill is intended to lock it up so that no man can enter in. There is a crying and a gross injustice against a certain section of this country. The honorable Senator from Texas may think that the interests of his State require that white immigration should be shut out of the Indian Territory; I do not know what he may think about that; but if he does he makes a great mistake. I could not give my consent to the bill without the amendment of the honorable Senator from Missouri. This bill affects in its operations the white people as well as the Indians, and if there is any benefit or advantage to be derived from it in favor of the Indians, I can see no reason why the Indians in the Indian Territory should be excluded from it.

Of course I do not include in this remark the five civilized nations, because they hold our land patents to their lands. As I understand, the patent reads that their title shall continue while water runs and grass grows. That title is irrevocable until we shall gain that period in our infamous conduct with our Indians, if you will allow me to characterize it as it has been heretofore, where we shall rob them of this title that we have conveyed to them by parchment. I therefore do not include them in my remarks. They are excluded by the amendment of the honorable Senator from Missouri.

But, Mr. President, I cannot subscribe to a policy which excludes the benefit of this enactment from the Indian Territory entirely, for the purpose of continuing the exclusion of white people who are hanging around there it is supposed for the purpose of getting in.

Now, I believe this with regard to the Indian: his hunting ground is gone and he is no longer a hunter. The Indian understands as well as any gentleman in the Senate that in the hereafter he is to support himself by his labor in some form or other, that agricultural labor is that which is best adapted to his want of education and skill in other pursuits, and that therefore he must become an agriculturist. The Indian understands also that when he is in the neighborhood of honest and good white people they are a protection to him rather than an injury. There will not be another Indian war of any magnitude in the United States while this Government lasts. These people have grown sick of it. Conquered by the very destruction of their natural sources of supply, disintegrated by the introduction of white men among them, they have become a feeble power; they are surrounded on every side; and they understand that question just as well as we do. They have buried the tomahawk; and they have done it forever, not because they have become cowardly or mean in spirit, but because they recognize the fact that civilization has at last absolutely conquered; therefore they finally surrender to it, and they are ready to stretch out their hand and work; and they ought to be permitted to do it like men. We ought not ruthlessly and by process of compulsion to undertake to force the Indians, in advance of their own convictions on this question, into an entirely new and different social system from that which they ever had before. Let the system grow upon them; give them the option; do not allow the President of the United States at his will and pleasure to take any tribe of Indians and pass them into tillers of the soil, until such time as they become satisfied that it is to their interest to do so.

There is one thing that I think I am justified in saying from my reading of history as well as from personal observation, that I have never known an Indian yet who was not willing to work—I do not mean to toil with his hands—but I have never known one yet who was so indolent in his nature as that he would not go out and participate in the activities of the chase, and take upon himself more labor and more hardship than almost any man in the world, for the sake of gaining his livelihood. These people, when they are brought in contact with a true civilization and are taught agricultural pursuits, as I hope they very soon will be, will not be found to be an inefficient or a lazy people. They will proceed in the cultivation of the soil with such success as has been mentioned in the letter read here today, until they will after a while become entirely self-sustaining.

Now, take the twenty-seven pueblo tribes down in the Arizona desert. You may pass over that desert and find corn-fields, and when you are approaching you see the tassels of the corn, when in full tassel, not more than a foot above the ground. You will find the Indian has scooped out a basin of two or three feet, in which he has planted the seed for the purpose of getting moisture by capillary attraction, there being no rains in that country and no chance for irrigation; and there they raise a hard corn of excellent character, corn that will keep better than any we have in our country, and not corn merely, but wheat, and an abundance of it; and there is not one of those pueblos that has not a year's supply for every man, woman, and child laid up in advance. Those Indians have cost the people of the United States not one penny. They have lost a great deal by depredations of roving bands of cow-boys and other white men; they have been disturbed frequently, and yet they have gone on living in villages, as they do, and have hoarded up the treasures of agricultural production, so that a man cannot find a pueblo without a year's supply of food for everybody garnered in their store-houses.

What does all this mean? It means that they are a more industrious people than we are, because you may take the liveliest Yankee that ever left Connecticut and you cannot put him on those plains and cause him to make a living under those circumstances. Of course he would not stay there and undertake it. The Indians have been compelled to do it; they have done it, and they have proved by that fact that they are capable of sustaining themselves by their own labor, and that we have nothing to do but to give them ordinary encouragement in this direction. The compulsory process has gone on long enough; and above all things, Mr. President, I do not want to leave these Indian tribes exposed again to the hardship and the wrong that will be inflicted on them by selecting out what are called their councilors and their chiefs for the purpose of disposing absolutely of the rights of private individuals. That is not the theory of our laws; it is not in accordance with our treaties or laws. One man has no right in this country to dispose of the property of another. Let him have his rights under the treaty, but do not put in this bill any compulsory enactment; and above all things, if you pass this law, adopt the amendment of the honorable Senator from Missouri, and let the law have its application to all the Indian tribes alike.

But I claim that the basis and principle of this bill is wrong. These are people of the United States. Whether they are citizens or not, they are people subject to our legislative action. We can repeal the treaties if we choose; but we cannot take away vested rights that have vested under those treaties without the violation of our own Constitution, because our Constitution when it prohibits us from divesting vested rights does not stop to inquire whether the man in whose favor a right is vested is an Indian, a negro, or a white man. The vested right must be protected. If you will not recognize the tribal relation sufficiently to treat with them, still you have the legislative power, and there is but one restriction upon it, and that is vested rights.

I claim that by this bill you put it in the power of two-thirds of an Indian tribe absolutely to break down and destroy the vested rights of the balance of the tribe, and that is a false principle of legislation. If you find yourselves able under the Constitution of the United States and the guardianship of your own conscience to take from the Indians their own property, march up like men and take it away; do not go to an Indian council and persuade two-thirds of the male Indians who may be there to barter away the rights of the balance of the tribe. That sort of bickering with Indian tribes is disgraceful to the country; and while the policy of the Secretary of the Interior has been lauded here to-day, I undertake to say that in reference to that particular, as well as many others, the dignity and honor of the United States have been absolutely sacrificed in these conventions with Indians to say whether or not our laws should go into effect in reference to certain tribes. Here it is proposed to take the minority of an Indian tribe and strip them of their rights, and, not daring to do it by open act of Congress, it is proposed to do it with the consent of two-thirds of the male Indians of the tribe. It is this feature of the proposed law that I specially object to. I cannot vote for a bill that has that principle in it. Legislate for your Indian directly or do not legislate at all.

A Plea for the Indian Citizens of
The United States
by Jennings C. Wise (1925)

One of the least known yet most stalwart defenders of Indian rights was Jennings Wise of California. He struggled for years in a futile effort to get the sacred Pipestone Quarry returned to the Yankton Sioux.

In 1925 Wise wrote the following essay in an effort to nudge Congress into accepting its responsibility to assist Indian people. In this essay, he brings forth some legal questions with respect to the recently passed Indian Citizenship Act that have relevance today. While some of his language may sound stilted, the issues that he raised give eloquent testimony that there have been champions who have come forth from the white race and demanded of their white brothers that justice be done.

Today, after nearly half a century of neglect, Wise's essay brings to us the serious question of Indian rights. What effect did the Indian Citizenship Act REALLY have? Did it place the due process and equal protection guarantees in the path of Congress? If so can the Termination Acts of the 1950's be challenged on these grounds? What does citizenship mean when it exempts "tribal and other" property from citizenship rights and responsibilities?

I.
THE POLITICAL STATUS OF THE TRIBAL INDIANS

In 1828 the Supreme Court of the United States, speaking through Chief Justice Marshall, defined the political status of the tribal Indians. The tribes were then declared to be dependent communities and the tribal Indians the political wards of the United States. By the act of Congress approved June 2, 1924, however, every noncitizen Indian born within the territorial limits of the United States was declared to be a citizen of the United States. Thus, 148 years after the United States had assumed political jurisdiction over the Indians they were elevated from the status of a dependent political wardship to that of full citizenship, and as citizens, with all the constitutional rights of such, assumed a definite place in the body politic of the Nation.

The effect of the transformation which they have undergone has not been fully recognized. Whatever the status of the United States with respect to the property of the political wards of the Nation may have been prior to June 2, 1924, the enfranchising act of that date, it is submitted, definitely fixed its status as the trustee at law of so much of the property of the Indians as remained in its hands. In the law of nations and the municipal law of the United States there is no sanction for any other relation between a sovereign state and its citizens of whose property it retains control.

The report of the Commissioner of Indian Affairs for 1924 shows that there are still about 150,000 full-blooded tribal Indians who, with other legal Indians hold in common tribal lands that have not yet been allotted in severalty. Under the existing law, the unallotted tribal lands of these Indians necessarily remain under the control of the United States, and, though the tribal Indians, like all others, are citizens, it is clear that until they are prepared and elect to take their lands in severalty the Government is morally bound to continue in the relation of political guardian while discharging the trust with respect to their property imposed by the act of June 2, 1924. Political history fails to disclose another instance of such a relation. It is a unique relation, even more peculiar than that existing with respect to the tribes between 1776 and 1924, and one that requires to be very carefully considered by Congress. Plainly, many of the laws and practices designed to meet the case of political dependents are no longer suited to the needs of citizens and are inconsistent with the legal relation existing between citizens and a sovereign trustee.

II.
THE EXECUTIVE POLICY OF THE UNITED STATES WITH RESPECT TO THE TRIBAL INDIANS

The executive policy of the United States with respect to the tribal Indians was initiated and first expressed by President Washington in 1790 in an address to the Six Nations in the following words: "The General Government will never consent to your being defrauded, but will protect you in all your just rights." Washington's executive policy has remained unchanged. In the celebrated *Cayuga* case, before the American and British Claims Arbitration, after referring to the political system of the United States with respect to the Indians, the Department of State in 1912 said: "Under that system the Indians residing within the United States are so far independent that they live under their own customs and not under the laws of the United States; that their rights upon the lands which they inhabit or hunt are secured to them by boundaries defined in amicable treaties between the United States and themselves; and whenever those boundaries are varied, it is also by amicable and voluntary treaties, by which they receive from the United States *ample compensation for every right they have to the lands ceded by them.*" (Italics added.)

III.
THE JUDICIAL POLICY OF THE UNITED STATES WITH RESPECT TO THE TRIBAL INDIANS

It was over 40 years after Washington established the executive policy of the United States before the Supreme Court was called upon to define the rights of the Indian tribes. In 1823 in the classic opinion delivered by Chief Justice Marshall in *Johnson v. McIntosh,* it was held that the tribal title was a right of occupancy. Affirming this first decision, in 1895 Chief Justice White said: "The Indian title against the United States was merely a title and right to the perpetual occupancy of the land with the privilege of using it in such mode as they saw fit until such right of occupation had been surrendered to the Government."

The Indians can convey no title without the consent of the United States; their title is conditioned upon actual occupation; settlement on their lands is prohibited by statute; grants thereof are made by the United States subject to the Indian right of occupancy; the Indian right can be extinguished only by the United States; title to Indian lands can not be acquired either by a third party or the United States by adverse possession; the doctrine of laches does not apply to the tribal Indians; the Indian right of occupancy is as sacred as the title of the United States to the fee; and even the United States can not extinguish that right save by the voluntary consent of the Indians or by the exercise of the sovereign right of eminent domain.

That Indian right of occupancy is a property right has never been questioned, and that it is property within the meaning of the Fifth Amendment of the Constitution which forbids the taking of private property for public use without just compensation has long been decided. In the celebrated case of the Kansas Indians, involving the right of occupancy of the Shawnee, Miami, and other tribes, the Supreme Court in 1866 said: "If they have outlived many things, they have not outlived the protection afforded by the Constitution, treaties, and laws of Congress". That an Indian tribe can sue as such is not doubted.

In complete conformity with the foregoing principles the Court of Claims in 1910 in the *Ute* case said:

"While it may be true that the Indian title of the plaintiffs to any territory prior to the treaty of 1863 was not such a title as the defendants would recognize, yet the plaintiffs were located within this territory and had the usual claim of occupancy of other Indians. Their claim was considered of such importance that the defendants, during the year following the Guadalupe Hidalgo treaty, entered into a treaty with them and secured from them a concession for the right of free passage through their territory. By the treaty of 1863 the defendants considered these claims to territorial occupancy of sufficient importance to obtain from them a cession of all 'claim, title, etc.' to lands within the territory of the United States, excepting certain lands which were set apart to them as their hunting grounds. By the treaty of 1868 the reservation in question was set apart to the plaintiffs, and by the third article of the treaty the plaintiffs relinquished 'all claims and rights in and to any portion of the United States or Territories except such reservation.' Even if they admit that they had no valid title to any lands, yet they claimed some title and honestly claimed it, and the yielding of such a claim to a party who wishes to purchase it is good consideration."

IV.
THE LEGISLATIVE POLICY OF THE UNITED STATES
WITH RESPECT TO THE TRIBAL INDIANS

The policy of Congress has conformed, in theory at least, with the original executive policy as expressed by Washington in 1790, and the judicial view pronounced by the Supreme Court in 1823. In report of the Committee on Indian Affairs of the United States House of Representatives, submitted in 1830, dealing with the constitutional right of Congress to remove Indian tribes from the domains claimed by them to the Indian Territory, it was said:

"The Indians are paid for their unimproved lands as much as the privilege of hunting and taking game upon them is supposed to be worth, and the Government sells them for what they are worth to the cultivator. . . . Improved lands or small reservations in the States are in general purchased at their full value to the cultivator. To pay an Indian tribe what their ancient hunting grounds are worth to them after the game is fled or destroyed as a mode of appropriating wild lands claimed by Indians has been found more convenient, and certainly it is more agreeable to the forms of justice, as well as more merciful, than to assert the possession of them by the sword. Thus, the practice of buying Indian titles is but the substitute which humanity and expediency have imposed in place of the sword in arriving at the actual enjoyment of property claimed by the right of discovery and sanctioned by the national superiority allowed to the claims of civilized communities over those of savage tribes."

In 1922 Justice Sutherland, speaking for the Supreme Court, said: "Congress itself, in apparent recognition of possible individual possession, has in several of the State enabling acts required the incoming State to disclaim all right and title to lands owned or held by any Indian or Indian tribes." Elsewhere in the same opinion Mr. Justice Sutherland said: "The fact that such right of occupancy finds no recognition in any statute or other formal governmental action is not conclusive. The right, under the circumstances here disclosed, flows from a settled governmental policy." From the foregoing it is apparent that Congress itself has never deemed it within its undoubted "plenary power over the tribal

177

relations of the Indians" to deprive them of their property rights without some form of compensation. Such a practice would not only be violative of the decisions of the Supreme Court of the United States, but would be contrary to the law of nations. Civilized states, though possessing plenary political power over their inhabitants, do not confiscate the private property of dependent peoples.

V.
THEORY AND PRACTICE

Nothing could be fairer than the policy of the United States with respect to the Indians than that which is to be derived from the executive and legislative declarations and the judicial decisions hereinbefore quoted. Unfortunately the governmental practice has not accorded with theory. The two have been wide apart. Without prejudice, without sentiment, let the facts of history be reviewed.

Although the Indians, measured by European standards, were the most moral people known to history, the colonial Englishman's church deemed them the "spawn of hell," to be extirpated in the spirit of the Old Testament. Desirous of their lands the frontiersman invented the useful fiction that a people who had occupied definite tribal domains from time immemorial, were nomads without attachment to the soil. Thus, when the United States assumed political jurisdiction in 1776 over these former subjects of the British Crown, the Americans along the frontier deemed the rights of the Indians and the buffalo to be on a parity. Said Brackinridge, a frontier editor, in 1782: "So far from admitting the Indian title, I would as soon admit that of the buffalo." Again: "The animals vulgarly called Indians, being by nature fierce and cruel, I consider their extirpation would be useful to the world while entirely honorable to those who would effect it."

With such a view extant among the so-called civilized whites, it was not unnatural that the Indian should have become fierce in the defense of his lands—at times cruel—and that the idea should have gained credence that "The only good Indian is a dead Indian."

In vain Washington, who knew his fellow countrymen and was not deceived by them, sought to prevent the massacre of the Indians and protect them in their admitted rights. The Constitution itself forbade the acquisition of their lands save by United States treaties. New York ignored the Constitution and the statutes. Georgia, with the tacit consent of John Quincy Adams and Jackson twice nullified the mandates of the Supreme Court, threatening a resort to arms to prevent their enforcement, while Alabama treated to secede from the Union if Indian statutes were rendered effective. Under Jefferson, Madison, and Jackson, dependent as they were for their political support upon the "new democracy" of the frontier, the Buffalo Party had free play. Harkening to the wisdom and justice of Washington and Marshall, in 1824 Monroe timidly proposed to give the Indians land individually in order that they might be emancipated from their aboriginal state and enabled to compete in the economic order of civilization. The Nation would not have it. He then proposed their concentration in the Indian Territory which was partly effected under Jackson as the means of driving them, despite the Supreme Court, from the white man's path. Even there they were molested and abused. Then came a veritable reign of terror for the Indians of the West. Along the Oregon Trail and in the gold fields of California and the Black Hills they were destroyed like the buffalo.

The Californians and Oregonians demanded that they be removed. Congress passed acts providing for the negotiation of treaties with the Indian tribes of the Pacific coast in which reservations were promised them for the lands surrendered. Pending the ratification of these treaties they were induced to remove. Political influence prevented the ratification by the Senate of the treaties. Thus deceived, dispossessed, betrayed, a quarter of a million helpless people who had been partly civilized and Christianized by the Spaniards, whose rights were secure under the laws of Spain and Mexico, and whose rights had been solemnly guaranteed by the United States in the treaty of Guadalupe Hidalgo, were harried from place to place, massacred at will, and left to become vagrants upon the earth. Today they are homeless, dependent upon charity, and reduced to less than 20,000 souls.

In addition to the gold seekers another enemy was soon to appear. In 1850 Congress adopted the policy of granting western lands to corporate interests in order to promote the construction of the trans-continental railroads. To this end grants aggregating 155,000,000 acres of land with slight regard to Indian rights were made. Then came the homestead act of 1862, which caused the remaining Indian lands to be deluged with white settlers. The Indians of the East and the Pacific coast having been entirely dispossessed, now came the turn of the plains Indians. In all, it was necessary for the guardian Government to wage over 50 official wars against its wards during the first century of its existence in the civilizing process which it brought to bear, though there is not one instance in which the Indians sought to defend themselves until after protection had been denied them. During this same period the Indians north of the Canadian border who were protected by their government, remained in unbroken peace.

It was a harsh tutelage which the Indians of the United States underwent. It was not until Grant became President that the responsibility of the Nation was recognized. With an integrity and a courage equal to that of Washington, he appointed a commission to examine into the Indian situation, and adopted the reservation system as the only possible expedient to save the Indians from complete destruction. It was never designed to be more than a temporary makeshift. At his instance the Indian homestead act of 1875 was passed and steps taken culminating in the general allotment act of 1887—measures designed to absorb the Indians in the economic and social order of the political society of the Nation. That absorption was to be expedited by education and allotment of land in severalty to the Indians. Those who took allotments were to become citizens. Inadequate provisions for Indian education having been made, allotment has naturally proceeded slowly. Yet, in 1917 the Indians were called upon to fight for the Nation. Responding with a spirit unequaled by the white or black citizens, and without regard to citizenship, they furnished 17,000 soldiers. Among all the Indians less than 250 sought exemption. As a reward they were enfranchised in 1924, but today, half a century after Grant instituted his wise reforms, over 150,000 tribal Indians remain enslaved to the outworn economic and social systems of an aboriginal race. The great-great-grandsons of the Nation's first Indian wards still speak only the Indian language. Instead of cultivating the lands of their ancestors, as their forebears did, in many instances they have been reduced to the hunter state by the civilization which displaced them. Far more has been done for the Negroes in 60 years, for the Filipinos and Hawaiians in 30 years, than has been done for the Indians in a century and a half. Though the political massacre of the California Indians is, perhaps, the most scandalous incident in the history of the United States, not an official hand has been raised to help them, while the efforts of the Indian Board of Cooperation of California—a private philanthropic association—have so far proved abortive.

It would be useless to attempt here an accounting as between the United States and its Indian wards for the purpose of determining whether or not the compensation paid for their lands has been "ample." Suffice it to say that if the acreage acquired by the United States, or the political guardian, from the Indians, or its wards, were placed in one column and the price actually paid therefor in another it would require a stretch of the imagination to construe the purchase price as "ample," or one that the Indians had in fact voluntarily accepted. History shows that the actual course of the Government of the United States in dealing with this dependent people, despite its high-sounding declarations to foreign governments, has ordinarily embodied the following steps:

1. Disputes over Indian lands between the Indians and white settlers.
2. Local violence to the Indians by white intruders.
3. Appeals to the Government by the Indians for the protection of their rights.
4. Failure of the Government to provide, or the provision of inadequate protection.
5. Efforts on the part of the Indians toward self-protection and sometimes retaliation for wrongs done them.
6. Official military restraint and often chastisement.
7. So-called treaties of cession at a price fixed by the guardian Government, sometimes procured fraudulently by shrewd negotiators and undue influence upon tribal representatives, sometimes compelled by threat of force, seldom voluntary.

Such, in brief, is the cold outline of the national history with respect to this dependent people. Deny it though we may, the facts are writ in large letters in the debates of Congress and the records of the fifty-odd wars the Nation has waged against this helpless race. It is not a record which supports the declaration that was made by the Government to Great Britain in 1912.

VI.
THE CONSTITUTIONAL RIGHTS OF THE INDIANS
PRESENTLY DENIED BY THE GOVERNMENT

It must not be thought that injustice to the Indians is a thing of the past. The mere conferring of citizenship upon them has not improved their lot. Today they are subject to disadvantages known to no other citizens. Their situation is without a parallel in history, a fact that must appear from a consideration of the attitude of those executive agencies having charge of them.

In 1924 the Solicitor General, in the discharge of his public duty as advocate for the United States, argued the case of *United States v. Title Insurance & Trust Co. et al.* in the Supreme Court of the United States. In that case the appellees sought to deny the Indian tribal title in order to derive an advantage against the United States. The Solicitor General contended with great weight of authority that the Tejon Tribe of Indians possessed under Spanish and Mexican law an undisputed right and title of possession and use of the tribal domain actually occupied by them at the time of the cession of California.

Citing, among other authorities, *Holden v. Joy* and *Worcester v. Georgia*, said the Solicitor General on behalf of the United States: "The Indian right was aboriginal, antedated the sovereignty of Spain and Mexico, and was not derived from either, but was recognized and protected by the laws of both." In addition to the *Ute* case, unlimited authority might be added in support of the Government's contention. Long since it had been declared by the Supreme Court that the hunting grounds of the Indians were "as much in their actual possession as the cleared fields of the whites, and that their rights to its exclusive enjoyment in their own way and for their own purposes were as much respected until they abandoned them, made a cession to the Government, or authorized a sale to individuals."

Over and over it has been declared that the tribal right of occupancy under the law of Spain and Mexico was a property right, and that the cession of California to the United States did not impair this right of property. In *Delassas v. United States,* Chief Justice Marshall said: "The right of property, then, is protected and secured by the treaty, and no principle is better settled in this country than that an inchoate title to lands is property." Plainly, it was in recognition of these fundamental principles that in the *Ute* case the Court of Claims in 1910 rendered judgment in favor of the Indians against the United States for the misappropriation by the Government of their tribal lands for use as a forest reserve.

From what has been said it is apparent that the executive departments of the Government, and especially the Department of Justice, are fully advised as to the rights of the Indians of California and that the property rights of all Indians are protected by the Constitution.

In the case of *Lone Wolf v. Hitchcock,* the Supreme Court said: "Plenary authority over the tribal relations of the Indians has been exercised by Congress from the beginning, and the power has always been deemed a political one, not subject to be controlled by the judicial department of the Government. The power to abrogate the provisions of an Indian treaty, though presumably such power will be exercised only when circumstances arise which will not justify the Government in disregarding the stipulations of the treaty, but may demand, in the interest of the country, that it should do so. When, therefore, treaties are entered into between the United States and a tribe of Indians it was never doubted that the power to abrogate existed in Congress and that in a contingency such power might be availed of from consideration of governmental policy, particularly if consistent with perfect good faith toward the Indians."

The Government knows that plenary authority over tribal relations is not absolute power to confiscate property—a power unknown to the Constitution. On this point Alpheus Henry Snow in his recent work, entitled "The Question of Aborigines in the Law and Practice of Nations," written at the request of the Department of State (1921) says:

"The Supreme Court has also held that the power which the United States has, by law of nations and its Constitution, over all colonies and dependencies is 'plenary' for the accomplishment of the object sought to be obtained. These objects can only be, and are, the extension of democracy, republicanism, and equality of opportunity. 'Plenary' power is the power which an agent has who is delegated to accomplish a certain object and whose mandate is limited only by the needs of the situation. An agent with plenary power—an agent plenipotentiary—represents the principal with full power to do all which the principal might reasonably do in the accomplishment of the object intended. *Plenary power is not absolute power,* but power limited to the needs of the situation. It implies that the supreme organs of the United States—its Congress, its President, its Supreme Court—acting for the United States, in fulfilling its fiduciary relationships under the law of nations respecting its colonies and dependencies, have full powers to do all which the United States might reasonably and legally do under the law of nations, consistently with the fundamental principles of the Constitution and the fundamental principles of human society recognized by civilized states.

"As the Constitution contains a Bill of Rights imposing certain prohibitions or conditions upon the action of all the organs of the Central Government respecting individuals under the sovereignty of the United States, all of the provisions of this Bill of Rights which are of universal application are applicable in all the colonies and dependencies of the United States from the moment of their acquisition." It has been shown that in the case of the *Kansas Indians* the Supreme Court held that the provisions of the Constitution were applicable to the Indians.

It must, therefore, come as a distinct shock to Congress and the people of the United States to learn that 148 years after the United States assumed political jurisdiction over the Indians, 138 years after the Constitution was adopted, the Department of Justice, on behalf of the Secretary of the Interior, the Secretary of Agriculture, and the Secretary of War, who together constitute the Federal Power Commission under the act of 1920, should argue in the Court of Appeals of the District of Columbia, the second highest court in the land, in effect that the Fifth Amendment to the Constitution guaranteeing private property rights is not applicable to the Indians of the United States—that Congress can confiscate their property without recourse on their part to the courts! But that is exactly what was done.

In the Government's brief submitted in the case of *Super et al v. The Secretary of War, The Secretary of the Interior, The Secretary of Agriculture, and The Federal power Commission* in the Circuit Court of Appeals of the District of Columbia, it was said:

"The *Lone Wolf* decision is our authority for these propositions: that plenary authority over the tribal relations of Indians has been exercised by Congress from the beginning and the power is a political one not subject to be controlled by the judicial department of the Government . . . ; that Congress has paramount power over the property of Indians by reason of its exercise of guardianship and may interfere or determine the occupancy rights of Indians in lands; and if injury be occasioned, the relief must be sought by an appeal to Congress and not to the courts for redress.

This argument is diametrically opposed to that of the Solicitor General hereinbefore mentioned. Shorn of all sophistry it seeks to set at naught the traditional executive and legislative policies of the United States, the law of nations, the Fifth Amendment to the Constitution and innumerable decisions of the Supreme Court, with respect to the Indian right of occupancy. How, let it be asked, can the Indian right of occupancy be as sacred as the title of the United States to the fee, if Congress can confiscate it at will without a legal remedy on the part of the Indians? Yet, this argument was made by assistants to the Attorney General on behalf of the Secretary of the Interior who is the executive agent in charge of the Indians, in 1924, coincidentally with the directly opposite contention of the Solicitor General hereinbefore mentioned. What is the explanation?

Simply this. In the one case it was to the advantage of the Government to sustain the Indian rights. In the other, in which Indians sought to enjoin the usurpation and flooding of their lands by the Government, it was to the advantage of the United States to deny the Indian title, so that without any definite policy or supervision over Indian litigation by the executive branch of the Government subordinate officers of the Department of Justice were left free to put up any argument against the Indians that they might find it expedient to make in order to win a case committed to them. Indeed, it is all but inconceivable that the President, the Secretaries of War, Agriculture, and of the Interior, and the Attorney General even know that it is being contended in the courts by the Government that Congress with impunity may confiscate Indian property.

That fact does not excuse the existence of such a situation. Any system of administering the affairs of the former political dependents and wards of the Nation under which their constitutional rights can be denied at this day and generation is faulty and requires reformation. Does Congress know that the constitutional rights of the Indians are being denied by the Secretary of the Interior in the highest courts in the land? That the Indians are being put to the expense of establishing those rights? In the face of what has been said, is it not natural that the Indians should have some doubts as to the meaning and value of citizenship?

If, from the mere fact that Congress has "plenary authority" over "tribal relations" of the Indians, and the equally undoubted fact that it may abrogate Indian treaties, is to be implied the power on its part to confiscate Indian property rights guaranteed by a foreign treaty, and that the constitutional guarantees that apply to all other citizens and dependents do not apply to tribal Indians, surely it is time to amend the Constitution. Meantime, and until the law is determined, it would appear reasonable to expect the guardian government not to appear on opposite sides of the same question in two contemporaneous litigations in the highest courts of the land, thereby putting the national wards to the burden and expense of meeting the guardian government or trustee on both sides of the same question. Such a confused, if not unconscionable, executive practice can only serve to destroy all confidence on the part of the Indians in the integrity of the Government as the trustee of their property and all faith in its declarations to foreign governments.

VII.
LACK OF COORDINATION IN THE GOVERNMENT

It has been shown how the executive and legislative branches of the Government failed to coordinate in the case of the California Indians. Waiting for the Senate to act upon the treaties negotiated with them on October 6, 1851, the executive agencies in charge of the Indians did nothing but persuade them to surrender their lands upon the promise of reservations. When the treaties were finally pigeonholed and at the mercy of squatters, who were affirmatively protected by the government of California, which has since confirmed title in the squatters. What lands belonging to the Indians were not confiscated in this way were misappropriated by the United States and converted into national parks and reservations. Under its own laws it could not acquire title to these lands free of the Indian right of occupancy, since it never extinguished that right, which was solemnly guaranteed by the treaty of Guadalupe Hidalgo. Yet the Government declared to Great Britain in 1912 that the Indians receive "ample consideration" for the lands surrendered by them to the United States.

Such a statement should not be made for the simple reason that it is false. It was bad enough to confiscate the property guaranteed by a treaty with Mexico. It was worse to make false representations in an international arbitration proceeding. Facts are facts. Whatever the explanation may be, let us look at them squarely. The Nation has not dealt with the California tribes in good faith, and there is no use in trying to avoid the facts of record. No wonder the ban of secrecy was placed on that record for half a century, since it disclosed an affirmative intent to take the lands of the Indians without their consent, contrary to existing law.

About such a course the Government is apparently without conscience. Thus, in 1924, in the case of *Super et al v. Weeks et al,* the Department of Justice contended on behalf of the Secretary of the Interior and the Government generally that the right of occupancy of the California tribes which had been guaranteed by the treaty of Guadalupe Hidalgo in 1848 was forfeited by the tribes because their claim to it was not presented to the Commission of Private Land Grants created in 1851. This, in spite of the fact that the California tribes held no grants from Spain and Mexico and that no less than three acts of Congress in 1850 and 1851 provided for the treaties to be negotiated with them on October 6, 1851.

In other words, the position of the Government in 1924 was that uncivilized tribes should have refused to deal with the treaty commissioners appointed by the President pursuant to the act of September 30, 1854, and sent among them with armed escorts; should have marched from the most remote quarters of California to San Francisco, in the face of armed opposition at every point, and presented to the Commission of Private Land Grants sitting there to pass on grants from the Spanish and Mexican Governments, grants which they never possessed. That such a contention could be made by the Government of the United States against its Indian wards in the good year 1924, in the Court of Appeals of the District of Columbia—one of the highest courts of the land—almost transcends the power of credulity. As declared by the Solicitor General, the Hon. James M. Beck, in a contemporaneous proceeding in the Supreme Court, such an argument was but to charge Congress with bad faith and to cloak the acts of Congress with a dishonorable design.

The facts cited are valuable as evidence of the technicalities to which the Government has all along resorted to defeat the rights of the Indians. Over and over this has been done.

Another striking instance is the case of the Yankton Tribe of Sioux Indians. In 1858 the United States entered into a treaty with the Yankton Sioux in which they were given certain rights in the celebrated Pipestone Quarry in Minnesota. By act of Congress of February 16, 1891, the Secretary of the Interior was directed to cause a Government educational institution to be established on the Pipestone Quarry Reservation. All of the reservation was appropriated by the Department of the Interior, according to an official report to Congress, whereupon the Indians set up a claim to their rights. The United States now entered into a treaty with the Yankton Tribe, which was ratified by the act of August 15, 1894 section 12 of which provided as follows: "If the Government of the United States questions the ownership of the Pipestone Reservation by the Yankton Tribe of Sioux Indians under the treaty of April 19, 1858, including the fee to the land as well as the right to work the quarries, the Secretary of the Interior shall as speedily as possible refer the matter to the Supreme Court of the United States, to be decided by that tribunal. And the United States shall furnish, without cost to the Yankton Indians, at least one competent attorney to represent the interest of the tribe before the court. If the Secretary of the Interior shall not within one year after the ratification of the agreement by Congress refer the question of ownership of the said Pipestone Reservation to the Supreme Court, as provided for above, such failure upon his part shall be construed as and shall be waiver by the United States of all its rights to the ownership of the said Pipestone Reservation, and the same shall thereafter be solely the property of the Yankton Tribe of Sioux Indians, including the fee to the land."

Plainly it was the purpose of Congress to quiet the dispute over the reservation and to give the Government *one year* to establish its right, if in fact it possessed one. The act of August 15, 1894, was no more nor less than a statute of limitations upon the Government designed to quiet the title involved.

The Secretary of the Interior referred the facts to the Attorney General, who advised that the institution of a suit attacking the title of the Indians was "impractical." No such suit was instituted. This left the Government in the position of having misappropriated land which belonged to the Indians and having erected a Government institution thereon. Accordingly, by the act of June 7, 1897, the Secretary of the Interior was directed to negotiate an agreement with the Yankton Tribe for the purchase of their rights. This was done, and in a formal agreement signed by them on October 2, 1899, they agreed to accept $100,000 for their rights. The agreement was transmitted to Congress with the approval of the Secretary of the Interior on March 24, 1900, and on April 4, 1906, after a lapse of six years, the Senate Committee on Indian Affairs rendered a favorable report thereon and recommended its ratification. Nothing was done by the Senate. As time went on the Yankton Indians, who were without both their land and the money offered them for it, against whom had run the statute of limitations barring a claim on their part in the Court of Claims, appealed to Congress. By a special jurisdictional act the Court of Claims was directed to find the facts, which were found by it and reported to Congress. Again Congress did nothing, until finally by the act of January 9, 1925, it empowered the Court of Claims to adjudicate this particular case, but making no provision for compensation of counsel for the Indians. Nevertheless the Yankton Sioux, who were in dire need of funds, employed counsel and brought their suit in the Court of Claims. In that proceeding the Government contended that the act of August 15, 1894, designed to quiet title to the Pipestone Reservation, was beyond the power of Congress, because it was impossible for the Secretary of the Interior to refer the question within one year to the Supreme Court, and that therefore the Indians only had a right under the treaty of 1858 to take pipestone from the quarry, and that their rights under the treaty had never been denied them.

Such an argument is but the veriest quibble. The circumstances show that Congress did not intend in the act of 1894 that a suit to quiet title should be instituted in the Supreme Court in the first instance. It is plain that Congress intended that unless the question of title should reach the Supreme Court—in other words, be referred to it—within a year through the proper legal channels the title to the fee should be deemed to be vested in the Indians. So, too, it is plain that the Indians are not free to enjoy the rights conferred upon them by the treaty of 1858. The weakness of such a contention is manifest. The treaty of 1858 provided as follows: "The said Yankton Indians shall be secured in the free and unrestricted use of the red pipestone quarry, or so much thereof as they have been accustomed to frequent and use for the purpose of procuring stone for pipes, and the United States hereby stipulate and agree to cause to be surveyed and marked so much thereof as shall be necessary and proper for that purpose and retain the same and keep it open and free to the Indians to visit and procure stone for pipes so long as they shall desire."

The Yankton Tribe numbers about 2,000 souls. It need only be inquired what would happen if the tribe in the exercise of the right conferred by the treaty should suddenly appear on the reservation which has been converted by the Government into a large and thriving educational institution boasting over 20 buildings, many other structures, and an experimental farm. In visiting the quarry at a great distance from their reservation in South Dakota the Yanktons would necessarily have to camp on the quarry reservation. Is it not obvious that the joint use of a small tract of 600 acres by the Government for an educational institution and demonstration farm with an Indian tribe is utterly impossible? It is extraordinary for the Secretary of the Interior to argue in 1925 that the Yankton Tribe has not been denied its right under the treaty of 1858 to the free and unrestricted use of the quarry when it was reported by the Secretary of the Interior as far back as 1900 that the entire Pipestone Reservation had been appropriated by his department to the use of the school erected thereon by the Government.

Oh, yes. The customary argument is anticipated—an old, outworn argument—that in the nature of things the governmental agencies can not assume the responsibility for ignoring technicalities. So, too, the weakness of the Federal Government in dealing with New York and Georgia and Alabama when they purposefully ignored the Constitution and the mandates of Supreme Court with respect to the Six Nations, the Creeks, and the Cherokees, is sought to be excused on the ground that the United States dared not enforce its laws against the States!

Such excuses have never helped the Indians in the least. The United States succeeded by act of the States to the sovereignty of Great Britain. The British Crown made a sincere effort after 1763 to protect the Indians, and has done so unfailingly ever since. The plain truth is, as declared by Presidents Washington, Harrison, and Grant, the American people have never taken enough moral interest in the race to dictate a proper policy in dealing with that race. Inherently directly responsive to the popular demand, until the American people had sated their desire for Indian lands, it was impossible for Congress to deny that demand or enforce the decisions of the courts.

The old conditions no longer exist. The equally plain truth now is that senior executives under the existing system know nothing of Indian litigation. The Indians are left to the mercy of subordinates who are naturally more bent upon winning their cases than they are in seeing that justice is done by the United States to the Indians. Again, without any personal charges whatever against executive chiefs or subordinates, and no lack of understanding of their natural limitations, it is the haphazard system of Indian administration that is at fault; not the servants of the Government.

But neither does this explanation help the Indians. Surely, now, at last for reasons of economy as well as good conscience, it is the duty of Congress to bring to an end the necessity of such litigation by the Indians as that described. Without regard to the legal merits of such cases and the intricate technicalities of the law by which Indian claims are defeated in the courts by the Government should the Indians be left to go on indefinitely consuming their paltry substance in such contests with a Government which possesses every advantage over them and under the existing law and system feels compelled to resort to every means to defeat Indian claims?

Is it not possible to establish a system of administration that will at least prevent inconsistent defenses being put forward by the Government against the Indians? A system that will at least insure a measure of coordination of policy by the several executive departments and full regard to the statutes of Congress and the intent of Congress with respect to the Nation's wards?

What, let it be inquired, would be the political effect should the Secretary of War and the Governor of the Philippines suddenly insist that the private property of Filipinos could be taken by them, without compensation, for the purpose of creating a public reservation? If the courts should then hold that the Filipinos had no remedy in the courts?

It is only because the Indians are disintegrated as a race, untutored, poor, and patient that the Government dares take such an attitude toward them. They have learned by a century and a half of sorrowful experience that their rights are deemed by the Government to be more or less on a parity with those of the buffalo—to be ignored when they stood in the way of the Government, notwithstanding the declarations of Congress and the courts. The will has all but vanished with the means of the tribal Indians to contend with the Government for their rights. Materially impoverished beyond the power of resistance, the spirit of the uncivilized Indians has been all but crushed. They have been reduced to a state of abject vassalage to a bureaucracy against which they almost fear to contend. They have been muted by injustice.

VIII.
THE PRACTICAL DISADVANTAGES OF INDIAN LITIGANTS

Not only are the Indians of the United States put to the burden by the Government of contending against it for the most fundamental constitutional rights, but they are subject to the gravest disadvantages in their legal struggles with the so-called guardian government.

In theory adverse possession and laches may not be pleaded against the national wards either by the guardian government or third-parties. Yet the practical effect of those equitable doctrines which the law invokes on their behalf is largely nullified for the reason that Indians, like other parties claimant, may only sue the United States in the Court of Claims within six years after the cause of action arose. The result is that in the great majority of cases the wards of the Nation must maintain lobbies before Congress to obtain relief, since it is seldom that they become advised of their rights before the general statute of limitations has run against them.

The case of *Super et al v. the Secretary of the Interior, the Secretary of Agriculture, and the Federal Power Commission, supra,* well illustrates the point. Recognizing the pre-existing right of occupancy of the Karok Tribe of California, which was guaranteed by the treaty of Guadalupe Hidalgo in 1848, in 1851 the Government caused a treaty to be negotiated with the Karok Tribe on October 6, 1851, in which the tribe agreed to cede its domain for a consideration. That consideration was a definitely specified reservation. The treaty failed of ratification and no attempt was ever afterwards made to extinguish the Karok title. In 1891 Congress passed the forestry act authorizing the President to set apart as forest reservations "public lands." Indian lands over and over have been held not to be *public lands,* and the Government has been forbidden by statute to designate them as such. Yet, acting, no doubt, upon erroneous advice, the President by proclamation on May 6, 1905, set apart the Karok tribal domain as the Klamath National Forest, over which the Secretary of Agriculture and the Federal Power Commission have since assumed to exercise control to the exclusion of the Karok Indians.

Plainly it was the duty of the guardian Government in 1905 to protect the rights of the Indians instead of misappropriating their lands to public use. But the Karok Indians were poor and scattered. Driven from place to place, they did not possess the means to procure legal advice. It was only in 1920 that the Indian Board of Cooperation of California, a private philanthropic society, investigated their case. The right of action of the Indians in the Court Claims had long since lapsed.

Should such a limitation as that imposed by Revised Statutes 1069 be enforced by the political guardian in its own favor against its dependent wards whose property it has misappropriated?

Is there any theory of justice that can be invoked thus to favor the political guardian as against the ward, the trustee against the cestui qui trust. Surely the United States should not avail itself of the inequitable advantage of obtaining possession of a public reservation by virtue of such a limitation upon its own wards, who without the understanding and means to protect themselves were helpless at the hands of the Government. Should they be put to the burden of continuing to lobby for remedial jurisdictional acts under which to obtain justice? Plainly, an end should be put to such injustice by one jurisdictional act conferring upon the Court of Claims power to hear any Indian claim against the United States without regard to when the cause of action arose.

But even where an Indian tribe possesses the organization and the means requisite to the litigation of its rights, it meets with the utmost difficulty in doing so. Under Revised Statutes 2103 the contracts between an Indian tribe and its attorneys are required to be approved by the Secretary of the Interior and the Commissioner of Indian Affairs. The policy of the Government is to approve only such contracts as provide for a contingent fee. A maximum fee of 10 per cent of the amount recovered is allowed, and the amount recovered is allowed, and the court may allow less. The attorney must advance all the costs and expenses of the litigation in the first instance and is not reimbursed therefor unless a recovery is bad.

A proper restraint upon such contracts is eminently wise in order to protect the tribes against fraud, to insure that the contract is authorized, to prevent the exploitation of the Indians by unscrupulous attorneys and their field agents, and to discourage by timely advice useless litigation. The fact is, however, the existing statute, coupled with the departmental policy of limiting the possible compensation of counsel to a contingent fee of 10 per cent of the amount recovered, leaving it to the courts to fix a lesser amount, at the same time casting on the attorney the risk of the expense of the litigation has operated against rather than for the Indians in at least two ways: First, purely contingent fees are not favored by the higher bar for reasons too numerous to require mention. In the case of the Indians, therefore, the executive policy of allowing only such fees tends to deny them the aid of eminent counsel, few of whom are available upon such terms. Second, it is not to be expected that the most able and conscientious counsel, even if they can afford to finance Indian litigation, will place at the disposal of their clients, with no hope of a reasonable remuneration of their services, the requisite funds, much less risk the loss of the same. Added to the risk of the costs now imposed upon attorneys for the Indians is the further deterrent that through lack of adequate accounting facilities available for Indian litigation a legal proceeding against the Government is apt to be prolonged for years.

In the very nature of things, therefore, these helpless wards of the Nation, who require the best possible legal advice and representation in a contest with the Government that is inherently unequal, are denied that aid. Instead of deterring their exploitation, the prevailing system tends to promote it.

Without throwing down the bars that experience has raised against the exploitation of the Indians by unscrupulous agents and attorneys who when once employed will have their pound of flesh, the whole system requires to be reformed.

The influence of the Department of the Interior and the Office of Indian Affairs, the duty of which it is to administer Indian property, should be wholly divorced from matters pertaining to the legal representation of the Indians. Since it is the duty of these executive agencies to furnish evidence in Indian litigation, absolute impartiality on their part in matters affecting their own administration is not only a very great but an unreasonable demand to make upon them. A statute might well be enacted providing that upon application to the Attorney General any Indian or tribe of Indians having a bona fide claim against the United States or any person, persons, State, foreign government, association, or corporation, by virtue of any treaty, agreement, or statute of the United States, should be entitled to select out of a list of attorneys approved by the President within the current year, a guardian ad litem to represent the applicant, and at the Government's expense, with the privilege of nominating attorneys for the approval of the President. In order to insure the willingness of competent attorneys to serve, all expense to them should be eliminated by providing for the payment to them of a reasonable retainer as in the case of other special counsel, and for covering by appropriation such additional compensation as the court might allow. It is a simple device that would do justice and at the same time discourage wasteful and useless litigation, eliminate incompetent and untrustworthy counsel in Indian litigation, and enlist in the service of the Indians the highest legal talent in the country. To that much they are fairly entitled in a struggle either with the trustee, or to enforce their rights against others where the Government has failed to do so. Certain it is that the Attorney General should be required to see that Indians are not put to unreasonable expense by inconsistent or dilatory defenses on the part of the Government.

Again, upon what theory of justice can the wards of the Nation be required to bear the expense of costly litigation to recover what is due them from the guardian trustee? If they are entitled to a judgment against the United States should they not receive the full amount net of what is due them? Plainly, it is only fair that the United States, which now occupies as political guardian the position of the legal trustee of the property of the tribal Indians remaining in its hands, itself should furnish them with a guardian ad litem when litigation of their rights becomes necessary.

In recent years, too, the practice has grown up of the Government deputing representatives to examine into local conditions among the Indians and charging the expense against the trust funds of its wards. Is this fair? Are the Filipinos, the Puerto Ricans, the Hawaiians charged individually with the cost of Government inspection? In what other case are citizens of the United States required, save through general taxation, to bear the cost of government?

The whole question of Indian litigation requires to be gone into very thoroughly and regulated by statutes insuring fair and adequate representation for the Indians.

IX.
THE DESTINY OF THE INDIAN CITIZENS

Enough has been said to disclose the imperative need of a new and definite national Indian policy. What should that policy be? Only the most careful study can determine. Yet, it may well be said that any policy that is determined upon should have full regard to the destiny of the Indian race. What that destiny is would seem to be clear.

In the *Handbook of American Indians,* published in 1910 by the Bureau of American

Ethnology, it is stated that upon the coming of the White Man there were 918,000 aborigines within the present continental limits of the United States including Alaska, and that in 1910 there were 403,000, including all degrees of admixture. (Pt. 2, p. 287.)

The Commissioner of Indian Affairs in 1924 reported that there were 320,497 Indians in the United States of all degrees of Indian blood, and that of these, 162,602 were full blooded. The figures as to the latter are much more apt to be correct than the number of persons claiming to be Indians for mere legal reasons. Thus, it is seen that on the basis of those figures there remains but 18 per cent of the original full-blooded population.

Of the 320,497 legal Indians reported in 1924, the Indian blood of some is as low as one sixty-fourth of 1 per cent, of many more only twice as great, and so on down to the full bloods. This fact, coupled with the census report of the number of Indians for 1920, or 265,683, is significant since from these figures it is obvious that in 1920 there were over 50,000 persons of Indian blood in the United States whose admixture was indiscernible to the census taker, or when not claimed for legal reasons, which fast, coupled with the evidence of the gradual amalgamation of the races in the past, would seem to indicate beyond the peradventure of a doubt the ultimate solution of the Indian problem—complete absorption of the Indians.

X.
A NEW AND DEFINITE POLICY REQUIRED

In the determination of a new national policy full regard should be had to the lessons which an unbiased study of the past affords. The chief cause of the decrease of the Indians during the past century and a half in order of importance may be said to be smallpox and other epidemics; tuberculosis; sexual diseases, whiskey and attendant dissipation; removals, starvation and subjection to unaccustomed conditions; low vitality due to mental depression under misfortune; wars. Smallpox has repeatedly swept over wide areas, sometimes destroying perhaps one-half of the native population within its path. One historic smallpox epidemic originating on the upper Missouri in 1781-82 swept northward to Great Slave Lake, eastward to Lake Superior, and westward to the Pacific. Another in 1801-02 ravaged from the Rio Grande to Dakota; and another, in 1837-38 reduced the strength of the northern plains tribes by nearly one-half. A fever visitation about the year 1830 was officially estimated to have killed 70,000 Indians in California, while at about the same time a malarial fever epidemic in Oregon and on the Columbia— said to have been due to the plowing up of the ground at the trading posts—ravaged the tribes of the region and practically exterminated those of Chinookan stock. The destruction by disease and dissipation has been greatest along the Pacific coast, where also the original population was most numerous. In California the enormous decrease from about a quarter of a million to less than 20,000 is due chiefly to the cruelties and wholesale massacres perpetuated by the miners and early settlers. These facts are a dreadful commentary upon the Nation which assumed jurisdiction before God over the aborigines of America. Yet they clearly point the way to the needed reforms.

In the reformation of the existing statutes and practices with respect to the Indians there must be a departure from the old methods. Provisions, including legislation, designed to benefit the Indians must have regard to Indian character, Indian understanding, and Indian sensibilities, and be designed to gratify the wishes of the Indians more and those of the whites less than in the past.

It must be recognized that however loyal and uncomplaining they may be, however little they may ask, the Indians by nature are not the same as white men. In the soul of the red man course cross currents still uncharted by the white man's mind. These the

Indians themselves should be allowed to mark out for the guidance of those whose different viewpoint of life often leads to the most extravagant blunders. This difference of viewpoint and consequent misunderstanding must be constantly borne in mind if the most conscientious purpose to help the Indians is not to be defeated. In other words, Congress must cease to regard the Indians through an opaque lens. The point is not difficult to illustrate.

The inherent dignity of the Indian has often been misconstrued as stolidity, if not sheer stupidity. Analyzed, the understanding of the white man often shows him to be the more stupid of the two. For instance, let us consider our understanding of the Indian language. Young-man-afraid-of-his-horse? What does such a name mean to the white man? Surely an absurd name for a warrior! To the Indian, however, it signifies a valor so great, a courage so dauntless, that the young soldiers or the recruits of the enemy feared even the prowess which the spirit of the knight had imparted to his steed. Thus, to the Indian mind, this gallant chieftain partook not of the nature of the soldier clown, but of a Cid or a Bayard! We missed the import of his name entirely. Rain-in-the-face? What a comical name—to the white man! But to an Indian's mind it is not comical in the least since it expresses the idea of one with a confidence, a faith, a courage so sublime that he can face without the slightest misgiving the storm of life and without flinching confront the wintry gales of adversity.

Another case of equal misunderstanding may be cited. A gallant Chippewa chief, killed in battle, was borne home by his victorious warriors to a widowed bride. Soon a son was born to her. On the little mother's mind there was the impression of darkened days, cloud and rain, sudden shadows and sobbing trees. Just as the sun of her life seemed to have set forever, all joy departed, its rays had broken through a rift in the clouds and like the rainbow of a new hope, had shone out across the saddened plain of her thoughts. A little lad is born to her—a rift in the clouds of her sorrow. Of this beautiful conception the Indian language—literally translated, conveys no other meaning than Hole in the Day. Such a name it was that the whites, seeking to do him honor, placed on the tomb of Rift-in-the-Clouds. Again a little girl, blue eyed and golden haired, won the hearts of the Mohawks. They gave her the name Gajajawox—a picture name suggestive of the wind listing through a field of flowers wafting their perfume as it came—the mingled perfume of the eglantine and honeysuckle borne on a summer breeze. Yet in our language there were no words that fitted Gajajawox. The white man called her Smell-in-the-Air.

No. It is impossible to interpret the exquisite beauty which Indian words often convey to the artistic sensibilities of the Indian mind. Yet, deep down in the Indian soul there is a sense of beauty of which the white man scarcely dreams. We know it only in our literature and music. For us it is a thing we must create out of a strained imagery. We are only conscious of it as a thing apart from workaday affairs. In the Indian mind it is omnipresent, a living, everyday force, untainted by the so-called modern art of civilization. Is it not something worth preserving in the nature of a people, something from the expression of which the whole Nation may profit?

But we need not resort to such qualities or any sentiment whatever for the Indian to justify a different policy from that of the past in dealing with him. As we refer to each decade of Indian history, invariably we find standing out among this people some towering stature, heroic in his moral proportions, unsubmerged by the flood of adversity which poured in with white civilization upon him. Were Philip or Pontiac, or Cornplanter or Little Turtle or Tecumseh, or John Ross or Osceola, or Chief Joseph of a quality morally or intellectually inferior to that of those whom with superb resolution they faced in the most unequal contest that was waged between their people and the whites? Men of such character were too numerous among the Indians to be accidental. Were there not thousands in this race of equal character? Yet, has the Nation ever afforded the Indians—a race of the highest potential capacity—an opportunity to express its aims and aspirations?

Despite the ceaseless recommendations of Washington and their own pleadings it was forty-two years after the United States assumed responsibility for this dependent people before the first dollar was appropriated by Congress for their education. The paltry annual sum of $10,000 then appropriated (1818) for frontier schools was not increased for over half a century. Such was the pitiful provision made for the uplift of half a million aborigines. Was it not natural that the two races with fundamentally hostile economic interests should have misinterpreted each other? What are we really doing today for their education—to prepare them to enjoy their citizenship? The current annual reports of the Commissioner of Indian Affairs indicate a very flourishing condition among the Indians. Nevertheless, there have been dreadful indictments on the floor of Congress in recent years of the Indian policy and conduct of Indian affairs. Unfortunately the issue has become a political one between the Indian Commissioners and their accusers. Again, the Indians have been lost sight of in the controversy that has waged.

Personal experience leads the writer to believe that the issue which has been raised is not one to which the Commissioner of Indian Affairs and his office are properly parties; that the Commissioner of Indian Affairs and his subordinates are imbued with a very high sense of responsibility for the Indians; that they are deeply interested in their welfare; and that they are efficient in the discharge of their duty under the law as it exists. Complaint over the situation of the Indians should be directed not against them but against the law. It is with the law and the system that has developed under it that the fault lies. So long as the present laws remain on the statute books the existing system of dealing with the Indians must persist, and the Indians will not be bettered by investigating this or that administration or Indian Commissioner.

If the present system be scrutinized in a broad way, it will be seen that it is not well designed to advance the welfare of the Indians socially or economically. Like the fifteenth amendment in the case of the negroes, which demanded much of untutored aborigines, but gave them no chart with which to steer their course upon a stormy sea toward economic freedom, our Indian system leaves the tribal Indian to wallow on toward citizenship almost rudderless in an obsolete craft. How can we expect the tribal Indians to overtake the economic vessel in these days of steam and electricity equipped only with an aboriginal paddle. The point may be well illustrated by the case of the Yankton Sioux of South Dakota, one of the finest and proudest groups of the red race.

Always friendly, these Indians received and entertained Lewis and Clark most hospitably during the winter of 1804. Upon the birth of one who was to become their head chief he was wrapped by Lewis in the American flag. The Yanktons came to honor and love that flag, and gave timely warning of the Minnesota massacre of 1862. They took no part in the Sioux uprisings of 1876 and 1891 and have never raised a hand against the government. In 1917 they sent forth their young men in a body to fight side by side with their white brothers in France. Among them there was not a single case in which exemption from military service was sought, and today they are peacefully litigating their rights against the United States in the Court of Claims at their own expense. Assigned to their reservation at Greenwood, South Dakota, is one of the finest, ablest, and most conscientious gentlemen who occupies the office of Indian superintendent in the United States—Mr. Robert E. Lee Daniel.

How have these proud, brave, dignified, peaceful people prospered in their traditional loyalty to the Government? A letter received by the writer from one of their chieftains, under the date of August 26, 1925, describes their present plight as follows:

"A committee meeting was called at Greenwood last Saturday, the 22nd, for the purpose of laying before you the awful conditions that some of the Indians are to face this coming winter. As you will remember we had a short crop last year, and many suffered for lack of food and fuel. In fact all the willows that grew along the river and on the little islands are gone, and soft coal is selling for $14 a ton. The reservation is going through one of the worst droughts since '94. Up until the 1st of July everything looked promising, but we haven't had a decent rain since. The Indians will have to do without their dried sweet corn, as we haven't got a roasting ear. I understand the superintendent has written the Indian office in the matter. I know he will do all he can.

"Antelope and Standing Bull were strong in their speeches, Saturday, that now is the time that help is needed. Antelope thought it may be possible that two or three months of rations could be gotten. I understand that credit has been shut off at the agency stores, and as many Indians were living on the strength of share rents, you can imagine conditions with such a season. Lawrence just returned from Cheyenne River and says the country was blessed with lots of rains, but the Indians were living on horse flesh. A complaint is made that a resident doctor had been promised after July 1 and instead we have a contract doctor who is paid $1,200 per year and figures he can't serve the whole tribe for that amount, and says he will serve just those who have no money. He'll find out that there are a whole lot without money. These are some of the things that I was asked to lay before you."

If such conditions as those represented by the Yankton chief exist among the proud Sioux, they must also exist elsewhere. Here it is to be observed, these people are not complaining, they are not asking for charity. They are only asking for aid in a cruel struggle with the elements. Are they misrepresenting conditions? What are the facts? Does Congress really know the facts? Will Congress take the risk of letting them perish for want? Can a government policy towards the wards of the Nation which makes it necessary 150 years after the Nation assumed responsibility for these people for them to sue for rations be said to have been designed to uplift these people?

Are the tribal Indians, still like the few remaining buffalo herded on reservations, to be left indefinitely in their present plight, not even speaking the language of the Nation that claims them as citizens? Since the receipt of that letter quoted, and at the interposition of the writer, the case of the Yankton Sioux has been investigated by the National Red Cross. While the tribe is very poor it would appear that less than 10 per cent require charitable aid. Even if conditions among them were found to be not as bad as those reported, it is a sorry reflection upon the Government's supervision and care of its wards that the facts respecting their true condition are a matter of doubt, and that any part of the tribe should require charitable aid, or aid over and above that which the Government is rendering.

XI.
THE NEED OF AN INDIAN COMMISSION

Now and then in the martyrdom of man an epical plea is expressed, so convincing of the woes of humanity, of some great moral wrong, that even the most callous of men will pause to hearken to the cry that rises to the high heavens. So it was in the case of Euripides' imperishable tragedy—The Trojan Women—which shook to its foundations the Greek civilization, introducing into the moral philosophy of his time a new principle of humanitarianism. Longfellow but reiterated in "Evangeline" the protest of Euripides. Sometimes the wrong is so indisputable, the right so overwhelmingly on the side of the reformer, that even the most craven of men will not take issue. Then, the potential energy of the moral conviction which has been stored in the conscience of men translates itself into the moving energy of some great reformative act.

So it was when Granville Sharp climbed over the side of an English slaver in the port of Greenwich with Lord Mansfield's writ of habeas corpus in his hand, leading directly to the early abolition of slavery in the British Empire. So it was later with Harriet Beecher Stowe's *Uncle Tom's Cabin*. A picturesque romance it was, of course, well calculated to inflame the passions of men, yet, it was compounded of pathetic though isolated truths each of which could not be denied before God. The travail of the negro was a present fact. His wrongs were not merely things of the past, lamentable but irreparable. The potential energy of the moral conviction which Sharp and Clarkson had generated was translated by Garrison and Stowe, however, impoliticly, however violently, into the moving energy of abolition.

So, too, the oft published speech of Logan, the old Cayuga chieftain, the heroic stories of Lamotachee, the Creek, and Osceola, the Seminole warrior, served to touch the national conscience and store up the potential energy of a great moral conviction of the wrong that had been done the Indian, and no man stood forth in 1881 to deny the appalling indictment against the Government of Helen Hunt Jackson's *Century of Dishonor*. Yet, ignorant of the present facts, the Nation conceived of the wrongs that had been committed against the Indians as crimes of the past. Moreover, uninspired by desire for political and economic gain as in the case of the abolition movement, and, since there was no one with whom to wage a conflict over the Indians, the passions of the people were not aroused by the revelations concerning them as they were by *Uncle Tom's Cabin*. Consequently, the potential energy of an almost unanimous moral conviction did not translate itself into a moving action. The mere spiritual gain that was to be had by the amelioration of the Indians' condition was left to the executive agencies of the Government, with the silent injunction that the indisputable crimes of a dishonorable past occur no more. For these reasons, *Romona*, the *Uncle Tom's Cabin* of the Indians, was not to lead to their liberation from the bonds of political injustice.

Sad were the years that intervened between Washington and Grant, sad were the futile struggles of the red man against whom a rapacious fate with mocking avarice had held down its thumb. In vain it is to regret that from the annals of the Nation may not be stricken out all record of the martyrdom of this helpless race; to rue the frenzied madness of the skin-deep humanity to which that race fell prey; to lament or to apologize for the unparallelled cruelty and neglect of a Government itself but recently born of a dreadful travail in the cradle of human justice. Let not the historian, with the smug apology that such a course was inevitable, brush over the mortifying facts, at the same time professing amazement over the carnival of blood that reigned in France, and today recurs in Russia, inspired as these madnesses were by centuries of oppression. Here, in free America, the soil of the Indian fatherland was saturated with the blood of a people that claimed only the right to exist.

Here a race was politically massacred, while in its defense not a single effective hand raised itself during the orgy of rapine and murder that marked the interlude between Washington and Grant. It was only when a man with all the courage and honesty of Washington, with nothing more to ask at the hands of the people, came into power—Grant—that the voice of the accuser was raised to touch the conscience of those whose interests were no longer affected. In the pulpits and among the settled portions of the country it was Grant who was first able to organize the counter force which eventually overthrew the revel of confiscation that for the reasons mentioned had continued a hundred years. Then, then only, could Congress, reflecting the dominant view, turn to the task of reconstructing the Indians.

After all is said and done, the American people can not shunt the blame to Congress, since any long-continued policy of neglect is but the expression of their own will. This being so, the policy of Congress has been analyzed not for the purpose of disparaging that body, but simply to fix upon the American people more conclusively the responsibility for all that Congress and the Government failed to do.

Again, let the historian speak the truth, not out of a bitterness of heart, not with a vindictiveness designed merely to brand with unanswerable accusations a people who profess to be repentant, but to make the world so deeply conscious of their sin that others may pause upon the threshold of conquest to ask God what is the obligation which civilization imposes along with the right of pre-emption that may be claimed in its name. The story can not be made too full, be told too frankly, to insure that governments, ministries, cabinets in asserting the undeniable rights of civilization will not again revert to a barbarism which has been shown to have been more savage than the savagery of savages. With the facts before the world, perhaps a governmental police, not designed to destroy the aborigines but to restrain the ill-subdued ferocity, the skin deep humanity of the white man, will hereafter precede the latter in uncivilized lands, denying to him the facile methods of the past.

Now, with only good will on the part of all for the Indians, free of all passion, with pride in their wonderful record in the late war, it is time for Congress to do what can be done by way of amends for the past. In the noble words of Grant— "Our superiority of strength and advantages of civilization should make us lenient toward the Indian. The wrong inflicted upon him should be taken into account and the balance placed to his credit. The moral view of the question should be considered, and the question asked, 'Can not the Indian be made a useful and productive member of society by proper teaching and treatment?' If the effort is made in good faith, we will stand better before the civilized nations of the earth and in our own consciences for having made it."

With little aid and in the face of well-nigh insurmountable obstacles all but 150,000 Indians have taken their place in the social and economic life of the Nation beside the other citizens. As to the tribal Indians, the duty of the Nation is as plain now as it was when Washington and Grant pointed it out in words which could have but one meaning.

What is the part of Congress?

The best policies become obsolete. Systems of administration become set and inflexible. New needs are ignored. It is inevitable that official bureaus and agencies should fail to respond to changing conditions even when recommendations are not resented and ignored simply because novel. It is time now for a nonpartisan commission, composed of the ablest obtainable men, to be entrusted with a complete survey of Indian affairs, in order that the Nation may not be misled into enacting laws designed merely to give expression to the white man's aspirations and ideas concerning the race.

The most reliable testimony—not that of their enemies, but of those who have lived and labored among them—is that deep down in the soul of the Indian there is still a living, burning ambition for leadership, a desire to do and to accomplish. Until now the Nation has felt that the white man must hold things in his own hands. But surely now there need be no fear to develop the Indian's power of leadership. Among a people who could furnish such faithful leaders as Cornplanter and Little Turtle, such restrained wisdom as that of John Ross, who but recently could furnish 17,000 soldiers for the defense of the common country, soldiers that could make the great sacrifice no less nobly than their white brothers, there can be nothing to fear. Among them, surely there are many who might, if given the chance, contribute much to the welfare of their race, as well as to the white man's understanding of what is best for it. By allowing them now to serve the country on a commission with white men, their powers of self-government could only be developed, at the same time their understanding of the Government's difficulties enlarged, and their influence for good among their own people enhanced.

If Congress could call upon these people to fight for the Nation, and enfranchise them, is it not time to give them a chance to be heard in their own behalf? Are they not entitled to that much at the hands of a nation which at last, whatever the past may have been, is strong in its desire to do them justice?

194

Shall the Nation continue to pour its wealth and aid into Armenia, Russia, Tyrjetm China, and Japan, and let its own Indian citizens starve upon inhospitable and blighted reservations, still ignorant even of the language of their guardian Government and those with whom they are left to contend? Should foreign policies, battleships, submarines, airplanes, road-building, harbor, drainage, and irrigation schemes, canals, post offices, and further economic developments designed to benefit the white man, take precedence over our duty to these people?

If not, what is the definite plan of Congress for their emancipation from the slavery of the aboriginal social and economic order to which the national policy has consigned them? Before God, it is time for Congress to consider these things and *to act* in such a way that will remove forever the continuing reproach that now rests upon the Nation.

A long time now we have been thinking of the Indians as a romantic race. We read Prescott and Parkman and Cooper, visit the Wild West shows, and in our minds picture them only as befeathered savages of the past. It is time now to think of them with less sentiment and more reality. Let us visit their country—what little of it is left to them—and see them as they really are—citizens bending over the national hoe and plow in a life and death struggle with nature. Let us think of their young men in olive drab upon the firing line in France—not merely as painted warriors upon the warpath of a century ago. Then we will have in our minds a true picture of the Indians.

Then let us ask if the yoke they bear is not too heavy even for this patient people.

For once—the first time—let him confide to us what is in their hearts. Let the Nation hear what they have to say as well as what comes from the departmental bureaus and out of the debates of Congress.

That is the first step, it is submitted, that should be taken in recognition of the citizenship of this people who but recently have contributed so freely of their loyalty and blood to the defense of this, the land of their forefathers. Then—then only we may be able truthfully to say to our sister nations—for all that is taken from the Indians they receive ample consideration.

VI

THE LONELY FIGHT OF THE INDIAN LEADER

The great champions of the Indian people have always come forth in the darkest hour to fight against impossible odds. Crazy Horse with his starving band in the Badlands of South Dakota, Chief Joseph with his women and children fleeing toward Canada pursued by hundreds of cavalry, Geronimo and his handful of Apache patriots tying up thousands of American soldiers—all are indicative of the heros of the Indian past.

So much emphasis has been placed on the spectacular achievements of the past that few people have come to recognize the leaders of today. Thus Indians, like some other minority groups, suffer from the curse of anonymity. The public has few Indians with whom it can identify. Whenever reports, statements or policy are required, Indians themselves are rarely asked to give their opinions. More often white experts who have established national reputations as "friends" of Indians come to the forefront as final authorities on the problems of Indian people.

This chapter is devoted to a presentation of the speeches of contemporary Indian leadership. Earl Old Person, for example, is presently the president of the National Congress of American Indians. Joe Garry is a former President of the N.C.A.I., and still a vigorous proponent of Indian rights. Governor Robert Lewis is one of the ablest leaders of the Southwest, a man fully demanding the respect of Indian and white everywhere and one of the ablest leaders in the history of the Pueblo people.

Over the years these men have given leadership to the Indian cause. They have worked without publicity, at great personal cost, and with the highest devotion to Indian people. Perhaps their unrecorded speeches are better than the selections included here. But what is vitally important for today is that noted Indian spokesmen be acknowledged by Indian and white alike for their accomplishments and significance. The tribes are still producing champions. From within the national Indian community wise and good men are still coming forward.

Protest of the Representatives of the Indian Territory
Against the Indian Allotment Act (1881)

In 1881, at the instigation of churches, railroads, land-hungry settlers, mining companies, and philanthropists, discussion was begun on a bill to divide up the great Indian reservations and allot to each Indian and his family an amount of land on which he could become a farmer. It was assumed, through some intangible and metaphysical revelation, that the mere presence of a piece of paper entitled "deed" in the hands of an Indian would inspire him to achieve the heights of agricultural efficiency.

The majority of the tribes were still but months removed from their traditional ways of life, the Custer battle having been a mere five years distant and the Geronimo campaign yet to be waged. Misrepresentations were made to the various tribes by which their consent was allegedly gotten to allot the lands in severalty. For the remote tribesmen huddled on the desert reservations the activities in Washington were unknown.

The only tribes capable of understanding the implications of the Allotment Act were the Five Civilized Tribes. They vehemently opposed the idea, not just for themselves but for all the tribes in Oklahoma. Thus when the bill was being discussed in the Senate of the United States, the headmen of the Five Civilized Tribes sent the following message to Congress to register their disapproval. It stands as another example of the eloquence of the Cherokee statesmen as a prime example of the "savage Indian" being smarter than the whites who were making decisions on behalf of the Indians, and as a tragic appeal for reason, understanding and good faith from one race to another.

The Five Tribes eventually fell before the onslaught of allotment in the early years of this century. Today they are among the poorest people in the nation having been thoroughly despoiled in the interim. But in their day they fought for what they believed.

To the Congress of the United States:

As representatives of the leading nations of the Indian Territory we desire to call your attention to several measures pending before you, the purpose of which is to change the condition and compromise the safety of the Indian people. We refer to the bills for sectionizing and allotting in severalty the lands of the Indians. We have understood that such bills were not intended to apply to the Indian Territory, as there is no provision for white settlement in that country, and the treaties define that this allotment in severalty can only be done on the request of the Indian nations.

We therefore appeal to you not to violate your pledges to us in treaties. Doing this for a single tribe in the Indian Territory, as would be the case in passing H.R. No. 6022 for allotting lands of Peorias, Weas, Miamis, Piankeshaws, and Kaskaskias, would lead to local disturbance and produce great mischief.

Our people have not asked for or authorized this, for the reason that they believe it could do no good and would only result in mischief in their present condition. Our own laws regulate a system of land tenure suited to our condition and much safer than that which is proposed to be established for it. Improvements can be and are frequently sold, but the land itself is not a chattel. Its occupancy and possession are indispensible to holding it, and its abandonment for two years makes it revert to the public domain. In this way every one of our citizens is sure of a home.

The change to individual title would throw the whole of our domain in a few years into the hands of a few persons. In your treaties with us you have agreed that this shall not be done without our consent; we have not asked for it, and we call on you not to violate your pledges with us.

There are other reasons involving prosperity and safety, why the limitations of sectionizing should not be thrust over us. A large portion of our country, and at least two-thirds of the Indian Territory, are only suitable for grazing purposes. No man can afford to live by stock-raising and herding who is restricted to one hundred and sixty or even three hundred and twenty acres, especially on lands away from water. The herds must be sufficiently large to justify the care of them. The pasture country of the

United States is fast being reduced. It is necessary for your prosperity, as well as our own, that what little is left of it should not be destroyed by vicious and ill-adapted systems of legislation. We would instance a single case outside of the Indian Territory. The Navajos, in New Mexico, do not number much more than one-fourth of the Cherokee Nation. Their reserve is as large as the reserved lands of the Cherokee Nation. Not more than one acre in twenty is suitable for cultivation. They live by pastoral pursuits. They are stated to have 800,000 sheep, 300,000 head of cattle, and 40,000 horses; by this business they live, comfortable, exporting wool and livestock. By sectionizing or reducing them to one hundred and sixty acres, you would pauperize and ruin a people who are now holding to your productive industries.

Again, there are several tribes now in the Indian Territory who have already suffered from this process. The Shawnees, Pottawatomies, and Kickapoos once lived in Kansas; it was provided by the treaty that they should take their lands in severalty, but they could not be alienated for twenty years unless they became citizens of the United States. White men were introduced among them; before five years every acre had been alienated and these tribes had to be gathered up and sent to the Indian Territory.

This program has seductive allurements for visionary persons who have not carefully studied the subject, but it is full of mischief for us. While we do not think the general policy, as at present pursued, is capable of producing anything but mischief, we only desire to call attention to the case of our own people and appeal to you not to violate your treaties with us.

> D.W. Bushyhead
> Principal Chief
> P.N. Blackstone
> George Sanders
> Cherokee Delegation
> Pleasant Porter
> Ward Coachman
> D.M. Hodge
> Creek Delegation
> Peter P. Pitchlynn
> Choctaw Delegation

The Fight Against Garrison Dam (1949)

After the Second World War the U.S. Army Corps of Engineers, restless and eager to continue its massive program of flooding America, began looking around at the many rivers which were virtually untouched by dams and hydro-electric plants. Spying the innocent tribes residing along the Missouri River they decided that here they had a victim ready for plunder.

But the Interior Department also had some ideas on developing the Missouri River and it was not about to take a back seat to an upstart and competitive group like the Engineers.

Two plans were advanced: the Sloan Plan and the Pick Plan. One sought to build massive earth dams at key points on the river, the other looked to a series of smaller dams on the tributaries of the Missouri. Not being determined to kill each other off when the pork barrel looked so promising, the Interior and War Departments combined their ventures under the name Pick-Sloan and promptly began the acquisition of millions of acres of Indian lands for their gigantic undertaking.

By methods more foul than fair they browbeat every tribe on the river and forced them to sell their lands to be flooded by the large project. The most seriously affected was the Fort Berthold Reservation on which lived the Mandan, Gros Ventre and Arickaree tribes, friends of the United States of longstanding. They had provided many of Custer's scouts against the Sioux and nearly a century before had given Lewis and Clark shelter against the Sioux who had opposed the march up river.

The tribal council of the reservation, now designated the Three Affiliated Tribes, fought desperately against the taking of their reservation for the dam. But they lost. Not only were their best bottom lands taken, but later the Army would claim they had also ceded any water and shoreline rights. The reservation was divided into four parts which became inaccessible one to another as a result of the flooding. Traditional patterns of tribal settlement were disturbed and the people were callously resettled according to the whims of the Corp of Engineers—thus breaking forever the reservation communities that had previously existed.

At the final hearing on the condemnation of the lands the government was still trying to avoid paying a fair price for the lands. The tribal council sent a delegation to Washington to protest the arbitrary cruelty of the government's position. Charging lack of good faith by the United States the delegation asked for justice citing the long history of friendly relations which the tribes had maintained.

An appeal to justice and good faith, when made to the United States by an Indian tribe, is like humming in a hurricane!!

Thus we have the finest statements of the Indian case falling on deaf ears. These presentations should not be left to wither, neglected and unavailable to red and white alike. Rather they document the anguish and heartbreak of Indians of all the centuries. In their bitterness is the story of humanity deprived and downtrodden by the goddess of progress.

At Fort Berthold also, we have had our warriors and statesmen.

TESTIMONY OF JEFFERSON SMITH, GROS VENTRE, AGAINST THE INJUSTICE OF THE GARRISON DAM

(April 30, 1949—Washington, D.C.)

Mr. Chairman, my name is Jefferson B. Smith, a member of the Gros Ventre Tribe, an official delegate of the Tribal Business Council of the Three Affiliated Tribes, comprising the Arickaree, the Gros Ventres and the Mandan and the individual members thereof.

The United States of America, before its advent as a Nation, was a haven for the oppressed of other lands. Political, religious, and economic oppression in Europe caused the Pilgrim Fathers to seek homes, freedom and greater opportunity in the New World. These Pilgrims, upon their arrival in 1620, were welcomed by the native Americans. They were given land and all that was within. In a short period of time, greed for gain became evident. The white man, motivated by a great desire to acquire additional territory, compelled the Indian to move thither and yon. Thus began the racial discrimination, plundering, stripping, despoiling him of his property; a delimitation of Indian tribal boundaries.

The Three Affiliated Tribes of North Dakota have always maintained utmost good faith and friendship with the United States. Many years ago, upon meeting his first white man, who aroused his admiration to a high degree, one of our chiefs decreed to his people that the white man was their friend and that there should ever exist a mutual and friendly relationship. When Lewis and Clark were designated to explore the land which comprised the Louisiana Purchase of 1804, they found a very friendly people in the three tribes. They were afforded food and protection. The famed Indian woman known as Bird Woman guided the expedition westward.

Many of our Indians joined the United States troops as scouts in the pioneer days and have rendered valuable services. The Commissioner of Indian Affairs in his report dated November 1, 1873, said of the Three Affiliated Tribes, pages 158 and 159:

> The Indians of these agencies deserve more from the Government than any other tribes in Dakota on account of their fidelity to the Government and the faithful services rendered by them as scouts in compelling other Indians to keep the peace.

Another report dated August 31, 1874, pages 159 to 160, contains the following:

> The military have found them the most brave and reliable of all Indian scouts. But notwithstanding their established friendliness, I found them in an intensively dissatisfied state of mind. They complained that while they had steadily kept the "straight path," the Government had not done so; the whites had lied to them, cheated them, and actually allowed them to starve, instead of feeding them and caring for them as promised in all their treaty councils. Unfortunately, and to our shame, their declarations are too true.

The proposal of the United States to negotiate treaties with the Arickaree, Gros Ventre, and Mandan Indians was gladly accepted as a kindly gesture.

The three tribes inhabited the Dakotas and eastern Montana. They were once populous tribes. It is a common knowledge among our older people than on or about the year 1837 a boat drifted down the river bearing some white men, one of which was allowed to remain at an Indian village. He had smallpox. Ravages of the disease nearly exterminated the tribes.

The United States entered into a solemn treaty with Arickaree, Gros Ventre, and Mandan Indians on or about September 17, 1851. The treaty lands as claimed by the three tribes were as follows: Commencing at the mouth of the Heart River, up the Missouri, Yellowstone, and Powder Rivers, to the headwaters of the Little Missouri River, to the foothills of the Black Hills, to the Heart River and the place of beginning, containing about 13,000,000 acres.

Across the span of our national history, it is inconceivable that treaties with Indians which have been sacredly solemnized and duly ratified have been violated by its author—the United States Government. The construction of the Garrison Dam which will inundate a large portion of our treaty land is a more recent violation of treaty. The Three Affiliated Tribes now deem that their faith and friendship with the Federal Government has worked largely to their undoing. It is quite evident that the Indians have done most of the giving and the United States Government most of the taking.

The native Americans, who in the remote past reigned supreme in all they possessed by immemorial right of occupancy, are an underprivileged minority group against whom many illegal forms of oppression and discrimination are practiced. Belonging to a minority group whose skin is pigmented seems to be a disqualification which serves as a bar in preventing participation in the benefits of American justice.

At one time in the past, the United States Government recognized the importance of fair treatment for the Indians and on July 13, 1787, it adopted the Northwest Ordinance, section 3 of which reads as follows:

> The uttermost good faith shall always be observed toward the Indians; their lands and property shall never be taken from them without their consent; and in their property, rights, and liberty they shall never be invaded or disturbed, unless in just and lawful wars authorized by Congress, but laws founded in justice and humanity shall, from time to time be made for preventing wrongs being done to them, and for preserving peace and friendship with them.

In 1944 Congress authorized five dams to be constructed on the main stem of the Missouri River, one of which was the Garrison Dam.

This reservoir, when completed, will destroy the homes, the lands and the economy of the Fort Berthold Indians. The Northwest Ordinance of 1787 was violated when the matter was not referred to the Indians for consideration. Preliminary work on the dam was well begun when a Colonel Freeman furnished us information that the Garrison Dam would flood some of the best land the Indian possessed, but that they would be given other land of equal value. The land offered included for the most part, the area known as the Little Missouri River Badlands. Much of the land offered is devoid of any vegetation. We refused the disgraceful offer. We have rejected other offers because we feel that our rights were not protected.

In July of 1947, Councilmen Packineau, Mahto, and I were present at the hearings before the Subcommittee on War Department Civil Appropriation Act, Public Law 296, to prevent, if possible, the flooding of our lands. The pleas we made to save our land, homes, and our economy was given a deaf ear. Our offer of an alternate plan and location of a dam was not considered. An offer of $5,105,625 was made.

We requested a compensation of a larger amount. There was disagreement and no further offer was made. We returned home to learn to our dismay that it was reported on the floor of the Senate Chamber that the Indians agreed to the offer. We did not agree to the offer and, hence, we charge that the offer was false and illegal. We protest the wrong being done to us by the illegal action and methods. The Indian has become inferior to the white man, he is forced to serve him and is subject to his master's orders. Because the Indian is weak and docile, he is wronged and imposed upon.

It has been a requirement of law that a contract be entered into by the United States Government and the Three Affiliated Tribes in the apportionment of the funds which was supposed to have been agreed upon by the Indians. The contract has been completed in compliance with the law. It is awaiting the ratification by Congress.

A grave situation confronts the Three Affiliated Tribes. The United States Government has entered into solemn treaties with the Indians. The treaties were made, composed, and devised by a commission authorized by the United States Government (Indians being illiterate and belong to a lesser social and economic caste), for the sole benefit and strictly in accordance with the desire of the Government. It has defaulted and broken the treaties. Will the present contract or treaty meet the same fate? The abuse and misuse of its ward Indians has created an atmosphere of suspicion and mistrust that no future time can repair.

The tribal business council of the Three Affiliated Tribes have signed the contract with tears in their eyes and heavy hearts. Being compelled to surrender about 155,000 acres of our best lands to the United States Government, thereby disrupting our homes and economy, the future looks dark and dismal to the Fort Berthold Indians. We are being punished for being Indians by a Christian nation.

The United States Government is the strongest, the wealthiest, and freest nation in the world. It has furnished billions of dollars to Europe, Asia, and Latin America, much of which will never be reimbursed. The Government owes its wards a moral obligation. It is the guardian and bound by every moral and equitable consideration to discharge its trust with good faith.

TESTIMONY OF CARL WHITMAN, JR.,
CHAIRMAN OF THE COUNCIL, FORT BERTHOLD RESERVATION
AGAINST THE INJUSTICE OF THE GARRISON DAM
(April 30, 1949—Washington D.C.)

For almost 100 years our forefathers and representatives of the Federal Government entered into a solemn treaty whereby our reservation lands were reserved for our use forever. We kept our promise and have worked to build up a strong and growing cattle industry and steadily expanding agricultural program. Just as we were in sight of economic independence you began to build a reservoir and to take away the heart of our reservation and divide it into five isolated segments. The homes which we built, the bottom lands on which 85 per cent of our people lived and on which cattle industry depended, our churches, our schools, our government, and our social life will be disrupted.

We did not want Garrison Dam built. We pleaded with you to find another place to build a dam. It was not that we wish to hamper progress. In fact, we voluntarily offered some of our other lands which were not so vital to our life as a place to be used to construct a dam. Our prayers and pleas were fruitless. The Government told us "Either you agree to some terms, or we'll take the land without your consent."

We were, therefore, forced to sign a contract with the Army. This contract was ratified by our people and our council over a year ago. Yet it is still unratified by the Congress with the result that some of its terms like a provision enabling us to use certain timber up to 1950 cannot be utilized by us. Every day that passes worsens our plight.

I have shown the necessity for prompt action now. Let me summarize the terms of this proposal—our brief explains in detail. The United States will make a settlement with my people for less than $15,000,000. It will obtain the right-of-way of Garrison Dam and Reservoir which constitutes the keystone of the five great dams on the main stem of the Missouri River and 100 large and small dams on the numerous tributaries of the river. The cornerstone of the Missouri River development program will thus be carried out by the Government obtaining Garrison Reservoir right-of-way at about two-thirds of its basic value and its annual use to the Three Affiliated Tribes.

Let me also discuss briefly two portions of this proposed agreement which will illustrate its wisdom in effectuating the Government's special responsibility for these tribes.

Three million dollars would be authorized for an appropriation to be used for land readjustment. Under the Indian Inheritance Act of 1910 estates of individual allottees have passed to heirs of even a third and fourth generation developing a complex picture of divided interest in various fractional interest scattered over the reservation. The resulting land situation is so confused that many members of the tribe are either landless or without sufficient or usable land to make a decent living. The land readjustment fund will be used to turn fractional interest into cash which will in turn be used to buy other lands for the individual. The consolidated lands will enable him to make a decent living for himself and for his family.

Another important provision which, I will briefly touch on, would harness a block of the power generated by the dam for use of the members of the tribe and for sale to others. This will bring electricity at a reasonable cost which will enable us to improve our standard of living and gain some of the advantages of modern technology.

We know that the heart of America bleeds for us. Hundreds of our fellow citizens throughout our great country have shown their sympathetic understanding of our loss. We know now that the United States Government will carry out the wishes of its people and use this great opportunity to help us help ourselves. Our task is very difficult. We must rebuild and reorganize a new life. Even if the bills and appropriations before you are passed quickly, we face 10, 15, or 20 years of hardship, unrest, reorganization and reconstruction. With your help, we must forget the heritage of our homeland guaranteed to us by a solemn and sacred treaty. We, the first Americans, the original owners of this land, feel confident that you will delay no longer. While you cannot restore the 155,000 acres of our best land nor the many losses that cannot be transmuted in money, we expect that you will do your part and be just to our people.

There is one point that I would like to make clear at this point, that this agreement made by the Indians was taken as the only recourse left to them. It was more or less forced on them. We did not willingly agree to it. That I wanted to emphasize at this point.

STATEMENT OF MARTIN CROSS, COUNCIL MEMBER,
FORT BERTHOLD RESERVATION
AGAINST THE INJUSTICE OF THE GARRISON DAM
(April 30, 1949—Washington, D.C.)

Mr. Chairman and gentlemen of the committee:

My name is Martin Cross. I reside at Elbowoods, North Dakota. I am enrolled as a member of the Three Affiliated Tribes of the Fort Berthold Indian Reservation. I appreciate this opportunity to appear and deliver my message orally to the committee. I have with me two petitions which combined have over 200 names that I am submitting as my credentials for this occasion. The petitions authorize me as their true representative and spokesman for the group. I am acting on those premises.

I earnestly request that my statements in their entirety and any colloquy that may ensue be printed as record and make it accessible to the Indians at home and other interested parties elsewhere in the United States.

I intend to speak frankly and freely—I will be as brief as possible. I will try to cover all the pertinent matters that pertain to my cause here. I feel hopeful that the committee will indulge me the time to do so.

The Indian people I represent are now under the control and guardianship of the United States Government. They own property, own lands in severality, have equity in tribal property and lands held in common. They have at no time attempted to sever their tribal relations with the United States Government. They beg to remain in firm and lasting harmony with the United States Government.

We are not in favor of ratifying of this legislation House Joint Resolution 33. I will carry on from here; my remarks will have the effect and force of the group. I myself have opposed this legislation all along and I am opposing it now. I am doubly convinced that my reasons for opposing it are on a sound basis, logical, and of deep concern both to the Indians and the policy of the United States Government. Therefore, I feel justified in enumerating them here, and file them into the record to be considered with analysis and study of this bill. I hope the members of the committee will give careful consideration to them. I have always adhered to the principle that the Subcommittee of Indian Affairs is set up for the express purpose of protecting the constitutional rights and privileges of the Indians foremost in every consideration of Indian bills; that they are open to suggestions and opinions both legally and morally from both sides of the question. So, therefore, I am speaking here on those terms without fear of any consequence. I do not seek to do any injustice, nor do anything that might result in disastrous or deteriorating effect on my people. I wish to prevent any mistakes that will have lasting effect in the well-being of the Indian people.

Permit me to say that I am well acquainted with my congressional Members here in the United States Congress from the State of North Dakota. There are only four of them, a small number in comparison with other States, but their ability as statesmen is second to none. I have only the highest regard for them. I have every reason to believe that they will do their utmost to support my contentions. I realize that because of their position their advice recommendations will have strong bearing on any situations in the State of North Dakota, including the Fort Berthold Reservation. I am also seeking help of other Members of the United States Congress. I am most anxious to carry my problem to final determination.

This is not the first time that public interest has sought to acquire the lands of the Fort Berthold Indians. It has been done before in the 1866 treaty which opened the territory for railroads and by subsequent Executive Orders of 1870 and 1880 which reduced some more of our territory without our consent, until now we have only 600,000 acres left of our original 9,000,000 acres. Is that not depreciation enough? No; the public demands some more. Do you argue why we protest against this further demand? It seems imperative for me to reiterate and remind Uncle Sam at this time of some of the principles involved in this proposition. What I am about to say is within the deep recesses of your mind. I would like to bring it up again to the surface for this occasion to illustrate my point in the following statement.

I oppose the ratification of this legislation House Joint Resolution 33 or similar legislation now pending in the mills of the United States Congress wherein the main purpose is to acquire further tribal and individual-owned Indian lands for public purpose.

If you allow the Indians by legislation to sell their best lands, as in the case of Fort Berthold Indians, it is to rob and permit expatriation of their wealth. It not only constitutes breach of promise, but out and out is a violation of treaty stipulation of article VII of Fort Laramie Treaty of September 17, 1851. The Fort Berthold Indians are parties of the second part to this agreement, and it has stood the test of the Court of Claims. I am no attorney therefore I have no knowledge of the procedure of the United States Congress—how they carry out their acts. However, I have grown up with the belief that our rights and title to our lands were safe and secure in the protective custody of the United States Government. I have lived all my life under that atmosphere and have become so accustomed to that philosophy that any transition from that principle would result in a disastrous revolutionary process. I began to wonder if the validity of the Fort

Laramie Treaty had become obsolete, or if the meaning had lost its charm. With all these facts and figures if such legislation as House Joint Resolution 33 is approved it will only lead to prove instability of our title to our lands and rights, and prove the hypocrisy of your wardship theory, and we do not wish to have that happen. We ask that Uncle Sam keep that predication intact.

We realize that the building of the Garrison Dam is a big item here in the United States Congress. Millions upon millions of dollars are being expended. The United States Army Engineer Corps is guaranteeing the job. Big names can be made. Everybody wants to get into the act. There is no opposition among the ranks of the United States Congress. It is a big issue. Any opposition raised is not strong enough against the irresistible force of the demand.

Mr. Benton Stong of MVA raises the issue that the feasibility of building such a big earth dam is unsafe. I want to side in with him. I oppose the Garrison Dam Reservoir because it will inundate the lands of the Fort Berthold Reservation and cause to be removed a whole community of Indians from their ancestral homes.

I feel that basically and morally, if Uncle Sam really wants to protect and respect the wishes of the Fort Berthold Indians it can do so without too much trouble. I think liberty-loving people will applaud and support such a stand.

We are classed as noncompetents. The Indian Bureau thrives on that fact. If we are really under the category of noncompetents, then legally we could not enter into contracts as parties.

Gentlemen, I would like to say a few words more, and then I will yield the floor.

That is the way the group that I represent feels. That is the attitude of the people who have sent me down here. They want to stand pat. They ask that the bill, House Joint Resolution 33 be not passed at this time for the following reasons:

The tribal council are unwilling to permit settlement of differences at home. Surely we do not want to burden the United States Congress to decide this matter for us. We feel that it will be a long time yet before the floodwaters of Garrison Dam will reach the doorsteps, and it is premature to feel any alarm today. We have ample time yet to make intelligent decisions. We know what we want. We know how to ask for it, if permission is offered us. It is not necessary for someone else to do that.

The lump sum offered is not a satisfactory way of making us feel safe in accepting or considering the proposition. It must be a definite thing. We are not playing marbles. We are playing for keeps.

The Indian Office personnel have been around making appraisals of lands, homes, and improvements, but they have never told anyone how much they will receive.

As far as I am concerned, I think it is better to take the condemnation proceedings and receive less, than to settle by arbitration and not be satisfied.

There are some men among the group that we have here who have no property at all. They are here to chisel in on this proposition.

I look at it this way: Only those people who have the chance of being actual losers should be given the first consideration, and not those that have nothing to lose in this steal.

I will put it this way: If you do not have anything you never miss it.

Do not permit any witnesses here with that kind of presentation. Please question each witness as to his occupation, and the real and personal property which is involved in this transaction.

I know that some have nothing to lose, and everything to gain, if this bill goes through. Then I think some provision should be made, if you are going to approve this legislation, for some financial assistance to have it ready for those of us who are going to be moved. It does not make any difference whether you give us $50,000,000 in the legislation, or something else, if you put it in charge of the tribal council or the Indian Bureau. It is pretty hard to get any money out of them. I do not have to repeat that. It is a fact.

Concerning House Report No. 2680 of the 83rd. Congress— A Resolution of the National Congress of American Indians (1954)

In an effort to browbeat the tribes who had gathered in Washington, D.C. in the spring of 1954 to oppose the Termination Policy being promulgated by Senator Arthur Watkins and Representative E.Y. Berry, the Joint Subcommittee of Indian Affairs struck back with a threatening report, H.R. No. 2680. In this report, which displayed an abysmal ignorance of federal-tribal relationships, veiled threats were contained, foremost of which was the repeal of the Indian Reorganization Act and the nullification of tribal constitutions which had been chartered under it. The Congressmen thought that without a functioning tribal government the Indians would be handicapped by lack of travel funds and official status and would therefore be unable to oppose the Termination Policy.

Looking around during the summer of 1954 the Indians discovered a noticeable lack of white allies and, with the exception of their tribal lawyers, the landscape looked barren indeed. The National Congress of American Indians met that year in Omaha, Nebraska. Faced with the impending report and the implications of its suggested policy, there was discussion as to what the Indian response should be.

The convention resolutions committee had several able leaders. With magnificent courage they decided to attack. Thus for two days Darcy McNickle, Frank Parker, and Frank George sweated over the statement against H.R. No. 2680 and presented it to the assembled delegates. It was passed by a large majority. The tribes had decided to draw the line.

The N.C.A.I. statement, of course, brilliantly shredded the contentions of the House Report and revealed the Joint Subcommittee and its staff as incompetents of the first magnitude. So piercing was the N.C.A.I. attack that it embarrassed those Senators and Congressmen who had previously remained silent. When Congress next convened the powers of Watkins and Berry were somewhat curtailed and the sharpness of the Congressional attack on the tribes was blunted. was blunted.

The statement on House Report No. 2680 belies the common complaint of non-Indians newly arriving on the Indian scene that "no one speaks for the Indians". At a time of extreme crisis the assembled Indian tribes took the final step of defiance and launched the attack breaking the impetus of the movement to destroy them.

An investigation was held some years later, but it was a perfunctory letter-writing request for information rather than the scathing revelation which House Report No. 2680 had implied was necessary. Even during the subsequent investigation, the N.C.A.I. held its own and emerged with solid credentials as a powerful Washington representative of the Indian tribes.

Whereas, House Report No. 2680 of the 83rd Congress, 2nd session, makes the charge that there exists "no adequate channel for the expression of overall Indian public opinion within local communities, or in the nation as a whole", and this report further reflects unfairly on the sincerity of purpose, and the motives of private organizations devoted to Indian matters, including the National Congress of American Indians, and proposes an investigation of such private organizations, and

Whereas, Indian tribes, bands, and groups throughout the United States and Alaska select their spokesmen and governing bodies in accordance with customary law or written constitution, and in either situation such spokesmen or governing bodies are fully responsible to the people they represent, the Indian people having followed democratic forms of government since long before the United States Government was organized; and

Whereas, the National Congress of American Indians invites and welcomes a fair and complete investigation of all of its activities, and does hereby urge that such a fair and complete investigation be conducted; and

Whereas, the National Congress of American Indians meeting in its annual convention in Phoenix, Arizona, on December 9, 1953, did adopt a resolution "condemning organizations, groups and individuals affiliated with subversive movements, and un-American activities designed to undermine American institutions," which Resolution is attached and made a part of this Resolution; and

Whereas, it is the intention and purpose of the National Congress of American Indians never knowingly to accept grants, or contributions from any individuals, or organizations of a subversive, or un-American nature; and

Whereas, Report No. 2680 contains many misleading, ill-considered, and factually inaccurate statements pertaining to Indian Affairs;

Now, therefore, be it resolved that the National Congress of American Indians at convention assembled in Omaha, Nebraska, November 18-21, 1954, authorize and direct that the attached statement commenting on House Report No. 2680 be adopted as voicing the views of the convention and that this Resolution with the attached approved statement be submitted to the Chairmen of the House and Senate Committees of Interior and Insular Affairs.

STATEMENT OF THE 11TH ANNUAL CONVENTION OF THE NATIONAL CONGRESS OF AMERICAN INDIANS CONCERNING HOUSE REPORT NO. 2680, 83rd Congress, 2nd Sessions, PURSUANT TO HOUSE RESOLUTION 89 TO INVESTIGATE THE BUREAU OF INDIAN AFFAIRS

The above-named report was prepared by some of the members of the sub-committee on Indian Affairs who were especially appointed and authorized by the Committee on Interior and Insular Affairs to conduct an investigation of the Bureau of Indian Affairs.

In view of the fact that some of the signers of this report exhibited intelligent concern for their Indian constituents and showed respect for the principle of fair dealing, we find it hard to believe that these men could have read the report on which their names appear. We say this because the matter contained in the report reveals a profound ignorance of Indian issues, while the recommendations offered in the report, if followed, would result in violations of fair play to which Indians are entitled.

These are unkind charges to lay against any group, in Congress or elsewhere, and the statements are made reluctantly. The Subcommittee's report assumes there is no good faith, or logic, or wisdom in any spokesman—Indian or non-Indian—who may have differed with the views expressed in this report. This leaves no room for charitableness.

With regard to the charge of ignorance, the report speaks for itself. The following are cited:

1. In the matter of tribal membership, referred to in the second paragraph of page 2 of the report, Indian tribes were deciding membership questions long before the Indian Reorganization Act of 1934 and the adoption of written constitutions under that Act. The power to make such determinations is inherent in an Indian tribe and was not delegated by the Congress to the tribe as the report asserts.

It is not clear who is being slurred by the statement that "certain elements" manipulate tribal rolls to suit themselves, but it is a fact, easily verified, that persons of little or no Indian blood were placed on tribal rolls by Government officials on many occasions *prior* to 1934. Any fair appraisal of the enrollment procedures followed by tribes *since* 1934 would certainly reveal a high standard of official conduct.

2. The recommendation in the middle of paragraph on page 6, that the authority of an Indian tribe to adopt a form of Government be "repealed" in case of a "demonstrated unwillingness or inability of an individual group to function in a reasonably satisfactory manner," is confused and ambiguous. Repeal of the Indian Reorganization Act, if that is what is intended, would not repeal the authority of an Indian tribe to govern itself either under a written constitution or in accordance with unwritten customary law. If on the other hand, the recommendation is to the effect that the constitution of an Indian tribe might be repealed by an Act of Congress, it is a very strange proposal to come from a body of men dedicated to a democratic form of government. Tribal constitutions under the Indian Reorganization Act of 1934 were adopted by a majority vote of the members of the tribe, and are open to amendment and to revocation by a vote of the same members, not by an Act of Congress.

3. The reference to the Handbook of Federal Indian Law in the following paragraph on the same page is silent on the Revised Edition of that Handbook which appeared in 1943. The intention here appears to be to stress the out-modedness of a book published in 1940, and the fact that the book was later revised would have minimized this point.

Anyone familiar with Title 25 of the United States Code must realize that it is no substitute for the Handbook of Federal Indian Law, even if the former should be revised to include a detailed index to legislation and treaties by individual Indian tribes. The value of the Handbook is the perspective it provides across the broad field of Indian legislation, treaties and Federal and State court decisions, and Federal regulations.

4. The discussion of Indian tribes and Indian census rolls in the last two paragraphs on page 9 reveals great confusion. The fact that the Federal Government for its own convenience settled Indian tribes (often with a prior history of hostility and of different culture and language) within the same geographical boundaries is here used as an argument in favor of ignoring all tribal units. Even where those jurisdictional hodge-podges occurred for administrative convenience, the census rolls continued to recognize tribal distinctions and a tribal designation was shown for each individual enrolled.

The comparison of Indians to immigrants becoming citizens is, of course, irrelevant and insulting to Indians—the First Americans!!

The recommendations offered by the Subcommittee, if offered by any other body of citizens would be ignored because of their short-sightedness and their callous disregard of the human problems involved. The fact that they are offered by members of Congress and may lead to legislative action (indeed, in certain details, have already produced legislation!!), demands the most careful study of this report.

The underlying purpose and intention of the Subcommittee is revealed at two places in the report. Under Item 4 on Page 2, the report states that "no law yet enacted in the field of Indian Affairs has had the effect of stimulation of Indians, as a group, to make an active effort to end Federal wardship." This suggests two things: First, that the members of the Subcommittee believe that the complex problems of human adjustment, changed ways of living, can be brought about by law alone (we know of no law in any other field that has stimulated other tax-exempt individuals or institutions to end their tax exemptions); and Second, that law be used as a club, if necessary, to make Indians conform to the wishes of Congress.

The other point at which the intentions of the Subcommittee members come into the open is found at Page 7, in the recommendation that surveys be made to obtain "authentic information regarding ownership, title, extent, and value of Indian lands which may ultimately be added to the local tax rolls." It is in keeping with this recommendation that, in the next to the last paragraph of that page, the members express the view the "the only permanent solution for the problem involved in the handling of Indian lands by the Bureau of Indian Affairs lies in the removal of Indian Bureau control."

THE DAY WHEN TRUSTEESHIP IS REMOVED ALTOGETHER WILL BE THE BEGINNING OF THE END FOR A PEOPLE WHO ONCE WERE MASTERS IN IN THEIR OWN HOUSE, BUT WHO ARE NO LONGER. In fact, the record on this is clear where tribes were persuaded to allot their lands and land sales at foolish prices have been taking place at the rate of hundreds of acres per day.

The recommendation in the first paragraph on Page 7 certainly goes beyond the scope of House Resolution 89 and seems very questionable from a policy standpoint. To translate this to some other field, perhaps the Interior and Insular Affairs Committee should undertake studies of adequacies of expression of organizations representing water users, forestry organizations, public power organizations, and other like groups.

It is difficult to square this recommendation with the last full paragraph on Page 10 and the statements on Page 12. If the Subcommittee is serious about requesting private organizations to assist Congress in its deliberations on Indian legislation, this seems a strange way to encourage such assistance.

The "final solution" which the Subcommittee proposes in the first full paragraph on Page 8, to avoid a repetition that a few Federal employees may, by dishonesty, involve the Federal Government in such scandal, the Subcommittee would grant patents in fee, apparently without regard to the capability of the allottee, so as to prevent dishonesty among government employees. It seems to overlook entirely the strong probability that this will result in countless frauds being perpetrated upon incompetent wards. In short, it would not eliminate fraudulent transactions; it would merely eliminate the temptation for Federal employees and relieve the trustee (the Government) of any responsibility. Likewise, the recommendation in the following paragraph is devoid of any consideration of the trust responsibility.

We well realize that Indian affairs are extremely complex, a fact alluded to in the opening statements of the report. Much of this complexity, oddly enough, results from actions taken by Congress in past years. Because of the complexity, it is understandable that members of Congress rarely find the time needed to study out any given Indian situation and to arrive at just decisions. For this reason staff members must be relied upon, and perhaps in the case of this Subcommittee Report, it is a failing of staff rather than of members of Congress which should be recognized. We know that individual members of the Subcommittee have been most helpful and most friendly to Indian delegations and to individual Indians. And so, repeat, it is hard to believe that these individual members have shared fully in the views and recommendations contained in the report.

These comments are directed at statements, including recommendations, contained in the report. It is equally important to remark on certain assumptions which are not expressed and to call attention to areas of concern to Indians on which the report is entirely silent.

With regard to the unstated assumptions, it is certainly naive to accept the premise that failure to solve Indian problems is the failure of a single department of the government; or that, in the alternative, transferring functions of the Bureau of Indian Affairs to other branches of federal or state government will solve these problems. Are we to believe that in the whole area of federal administration only one minor branch in the federal household is incompetent?

Another unuttered assumption is that Congress in its decisions in the field of Indian Affairs can do no wrong. The history of Indian Affairs administration will not support any such contention. The Executive Branch may do a poor job of administration but basically it can only act within the framework of policy and budget limitations laid down by Congress. Any failure therefore must be jointly shared by the legislative and Executive Branches, and this leaves no room for infallibility on the part of either.

Where this report is wholly silent is in the broad field of human and physical resource development. Indians are not trained for skilled jobs, not because of any ineptitude on their part, but because basic training facilities have not been made available in sufficient quantity. The fact that millions of acres of Indian lands, including timber, irrigable lands, and mineral-bearing lands, have not been developed is not due to any underlying indifference on the part of Indians to use their resources, but primarily the result of the lack of investment capital which only the federal government has been in a position to provide.

No part of these failings is mentioned in the report. The report tells us only that the easiest solution to the Indian problem is to transfer it from federal to state and local responsibility, and in many cases the states are unwilling or financially unable to accept this burden.

For years the National Congress of American Indians has been insisting that what is needed most basically to help the Indian people of the United States and Alaska is a domestic Point Four Program which will provide educational and health benefits in adequate measure and promote the economic well-being of the Indians through proper development and use of their resources. Relieving poverty, ill-health, educational deficiencies, and lack of adjustment in the Indian population will directly benefit every community in which Indians reside. "Assimilation", in fact, and "termination", with honor, will then follow.

> 1954 Convention of the National Congress of American Indians
> 11th Annual Convention
> Omaha, Nebraska

The Proposed Senate Concurrent Resolution
No. 3 (1957)

Because of an overwhelming demand that the termination policy be changed to a policy of human and economic resource development, the Senate Interior Committee was reluctantly forced to call a hearing to change the policy in 1957. The proposal, drawn up primarily by the National Congress of American Indians in conjunction with friendly Senators who sympathized with the tribes, was Senate Concurrent Resolution No. 3.

Although it was not passed, nor has any subsequent Resolution been passed, it did mark the beginning of the offensive for the tribes of the nation which had been on the defensive since early in 1950.

It was in response to this Resolution that Joseph Garry, then President of the Northwest Affiliated Tribes and the National Congress of American Indians, presented the platform of the national Indian community.

Whereas, it is the understanding of Congress that its responsibility in the American Indian problem cannot be fulfilled by the dispersal of Indian communities, but by the continuous development of their human and economic potential; and

Whereas, it is recognized that Indian communities cannot be considered to have reached the American level of well-being until the principles of consent of the governed, self-determination, and local self-government are operative, nor until Indian opportunities in economy, education, and health are measurably equal to those of their fellow citizens; and

Whereas, the American "point 4 program," as it has been applied successfully in underdeveloped areas of the world, reveals tested techniques whereby American Indian communities may be so developed: Now, therefore, be it

Resolved by the Senate (the House of Representatives concurring), That the Bureau of Indian Affairs shall be, by definition, an agency to assist American Indian communities to reach the level of well-being enjoyed by other communities in the United States, and the governing program of the Bureau of Indian Affairs shall be an American Indian point 4 program.

213

It is declared to be the sense of Congress that this program shall be offered to the American Indian communities without exacting termination of Federal protection of Indian property or of any other Indian rights as its price; that Indian culture and identity shall not be restricted or destroyed; that technical guidance and financial assistance shall be made available; that the request for assistance shall come from the Indians themselves after each Indian group has studied itself in terms of its own needs; that an impartial effort shall be made to deal with the development of natural resources to maximum capacity, to develop full capabilities of industrial and agricultural production, of improvements in housing, nutrition, clothing, sanitation, and health, and of the resettlement on their initiative of individuals and families in other areas; that technical assistance shall be given to long-term general, vocational, technical, and professional education to enable American Indians to share fully in our total American society and to contribute to it; and that older, revered values shall be respected and used as new forms of living are introduced.

It is further declared to be the sense of Congress that the Secretary of the Interior shall review all programs of the Bureau of Indian Affairs in order to develop its activities to further an American Indian point 4 program, and that he shall report to Congress at the earliest possible date his recommendations for such legislation as may be necessary to accomplish the purposes of this resolution.

Finally, it is declared to be the sense of Congress that Federal protection and services shall be ended for any tribe, band, or group only when such unit shall have adopted a plan for its organization and operation under State law, and such plan shall have been approved by the appropriate State and by the Secretary of the Interior prior to its submission to the Congress.

Testimony of Joseph R. Garry in Support of Resolution No. 3

The bitter struggle against the irrational policy of termination of federal services brought forth many Indian spokesmen. Perhaps none was more representative of the struggle to protect Indian rights than Joseph R. Garry, grandson of Chief Spokan Garry of the Spokane Tribe. Joe was elected to the chairmanship of the Coeur d'Alene Tribe year after year and his terms of service to the tribe stand out in the annals of Indian history as brightly as do those of Red Cloud, Chee Dodge of the Navajo, Chief Joseph and others.

Six times Joseph Garry was elected President of the National Congress of American Indians. These were years of toil, deficit budgets, weary car trips east in the middle of the winter to testify on legislation, and the bitterness of betrayal by a government whose solemn promises were written on the water. Yet among the Indians who fought for Indian people there has been no one in the last half century who has given as much to the national Indian community as has Joe Garry. To Joe can be credited the defeat of the termination policy and the establishment of the great Northwest alliance of tribes.

Joe resigned the Presidency of the N.C.A.I. to enter the primary race for Senator in Idaho. He was the first major Indian political figure to take such a step. He was elected several times to the Idaho state legislature. The following excerpt is from Joe's testimony before the Senate Interior Committee on a bill which we have already seen was designed to create a new Indian policy to replace House Concurrent Resolution No. 108.

The white world cooed and applauded when Oliver LaFarge sent his well publicized letter to President Eisenhower asking for justice for Indians. Movie stars become instant authorities on Indian problems merely by indicating that they have an interest. It is time the white world discovered the life and work of Joe Garry who truly defended Indian rights and who rallied the broken forces of scattered Indian nations to oppose and defeat the men in Congress who sought nothing less than the total extinction of Indian people. Had Joe been a white living in the east with access to the seats of power he would have been trumpeted far and wide as the greatest Indian defender in all American history.

But he was simply a poor Coeur d'Alene tribal chairman who did his best and did not seek the publicity and fanfare which one needs to gain a national reputation. Joe is, and has always been a man of the people. If nothing else, read his testimony and know that we have had our spokesmen and heroes in this age also.

I am president of the National Congress of American Indians and president of the Affiliated Tribes of the Northwest and, as Mr. Church also mentioned, I am a member of the State Legislature of Idaho.

I am also chairman of the Coeur d'Alene Tribal Council and am a veteran of World War II and the Korean campaign.

On behalf of the two Indian organizations—the National Congress of American Indians and the Affiliated Tribes of the Northwest—of which I have the honor to be presently the president, I wish to give wholehearted support to Senate Concurrent Resolution 3 as the singlemost constructive measure to restore confidence of Indians and motivation to renew their efforts in their own behalf.

I should first like to emphasize that I believe that the United States Congress in 1953 passed House Concurrent Resolution 108 in good faith, believing that the policy set forth in this resolution was in the best interest of the Indian people.

I also believe that the individuals and groups that brought about the general allotment act in 1887 felt that they were acting in the best interest of Indians, but highly respected institutions and groups and time have shown that this policy and this act results in dispossession of Indians, worsens their conditions, and is a shame to the United States as trustee.

Likewise, many conditions have grown out of House Concurrent Resolution 108 which are not in the best interest of Indian people, and I submit the following as examples:

No. 1: soon after House Concurrent Resolution 108 passed in 1953, the impression became prevalent that the paramount feature of this policy was that all Indian property must be liquidated along with the termination of the trust relationship between the various tribes and the United States Government.

This created confusion, chaos, unrest, and fear. Oldtimers, non-Indian lessees, neighbors of Indians, were so aroused that they began to put pressure, not only on Indian allottees and tribal officials, but on the Federal Government to buy Indian land.

No. 2: less friendly and more greedy non-Indians began to paint pictures showing liquidation of reservation property to be consistent with progress, freedom, equality, and first-class citizenship.

No. 3: local non-Indians in fear of competition from larger interests from farther away, were prompted to put even greater pressure on individuals to sell trust lands.

No. 4: when it was assumed that House Concurrent Resolution 108 was going to bring about the sale of individual Indian allotments local real-estate agents called in members of tribes as well as tribal council officials and attempted to persuade them that land should be sold through them for better prices.

No. 5: House Concurrent Resolution 108 immediately stirred up the officials of local government, State, and county. For them this resolution meant the taxation of Indian land was near at hand and they seized on this as a possibility for increasing local tax revenues.

No. 6: in addition to these pressures which the Indian people have had to withstand from outside interests, many employees of the Bureau of Indian Affairs, the Indians' own trustee, were discouraging continuation of expense of tribal enterprises, everything pointed toward disbanding the Indian tribes.

They hinted, but they did not make such statements outright. Based on the policies spelled out in House Concurrent Resolution 108, numerous bills emanated to carry out the purposes of the resolution. There were bills to terminate individuals and families, to terminate bands, tribes, groups of tribes, and all the tribes in the State, to terminate by branch of service, to terminate by amending the United States Constitution, to terminate by abolishing the Bureau of Indian Affairs, and to terminate even by blood quantum.

These bills kept the Indians so busy defending themselves they had no time or even energy for constructive planning or actions.

I feel sure that most Members of Congress are unaware of the damaging effects of House Concurrent Resolution 108 as it has been used.

Whether Congress intended it to be a mandate or not, the Bureau of Indian Affairs has considered it to be a mandate and is carrying out piecemeal termination regardless of the action by Congress.

I wish therefore to repeat again our support of Senate Concurrent Resolution 3 and also Senate bill 809 as one means of carrying out the policy resolution. This would be in effect a return to the philosophy of the Indian Reorganization Act, which by no means ever did mean, or ever will mean, making Indians museum pieces.

Rather, it will be a meaningful, effective, and long step toward solving the Indian problem and restoring dignity and justice in dealings of the United States toward the first American trust beneficiaries.

Reaffirmed N.C.A.I. Policy Resolution for Indian Program
(1959)

The readers of Indian anthologies have always been led to believe that no significant statements were made by Indians in modern times until the great

Chicago Conference of 1961. Then, in a typical collection of documents sections of the "Declaration of Purpose" from that conference are quoted at length showing that, under the sponsorship of friendly people, Indians can gather and present an intelligible statement of their needs. But if one is familiar with Indian Affairs such statements demean the intense work done by hundreds of unpublicized Indians over the years.

All through the Eisenhower administration, without fanfare and publicity, the members of the National Congress of American Indians fought a valiant struggle against the forces of Congressional oppression. As the decade was ending the assembled convention at Phoenix, Arizona passed a resolution of historic significance reviewing their long struggle to reverse Congressional policy and create a favorable climate for Indian people. The reaffirmed resolutions passed in 1956, 57, and 58 showed beyond doubt that the Indian people had consistently spoken out on their own behalf defining their own policies and programs. EXCEPT NO ONE HAD LISTENED.

It was a mere formality, then, when the Chicago Conference arrived at its conclusions. For five years previous the Indian tribes had consistently adhered to the positions outlined at Chicago. Instead, therefore, of a new spirit being revealed at Chicago, it was merely the first time that a certain group of scholars began to understand what had been happening in Indian country over the previous decade.

WHEREAS, by far the great majority of the Indians of the United States continue to exist in poverty and under economic circumstances which offer little or no opportunities for advancement; and

WHEREAS, the Indian health is deplorable in comparison to the Nation as a whole, as revealed in countless surveys; and

WHEREAS, Indian education lags far behind the national average; and

WHEREAS, the Congress of the United States, in House Concurrent Resolution 108 (83rd Congress) used certain language which has been interpreted to require the termination of federal supervision and assistance to the Indians as rapidly as possible; and

WHEREAS, we are well aware of the earnest desire of the Congress of the United States and of the Executive Branch of the United States Government to bring about the honorable discharge of the responsibilities and obligations assumed by the United States; and we, speaking for the Indians' tribes and many individual Indians of the United States, having a desire to promote the ultimate adjustment of Indian life ways within the larger American community in a manner to preserve Indian cultural values; and

WHEREAS, the Congress of the United States and the Commissioner of Indian Affairs have repeatedly indicated a desire not to bring about termination for any group of Indians until the people in such group were prepared to take their place in the American society; and

WHEREAS, in spite of such indications however, the Congress of the United States and the Commissioner of Indian Affairs have moved rapidly to terminate Indian groups whose people are in dire and desperate straits from the standpoint of health, education, and economic opportunity; and

WHEREAS, such movement toward termination has been carried on, not only directly, but indirectly, through regulations and administrative practices, designed to divest the Indian people of their lands, thereby aggravating further their economic status; and

WHEREAS, such premature termination can only lead to tremendous suffering by the Indian people, and will result in substantial and continued expense to the various states and counties which will be required to assist such people; and

WHEREAS, this body at the 1956 NCAI Convention, Salt Lake City, Utah formulated a STATEMENT OF POLICY, in the form of RESOLUTION Number 1, which we earnestly believed would assist in the solution of many of the aforementioned difficulties; and

WHEREAS, the 1957 NCAI Convention, Claremore, Oklahoma, reaffirmed said policy; and

WHEREAS, the 1958 NCAI Convention, Missoula, Montana, reaffirmed such policy:

NOW THEREFORE, BE IT RESOLVED by the 16th Annual Convention of the National Congress of American Indians, assembled in Phoenix, Arizona, December 7-11, 1959, that after further consideration and deliberation, and being satisfied that the aforesaid STATEMENT OF POLICY is fundamentally sound, we do hereby reaffirm said STATEMENT OF POLICY, urge the immediate reconsideration of House Concurrent Resolution 108 (83rd Congress), insofar as it declares a policy of termination of federal supervision "as rapidly as possible" and urge the substitution thereof the following as a STATEMENT OF NATIONAL POLICY, and as a guide to administrative action:

1. A plan of development be prepared for each Indian group, whose lands or other assets are held in trust, whether such lands or assets are fully defined or not, such plans to be designed to bring about maximum utilization of physical resources by the dependent population to its full potential, such plans to be prepared by the Indians of the respective groups, with authority to call upon the agencies of the federal government for technical assistance, and the ultimate purpose of such planning to be the growth and development of the resources of the people, rather than the heedless termination of federal responsibility for such people;

2. That requests for annual appropriations of funds be based on the requirements for carrying into effect these individual development plans, and the annual operating budget for the Bureau of Indian Affairs to include sufficient funds to carry out the program needs of each planning group;

3. That such annual budgets include adequate funds to provide for the credit needs and for capital investment, required for the full development of Indian resources;

4. That determination with respect to the disposition of property or actions which may affect treaty rights or agreements be based on agreement between an Indian tribe or group and the United States;

5. That any transfer of services now provided by the United States for the benefit of Indians be jointly planned with the Indians;

6. That Public Law 280 (83rd Congress) be modified to provide that the assumption by states of jurisdiction in criminal and civil actions on Indian reservations be brought about only after negotiation between a state and an Indian tribe, and only to the extent, from time to time, agreed upon by the Indian tribe;

7. That the Indian groups be kept fully advised at all stages of pending legislation in which their interests may be involved and that the Secretary of the Interior likewise keep them advised of regulatory measures which may be proposed for adoption, and accord full opportunity to the Indian groups, and their representatives, to be heard, and have their needs and views considered in the formulation, modification or repeal of regulatory measures; and

8. That a concentrated effort be made to retain, rather than dispose of, Indian lands in order to allow the Indians sufficient economic units upon which to improve their economic conditions; and that administrative regulations and practices be reviewed, modified, and amended to bring about such result.

16th Annual Convention
Phoenix, Arizona

Statement of Earl Old Person, Chairman
of the Blackfeet Tribe, Montana,
Against the Omnibus Bill (1966)

In 1966 the Bureau of Indian Affairs held extensive hearings throughout the country ostensibly to determine what the tribes wanted in the area of legislative proposals to be sent to Congress. That tribes already knew that the Interior Department had drawn up a piece of legislation and was ready to submit it the moment it felt the tribes had been properly hoodwinked about consultation.

But the tribes were not fooled. At Spokane they got Commissioner Robert Bennett to admit that Interior had already written up the legislation. At that Conference one of the greatest speeches of modern times was given by Earl Old Person, then chairman of the Blackfeet Tribe of Montana and currently President of the National Congress of American Indians. When Old Person finished speaking there was sustained and hearty applause. The following are excerpts from his talk.

It cannot be denied that every time the Bureau of Indian Affairs goes to Congress for money, they justify their request for appropriations on the grounds that they are trying to "get themselves out of the Indian business." This means termination to members of Congress and to Indians.

It is important to note that in our Indian language the only translation for termination is to "wipe out" or "kill off". We have no Indian words for termination. And there should be no English word for termination as it is applied to modern day terms regarding the relationship of the U.S. Government and the American Indian. Why scare us to death every year by going to Congress for money and justifying the request on the grounds that the money is necessary to "terminate the trust relationship of the U.S. to the American Indian?"

You have caused us to jump every time we hear this word. We made treaties with the U.S. Government which guaranteed our right to develop our reservations and to develop as a people free from interference. In order to bring about this development, careful planning must be done on the part of not only the agencies of Government, but by the tribes themselves. But how can we plan our future when the Indian Bureau constantly threatens to wipe us out as a race? It is like trying to cook a meal in your tipi when someone is standing outside trying to burn the tipi down.

219

So let's agree to forget the termination talk and instead talk of development of Indian people, their land, and their culture.

Land and the animals it fed are the backbone of Indian existence. We worshipped the Great Spirit who created the land; we worshipped the Sun who gave life to the grasses and plants that provided food and clothing for us; and we worshipped the water and the rain by praying to the Great Spirit that he give us water and rain to make the plants and animals plentiful. That was the way of our ancestors. Now we realize that the ways are disappearing, and we must find new ones to take their place. The old ways of the Indian Bureau have disappeared also. And we hope you find new ones to take their place.

In the past 190 years, the U.S. Government has tried every possible way to get rid of the troublesome Indian problem he feels he has on his hands. First the Government tried extinction through destruction—where money was paid for the scalps of every dead Indian. Then the government tried mass relocation and containment through concentration—the moving of entire tribes or parts of tribes to isolated parts of the country where they were herded like animals and fed like animals for the most part. Then the Government tried assimilation—where reservations were broken up into allotments (an ownership system the Indians did not understand) and Indians were forced to try to live like "white men". Indian dances and Indian hand work was forbidden. A family's ration of food was cut off if anyone in the family was caught singing Indian songs or doing Indian hand craft. Children were physically beaten if they were caught speaking Indian languages. Then termination was tried by issuing forced patents in fee to Indian land owners—land was taken out of the trust relationship with the U.S. Government and an unrestricted patent in fee was issued to the Indian whether he wanted it or not or whether he understood what was going on or not.

None of these policies worked. They only seemed to make the Indians more determined than ever to keep their Indian ways and their Indian identity.

The first breakthrough came with the Indian Reorganization Act of 1934. This permitted a Government policy of organization by allowing tribes to adopt constitutions which provided terms for managing their own affairs. But the Indian Bureau became impatient with the progress of Indians under this system. So in 1953 they again turned to the policy of termination. Several tribes were terminated as a result of this old policy revived and sold to Congress. I do not need to tell you of the poverty and hopelessness these terminated tribes now suffer.

Again I say, "Let's forget termination and try a policy that has never been tried before—development of the Indian reservations for Indians and development of Indians as human beings with a personality and a soul and dreams for a bright future." Why is it so important that Indians be brought into the "mainstream of American life". What is the "mainstream of American life"? I would not know how to interpret the phrase to my people in our language. The closest I would be able to come to "mainstream" would be to say, in Indian, "a big wide river". Am I then going to tell my people that they will be "thrown into the Big, Wide River of the United States"?

As first Americans, we had a truly American way of life. And we mixed this with the way of life of the white man who came to live among us. The result is the most democratic form of government in the world.

On this point, will the mainstream of American life as we know it now be the same fifty, or even twenty-five years from now? Is it the same now as it was twenty-five years ago?

The white man has borrowed much from the Indian way of life. For example, the Indians probably saved the United States when they taught the white man to grow corn and plant potatoes. We feel that we can contribute still further to a better way of life for all Americans by an example of co-operation which we can hold up to the world as a model.

Let's do what the President asked at your swearing in ceremony, Commissioner Bennet. Let's also say to Indian people, "We are not going to force anything upon you which you do not want. We will give you time to develop your land and your people in your own way. The policy of each Indian tribe will be the policy of the Bureau of Indian Affairs."

Our people are eager to learn. They are proud of being American. They are proud of being Indians. They are proud to welcome non-Indians onto the reservation. We feel that we have dealt with honor with the Government through the many treaties we have made. We respect these treaties and expect the Government to do the same. We do not demonstrate in the streets to get our rights. We feel we have rights guaranteed to us by these treaties and we trust the Government to respect these rights.

We accept your word that Indians will be furnished copies of any legislation affecting their rights before such legislation is proposed to Congress. We hope that after reviewing such legislation, we will have another series of meetings to keep what is good for the Indians and take out what Indian people feel is not in their best interests at this stage in their development.

We have learned to live with what we have while we hope for a better future for our children, more dignity for our old people, and better opportunity for ourselves. All we need is time and cooperation. We do not need termination or all the other programs that have not worked in the past. And what will it cost for the Indian Bureau and the Congress to say, "Go home and develop your plans. You do not have to be afraid to take the time you need. We are not going to sell your land out from under you or force your people off the reservation."

If this is done, the time will surely come when Indian people everywhere can say in both word and deed that a special agency to handle their affairs is no longer needed. In closing, I would like permission to submit a statement at a later date proposing specific approaches to our problem.

Testimony Against the Civil Rights Bill of 1968

In 1968, as part of the Civil Rights Bill of that year, the United States Congress extended the provisions of the Bill of Rights unilaterally over the Pueblos of New Mexico. These people had governed themselves for centuries without finding it necessary to depend upon Anglo-Saxon ideas of jurisprudence. In many ways their ideas of justice were superior to those of the United States. In fact, it should have been the Pueblos who extended the ways of peace for which they are noted over the United States which at that time was itself carrying on any number of undeclared and unpublicized wars against other nations in violation of its own Constitution.

Requesting another hearing on the legislation in the hopes of amending the law to exempt them from its operations, the theocracies of New Mexico presented a reasonable and historically accurate case. The legislation is still before Congress and the Pueblos are still hoping to stop the interference of the United States with their ancient religious customs and practices.

Even in their adversity, the defenders of the Pueblos made their case far better than could any of their white supporters. While numerous friends attempted to raise the issue the best statements on this subject are those made by the Pueblos themselves.

HISTORY OF SAN FELIPE PUEBLO PEOPLE

In response to the Ervin (Senate) Bill 1843, the Tribal Officials with the Tribal Council of San Felipe Pueblo wish to be recorded as having reviewed and considered the Ervin Bill. Though it proposes to establish rights for individual Indians in their relationship with their Indian tribes and for other purposes, the Council finds the Bill most intruding on what was theirs in the beginning. The free sovereign exercise of self-government was theirs, shaped and given to them intangibly by the Spirit. Specifically, said the Council, should Titles I and II of Bill 1843 become law the Federal Government will empower and arm the Secretary of the Interior with another lethal weapon to push the so-called "Model Code of Justice" down the Indians' throat. Wherein a final holocaust of Titles I and II of the Congressional Act will result in the alienation of the democratic tradition of the Indians to exercise its sovereign government now practiced by the Indian tribes everywhere. It is for this reason the Tribal Officials with its Council of the sovereign Pueblo of San Felipe, situated in the sovereign State of New Mexico, has decided to review the history of its people as a method of counterattacking the composite pending legislation herein specifically mentioned, and to share this review with its fellow tribesmen and with the United States Congress, hoping to clarify its reasons and desires to remain free from further inundation with premature legislations the Congress of the United States may think to pass for the benefit of the so-called "American Indians." It is the Council's earnest desire to retain the sovereignty of self-government for the sake of heritage, and to preserve other basic values of Indian heritage while making slow but continual adjustment, though sometimes superficial, to the economic and political demands of the Whiteman society.

Thus the Council solemnly began its recollection of the ancient ancestors, those of the great great grandfathers, great grandfathers, and grandfathers of long ago, first, as people of spiritual beliefs, and secondly, as people of material contributors to the new continent. For the Indians had in the beginning what the world has finally and irretrievably lost, and we have it yet as it is, "a way of life." The Council in telling the spiritual legend of the ancient people remember them telling of the fortunes of the spirit world, the egress or emergence into the world, and the ingress or returning to the hereafter, whence we came. They remember too, that the emergence into the world was a great act of the Spirit for it came about with reverence and love for what was left behind in the spirit world, and of fear and respect for what was found above, on earth and in the sky. So it came to reality long ago that all life came forth from the womb of the earth, said the Council.

With them came the Spirit, and the Spirit guided the ancient people through all sorts of arduous tasks of everyday life. Age after age the Spirit, the guardian and leader of the Pueblo Indians, took the ancient people across this great continent southward, until they came to settle temporarily in the places of today's National Parks and National Monuments. Everything they planted was harvested and was eaten along the route.

Maybe to preserve the human race from total annihilation of any attack which may befall them, the Spirit caused the people to migrate in groups in separate directions from these places of historic settlements. He continued to guide each group on their trek until he brought them to a region where they can readily be safe and begin their tribal settlemen.

So said the Council. This was how it came about that the ancestral people of San Felipe Pueblo were guided into the region of the valley of Rio del Norte where they were eventually settled for sometime by the Spirit on the west bank of the Rio Grande River atop the black mesa north of the present San Felipe Pueblo. Their first settlement was in the proximity northeast of the present main bridge over the Rio Grande River and southwest of te-me-teh, a lonely hill standing on the northeast side of where the railroad track transverses the Tonque arroyo. Because of the imminent dangers of disasters they were gradually moved west across the Rio Grande River and to the top of the black mesa. Here as well as on the east side, and throughout the entire region of pueblo settlement, the Spirit began to give final instructions to the people. They were reminded of the past trials and dangers they had endured; the sorrows and joys they experienced together; the unity they showed each other at working and living together in a community, and the necessity of planting and farming crops for survival. The ancient people remembered these experiences well and began to show great concern. Now the Spirit was telling of another plan, he pointed out indigenous plants that grew wild and abundantly which the people can use as food; teaching the people to respect and obey the laws of nature and the orders of its chief, the Cacique. The Cacique, said the Spirit, will guide you henceforth, and as the head of the tribe he will be concerned with your spiritual lives as well as with your government when the need for it arises. With these revelations, the Spirit empowered the Cacique with spiritual properties and with jurisdictional powers by which to make laws and govern his people. Hitherto, said the Spirit, it is the only way you and your children can live and give protection to each other. Thus, the plan was revealed to the ancient people and it was truly a way of life and living.

However, the people were not without dangers. They were warned of the dangers to come as more people inhabit the new continent. Here again, the Spirit reminded her people of their past experiences of building dwelling places in fortress style. "This you must do," said the Spirit. Then before secluding, the Spirit promised the people protection from the dangers of war when the time was near. Perhaps then sometimes between the first and the second settlement in the region of Rio del Norte marks the beginning of the famous legend of the Pueblo people about the twin boys known to them as Masewi and Oyoyewi. They were the young gods of war who protected their people by killing their enemies, and when not at war, they attended to prayers asking the Great Spirit to grant them courage and valor with which to guide their people towards peaceful settlement. Some Councilmen remember the twins as more than gods of war, they were also more or less explorers of the nature, constantly seeking out better land for cultivation and for permanent settlement. This is true in the case of San Felipe people where they gave credit to the twin boys for having made the final move of the ancestral people from the top of the black mesa to the present location of the Pueblo down in the valley of Rio del Norte as the Spanish had named the Rio Grande River.

From the time the Spirit had secluded, the people have lived everafter under the guidance of the Cacique, and obeyed his orders for they all knew he was empowered by the Spirit. Everything went according to the prophesy of the Great Spirit. Wars were encountered courageously under the leadership of Masewi and Oyoyewi, and the preparation for better livelihood were made under the leadership of the Cacique. However, as the population increased and civilization took roots many problems begin to burden the Cacique. Naturally, more and more this took the attention of the Cacique away from his primary duties of devotion to prayers for spiritual livelihood of his people. Constant prompting of the Spirit to exercise the power vested in him, the Cacique began on a plan to formulate a sovereign government by which his people can be governed. Calling upon the assistance of the Great Spirit, for he did no important act without the ritual, he began to work on a momentous plan for his people and his community. The work, said the Council, had to first meet with the criterion of the Spirit. This being done, the Cacique felt encouraged to call forth the first office, the War Chiefs. Having honorably guided their people through war and having had the blessings of the Spirit, the Cacique felt honored to assign this Office to the twin boys, Masewi and Oyoyewi, to handle the traditional ceremonial activities as well as assisting the Cacique in related matters of religious beliefs of the people of the community. Creating the first Office he then searched his mind solemnly for other offices, upon which he then called chronologically the second and third offices respectively.

Fortunately, for the people, about this time into our world entered a new breed of people from another world. These new people called themselves Spaniards. And in keeping with the forecast of the Great Spirit these new people also suggested and contributed to the newest positions in our hierarchy of government. The second Office, ta-pooph, or the Governors, were assigned to a couple of honorable men of the community (to head the Office, and) to handle civic and temporal affairs of the people. The third Office, pe-scar-lee or the Fiscales, were assigned the Office in a similar manner to a couple of honorable men to coordinate Christian church activities, and to assist the Padres in achieving its assigned missions.

Having established each Office chronologically for his people he blessed and empowered each Office, and enjoined each Office to serve the people of the community henceforth honorably; and to exercise the power of authority judiciously on the problems and on the people of the community. Justice, in the mind of the Cacique, must at all times be attuned to the dictates of the Spirit. Then the Cacique said, "Those persons who shall serve in the Offices will become members of the tribal council for a lifetime, unless duly retired by the Cacique for reasons of acts contrary to the design of justice of the government." With these words he empowered the tribal council to function as advisory and approving body in the internal and civic affairs of the tribal government with some authortiy to make settlements when the Officers of the Government are reluctant to go at it alone. In a similar manner, with the judicial matters of the tribe the Tribal Council functions as a jury in the tribal courts, and has the authority to make a final decision on the case making it relative to the Governor and the rest of the head tribal officials. The power to convene the councilmen rested with the Governor of San Felipe Pueblo. Through the centuries then, prior to the discovery by the whiteman, the ancient people of San Felipe operated under this system of government, and all took part in the functionings of the tribal government. All this took place long ago said the Council, for they themselves do not know how long ago it was. There were no records kept by the ancestors and everything depended on the mind or memory.

Today the setup of the tribal government of San Felipe Pueblo is still the same and its function, in nature, is similar to the olden times except with minor changes made by the people where feasible. Simply, then, this sparsely constitutes the history of the San Felipe Pueblo and its people, and most assuredly of the other Pueblos in general. One then can see at this point that the idea of sovereignty and self-government are deep rooted in the history of the Pueblo people.

Perhaps at this point it is appropriate to turn to some recorded histories of today which has depicted the noble side of the American Indian and which the Congress of the United States and the American public may have sparse knowledge of the aborigines. When the European or the Spaniards, who called them savages, discovered the Pueblo people in the 16th century they were quite amazed to find a distinct and in some respects highly developed civilization. The simple human decency and the amenities of daily life, and the disciplines of its government were observed in them in the relationship between man and man, and between man and his God. As the Council had remembered in the opening paragraphs of this review, the ancient people were material contributors to this continent. The changes that these people worked into the lives of the "white pioneers" were far more impressive and less destructive than any changes the white teachers have yet brought to the Indian life. In the realm of the intangible the Indian gave more. The orderliness of the political ideas of young America owed much to the Indian democratic tradition. On many occasions Thomas Jefferson recognized this debt by making numerous references to the freedom and democracy of the Indian society when he said: ". . . had achieved the maximum degree of order with the minimum degree of coercion." Felix Cohen, the late noted scholar and Indian legal authority, remarked: "Those accustomed to the histories of the conqueror will hardly be convinced, though example be piled on example, that American democracy, freedom, and tolerance are more American than European, and have deep aboriginal roots in our land." The habit of treating chiefs as servants of the people instead of Masters, the insistence that the community must respect the diversity of men and their dreams, all these things were part of the Indian way of life before 1492.

The Council recalls at this point a recognition of credence given the Pueblo Indians, first, by the Spanish Government then next by the Mexican and the United States Governments respectively, "that the Indians' right to self-government is not a right derived from these Caucasian Governments, but a right which they held prior and maintained subsequent to the discovery of this continent." Since this discovery said the Council, the Indians did not ask for recognition, but it came forward spontaneously because of the respect and understanding the conqueror and the whiteman had for Indians' primacy of self-government. Upon this a covenant was made respectively by the Spanish, Mexican, and United States Governments to recognize the sovereignty of government of the Pueblo Indians by bringing the Canes of the Country's King or President to each Pueblo Government as a symbol of the solemn covenant and recognition. The Spanish kingdom in the 16th century and then the United States Government under the administration of President Abraham Lincoln in 1863 gave its recognition of the Pueblo Indian Governments. Today the Governor of San Felipe Pueblo uses these Canes as a symbol of authority of the Governor. Now this covenant is about to be amissed by Titles I and II of the Senate Bill 1843.

At this point one may well ask: "Of what relevance is this buried legacy to the present and future?" First, there is still much that the Indian can contribute to America's cultural enrichment. Second, recognition by legislators, administrators, and the American public of the true nature of our Indian heritage has great importance in freeing the Indian from a haughty and stupidly silly stereotype. It also may diminish the persistent themes of pity, superiority and the whiteman's burden, which have been twisted into vicious weapons of legislations against Indian culture. Third, the respect for different cultures may bring about a reasoned and humane policy which will fulfill Indian desires to achieve a higher living standard and still maintain his ethnic identity. Fourth, the Indian needs of stability and rights to their government should be left to the tribes to rectify through their unique aspects of the Indians' membership in special political bodies, or tribes, which largely take the place that states and municipalities occupy for other American citizens.

What then does the American Indian want of the United States Congress? Certainly, their dependency on and control by, the Federal Government is much greater since 1848 because of the tacit and implicit trusteeship relationship between the United States

Government and the Indian Tribes. Since then too, the Indian has sacrificed many of its youth in the whiteman's wars so as to have a free Nation of discriminating views, and today continues to sacrifice its youth in the commitments of the great "White Father" to wars of foreign Nations. How is it then the American Indian is involved in these wars? Certainly it is not for want of war, nor for greed of wealth, nor for fear of disgrace, but of respect to fellowman and to its Nation under one God that the Indian took up the challenge so that we may all enjoy the freedom, liberty and justice for all together. With these point of views the American Indian wants to be given justice of being involved in making his own plan of change and be given greater voice on all and any legislation to be proposed in committee or the Congress affecting both his Reservation and his freedom of self-government. Perhaps then the type of Indian's needs of real liberal system of justice can best be summed up in the view of the 1958 congressional proposal establishing a technical assistance program modeled after the so-called Point Four Program of Foreign Aid. The pertinent section of that proposal reads: "It is declared to be the sense of Congress . . . that Indian culture and identity shall not be restricted or destroyed; that technical guidance and financial assistance shall be made available; that the request for such assistance shall come from the Indians, after each Indian group has studied itself in terms of its own needs. . . ." Unfortunately the proposal dies in committee. Such a legislation of this calibre is most urgently needed for the Indian Reservations, and in the final analysis would achieve the liberal justice so much desired for the American Indian.

In summary then, the Ervin Senate Bill 1843 is well intended, but the Council of San Felipe Pueblo is not ready to implement such a proposal because it is premature in nature that no voice of the Indian tribes was involved to determine whether state criminal and civil laws should apply on their reservations. That rights of Indians to self-government are inherent in their backgrounds and should not be coerced to be alienated from the long history of democratic practice of their traditions. Finally, in view of the Indian history, it is self-evident that life, liberty and right to sovereign government was the forethought of the ancient people to which we give whole hearty support to earnestly ask for understanding of our desire to preserve our Indian heritage, in any shape or form, for here lies the true foundation of America's history. In conclusion then, we the Tribal Council of the Sovereign Pueblo of San Felipe solemnly decline to accept Titles I and II of the Senate Bill 1843 in its present form, and respectfully refuse to alienate our people, and ourselves, from the sovereign government, to wit, of San Felipe Pueblo.

CONSTITUTIONAL RIGHTS OF AMERICAN INDIANS
STATEMENT OF GOV. ROBERT E. LEWIS
ZUNI PUEBLO, NEW MEXICO

My fellow leaders and I, of different Pueblo tribes in New Mexico have come a far piece to convey to you in simple truth our situations upon which we have no room to exaggerate nor elaborate upon. We come before you as elected leaders from your respective States, which makes us mutual public servants. The one main difference being that we still communicate with our people in two languages, whereas you use only one—the language we are now using.

I know for a fact that the majority of you have never been to my Pueblo. Perhaps you have been to some, but not long enough to become acquainted with our situations and problems. So putting it bluntly, you really know nothing about us. We, in Zuni, understand that S. 1843 and H.R. 15122 are based on hearings set up in various places off the reservations in 1961. No recent followup investigations of what we are now planning and doing have been made. Why?

If this had been done, it would have been found out that several of our Indian tribes have their tribal constitutions, as well as now operating under their own tribal codes. Some, as in Zuni, have been drafting theirs. Using two languages, this takes time. Besides working on these matters, we are all very much involved in economic development programs which we know will bring up our economic structures to a better level. Poverty programs are also in operation. All these things mean practical training and education, to many of us, in planning and administration.

To prove to you that we are actually doing what needs to be done, I am presenting the committee a copy of our tribal constitution in draft. This backs up the statement of former Gov. Warren Ondelacy in answer to your questionnaire of August 1961, regarding a document which would have in writing those things concerning civil rights to individuals, as well as a law-and-order code.

In these days when all governments, from the local level to the very top, are swamped with workloads far beyond their capabilities because of limited personnel and funds, and everything operates on limited time basis, it is very difficult to get across the main points to do any good or be very effective, in many cases. Although we try to be brief, where we are concerned, this is very difficult. There are some factors that we have to go into and we are sincerely hoping that time will be taken to read our statement. A bit of history even has to be included to bring the picture into clearer focus, and because up to the present the communications gap from us to you is so evident, we cannot afford to be stingy with words.

There is a distinct difference between the Pueblo Indian and the nomadic tribes. This is very important to keep in mind because it has a direct bearing on the legislation we are discussing at this time. This is why:

Long before the first Norsemen, or whatever, touched the shores of what is now our United States, the Pueblo Indian was here as the first builder. Ruins all over our Southwest indicate and prove this fact, as well as our existing Pueblos. In all the places they built multi-storied pueblo communities, there apparently were no hostile marauding tribes. It takes several years to build such structures and live, no one knows how long, in these places if there is not a feeling of safety. He was an agriculturalist and a craftsman also. But the best part is that their government setup was so good that it is still evident today.

Through Spanish rule and up to now, the Pueblo Indians have kept together, are still together. A lot of our custom laws handed down are still being used. Our two-court systems mete out justice in the fullest sense and outside courts can look to these and learn something. Civil rights are not new to any of us. Our courts have operated in a more than satisfactory manner, and there has never been any complaints about the fairness of the system. Changing times force changes to be made in many areas. As far as Indians are concerned, we have a lot of adjustments to make. But we know our problems. Concerning our judicial situations, we understand the streamlining that we need to do to comply with today's needs. So we are doing something about this.

We cherish our rights and freedoms, and are very close to our lands, what little we have left. We take pride in the fact that our tribal government has endured all these centuries and we firmly believe that if we did not in our own way and in our governments, indicate these to individuals, we would long ago have disbanded as tribes, and sought a better way somewhere else. We are also proud to share democracy with all latecomers who came here seeking the freedoms and liberties they did not have in their own countries. Let us work together to preserve these. Let us prove that we can build around the good things we have and we assure you that it will conform to everything required.

VII

DEALING WITH INDIANS

Over the years there have been numerous unrecorded incidents that give a far better view of Indian life than many scholarly volumes. Some of the best stories are now lost forever. Yet there remain recorded sufficient incidents, events, and speeches to give good insight into the nature of Indian society, the abuses that we have suffered and the humor inherent in our people. It is far beyond the ability of any generation to describe the real feelings of Indian people as they have been experienced by the many Indian tribes. Yet the humor, pathos, oppression, and strength of Indians shine through.

For over four hundred years the white man has had to "deal with Indians" and with the "Indian problem". No book would be complete without a smattering of selections showing how—in a multitude of ways, and with varying motives— the dominant white society has "dealt with Indians". With every indication that the future may not differ the slightest bit, let us look at some of the ways that whites have dealt with Indians in the past.

United States v. Lucero
(1869)

The following selection may appear at first glance to be a landmark case in the struggle for the preservation of Indian rights. It is not. As white settlers moved into New Mexico Territory after the Civil War they were faced with a dilemma. Under the treaty of Guadalupe Hidalgo the Pueblos of New Mexico were given full rights to the lands they occupied. With Indian settlements scattered along the Rio Grande occupying the best farm lands it was obvious that the whites would have to take the desert lands that were not occupied. Standing in front of them barring the way was the power of the federal government protecting the Indian title.

In the *Lucero* case the New Mexico Supreme Court judge solved the problem. Realizing that if the Pueblos were not classified as Indians there would be no necessity for checking with the federal government before defrauding them, the court promptly discovered that they were not Indians at all but merely "Mexicans" and therefore available for exploitation.

Perhaps the best part of the case presented in this selection is the incredible lengths to which the judge is willing to go to ridicule the need for federal protection. It is unimaginable that a decision such as this could be written by a Supreme Court of any state and be seriously considered as a legal decision. But the case was never appealed. The Pueblos were defrauded of their lands by the god-fearing citizens of New Mexico Territory. It was not until the Sandoval decision of 1912 that the validity of the Pueblo land titles was upheld. The Sandoval decision threw land titles in New Mexico into question creating the need for the

Pueblo Lands Act of 1924 which set up a commission to solve the problem. Had the Pueblos been given their rightful protection nearly 80 years before, all of this confusion could have been avoided.

This suit is an action of debt on statute, and the statute upon which it is founded reads as follows:

Section 11. And be it further enacted, that if any person make a settlement on any lands belonging, secured, or granted by treaty with the United States, to any Indian tribe, or shall survey, or attempt to survey, such lands, or designate the boundaries by marking trees or otherwise, such offender shall forfeit and pay the sum of one thousand dollars. And it shall, moreover, be lawful for the President of the United States to take such measures and employ such military force as he may judge necessary, to remove from the land as aforesaid any such person as aforesaid.

It will not be forgotten that the intercourse act, which contains this penal section, was passed on June 30, 1834. The petition in this case charges Lucero with having entered upon lands belonging to the pueblo tribe of Indians, of the pueblo of Cochiti, and then sets out the boundaries of the land upon which Lucero settled, belonging to the pueblo, secured to them by patent from the United States.

This settlement of Lucero is alleged to have been made on the first day of January, 1866. February 27, 1851, congress passed an act, the seventh section of which was as follows:

Section 7. And be it further enacted, that all the laws now in force regulating trade and intercourse with the Indian tribes, or such provisions of the same as may be applicable shall be and the same are hereby extended over the Indian tribes of New Mexico and Utah.

A careful consideration of this act thus extending over New Mexico, the acts and all the acts regulating trade and intercourse, will satisfy the most incredulous, that, in the opinion of congress, some of these acts were, in some of their provisions, unsuited to be extended over all classes of people in New Mexico called Indians. The question now presents itself: Is there a class of Indians in New Mexico who do not come within the letter or spirit of said acts, and who are not operated upon by said acts, unless specially named and designated by congress as being within the provisions of those acts? When the Intercourse Act of June 30, 1834, was passed, and for ten years thereafter, New Mexico constituted a part of the Republic of Mexico, and within the extended jurisdiction of the United States there existed no class of Indians called pueblo or town Indians. The term pueblo Indian is a term used to separate and distinguish them from the general class of Indians, such as existed within the United States in 1834; no such Indians then existed within the limits of the United States, and the law then passed could not have been intended to operate upon or affect a class of Indians differing widely from the Indians of the United States in their habits, manners, and customs. Who and what are the Indians for whom said laws were passed, and upon whom they were intended to operate? They were wandering savages, given to murder, robbery, and theft, living on the game of the mountains, the forest, and the plains, unaccustomed to the cultivation of the soil, and unwilling to follow the pursuits of civilized man. Providence made this world for the use of the man who had the energy and industry to pull off his coat, and roll up his sleeves, and go to work on the land, cut down the trees, grub up the brush and briers, and stay there on it and work it for the support of himself and family, and a kind and thoughtful Prov-

231

idence did not charge man a single cent for the whole world made for mankind and intended for their benefit. Did the Indians ever purchase the land, or pay anyone a single cent for it? Have they any deed or patent for it, or has it been devised to them by anyone as their exclusive inheritance?

Land was intended and designed by Providence for the use of mankind, and the game that it produced was intended for those too lazy and indolent to cultivate the soil, and the soil was intended for the use and benefit of that honest man who had the fortitude and industry to reclaim it from its wild, barren, and desolate condition, and make it bloom with the products of an enlightened civilization. The idea that a handful of wild, half-naked, thieving, plundering, murdering savages should be dignified with the sovereign attributes of nations, enter into solemn treaties, and claim a country five hundred miles wide by one thousand miles long as theirs in fee simple, because they hunted buffalo and antelope over it, might do for beautiful reading in Cooper's novels or Longfellow's *Hiawatha,* but is unsuited to the intelligence and justice of this age, or the natural rights of mankind. The government of the United States, while thus dignifying these savages with the title of *quasi* nations, with whom the United States has, from time to time, and quite often, entered into stipulations to purchase their lands, have generally purchased at an average of about two cents an acre, and then sold it out to the people at from one dollar and a quarter to ten dollars and fifty cents per acre, thus making a speculation off of the Indian lands of over fifty millions of dollars, if their title is anything but an ingenious and benevolent fiction. This property of over fifty millions of dollars, the treaties with the Indian tribes and sales of public lands to the people will demonstrate. Let us now look at the pueblo Indians of New Mexico, and see if there is anything in their past history or present condition which renders applicable to them a set of laws designed and intended to regulate the trade and intercourse of civilized man with wandering tribes of savages. Columbus, the daring hero of the seas, discovered America in 1492. December 11, 1620, the pilgrim fathers landed on a granite boulder lying on the shore of Plymouth bay, in the new world. Now, it is worth while to know, that in 1530, ninety years before that event, Alsar Nunie Cohega de Bace, Alonzo del Castillo, Alejandro Andres Dorantes, and Estefana, a blackamoor, passed from the gulf of Mexico through Louisiana and Texas into New Mexico; spent several years in this valley of the Rio Grande, visiting the various villages of pueblo Indians in New Mexico during the year 1534, and passing south west in May, 1536, and near the Pacific ocean, at the village of San Miguel, in Sonora, and finally reached the City of Mexico, after seven years' wandering in the wilderness. Our timid forefathers, who peeped out into the wilderness from their colony of Plymouth, are not to be compared to the true Spanish adventurers who planted the cross of civilization two thousand miles distant, in the valley of the Rio Grande, ninety years prior to their arrival in the new world.

The theory, promulgated by some, and believed by many, that the Spanish adventurers found the pueblo Indians of New Mexico a wild, savage, and barbarous race; that they conquered them, and reduced them to subjection, placed them in villages, and taught them the arts of civilized life, is a pure and unadulterated fiction, and contradicted by the uniform history of the Spanish adventurers for over two hundred years. They found the pueblo Indians, on their advent into New Mexico, a peaceful, quiet, and industrious people, residing in villages for their protection against the wild Indians, and living by the cultivation of the soil. Their villages are described, their locality mentioned, their habits and pursuits delineated, and we learn that the old palace, not one hundred feet from where we are now holding court, was built upon the site of one of their ancient towns. That the Spanish placed them under subjection, treated them with cruelty, but planted the Catholic religion among them, and improved civilization, is true; but they found them civilized, peaceful, and kind, and on that account they became an easy victim of their cupidity and despotic rule. This condition of domineering on the part of the Spaniards, and meek obedience on the part of the pueblo Indians, continued until 1670, when the pueblo Indians rebelled against their Spanish masters, and expelled them all from New Mexico. It was not until 1688, that the Spaniards obtained sufficient force to conquer, subdue, and chastise them. At the date of 1689, and within a few years subsequent, was executed to the various pueblos of New Mexico their titles to their lands. The Spaniards acknowledged their title to the land on which they were residing, and had resided timed whereof the memory of man runneth not to the contrary, and a written agreement was executed and delivered to them; and so long as the Spanish rule was continued in America, these titles were respected. Upon the establishment of the independence of Mexico from Old Spain, these title continued to be respected, and the government of the United States in the treaty of Guadalupe Hidalgo pledged her faith as a nation to maintain and respect them. When the Republic of Mexico was compelled by the chances of unsuccessful war to part with a portion of her territory and people, she threw around them by treaty all the safeguards to their civil, religious, and political rights arising out of honor among men and faith among nations.

In the treaty of Guadalupe Hidalgo, signed on the second of February, 1848, ratified on the twelfth of March, 1848, exchanged at Queretaro the thirtieth of May, 1848, and proclaimed on the fourth of July, 1848, ample protection is promised and pledged to the people of New Mexico, and expressly stipulated in the treaty itself, and particularly in the eighth and ninth articles of said treaty "The citizens of New Mexico can remain in New Mexico or remove to Mexico," and whether they go or stay, it is expressly stipulated that they have the right of "removing the property which they possess in said territory, or disposing thereof and removing the proceeds wherever they please without their being subjected on this account to any contribution, tax, or charge whatever." It was further provided in the said treaty, that property of every kind now belonging to Mexicans not established there, shall be inviolably respected. The present owners, the heirs of those, and all Mexicans who may acquire said property by contract, shall enjoy with respect to it, guaranties equally ample as if the same belonged to citizens of the United States. In the ninth article it is provided, that "Mexicans, who in the territories aforesaid, shall not preserve the character of citizens of the Mexican republic, conformably with what is stipulated in the preceding article, should be incorporated into the union of the United States, and be admitted at the proper time (to be judged by the Congress of the United States), to the enjoyment of all the rights of citizens of the United States, according to the principles of the constitution, and in the mean time shall be maintained and potected in the free enjoyment of their liberty and property, and secured in the free exercise of their religion, without restriction:" See 9 Stat. at Large, 927, 928. Under this treaty the pueblos could have sold out and gone to Mexico. But if such protection had not been especially stipulated in that treaty, still the right of the people to have their title to their property recognized and confirmed by the new sovereign is plain and obvious. The Supreme Court has forever settled it to be the law of nations, of justice, and of right, that by conquest and annexation, the allegiance of the people is transferred from one sovereign to another, but the rights of the people to their property remain undisturbed, and their relations to each other: See *United States v. Percheman*. In the case of The *United States v. Arredondo* it was decided by the Supreme Court, that congress has adopted as the basis of all their acts the principle that the law of the province in which the land is situated is the law which gives efficacy to the grant and by which it is to be tested, whether it was property at the time the treaties took effect.

Let us now pass the consideration of the status of the Indian pueblo of Cochiti and its people as to the Republic of Mexico, and the title by which they held their land at the date of said treaty in 1848, when they passed out of the sovereignty of the Republic of

Mexico, and came under the sovereignty of the United States. Were the pueblo Indians of New Mexico, at the date of the treaty of Guadalupe Hidalgo, citizens of the Republic of Mexico, and as such entitled to all the protection and benefit of all articles in said treaty, made for the protection of the Mexicans?

1. What was the relation of the pueblo Indians of New Mexico to the Republic of Mexico prior to the treaty of Guadalupe Hidalgo as to citizenship?

In considering this question, it is worth while to notice that after the conquest of the city of Mexico by Cortez in 1521, the Spanish viceroys in Mexico assumed and exercised all the privileges of royalty. He was commander-in-chief of the troops, and filled up all vacancies; judgments and decrees bear his signature, and from his decision there was no appeal or writ of error. In everything but name he was a despotic sovereign. Cortez, with his handful of Spaniards, was joined by one hundred and fifty thousand Indian allies, and the great multitude of people found by him in the valley of Mexico, numbering several millions, lived in towns, cultivated the soil, and irrigated the country by means of extensive ditches and canals, and were called Indians, and it will be found that at as late a date as 1851, the population of this Republic of Mexico consisted of one million of whites, four millions of Indians, and six thousand negroes.

The Spanish rule in Mexico was partial and unjust. Its few favorites of the Spanish Crown held all the offices in church and state, made the laws, executed the laws, and considered the great body of the Mexican people, equally honest and more industrious than themselves, a sort of upper servants and peons to the wants of their whiter skin and more refined civilization. The Indians and Mexicans rebelled against such tyranny and injustice, and under the leadership of Iturbide, struck for independence and successfully maintained it. The Indians, as they were called of Mexico on account of their numbers, their courage, their patriotism, rendered easy the overthrow of the unjust, arbitrary, and partial rule of the viceroys of Spain, and they established upon its ruins the empire under Iturbide, their successful leader. The Spanish scholar will not fail to remember that when Spanish law books and Spanish legislators speak of Indians, they mean that civilized race of people who live in towns and cultivate the soil, and are often mentioned as *naturales* and *pueblos,* natives of the towns, and as *Indios del pueblos,* Indians of the towns; and for the other distinct and separate class of Indians whose daily occupation was war, robbery, and theft carried on against the pueblo Indians, as well as the Spaniards, the term savages (salvajes) or barbarous Indians (Indios barbaros), was the expression used.

An examination of the eleventh article of the treaty of Guadalupe Hidalgo will demonstrate, that in speaking of the Indians, no reference was had, or intended to be had, to the pueblo Indians, for the term is *tribus salvajes* (savage tribes). When the term Indian is used in our acts of congress, it means that savage and roaming race of red men given to war and the chase for a living, and wholly ignorant of the pursuits of civilized man, for the simple reason that when those laws had been enacted, no such class of Indians as the pueblo Indians of New Mexico existed within the existing limits of the United States.

Neither the Spanish crown, its viceroys in the new world, nor the Mexican Republic ever legislated for the savage class of Indians. They would as soon have thought of legislating upon what time the wolf should be admitted into their sheep-fold, the bear into their corn-fields, the fox into their hen-roosts, or the skunk into their parlors. The revolutionary government of Mexico, on the twenty-fourth day of February, 1821, adopted what is called the Plan of Iguala, a short time previous to the subversion of the Spanish power in New Spain, and by that plan it is declared "that all the inhabitants of New Spain, without distinction, whether Europeans, Africans, or Indians, are citizens of this monarchy, with a right to be employed in any post, according to their merits and virtues."

On the twenty-fourth day of August, 1821, the independence of New Spain was for the time established by the treaty of Cordova, made between the Spanish viceroy and the revolutionists, and in this treaty the principles of the Plan of Iguala were fully recognized and affirmed. On the twenty-eighth of September, 1821, the Declaration of Independence was issued, and that declaration asserts and reaffirms the principles of the Plan of Iguala. The Mexican congress, shortly after their first organization, passed two acts upon this subject, the first on the twenty-fourth of February, 1822, and the second on the ninth of April, 1823. By the act of the twenty-fourth of February, 1822, the sovereign congress declared "the equality of civil rights to all the free inhabitants of the empire, whatsoever may be their origin in the four quarters of the earth." The act of the ninth of April, 1823, reaffirms the three guarantees of the Plan of Iguala: 1. Independence of New Spain; 2. The perpetuity of the Catholic religion; and 3. The union of all Mexicans, of whatever race. It will thus be seen that the Indian race of Mexico and that portion, and a vast portion, of the inhabitants to whom that term was properly applicable, were recognized as citizens of the Republic of Mexico, in all her plans of government and acts of solemn obligation putting into practical operation that plan. Now, if there is no law of the Republic of Mexico (and we are unable to find any) taking away the right of citizenship with which the Indian race was invested as far back as the twenty-fourth of February, 1821, the conclusion is forced upon us, that they (the Indian race) were in fact Mexican citizens at the date of the treaty of Guadalupe Hidalgo, and are entitled to the benefit of all the articles in said treaty designed to protect the life, religion, and property of Mexicans under the new sovereign, in whose hands the destinies of war had placed them.

If the Republic of Mexico has never passed any act taking away from the Indians their rights of citizenship, it must be evident that at the date of the treaty of Guadalupe Hidalgo the Indian race, in the Spanish sense of the term, were as much and fully citizens of the Republic of Mexico as Europeans or Africans. On the seventeenth of September, 1822, the Mexican congress passed a preamble and act carrying into effect these fundamental principles of the new government, as follows: "The sovereign Mexican Constitutional Congress, with a view to give due effect to the twelfth article of the Plan of Iguala, as being one of those which form the social basis of the edifice of our independence, has determined to decree and does decree: Article 1. That in any register, and public and private documents, on entering the name of citizens of this empire, classification of them with regard to their origin shall be omitted."

Let us now consider the stipulations of the eighth and ninth articles of the treaty of Guadalupe Hidalgo. That article gives the Mexicans established in New Mexico the right to retain the title and rights of Mexican citizens, or acquire those of citizens of the United States, and the election was required to be made within one year after the exchange of ratifications of that treaty. Colonel Washington made proclamation requiring the people to elect by signing a declaration before the clerk of the courts in the different districts, if they wished to retain the title and rights of Mexican citizens. In that test, which is a public printed document, the name is not found of a single pueblo Indian; and hence, by the express terms of the eighth article of the treaty, they became citizens of the United States, as they were previously citizens of the Mexican republic. The ninth article provided "that Mexicans who, in the territories aforesaid, shall not preserve the character of citizens of the Mexican republic, conformably with what is stipulated in the preceding article, shall be incorporated into the union of the United States, and be admitted at the proper time (to be judged of by the Congress of the United States) to the enjoyment of all the rights of citizens of the United States, according to the principles of the constitution, and in the mean time shall be maintained and protected in the free enjoyment of their liberty and property, and secured in the free exercise of their religion without restriction." Whether the right to vote shall be given to the African or taken away from him;

given to the Mexican or taken away from him; given to the American or taken away from him; given to the pueblo Indian or taken away from him; are questions not properly before us, and are to be judged of by the Congress of the United States. It is to be presumed that congress has the right, if congress thinks proper to exercise it, to repeal the organic act, disfranchise all the citizens and legislate hereby directly for this territory without the aid of the legislative assembly; and whether political rights are given or withheld by congress, is no business of ours; but it is the right and duty of the courts to see that every citizen of the territory of New Mexico, in conformity with the ninth article of the treaty of Guadalupe Hidalgo, "shall be maintained and protected in the free enjoyment of their liberty and property, and secured in the free exercise of their religion without restriction."

This court, under this section of the treaty of Guadalupe Hidalgo, does not consider it proper to assent to the withdrawl of eight thousand citizens of New Mexico from the operation of the laws, made to secure and maintain them in their liberty and property, and consign their liberty and property to a system of laws and trade made for wandering savages and administered by the agents of the Indian department. If such a destiny is in store for a large number of the law-abiding, sober, and industrious people of New Mexico, it must be the result of the direct legislation of congress or the mandate of the Supreme Court. This court feels itself incompetent to construe them into any such condition. This court has known the conduct and habits of these Indians for eighteen or twenty years, and we say, without the fear of successful contradiction, that you may pick out one thousand of the best Americans in New Mexico, and one thousand of the best Mexicans in New Mexico, and one thousand of the worst pueblo Indians, and there will be found less, vastly less, murder, robbery, theft, or other crimes among the thousand of the worst pueblo Indians than among the thousand of the best Mexicans or Americans in New Mexico. The associate justice now beside me, Hon. Joab Houghton, has been judge and lawyer in this territory for over twenty years, and the chief justice for over seventeen years, and during all that time not twenty pueblo Indians have been brought before the courts in all new Mexico, accused of violation of the criminal laws of this territory. For the Indian department to insist, as they have done for the last fifteen years, upon the reduction of these citizens to a state of vassalage, under the Indian Intercourse Act, is passing strange. A law made for wild, wandering savages, to be extended over a people living for three centuries in fenced abodes and cultivating the soil for the maintenance of themselves and families, and giving an example of virtue, honesty, and industry to their more civilized neighbors, in this enlightened age of progress and proper understanding of the civil rights of man, is considered by this court as wholly inapplicable to the pueblo Indians of New Mexico.

What is the true character of all the tribes of wild and roaming Indians west of the Mississippi, and what has it been for over seventy years last past? Take the expedition of Lewis and Clark, from the Mississippi to the Pacific ocean in 1804, and expedition of Lieutenant Pike in 1806, to the Rocky mountains, and then take the vast multitude of reports resting in the pigeon-holes of the Indian department, upon the subject of the thefts, murders, and robberies of the Indians, which have never seen the light, and never will, if that department can prevent it, and it will be found that not a single tribe, beyond the Mississippi, of wild Indians can be found whose constant habit is not to steal, rob, and murder the white man, and to war against their own neighboring tribes and plunder one another, whenever a suitable occasion presents itself. This utopian idea, that kind treatment and a few agents and missionaries can civilize and christianize these wicked and wild savages in a few years, is a sad and fatal delusion. When you can tame a million wild buffalos by sending a yoke of oxen among them; when a single tame pony let loose among a herd of wild horses will reduce them to subjection; or when you can clear the muddy waters of the great Mississippi by running a spring branch into it, then, and not till then, will you accomplish these utopian schemes of elevation and civilization. Experience has proved that these agents and missionaries will descend to the habits and customs of the Indian, instead of elevating the Indian to the habits and customs of civilized life. Indians, in their nature and habits, are like other animals. The horse, the cow, the sheep, the chicken, can be tamed and made useful. The tiger, the bear, the panther, and wildcat can not be tamed or reduced to subjection, except by commencing when young, and bestowing years of labor in the undertaking. It is the same with Indians. Some tribes can easily and readily adopt the pursuits and habits of civilized life; but in other tribes, the civilization of those of mature age is impossible; and even when taken young, civilization is rarely accomplished under half a century. To extend over all the same system of laws is the height of folly and injustice.

In the argument of this case, it is contended, by the attorney for the United States, that this question has been settled by the Supreme Court of the United States, in the case of *United States v. Holliday,* 3 Wall. 407. This court has studied with great care and attention the decision of the able and learned Justice Miller, who declared the opinion of the court in that case, and the facts, material facts, are so different, as to take the case out of the consideration. In the case of *Holliday,* Otibsko, to whom Holliday sold liquor, was a Chippewa Indian. He was a member of a tribe under the care of an agent, authorized by congress, under treaty stipulations with that tribe and the United States. How different the facts in this case: 1. The pueblo of Cochiti has never had any treaty with the United States. 2. No act of the executive or political department of the government has ever authorized any agent to be appointed for the pueblo of Cochiti. 3. A treaty with a sister republic made the people of the pueblo of Cochiti citizens of the United States. Had there been no treaty with the United States and the Chippewas; had there been no agent over them, and no annuity received by them; and had Otibsko been made a citizen, not of the state of Michigan, but of the United States, by treaty with Mexico; and had it been shown that Otibsko lived on his own land, granted to his father's father by a foreign grant in 1689, and confirmed to him by the Congress of the United States; and that Holliday sold him a quart of liquor at his own house on his own farm, the opinion of Justice Miller would have been that it was no violation of the United States laws, for Holliday to sell liquor to a citizen of the United States on his own farm in a sovereign state.

It has already been shown that the people of Cochiti are a corporate body, and that a full and ample remedy is given them to protect and defend their title to their individual and common lands, and that they do not need any assistance from the penal statutes of the United States to accomplish that purpose. There is a world of influence produced upon individuals and whole communities by the suggestions of a single word or sentence. You take the healthiest village in the world, where no person ever died with disease, and where a doctor had never been for half a century, and just let a neat shop be fitted up with a bay window, and big bottles with different-colored water, and then hang up a neat sign with Doctor J. Snooks, physician and surgeon, painted on it; and one third of the people will imagine that premonitory symptoms of consumption are upon them, and in less than one year, the doctor will be engaged by the year as family physician, and papa will have to drop his pen in the midst of a half-finished opinion and run for the doctor if the baby sneezes. Take the case of a peaceful community, where they have not had a lawyer or a lawsuit for half a century, and let a young lawyer put up his law books on nice shelves, hang out his sign, O. Gammon, Esq., attorney and counselor at law, and in less than six months, one half the village will have hatched up a lawsuit against the other half; and no man will pass the counselor's law office, without trying to arrange in his mind a lawsuit for the counselor. So let the Indian department have placed under their control the twenty-one pueblos of New Mexico, and get the laws of trade and intercourse, designed to regulate the commerce of the country with savages, extended over these peaceful and industrious citizens, and in less than six months they will have fifty lawsuits on hand about questions settled by a former government fifty years ago.

The object and purpose of the eleventh section of the act of June 30, 1834, was to protect Indians in the peaceable enjoyment of lands set apart for their use by treaty with the United States; they were considered as the tenants of the government, and that the government was bound to protect them from intrusion and trespass. But does any such right or obligation exist where title is not held by treaty with the United States? By no means.

Let us now consider some points arising upon the face of this petition proper to be noticed if the pueblo Indians of Cochiti have been legally and rightfully stripped of their citizenship, and properly placed by the mandate, not of any treaty or law of congress, but of the commissioner of Indian affairs, under the Intercourse Act designed for savages.

The statute, upon which this debt of one thousand dollars is claimed to be due the United States, is in its nature penal, but the Supreme Court, in the case of *Taylor v. The United States,* decided "that statutes for the prevention of fraud, for the suppression of public wrong, or to effect a public good, are not in a strict sense penal, although they impose a penalty."

The fine in this case does not come under the above class. The penalty is found in an act to regulate trade and intercourse, and in the case of the *Mayer v. Davis,* it was decided, that "so far as statutes for the regulation of trade impose fines or create forfeitures, they are doubtless to be construed strictly as penal, and not literally as remedial laws."

In declaring for a penalty upon a penal statute, the case must be fully brought within the terms of the statute. The penalty is not imposed for settling upon lands secured or granted to the Indians generally; but to expose a citizen to that penalty it is required to aver in the declaration that the lands settled upon by the defendant belonged to the Indians "by treaty with the United States," and this court is of opinion that the omission of that averment renders the declaration bad on general demurrer. The court also finds that there is a fatal misdescription of the land in this case said to have been settled upon. The petition says: "Lands of the pueblo tribe of Indians of the pueblo Cochiti." Now, the title given, the title presented, and the title conferred was to the "pueblo of Cochiti," without alluding in the most distant manner to their being a "tribe of Indians." We are also of opinion that it was the intention and object of this statute to protect lands consecrated to the use of Indian tribes by treaty with the United States, from an unlawful settlement or wrongful settlement, and in the petition claiming the penalty of one thousand dollars, it ought to be stated that the "settlement" which subjected the offender to so heavy a penalty was either unlawful or wrongful. The chief justice who decided this case in the court below, has passed from this life to the life to come, and as a suitable tribute of respect to an honest, good friend and true patriot, we append his opinion in the court below, in a case identical with this, as a part of our opinion in this court, which is as follows:

"In the United States district court, of the first judicial district of the territory of New Mexico.

"THE UNITED STATES v. BENIGNO ORTIZ. Debt on Statute.

"Opinion. This action is brought as alleged, to recover the statutory penalty, for settlement upon lands belonging to an Indian tribe, in violation of the provisions of section 11 of the act of congress of June 30, 1834, entitled 'An act to regulate trade and intercourse with the Indian tribes and to preserve peace on the frontiers,' and commonly called the 'Intercourse Act,' which section is as follows:

" 'Section 11. And be it further enacted, that if any person shall make a settlement on any lands, belonging, secured, or granted by treaty with the United States to any Indian tribe, or shall survey, or shall attempt to survey, such lands, or designate any of the boundaries by marking trees or otherwise, such offender shall forfeit and pay the sum of one thousand dollars.'

"The petition filed herein alleges that the defendant, at the time named therein, 'did make a settlement on, and now occupies and is settled on lands of the pueblo tribe of Indians, of the pueblo of Cochiti, said lands, then and there, and at the time of bringing this suit, belonging to the said pueblo tribe of Indians of the pueblo of Cochiti aforesaid, and secured to them by patent from the said United States.'

"To the petition the defendant filed a demurrer, raising questions, not only of form, but of substance. As a question of substance disposes of the cause, the court will not consider those of mere form in this opinion.

"The demurrer and the argument of counsel thereon raise the fundamental question as to whether the pueblo Indians of the territory of New Mexico are a tribe of Indians such as those contemplated in the Intercourse Act referred to, and in the subsequent act of congress, that of February 27, 1851, which provides as follows, viz.:

" 'Section 7. And be it further enacted that all the laws now in force regulating trade and intercourse with the Indian tribes, or such provisions of the same as may be applicable, shall be, and the same are hereby extended over the Indian tribes in the territories of New Mexico and Utah.'

"If the pueblo Indians are not such an 'Indian tribe' as is contemplated in the foregoing section, which contain all the law upon the subject; or if the laws of the United States do not, without violation of the letter and spirit of the constitution, and treaties of the government, recognize them as coming within the provisions, then this action must fail.

"The court will now proceed to the consideration of this question. In its discussion, the first question is: What was the intention of the law-making power of the government in enacting these laws? And what is meant by Indian tribes therein? At the time of the passage of the Intercourse Act, nearly all of the uncivilized tribes of Indians within the then limits of the United States were within the region described as the Indian country in the first section of that law, viz.: 'All that part of the United States west of the Mississippi river, and not within any state to which the Indian title has not been extinguished.'

"The area referred to at that time was, with the exception of Missouri and Louisiana and the territory of Arkansas, almost entirely uninhabited by the white race, and was in the almost exclusive possession and occupancy of the savage Indian tribes of the whole country, many of which were originally there, and others of which had been removed there by the government. Within the region excluded from the description, 'Indian country,' to wit, that part of the United States peopled by the whites, and organized as states, civilized Indians were permitted to remain, and were exempt from the operations of this law. That it was the intention of the lawmaking power to exclude from the operations of the law the Indian tribes within the settled regions of the country is further evidenced by the fact that the states of Missouri and Louisiana and the territory of Arkansas, all lying west of the Mississippi river, were excepted, as well as the states lying east of that river.

"The intention, therefore, was manifestly to legislate with reference to Indian tribes beyond the settlements, or on the frontiers; the savage and uncivilized tribes there found, and not with reference to the civilized Indian tribes to be found within the settlements. This view is strengthened by the declaration of the title of the law, that one of its purposes was 'to preserve peace on the frontiers.' With civilized Indians, and those within the settled region of the country, no law was necessary for the preservation of peace. It was only on the frontiers that danger was to be apprehended, and for the protection of which legislation was required. If this position is correct, was the effect of the law of February 27, 1851, with reference to this region, more than to extend the provisions of the law of June 30, 1834, so far as same were applicable to the wild or savage and uncivilized Indian tribes of the territory of New Mexico? There is nothing to justify the conclusion that it was intended to extend the Intercourse Act over the civilized Indians, those living within the settlements of that territory. As to the applicability of these statutes to the pueblo Indians, more hereafter.

"Now let us inquire as to the character of the pueblo Indians. Greenleaf on Evidence, vol. 1, c. 2, in speaking of things taken notice of by the courts without proof, says that, among other things, 'the general laws and customs of their own country, as well ecclesiastical as civil,' 'matters of public history affecting the whole people,' 'public matters affecting the government of the country,' 'of whatever ought to be generally known within the limits of their jurisdiction,' etc., the courts judicially take notice of without proof; and 'where the memory of the judge is at fault, he resorts to such documents of reference as may be at hand, and he may deem worthy of confidence.' In the case of *United States v. Turner,* it is held, that the Spanish laws which prevailed in Louisiana before its cession to the United States, the courts take notice of. These rules are as good for the territory of New Mexico as elsewhere. This court is therefore justified in taking judicial notice of the past history and present condition of the pueblo Indians, as well as their status under the laws of the Mexican republic, and their present status under the laws of the United States and this territory. The court, for the attainment of the requisite information to decided this question, has consulted documents and other matters of reference worthy of confidence.

"For centuries, the pueblo Indians have lived in villages, in fixed communities, each having its own municipal or local government. As far as their history can be traced, they have been a pastoral and agricultural people, raising flocks and cultivating the soil. Since the introduction of the Spanish Catholic missionary into the country, they have mainly been taught, not only the Spanish language, but the religion of the Christian church. In every pueblo is erected a church, dedicated to the worship of God, according to the form of the Roman Catholic church, and in nearly all is to be found a priest of this church, who is recognized as their spiritual guide and adviser. They manufacture nearly all their blankets, clothing, agricultural and culinary implements, etc. Integrity and virtue among them is fostered and encouraged. They are as intelligent as most nations or people deprived of means or facilities for education. Their names, their customs, and their habits, are similar to those of the people in whose midst they reside, or in the midst of whom their pueblos are situated. The criminal records of the courts of the territory scarcely contain the name of a pueblo Indian. In short, they are a peaceable, industrious, intelligent, honest, and virtuous people. They are Indians only in features, complexion, and a few of their habits; in all other respects superior to all but a few of the civilized Indian tribes of the country; and the equal of the most civilized thereof. This description of the pueblo Indians, I think, will be deemed by all who know them, as faithful and true in all respects. Such was their character at the time of the acquisition of New Mexico by the United States, and such is their character now.

"Looking at the intention of congress as manifested in the Intercourse Act, etc., and the character of the pueblo Indians as thus presented, this court would be justified in declaring that such laws were not applicable to this people, the question of the applicability of those laws being a question addressing itself to the sound judgment and discretion of the courts. The exercise of these necessary judicial qualities impels this court, in view of the law and the facts, to declare the inapplicability of the laws referred to, to the pueblo Indians.

"Here the court might stop; other strong reasons, however, suggest themselves stronger than logical conclusions, viz., positive law upon the subject, and time-honored acquiescence therein. The pueblo Indians, having assisted the Mexicans in throwing off the yoke of Spain, were recognized as citizens of Mexico; and as a further token of the appreciation of the people of that government of the value of their services during the revolution, they were granted the lands upon which their pueblos or villages were erected, by grant since confirmed by the government of the United States, and for which patents have been issued conveying whatever of interest the United States government might have therein to them, as well as to their successors and assigns.

"The Plan of Iguala, adopted by the revolutionary government of Mexico, twenty-fourth February, 1821, declares, 'that all the inhabitants of new Spain, without distinction, whether Europeans, Africans, or Indians, are citizens of this monarchy, with a right to be employed in any post according to their merit and virtues,' and that 'the person and property of every citizen will be respected by the government.' The treaty of Cordova, twenty-fourth August, 1821, and Declaration of Independence of twenty-eighth September, 1821, reaffirmed these principles, as subsequently did the first Mexican congress, by two decrees, one adopted twenty-fourth of February, 1822, the other ninth of April, 1823. The first, 'the sovereign congress declares the equality of civil rights to all the free inhabitants of the empire, whatever may be their origin in the four quarters of the earth;' the other reaffirms the three guarantees of the Plan of Iguala: 1. Independence; 2. The Catholic religion; and 3. Union of all Mexicans, of whatever race. By an act of September 17, 1822, to give effect to the Plan of Iguala, it was provided that 'in the registration of citizens, classification of them with regard to their origin shall be omitted,' and that there shall be no distinction of class on the parochial books. Upon the subject of citizenship of Mexico of the Indian races, in the case supreme court of *The United States v. Ritchie,* Justice Nelson, who delivered the opinion of the court, says: 'these solemn declarations of the political power of the government had the effect necessarily to invest the Indian with the privileges of citizenship as effectually as had the Declaration of Independence of the United States of 1776, to invest all those persons with these privileges residing in the country at the time, and who adhered to the interests of the colonies,' and refers to 3 Pet. 99, 191.

"That the pueblo Indians were declared at that time 'Mexicans' and citizens; that they were recognized as such, no one familiar with the history of the Mexican government can question. That they are still recognized as citizens of the Republic of Mexico is evidenced by the fact that the present President of that republic is a full-blood pueblo Indian. Did they retain the character and description of 'Mexicans' or citizens, at the time of the acquisition of New Mexico? It is true that subsequently qualifications were annexed to the exercise of the right of suffrage; the freedom of many of the citizens of the Republic of Mexico was abridged and narrowed; but I can not find that by any legislation or judicial decisions the character of 'Mexicans' or citizens was taken away from the pueblo Indians as a class of people.

"The robbery of our territorial library during the late rebellion, of its Spanish and Mexican authorities, renders it difficult to obtain definite information upon the subject; but this we know, that as late as the year 1851, the pueblo Indians of this territory, without question or interruption, not only voted, but held both civil and military offices. In many localities, they, by their numerical strength, controlled the political destinies of the same. This period (1851) was more than two years after the treaty of peace between the United States and Mexico, and the erection of a government under the United States over the people of the territory. In the absence of law or decision on the subject, are we not at liberty to conclude from these facts that the laws, the decisions of the courts, and the acquiescence of the people, all recognized the pueblo Indians as citizens, as 'Mexicans'? We do so conclude.

"Now, if the pueblo Indians were 'Mexicans,' or citizens of the Republic of Mexico, what effect has the treaty of Guadalupe Hidalgo upon their present status? The federal constitution declares: 'All treaties made or which shall be made, under the authority of the United States, shall be the supreme law of the land.' As such, the executive, the legislative, and the judicial branches of the government are all alike bound by all treaties so made. The treaty of Guadalupe Hidalgo, made the second of February, 1848, declares, that Mexicans, 'who shall prefer to remain in the said territories (including New Mexico), may either retain the title and rights of Mexican citizens or acquire those of citizens of the United States; but they shall be under the obligation to make their election within one year from the date of the exchange of ratifications of this treaty; and those who shall remain in the said territories, after the expiration of that year, without having declared their intention to retain the character of Mexicans, shall be considered to have elected to become citizens of the United States.'

"Again, if the pueblo Indians were Mexicans, or citizens of the United Mexican States at that time, and did not, within the time limited, make their election by declaring their intention to retain the character of Mexicans, they became by virtue of the said treaty, citizens of the United States. The history of the times and country shows that they did not so elect, and thereby they became invested by law with the rights and privileges, and entitled to the title of citizens of the United States. They, although still called Indians, have never, since the acquisition of this territory, been subject to such legislation as that authorized by the constitution, and found in the Intercourse Act of congress. They should be treated, not as under the privilege of the government, but as citizens, not of a state or territory, but of the United States of America.

"It has been argued that, because of the Secretary of the Interior, the Commissioner of Indian affairs, etc., have considered the pueblo Indians as tribal Indians, and not citizens, by sending an agent to them; and that under the authority of the decision, in the case of *United States v. Holliday,* this court is estopped by such action of the departments, etc., from the adjudication of the question. This position would be true if the pueblo Indians were such Indian tribes as is contemplated in the acts of congress, under the constitutional authority, to regulate commerce 'with the Indian tribes.'

"That agents have been sent to them by the representatives of the government argues nothing, unless it argues ignorance of the status of this people, or as an intention on the part of the government simply to become advised with reference to them, and to assist them by the direction of their energies and intelligence to a higher degree of civilization or perhaps enlightenment. As they own their homes, are christianized, and are entirely self-sustaining, an agent for them is little else than what we have described.

"It is proper to add that the people of this territory who are most familiar with the pueblo Indians, have recognized their capacity and character by passing a general act of incorporation of their pueblos enabling them to sue and be sued in their corporate name, etc. This is more striking when we consider the fact that none of the other cities, towns, or villages of the territory have been incorporated.

"The federal constitution guarantees to all citizens the same privileges and immunities and protection to life, liberty, and property. These rights are as much guaranteed to pueblo Indians as to any other class of citizens of the United States."

The Faithful Apache Scouts

The way to "deal with Indians" has sometimes been so savage that one cannot begin to justify the means employed. In the 1880's Geronimo broke out of the confining reservation at San Carlos where he and his little band were facing a death of certain starvation. In short order he proved himself the most fearless opponent the United States had ever faced. The endurance of the Apaches while being pursued by thousands of United States soldiers over the deserts of New Mexico and Arizona has never been equalled in the history of warfare.

With the aid of hundreds of friendly Apache scouts General Miles was finally able to track down Geronimo in Mexico and corner him in a canyon where the little group was forced to surrender. Had there been no Indian scouts in Miles' service it is doubtful if the Apaches would yet be on reservations.

How did the United States treat its scouts who had brought the mighty Geronimo, their kinsman, to bay? Read the following excerpt and discover what happens after the smoke has cleared and it is time for the United States to reward its Indian allies.

Mr. DAKLUGIE: Why, along in 1886—I believe it was in September—Geronimo surrendered to the United States Government. At the same time Geronimo surrendered the peaceable Indians were kept at Fort Apache. They were all arrested by General Myers and placed in confinement and shipped to the East at a place called Fort Mann, in Florida. When this happened the Indians were placed as prisoners of war. There were about 750 of them. At the time Geronimo was taken, the agent at Fort Apache or other military officer was in charge of these United States Indian scouts and told them they were not to suffer anything; that Geronimo was to be confined. The officers told them—the United States scouts—to go and surrender themselves, the same as Geronimo. Therefore, they said, after you do this, do it in a peaceable way, as the Government wants you to do, and be prisoner, and at the time you leave here you will receive $2 a day for the time you served as prisoners of war. That was the sentiment from one of these Indian agents at the time and some of the military officers known to be acquainted with our people are living to-day.

Now, for that reason they charge that the Government should pay for punishing the innocent Indians that had not done the things that Geronimo did. The peaceable Indians defended the Government and defended the people and let the country be settled like it has been done, and they punished them just the same as what they did with Geronimo. So they think they have been unjustly treated by the Government in so doing. That is what these Indians complain about.

Senator THOMAS: How many Indians belonged to Geronimo's band at the time he surrendered?

Mr. DAKLUGIE: I do not know. I think they all died out.

Senator THOMAS: How many, approximately?

Mr. DAKLUGIE: There must have been about 25, maybe 40.

Mr. SCATTERGOOD: How many of these peaceable Indians were with him?

Mr. DAKLUGIE: There were about 700.

Senator THOMAS: So when Geronimo surrendered there were about 25 to 40 Indians and 700 peaceable Apaches likewise surrendered?

Mr. DAKLUGIE: Yes, sir.

Senator THOMAS: You understood that during the time they were to be kept prisoners of war they would be paid by the Government the sum of $2 a day?

Mr. DAKLUGIE: Yes, sir.

Senator THOMAS: These Geronimos of 25 to 40 in number were taken to Fort Mann and kept there for awhile, during which time great numbers died?

Mr. DAKLUGIE: Yes, sir.

Senator THOMAS: And from there they were sent over to Georgia?

Mr. DAKLUGIE: Alabama.

Senator THOMAS: Sent to where?

Mr. DAKLUGIE: Mount Vernon, Ala.

Senator THOMAS: How long were they kept there?

Mr. DAKLUGIE: They were kept there, I think, about seven to nine years.

Senator THOMAS: During your time there great numbers died?

Mr. DAKLUGIE: Yes, sir.

Senator FRAZIER: Were they military prisoners over there in Alabama?

Mr. DAKLUGIE: Yes, sir.

Senator THOMAS: All the time they were prisoners of war?

Mr. DAKLUGIE: Yes, sir. All the time they have been prisoners of war, for 26 years.

Senator THOMAS: Later on they were sent from Alabama to Oklahoma and confined on the Fort Sill military reservation?

Mr. DAKLUGIE: Yes, sir; in 1894, I think, they were sent to Fort Sill. They were there—

Senator THOMAS: At the time they were liberated in 1914, how many members were left of the two bands, the Geronimo band and the peaceable band?

Mr. DAKLUGIE: I think 8 or 10 were left of the Geronimos.

Senator THOMAS: How many of the peaceable tribe?

Mr. DAKLUGIE: All the rest of them, I think 200 or 300; about 300. A lot of them died. On this reservation on the list I think 166 of those prisoners of war served under the Government.

Senator THOMAS: What I was trying to bring out was this: Of these 750 Indians taken prisoners of war and kept prisoners in Florida, Alabama, and Oklahoma, for 26 or 27 years, during which time the band died off until there were only between two or three hundred left; is that right?

Mr. DAKLUGIE: Yes, sir.

Senator THOMAS: Now, there are only a few of the prisoners left and these former prisoners are asking that the Government pay them what they understood was agreed to be paid to them; that is, $2 a day during this period?

Mr. DAKLUGIE: Yes, sir.

Senator THOMAS: That forms the basis of your claim against the Government?

Mr. DAKLUGIE: Yes, sir.

Senator THOMAS: At the time Geronimo surrendered you had among the peaceable band a number of men enlisted in the army known as scouts?

Mr. DAKLUGIE: Yes, sir.

Senator THOMAS: Were they taken prisoners as well?

Mr. DAKLUGIE: Yes, sir.

Senator THOMAS: And kept prisoners for all these years?

Mr. DAKLUGIE: Yes, sir.

Senator THOMAS: Some of these men who were prisoners for all these years, former scouts, are drawing pensions from the government?

Mr. DAKLUGIE: Yes, sir.

Senator THOMAS: Indicating a judgment on the part of the Government that at no time should they have been considered prisoners, in my opinion?

Mr. DAKLUGIE: For 26 years.

Senator FRAZIER: They were prisoners, but the fact they now draw pension is evidence to me they should never have been prisoners.

Mr. DAKLUGIE: They should not be.

Mr. SCATTERGOOD: Why was it that the Government treated the peaceable Indians in the same way that they treated the Geronimo band who were enemies?

Mr. DAKLUGIE: That is what they would like to know and I would like to know that myself.

Mr. SCATTERGOOD: Is there no answer to it? There must have been some reason for it.

Senator THOMAS: If there is I would like know it.

(Conditions of Indians in the United States, Hearings, U.S. Senate, Part 25, pp. 13629-13631, 1929.)

An Act of Indian Territory

There have traditionally been two kinds of Indians in Oklahoma—the "civilized" tribes who were probably more civilized than any comparable white community in American history, and the "wild" tribes—the Kiowa, Comanche, Cheyenne, Arapaho and others in western Oklahoma who fought hard and well against the white invaders. Even today the state of Oklahoma is divided into two Area Offices of the Bureau of Indian Affairs reflecting the historical differences between the tribes.

It was pretty difficult to keep the western tribes in order. They had been hunting, roving tribes who cherished their freedom and the existential nature of the hunting life above mere existence itself. Thus when they were confined to the western reservations they felt miserable and downhearted like caged animals. It was from these bleak western Oklahoma reservations that Chief Dull Knife and his Cheyennes broke away on their epic fight for their ancestral homes in Montana.

Even to those Indians who stayed there was a deep sense of rebellion and yearning after the old ways. Thus it was not out of order for them to do little acts of civil disobedience to protest their condition. With the extreme paranoia that characterized Indian Service employees any act of resistance was considered the prelude to a general uprising. Therefore the following act was passed to prevent the little incidents that happened from time to time. It was federal law and it was enforced. It was about as important as your home town curfew ordinance. It was one more way of dealing with Indians.

An Act making it unlawful to shoot at or into any railway locomotive or car, or at any person thereon, or to throw any rock or other missile at or into any locomotive or car in the Indian Territory and for other purposes.

Be it enacted, That every person who, in the Indian Territory, shall willfully and maliciously shoot at or into any locomotive, caboose, postal car, passenger coach, express, or baggage car or any railway train, or at any person thereon, or shall throw any dangerous missile at or into any locomotive, caboose, postal car, passenger coach, express, or baggage car or any railway train, or at any person thereon, or shall derail or attempt to derail any locomotive or train, shall be deemed guilty of a felony, and on conviction thereof shall be sentenced to imprisonment at hard labor in the penitentiary for any time not more than twenty years.

Provided, That is any persons shall be killed, either directly or indirectly, by reason of said shooting, throwing, or derailing, the person causing the death shall be deemed guilty of murder, and upon conviction thereof shall be punished accordingly.

SECTION 2. That any person who, in the Indian Territory, shall willfully shoot at or into any freight, stock, postal, baggage or other car of any railway train, whether such car is attached to a locomotive or not, or shall throw any dangerous missile at or into such car, shall be guilty of a misdemeanor, and upon conviction thereof shall be punished by imprisonment not exceeding ninety days or by fine not exceeding three hundred dollars, or by both such fine and imprisonment.

(May 25, 1896)

Early Reservation Days — Martin Mitchell
Fort Peck Assiniboine Indian

The most important aspect to settling Indians on the reservations in the 1880's was to break their spirit so severely that they could no longer respond or react. In the 1920's a Congressional investigating committee heard the following account of the early reservation days of the Assiniboine tribe now living on the Fort Peck reservation. It shows without a doubt how the United States was able to bring the plains tribes to civilization rather quickly.

Martin Mitchell, being first duly sworn, on oath deposes and says: I am now 57 years of age, a member of the Fort Peck Assiniboine tribe, born in Montana, and residing in the city of Wolf Point, Mont.

If we are poor to-day it is not our fault; it is the Indian Bureau's fault. If the Indian Bureau left us alone we would be better off.

In about 1880 these Indians (Assiniboines) were about 2,000 in number, but to-day they are a little over 600. In 1881 the Indian Brueau gave orders to kill off all the buffalo. Before the buffalo were killed the Indians were all strong and healthy and no disease among them. After the buffalo were all killed I remember the Indian agent told the Indians, "Now your buffaloes are all killed and gone, and now you have to stay here on the reservation and we are going to feed you." And that winter it was a hard winter; the Indians were starving. They gave us rations once a week, just enough to last one day, and the Indians they started to eat their pet dogs. After they ate all their dogs up they started to eat their ponies. All this time the Indian Bureau had a warehouse full of grub. They

246

stationed seven Indian policeman at the door so the Indians could not get at the food. This all happened in the winter of 1883 and 1884. Some of the Indians, their whole families starved to death. Early that spring, in 1884, I saw the dead bodies of the Indians wrapped in blankets and piled up like cordwood in the village of Wolf Point, and the other Indians were so weak they could not bury their dead; what were left were nothing but skeletons. I think the Indian Bureau should have been prosecuted for murder or manslaughter at that time. That was the hardest time endured by the Assiniboine Indians since coming on this reservation.

Now I think we are about to go through the same thing.

About a year after our hard times the Government issued a cow to each of them. It was no time when every one of us had a nice bunch of cattle. Every fall we used to ship a trainload of cattle to the markets in Chicago. We were happy; we had plenty; we had nothing to worry about. But this did not look good to the Indian Bureau. They leased our reservation to a big cattle company against our will and protest. In one year after that we were broke. We were flat broke again. Then we sold a gravel pit to the railway company and we got $2,000; then we bought sheep with that money—400 ewes; tribal herd. We all pitched in and built sheds and put up the hay. Our intentions were when we got about 5,000 head we were going to divide upon among the Indians and go into sheep business; that was our intentions. When we got about 2,000 head, the Indian Bureau sold them all, and then they bought us some poor heifers and we got one apiece. Now we started in the cattle business. It was not long when we had a bunch of cattle, every one of us; we were happy again, every one of us; we were happy again. Then the Indian Bureau leased our reservation to big cattle outfit again, and in one year we were all flat broke. So we do not know what to do now if the Indian Bureau does things against our will and keeps us broke all the time. The way it looks to me, we could be better off a hundred times without the Indian Bureau.

It just puzzles me how these Indians are going to pull through this winter. We had no crop and no hay; we had a per capita payment this month of $50 apiece, but we were broke the next day. The traders were good enough to keep us from starving, and we gladly paid our bills. Of course, we did not all get the $50, because the Indian Bureau collected as much as they could for reimbursable loans. Now we can't stand it much longer under the present administration. The Indian Bureau has got to change their system; they ought to reorganize it, and if they do first thing they ought to call in all the Indian inspectors and pay them off. They are the ones who cause us all our troubles. They just go around whitewashing everything. The Government can't find out anything about the true conditions of the Indians from those sports; you must have special inspectors if you want to find out anything. Ever since I can remembers there have been over a thousand inspectors visited us; only one, F.E. Leupp, did the right thing. He was sent by President Roosevelt.

If given an opportunity I will present more facts and evidence about the hardships the Indians would have to endure during this winter, that possibly some of them would starve to death, unless aid was extended to them.

I know this is going to be pretty tough on me for making this statement, but I must tell the truth, and I don't care what they do to me I want save my people.

(From Survey of Conditions of Indians in the United States, Part 26, 1930)

The Campbell Ranch

During the Kinzua Dam struggle one of the arguments raised against the Senecas was that they had had the land for centuries and "What did they ever do with it?"

This theory that whites are so much smarter than Indians and can make so much better use out of the same lands has been with us for centuries. For years everyone pointed with pride at how much better the Campbell Ranch on the Crow Reservation was managing the land than did the Crows when they had charge of it. In the 1920's as part of the continuing investigation of Indian Affairs which ultimately led to the passage of the Indian Reorganization Act the history of this little venture was included in the testimony on Montana Indians. It was brought to the surface by a special investigator who apparently roamed at will turning up the most embarrassing facts about the management of Indian lands by the Bureau of Indian Affairs.

In order that this startling part of history not be forgotten it is included in this selection as a prime example of how to deal with Indians. In turn, I sincerely believe that if Indians had the weapons at their disposal that whites have had they could make a go of it also.

About 200,000 acres of Indian-owned land on the Crow Reservation is leased for agricultural purposes at prices ranging from 50 cents to $1.25 an acre in cash, and for one-fifth on crop share basis which sometimes amounts to as much as $10 an acre in the case of beet crops. Thomas C. Campbell is the largest single lessee, and at the present time has 80,000 acres under lease, most of it at 60 cents per acre.

Campbell first came to the Crow reservation in 1918, when the World War was still raging. He then was manager of the Montana Farming Corporation, the directors of which were J.P. Morgan, James A. Stillman, Charles D. Norton, Charles H. Sabin, Francis H. Sisson, J. Gilmore Fletcher, and Maxwell M. Upson, all of New York, and J.S. Torrance of Los Angeles. The stockholders list looks like a roster of Wall Street bankers.

The Montana Farming Corporation signed a contract with Secretary of the Interior Lane whereby it was authorized to select lands on any Indian reservation and to negotiate leases on a crop share basis ranging from 7½ to 10 per cent of the crop for the first five years. All these negotiations were carried out under the cloak of patriotism on the pretext that more wheat must be raised in order to help America win the war. It is noteworthy that the war ended before the Montana Farming Corporation had raised a single spear of grain, but the operations continued and no more money was paid the Indians who had been induced to sign away their lands for insufficient rents—after being harangued to do as patriots.

Most of the Crow Reservation leases, amounting at first to about 40,000 acres, were negotiated by F.A. Thackery, then agricultural inspector for the Indian Bureau. Mr. Thackery spent most of his time for several months signing up leases for the Campbell Corporation on the Crow and Fort Peck Reservations and frequently rebuked the Indians for their lack of patriotism for not being willing to accept the low rentals offered by Campbell. When all the leases were signed and Mr. Thackery could accomplish nothing more in his official position, he promptly resigned and bobbed up as manager of the Campbell Corporation on the Fort Peck Reservation.

Originally the Montana Farming Corporation leases provided for payments of 50 cents for the first year, 75 cents for the second year, and $1 each for the third, fourth, and fifth years on the Fort Peck Reservation, and 7½ per cent of the crop delivered at the elevator for the first five years and 20 per cent of the crop for the second five years.

The inadequacy of these leases—sanctioned—yes; practically made by the Indian Bureau as the result of coercion—require little comment. The World War was raging when the leases were signed. Wheat was selling at $2.95 per bushel in the United States and was bringing $5 and $6 per bushel when delivered abroad. Land capable of raising wheat was in demand. White landowners were offered 50 per cent on a crop-share basis for irrigated land and 33 1/3 per cent of the crop for the use of dry land. When the Interior Department and the Indian Bureau conspired to give a group of Wall Street bankers some 200,000 acres of the choicest wheat land in the country they had every reason to believe that enormous profits would be made by the Montana Farming Corporation. Nevertheless, the Indians were bullied into signing away their land for a mere pittance—on the grounds of patriotism, of course—and all throughout the proceedings high and low Government officials acted as if they were the paid advocates of Campbell and his Wall Street backers.

It is rather refreshing to learn, despite uncounted columns of publicity in which Mr. Campbell has created the illusion that he has found the one profitable method of farming, that the Montana Farming Corporation miserably failed to make its expected profits. In 1921, after four years of operation, the Montana Farming Corporation's books showed a total loss of $2,006,308.85 and Mr. Campbell's Wall Street backers threw up the sponge. They pocketed their enormous losses and Mr. Campbell purchased several hundred thousand dollars worth of machinery for less than $50,000, and after canceling the Fort Peck leases—which required cash rentals—proceeded to continue his crop-share operations on Crow Reservation.

Aided by Indian Commissioner Burke, who wrote a letter to Superintendent Asbury plainly stating the Indians would lose what was owed them unless they modified the terms of their existing contracts, Campbell reduced his share of the crop to 20 per cent for only three of the last 5-year period, instead of for the entire term, and increased his acreage materially.

Campbell's occupancy of the Crow Reservation land was marked by numerous high-handed acts, which he was enabled to pull off with the connivance of Indian Bureau officials.

First of all, E.L. Dana, who has a lease on 30,000 acres coveted by Campbell, was told that his lease would be canceled unless he allowed Campbell to use the land. Thackery, the Indian Bureau farm supervisor, threatened Dana on several occasions, telling him the land was needed for war purposes and would be commandeered by Washington officials unless he voluntarily relinquished his lease.

In the second place, land desired by the Sheridan Sugar Co. was practically pre-empted by Campbell, and at one time the sugar company officials were told they could not negotiate leases, although they offered the Indians from $2.50 to $5 an acre, far more than they ever received from Campbell.

In the third place, the lands of many Indians were arbitrarily taken from them and farmed by the Campbell corporation at low rental. One flagrant example of this was the case of William Brass, a full-blooded Crow Indian, 50 years old, whose 80-acre hay meadow, on which he had raised $700 worth of hay the year before, for which he was paid less than $80 a year. This land was taken without Brass's consent and the meadow was permanently ruined by plowing.

I made efforts to ascertain the cash value of the crop share rental paid by Campbell, and find that is has averaged considerably less than $1 an acre for the 10-year period since

1918. Some years there was almost complete crop failure, and consequently the Indian got nothing at all, although his land was used. When the land was summer fallowed, the Indian got no payment. For the entire 10-year period it is very doubtful if the Indians averaged 75 cents a year. This is lower than the prevailing rental for dry land, and it must be remembered that Campbell's leases included more than 10,000 acres of irrigated land.

Many Indians complain that there were long delays in paying the crop-share lease, and others complain that sufficient precautions were not taken by the agency to check up whether the proper division was made. It would be impossible at this time to verify the truth of these complaints, and the agency lease clerk vehemently denies there is any justification for these charges.

The Campbell leases on 80,000 acres were renewed on August 19, 1927, for a 5-year period ending December 1, 1933. The leases now are on a cash basis, but the prices are far too low for land of this character. Prices range from 60 cents to 80 cents an acre, but the majority of land—some 50,000 acres—is leased at the lower rate. In fact, Mr. Campbell has leased 4,000 acres of irrigated land for 50 cents an acre and water charge. This is far too low.

(From Survey of Conditions of Indians in the United States, Part 26, 1930.)

The Story of Hill 57

When the Bureau of Indian Affairs wants to act arbitrarily with respect to Indian rights there is nothing in the world short of an act of God that can affect them. For a long time there has been an orphan band of Indians known as Chief Little Shell's band of Chippewas. During the days when the various tribes were being restricted to reservations there were too many Indians at the Turtle Mountain Reservation. Crowded and unhappy the members of Chief Little Shell's band decided to visit their relatives in Montana and began the trek westward. The result of their wanderings was a deprivation of their rights on the Turtle Mountain Reservation and the establishment of numerous homestead allotments for individuals of the tribe. Thus the Turtle Mountain Allotments have been strung out arbitrarily from the Turtle Mountain Reservation in North Dakota westward to Great Falls, Montana.

The Bureau, in order to punish the Chippewas, refused to organize them in the late 1930's when almost every other tribe was given the choice of organizing under the Indian Reorganization Act. Thus they are eligible for organization under the Act, having never rejected it.

In 1957 the two Senators from Montana asked the Bureau of Indian Affairs to accept some land donated by white friends of the Indians and to organize them under the I.R.A. The following correspondence ensued with Commissioner Glenn Emmons—not only refusing to act in accordance with the wishes of Senators Murray and Mansfield but deliberately twisting the facts of federal law to justify his conclusions. Emmons stated that he was forbidden by the act of March

3, 1927 from establishing any new Indian reservations. This was not true. Under the Indian Reorganization Act there was blanket authority to organize any 'tribe', 'band' or 'group' of Indians which definitions the band at Hill 57 easily qualified under.

The following selections are, therefore, indications of how bureaucrats can thwart the policies of the United States, the wishes of the Indians, and the requests of the Congress with relative impunity. It should be a lesson to red and white alike that benevolence is an ideal, not a reality. The tragic aspect of the incident is that even today the Indians can be organized under the I.R.A.—if the Bureau really wished to do so. It doesn't.

THE TURTLE MOUNTAIN ABANDONED CHIPPEWA INDIANS

In order to have a full and complete understanding of the affairs of the Turtle Mountain abandoned Chippewa Indians, of how they were deprived and forced to leave their lands, it will be necessary to go back to the time the Turtle Mountain Reservation was set apart for their use and occupancy in North Dakota.

In the year 1882 approximately 22 townships were set apart for the Turtle Mountain Chippewa Indians by order of the President of the United States, out of territory claimed by them at that time. A tribal roll was prepared and all Chippewa Indians of the band of Chief Little Shell, who were at that time living within this reservation, were carried on this tribal roll. These Indians, mostly mixed-bloods or half-breeds, immediately started to build homes for their families and to cultivate the lands they had selected for their homes. Everything went well enough for a few years. The Government furnished them with food, livestock, farm implements, seeds, etc., with which to carry on their farming activities. These people were quite industrious and saw the necessity of settling down and making a living out of the soil. It was evident they could no longer depend on hunting and fishing for a living upon which they had subsisted for many years.

In the year 1884, by Executive order, presumably at the recommendation of the Indian Bureau, the reservation was diminished, reserving two townships of the poorest land for the Indians and the rest was thrown open to white settlers. A tribal roll was again prepared and all Indians who were not carried on this new roll and who were not living within the two townships were told to homestead the lands they had selected, which they refused to do at the counsel of Chief Little Shell and other leaders of the tribe. Little Shell said, "We can not allow the Government to take all of our land away from us; they must give us back what they have taken away." This controversy over the land between the Government and the Indians went on for a number of years, but the land was never restored to them. At about this time white settlers began coming in, and the poor Indians, who were living outside of the two township reservation, were forced to leave their homes, in many instances at the point of a gun. Many of them came to Montana where they have remained ever since.

Chief Little Shell was greatly incensed at the treatment accorded his people by the Government and shortly thereafter left the Turtle Mountain Reservation and came to Montana, primarily for the purpose of finding suitable land upon which to place his people and ask the Government to establish a reservation for them. Nothing was ever done; broken down in health and in spirit, Little Shell was forced to go back to Turtle Mountain, where he died some years ago.

In 1910, through the recommendation of some former superintendent of the Turtle

Mountain Reservation, the unalloted Turtle Mountain Chippewa Indians were allowed to make allotment selections on the public domain under the fourth section of the general allotment act. Many of these Indians availed themselves of this opportunity. After spending much time and money in endeavoring to improve the land, their applications were rejected and allotments canceled by the General Land Office at the recommendation of the Indian Bureau. On some pretext or other, the Indian Office advised the applicants that the land was valuable mineral land and was not subject to allotment, or the applicants were not affiliated with the Turtle Mountain Indians and therefore not entitled to allotment, or that they were Canadian Indians.

The Turtle Mountain Chippewa Indians, like other tribes of Indians of the Great Plains, depended entirely on the chase for a livelihood. They were buffalo hunters. It was often necessary for them to go into Canada in pursuit of wild game, and that is probably the reason why the Indian Bureau calls them Canadian Indians. Regardless as to what the Indian Office records may show, all of the Turtle Mountain Chippewa Indians sprang from the great Chippewa Tribe of Minnesota and Dakota. We have to-day many Indians in Canada who rightfully belong to the United States. It has always been the contention of the Indians that no boundary line existed for them. They were at one time the owners of the whole of North America with the privilege of settling down in either country when reservations were set apart for them.

After a great deal of correspondence in 1924 between the Indian Office and these Indians, by letter, they were advised to make application for enrollment, and in compliance with this request, applications, in affidavit form, were prepared and submitted. In reply the Indian Office said that under existing law the Turtle Mountain abandoned Chippewa Indians could not be put back on the Turtle Mountain tribal rolls; that there was nothing that the Indian Office could do for them; that any relief for these Indians could only be granted by congressional action.

Recommendation: Therefore, we hereby respectfully request, through our Representative in Congress, that at the coming session of Congress some kind of legislation be enacted authorizing the Secretary of the Interior to enroll or cause to be enrolled any member of the Turtle Mountain Chippewa Band found to be entitled to enrollment. That these Indians be accorded the same rights as were given other members of the band, to land and other tribal rights, in conformity with the provisions of the act of February 8, 1887. (24 Stats. 388.)

Respectfully submitted on behalf of the Turtle Mountain Abandoned Chippewa Indians.

David La Roque

(From Conditions of Indians in the United States, U.S. Senate, Part 23.)

DEPARTMENT OF THE INTERIOR,
BUREAU OF INDIAN AFFAIRS
Washington, D.C. April 18, 1957

Hon. James E. Murray
United States Senate
Washington, D.C.

Dear Senator Murray:

We have had several letters from you since March 21 regarding the establishment of Bureau facilities for Indians on Hill 57 near Great Falls, Montana. While the intentions of some of the citizens of Great Falls, Montana to find ways and means of alleviating the conditions on Hill 57 are laudable, the suggestion they have advanced to designate this particular area as a reservation is one which cannot be accepted by the Bureau.

This Bureau does not have and cannot assume authority over or responsibility for this particular group of Indians any more than it could over any particular community or grouping of off-reservation Indians in any other part of this country. For years, Indians have been leaving the reservation areas and settling in other communities. Some have settled in metropolitan areas under quite unsatisfactory living conditions. Such situations, like those prevailing on Hill 57, are community problems and responsibilities of the State and its political subdivisions. The Federal Government could not discharge this task.

The many services extended to Indians living on reservation lands, including primarily services which are generally provided to our citizenry through State and local governmental auspices, have been enabled and justified as Federal responsibilities on the basis of Indian residency on trust (therefore tax-exempt) lands. The Bureau of Indian Affairs cannot, and should not, follow the Indian wherever he might go with a full gamut of services which duplicate those offered by local governments on the basis of residency rather than ethnic origin.

We understand that the great majority of the Indians who have congregated on Hill 57 near Great Falls are enrolled at the Fort Belknap and Turtle Mountain Reservations. Admittedly, these reservations are grossly overpopulated in relation to the resources base available there to afford them a living. But the Bureau does offer them alternatives in the form of very generous assistance to relocate in centers of maximum opportunity in a wage economy. Their failure to avail themselves of those services indicates a gravitation to Hill 57 by choice rather than by dint of necessity.

As you are probably aware, the act of March 3, 1927 (44 Stat. 1347; 25 U.S.C. 398d), has been construed to prohibit the establishment of new Indian reservations without enabling legislation by the Congress. Therefore, we are returning the deeds to land on Hill 57 which Messrs. Mallette propose to donate for the purpose of establishing a reservation. We would suggest that legislation not be introduced to create a new reservation, but rather we will pledge to offer to every eligible Indian who applies in person at his reservation the special relocation assistance to find a better way of life in areas where it is really available to those who are motivated to meet this challenge.

Sincerely yours,

Glenn L. Emmons, Commisioner

UNITED STATES SENATE,
COMMITTEE ON INTERIOR AND INSULAR AFFAIRS,
April 25, 1957

Mr. Glenn L. Emmons,
Commissioner of Indian Affairs,
Department of the Interior, Washington, D.C.

DEAR MR. EMMONS: Several weeks ago you were informed of the willingness of citizens of Great Falls, Mont., to donate land on Hill 57 for the purpose of establishing a reservation there. In your letter of April 18 you state that this suggestion could not be accepted by the Bureau.

You also ask that legislation to create a new reservation not be introduced. Your suggestion regarding Hill 57 and the Indians there is "relocation."

"We will," you wrote, "pledge to offer to every eligible Indian who applies in person at his reservation the special relocation assistance to find a better way of life in areas where it is really available to those who are motivated to meet this challenge." You gave no alternative to relocation, a program for which those Indians on Hill 57 who are not enrolled members of a tribe are ineligible.

As for those Indians who would be eligible, we would like to point out to you that, while we support the program, relocation in itself is no answer to the problems on Hill 57 and on the reservations of Montana and other States. Many Indians who want to relocate will do so whether or not there is a special relocation program. Others choose not to leave the land of their fathers. They are willing and anxious to work, if job opportunities are available nearby, and they have proved themselves to be skillful and competent workers in those few areas where jobs have been made available.

The Federal Government and the Indian Bureau, Mr. Emmons, do not fulfill their obligations to the Indians by offering only relocation, which frequently means moving from a rural slum to an urban slum. The Federal Government and the Bureau which you head have further obligations to our Indian citizens. One of the best ways to help the Indian people develop their own human resources and, incidentally, become taxpayers instead of tax recipients, is through the establishment of industry and more jobs in Indian country.

We are aware of the modest efforts in this field by the Indian Bureau. If your Department supported industrialization with the enthusiasm with which it supports relocation, there would be no cause for complaint.

However, we note, for example, that the amount of money loaned to tribes for purposes such as industrial development has steadily decreased under your administration. As of June 30, 1956, the outstanding loans receivable and the cash balance in the revolving loan fund under the jurisdiction of your Bureau totaled $15,548,591. The amount of money on loan to the tribes has steadily decreased. The approximate amounts, by year, are: 1952, $11 million; 1953, $10.2 million; 1954, $9.5 million; 1955, $8.3 million; 1956, $7.7 million. What is your explanation of this decrease in the use of available money for development of tribal resources?

Your annual credit report for the fiscal year ending June 30, 1956, states that financing through the Bureau has increased from $22,991,070 in 1952 to $29,961,299. But included in these total is $8,737,444 from tribal funds in 1952 and $21,216,541 in tribal funds in 1956. In other words, some tribes were able to increase their own financing, which is commendable. However, many tribes, including several in Montana, have practically no tribal funds. They could put to good use the money which has been steadily accumulating in the tribal-loan fund under your administration.

We note, too, that the Indian Bureau has not yet submitted to the Banking and Currency Committee its views on S. 964, the area redevelopment bill which we co-sponsored along with Senator Douglas. A departmental report was requested 3 months ago and hearings have been in progress for some time. Passage of this bill would, in our opinion, be of tremendous benefit to Indian tribes, in that the bill would establish their own industries. We cannot help but contrast your enthusiasm last year for the Indian help features of this legislation with your inaction so far this year.

To refer specifically to some of the industrial possibilities in Montana, we are following with great interest the negotiations for development of a pulpwood industry and establishment of a small sawmill on the Rocky Boy Reservation. We are hopeful that these new industries, which would provide jobs for a number of Indians, can get underway by this fall, and we shall appreciate such help as you can provide in this undertaking.

We would also like to receive from you verification of the statement, made to us verbally by Bureau officials, that arrangements will be made shortly for the Northern Cheyenne Tribe to utilize its coal deposits on the Tongue River Reservation.

Along with our House colleagues, Representatives Lee Metcalf and LeRoy Anderson, we are willing and anxious to do all that can possibly be done to help our Indian citizens. We recognize the difficulties and burdens inherent in your task as Commissioner of Indian Affairs and hope that you can, as you suggested to the Indians in your letter of April 18, "meet this challenge."

We shall appreciate an early report from you on these matters, which we can discuss in greater detail at forthcoming hearings on Indian legislation.

Sincerely yours,

JAMES E. MURRAY
MIKE MANSFIELD

The Problem with the Senecas

In 1965 the House Interior Committee sent out questionnaires asking the respective government agencies of their estimation of the value of a contemporary study of Indian treaties. One division of the U.S. Army Corps of Engineers shows the basic problem of differences in attitudes in its answer to one of the questions.

The Pittsburgh District and the Senecas

Question 11. From the standpoint of your agency should a study of Indian treaties discuss or evaluate the attitudes of individual Indians and of Indian tribal councils to assumed provisions in their historic treaties?

Answer. On the basis of the experience of the Pittsburgh engineer district with the Seneca Nation of Indians on the Allegheny Reservoir project, a study of Indian treaties should discuss or evaluate the attitude of individual Indians and of Indian tribal councils to "assumed" provisions in their historic treaties.

The Pittsburgh engineer district encountered a feeling among the tribal officials and some individual Senecas that the Seneca Nation was a sovereign power and independent of the United States. In illustration, a prominent Seneca in making a public speech at a public meeting of the Senecas on the Allegheny Indian Reservation addressed the audience on the subject of the 1794 Treaty in the Seneca language, and, in changing to the English language, stated that he would now address them in a "foreign" language. This received loud applause.

The difficulty of conducting negotiations with Indians in such a climate is obvious.

(Federal Opinion on Treaty Study, House Report 1044, 89th Congress)

On the other hand, dealing with Indians has not been such a terrible burden if the person dealing with them has had wisdom, foresight, imagination and initiative. Recognizing that adult Indians like to "play", as do all childlike aborigines, J.R. Venning, whose job was in fact law enforcement on reservations, took pen in hand one day and created one of the more enlightening memorandums ever produced by a federal employee.

The memorandum does indeed suggest other practical uses of scrap wood material. Upon discovering this memo I suggested to Ron Roberts of the Nooksacks that the tribe embark on whittling new heads for the employees of the Bureau of Indian Affairs.

Tulalip Agency
Tulalip, Wn.
March 20, 1946

Memorandum to the Tribal Organizations,
Tulalip Jurisdiction.

I have received the following article from the Indian Office with a statement to the effect that a number of Indians under the Tulalip jurisdiction can do a good job on this sort of thing, if this can be brought to their attention. I am therefore submitting it to you in hope that you will pass it on to as many members of your Tribe as possible.

"A SUGGESTION—Indians can make many useful or ornamental articles out of apparently worthless scraps. Here is a suggestion for utilizing scraps of wood. In the wood scrap piles in school and agency carpenter shops, and at building construction or remodeling jobs, may be found nice scraps of wood. For example, pick out scrap 2" x 4" studding, or 2" x 3" pieces. They usually come from the mill "smoothed on four sides". Saw them into 8" lengths; sandpaper them to a smoother finish (a sandpaper holder obtainable at a dime store makes the job easier); keep them clean; on the top, sides and ends draw Indian designs and pictures; color them; give them a coat of clear shellac (white); then clear varnish; they make splendid paper weights—for both ornament and utility. Adult Indians who like to "play" with wood and who have spare time on their hands, also student Indians practicing art work, will find this an interesting pastime, capable of bringing out their artistic genius. There should be a considerable sale for such articles on display. A more elaborate job could be produced by those Indians who are handy with a whittling knife. I have one on my desk now which I prize, and which has aroused a great deal of interest, admiration, and wishes for one like it. This is not intended as a suggestion for a commercial saw-mill enterprise on a basis of cost of time and new material. On the contrary, much Indian artistic work is done in spare time and with materials not represented by a purchase of cost price. This suggestion will probably bring to mind other practical uses of scrap wood material."

J.R. Venning
Chief Law & Order Section
Indian Office, Chicago

ss F.A. GROSS
F. A. Gross,
Superintendent

Basil Two Bear

Occasionally there appears an Indian who is simply enjoying life to its fullest. He somehow knows the complexity of life and is nevertheless able to pierce the veil of sober respectability with its own darts. A number of years ago there were Congressional hearings being held to determine the state of the Sioux Indians in South Dakota. One of the delegates to attend the hearings was Basil Two Bear and he provided the favorite speech of the plains Indians. Basil's statement has been repeated wherever Indian people have gathered. It is reproduced here to indicate that it has not always been easy for people to deal with Indians.

STATEMENT OF BASIL TWO BEAR, A RESIDENT
OF THE STANDING ROCK RESERVATION, N. DAK.
(before the Subcommittee on Indian Affairs
Thrusday, March 17, 1949)

My friends and honorable gentlemen, my name is Basil Two Bear from Standing Rock Reservation, a big Sioux chief, and at the same time I was an Indian cowboy.

I did not have very much education, but at the same time I am not afraid to talk to anybody. You may have to ask a question or two now and then before I can make myself clearly understood.

I worked under a lot of superintendents of that reservation up to 1923. As my cousin, Mr. Gates said, he was a politician. I was working on that politics but I finally quit. I found it unprofitable. I resigned the job. I am going to tell a story before I am going to come to this discussion.

I live quite a distance from here, from this city, and I know there are two factions, the Republican and Democrat; but it doesn't make any difference who is elected, I come to kneel down before you fellows and what I want for my Indians is this: I am getting old, but still I sit on my saddle. As I told you, I was an Indian cowboy.

The last 30 days I was working with the Government officials, and one day a fellow named Dewey had a headache and something wrong, so he went to a doctor. The doctor told him, "Your brain is all full of blood and no good, and so I have to clean it." And so he cut off the top of his head and took the brain out and put it in a glass, and just then a fellow stepped in and he said, "Dewey, your house is on fire." And so he left right away, and slipped the bone on and left his brain there on the table, and he didn't come back for 2 days. Well, pretty soon he was coming back on the other side of the street, and the doctor was looking outside and he said, "Say, Dewey, don't you remember you forgot something here?"

"WHAT IS IT?" he said.

And the doctor said, "Your brain. That is already cleaned."

And he said, "Never mind, Doctor; I don't need it because I is with the Indian Service".

They don't have to have very much brain flow in working with the Indians. There was something wrong for many years. Now there is something wrong that all different reservations, you hear my friends, that they are calling on you to help and to help and to help. I am getting tired of hearing about it.

Suggested Reading for Further Study

The major sources of legal documents relating to Indian rights are to be found in the reports of cases decided in the federal courts. Any standard law library will contain the various sets of federal reports. The Supreme Court reports cover every decision of that court. In this book cases from volumes 5 (Wall), 109, 112, 163, 314, and 391 were used. These volumes generally have the designation "U.S." but in recent years the abbreviation "S. Ct." has been used to indicate the series. Few Indian cases actually get to the Supreme Court.

Students researching the reported cases will find more information in the Federal Reporter Series. In this series the cases decided in the U.S. District Courts and U.S. Circuit Courts prior to 1880 (which had been known as Federal cases) have been continued in two series, Federal Reports, 1st and 2nd series. Decisions in the District Courts until 1932 are reported in the Federal Series, since that year they have been classified in the Federal Supplement Series.

For students needing information on Indian land claims, the Federal Reports series is helpful only for the years 1929-32 and since 1960. Reports of the Court of Claims from 1932 to 1960 are published in the Federal Supplement. In this book selections have been taken from volumes 143, first series, and 272 and 342 of the second series of Federal Reports, and volumes 119 and 146 of the Federal Supplement. One case, decided before the Court of Claims reports were added to the Federal Reports, is taken from volume 29 of the Court of Claims reports. All of the reported cases decided in Federal Courts are published in volumes thoroughly catalogued and cross-indexed by the West Publishing Company of Saint Paul, Minnesota. Anyone seriously considering extensive use of these reports would be well advised to purchase WEST'S LAW FINDER, a booklet published by the West Publishing Company detailing how the West Key Number System of reporting can be most efficiently used. It is available in most college book stores.

In addition to the Federal Court system each state has a series of reports that give the cases decided in its own court system. From the extensive state reports, volume 3 of the Alaska State Reports and volume 1 of Stewart and Potter's Alabama State Reports have been used as well as volume 1 of the New Mexico State Reports. State reports generally do not have many cases involving the rights of Indians or Indian tribes. The major reason for this situation is that most tribes and individual Indians are litigating their cases in the Federal Courts. Thus legal problems involving treaty rights, titles to land, taxation, and often civil and criminal jurisdiction begin and end in the federal system without ever having made their appearance in the courts of particular states.

All legislation affecting the federal rights of Indian tribes and individuals appears in the United States Statutes at large. The legislation of each Congress, resolutions, memorials and Indian treaties until 1871 are published in the individual volumes. Volume 7 contains the Indian Treaties through the early 1830's. After that each volume reports only those treaties ratified during the life of that Congress. From the U.S. Statutes at large certain pieces of legislation have been taken. These are volumes 4, 12, 23, 25, 26, 43, 48, and 60. In each case the legislation was selected in its entirety for reproduction here. In that way the reader can determine the context of the clause or phrase he is interested in without lifting the phrase out of its natural context.

Another excellent source of material on Indian problems is the Congressional Record. In this book the speeches of Senators Teller and Morgan on the Allotment Bill, recorded in the proceedings of the 46th Congress, 3rd Session, Volume XI, June 10, 1881 were taken. These volumes are sometimes difficult to find in the libraries of small colleges. Many colleges have this material on microfilm and the reader who seriously seeks further information must have a specific citation to avoid tedious hours of searching. When the reader gets into the early years of this century he generally finds that most college libraries have copies of the Congressional Record for most of the Congresses. Thus Jennings Wise's essay on Indian rights appears in volume 67, 69th Congress 1st session, pages 502-511 and is generally available in volume form to the interested reader.

The great source of collected documents on Indian Affairs is, of course, Charles J. Kappler's massive compilation of legal material on Indians known as INDIAN AFFAIRS, LAWS AND TREATIES published by the U.S. Government Printing Office, Washington, D.C. 1904. The problem with this set is that it is now 66 years old, many copies have long since disappeared or been lost, and finding a set of Kappler's is a significant event in one's life. Owning a set is even more extraordinary. Under the 1968 Civil Rights Act an amendment was added directing the Secretary of the Interior to update and republish the Kappler's series. To date nothing has been done to fulfill this Congressional directive.

An additional source of materials on Indians is the reports of the various Congressional committees which have conducted investigations and hearings on subjects related to Indian Affairs. For those readers who wish to read the entire reports that have been published in abridged form in this book the following list is offered:

"Federal Opinion on the Need for an Indian Treaty Study", Report of the House of Representatives Committee on Interior and Insular Affairs, U.S. Government Printing Office, Washington, D.C. (1965) 89th Congress, 1st Session

"Federal Indian Policy", Hearings before the Senate Committee on Interior and Insular Affairs, 89th Congress, 1st Session, U.S. Government Printing Office, Washington, D.C. 1957

"Rights of Members of Indian Tribes", Hearings before the House of Representatives Committee on Interior and Insular Affairs, U.S. Government Printing Office, Washington, D.C. 1968, 90th Congress, 2nd Session

"Massacre of Cheyenne Indians", Report of the House of Representatives, 38th Congress, 2nd Session, January 10, 1865, U.S. Government Printing Office, Washington, D.C. 1865

"Wounded Knee Massacre", Hearings before the House of Representatives Committee on Interior and Insular Affairs, 75th Congress, 2nd Session, U.S. Government Printing Office, Washington, D.C., 1938

Of the reports listed above the last two, covering the Sand Creek and Wounded Knee Massacres are now out of print. Many libraries have copies of these reports acquired at an earlier time and fortunately retained by the library. Other reports are more recent and could probably still be obtained from either the staff of the respective Congressional committee or from the U.S. Government Printing Office.

The best series of reports, undertaken by the Senate Interior Committee in the late 1920's and published in 1931 and 1932, are called "Survey of Conditions of Indians in the United States". This series of field hearings lasted a number of years and conditions on nearly all of the reservations in the nation were recorded. From the scandalous situation that emerged came the impetus for the passage of the Indian Reorganization Act of 1934. Any person interested in obtaining first hand materials on the problems of Indians in this century should obtain these hearings. They were made while some of the original chiefs and head men from the major tribes were still alive. Thus their sense of what the treaties actually meant is greatly heightened. Selections in this book were taken from volumes 15, 23 and 25. While this series was published and released by the U.S. Government Printing Office it is extremely doubtful that one could obtain copies of the reports from that office today. Major college libraries should have them however.

In 1966 the Bureau of Indian Affairs conducted field hearings at a number of cities central to the regional groupings of tribes. Each tribal council was invited to send a delegation to these meetings and spell out the legislative and administrative changes it desired as part of the ongoing federal program for Indians. These field hearings were published in mimeograph form and distributed to all tribal councils and interested parties. They are the finest contemporary data of problems on a reservation by reservation basis. Copies can still be obtained from some of the Area Offices of the Bureau of Indian Affairs.

The last source of material for the selections in this book is the mimeographed booklet published by the National Congress of American Indians in

1966. It is a reproduction of the important resolutions passed at the annual convention of the N.C.A.I. Even with its ups and downs the N.C.A.I. has been the only consistent voice for the Indian tribes. It has fought a number of important battles over the past two decades and several times has stopped bad legislation and reversed detrimental policies. Copies of the annual resolutions of the National Congress of American Indians can be obtained from its Washington headquarters. Anyone seriously contemplating a study of the problems of Indian people should obtain the N.C.A.I. resolutions. They represent the concerns of the Indian community as it convenes annually to discuss ways and means of solving its problems.